A SHEPHERD TO FOOLS

A SHEPHERD TO FOOLS

Drew Mendelson

Copyright © 2021 by Drew Mendelson.

Library of Congress Control Number:		2021915694
ISBN:	Hardcover	978-1-6641-8783-2
	Softcover	978-1-6641-8782-5
	eBook	978-1-6641-8781-8

All rights reserved. No part of this book may be reproduced or transmitted in any form or by any means, electronic or mechanical, including photocopying, recording, or by any information storage and retrieval system, without permission in writing from the copyright owner.

This is a work of fiction. Names, characters, places and incidents either are the product of the author's imagination or are used fictitiously, and any resemblance to any actual persons, living or dead, events, or locales is entirely coincidental.

Any people depicted in stock imagery provided by Getty Images are models, and such images are being used for illustrative purposes only.
Certain stock imagery © Getty Images.

Print information available on the last page.

Rev. date: 08/12/2021

To order additional copies of this book, contact:
Xlibris
844-714-8691
www.Xlibris.com
Orders@Xlibris.com
827994

I dedicate this book to my wife, Susan Aguilar and to our kids, Alekka, Eric, Max and Jacob, and to our grandson, Kevin.

Frontispiece

*I was a shepherd to fools
Causelessly bold or afraid.
They would not abide by my rules.
Yet they escaped. For I stayed.*

—*Epitaphs* by Rudyard Kipling

> *Some die shouting in gas or fire;*
> *Some die silent, by shell and shot.*
> *Some die desperate, caught on the wire;*
> *Some die suddenly. This will not.*

—*"A Death-Bed"* by Rudyard Kipling

SSG Frank Rosenbaum died bellowing in a cave near Laos along with a squad of Viet Cong, shattered in the blast of his own grenade.

PFC Carlos Ramirez died needlessly, smothered in the smoke of a brush fire LTC Prentice Mattier's negligence had caused.

Mattier died from a bullet to the head, his arrogant ignorance intact to the end; some called it a fragging, others a mercy killing, for the men he commanded despised him.

Y Beo, a Montagnard mercenary, died where he'd fallen, limp and torn after taking a bullet, stoic till death, his wife in mourning, his spirit—as the Yards believed—joined with the earth again.

LTC Maxwell Bowie died sadly, perhaps heroic, yet too late repentant, pinned like an insect in a helicopter crash.

SP5 Django Danis died of a mortar shard, a wound so small you'd have to hunt to see it, a moan of pain and wonder escaping him as he slid into death.

A score or more of Khmer Rouge soldiers died in spasms, their breath a bloody froth, killed by the phantasm of the worst of the worst.

Some died nobly, some in wide-eyed terror. Some died struggling; some unmoving as if already dead. All lost to us; their deaths an end but not a destination.

CHAPTER 1

CPT Hugh Englander smiles while the frantic voice begs behind the door. *"Xin đừng, xin đừng!"* (Please stop!) A cry of pain. A reply, *"Ở đâu?"* (Where?), and then, *"Tôi không biêt!"* (I don't know!) Finally, there is a formless yelp of fear and a gunshot.

After the crack of the shot comes the single wordless exclamation, "Uh!" The door opens, and Englander's Vietnamese counterpart, the Montagnard CIDG unit's *đại úy*, steps through holstering a pistol, a thread of blood on his fatigues. He looks at Englander and says, "No," shrugs, looks at me, and shakes his head.

Englander says, "Fuck, all that and nothing?" He leans out of the operations shack's door after the departing đại úy and shouts, "Next time, catch one who knows something, dickhead." Then, "Goddamn Yards," to me.

I catch my breath at the sound of the shot and make to move to that door after the đại úy passes, but Englander steps in my way. "You don't want to get into that, man," he says to me. "Yards do things their way. We don't interfere." He says it as a fact, blandly, his voice empty of passion, but it strikes me that he means with all his heart that I won't like the universe I enter if I look at what is behind that door. Somehow, in my dreams of it, I never take my outrage much further. Yet it isn't fear of the captain that causes me to cram my revulsion down, and so I have wondered since why I did so little about it. The answer that comes, hard as it is to accept, is that I'd been in-country in Vietnam a long time by then, almost a year, and was too familiar with dink-on-dink death for this to matter.

When I first meet Hugh Englander at the Téthian camp on the Sông Re River in the late summer of 1970, I am still a senior first lieutenant in the artillery. Englander, a newly promoted captain, is the camp's commander. My first impression of him, which will change only a little and mostly for the worse over the months I'll know him, is of a humorless bastard, sneering and discourteous. His blond hair is an unmilitary mop, and his blue eyes are mild, but this show of grace fails to disguise his underlying bitterness. I've previously worked with Special Forces units at the Minh Long and Ba To camps, coordinating defensive artillery fires for them. I've found them to be, as 1SG Schlagel (the top sergeant for the infantry company I'd first been assigned to as artillery forward observer in Vietnam) had once pithily described them, "The best fucking soldiers in the whole fucking army, bet your ass."

CPT Englander is the exception that proves this rule. It is my bad luck to have to deal with him.

The camp is adjacent to the Montagnard hamlet of Téthian along a remote stretch of the fertile Sông Re river valley in the western mountains of Vietnam's Quang Ngai Province. Here, the river sweeps briefly west and then north again, placid in the dry days of summer, a raging dragon of a river in the months of the monsoons. The ground here, beyond the western reach of regular U.S. Army patrols, is bare of the crudely dug circles of foxholes that mark every strategic rise and clearing throughout the lower hills and coastal plains of eastern Vietnam. The trees and shrubs—teak and mahogany and philodendron—that climb the steep mountainside to the east of Téthian in a triple canopy of rainforest are green and vigorous, nothing like the ruined, defoliant-ravaged forests nearer the coast.

One might think this—like the Ba To and Minh Long camps I have visited before—is a Special Forces camp. Like the others, over the Téthian camp's main gate, a sign declares the Special Forces' apothegm, *De Oppresso Liber* (To liberate the oppressed). But it is impalpably different, with a rawness and subtle disorder that is both very military and very odd.

I am visiting the camp because MAJ Perkins, who commands the Special Forces local battalion, wants his units to make better use of artillery.

My own artillery battalion commander, LTC Dolby, has told me, "They're so highly trained in every sort of unconventional tactic and operation, they think nothing else is worth knowing. They're schooled in artillery but don't seem to trust it and mostly avoid calling for artillery support when it could do them some good. So I want you to get out to Téthian and teach them about what we can do."

"All you've got to support us here are some big-ass 175-millimeter guns way up at Minh Long," Englander says to me. "Tell me if I'm wrong, but those 175s couldn't hit shit if you magnetized it. Could they?"

"They're what we've got with the range to reach targets out here, Captain," I say. "They've got good gun crews, and, by themselves, they're pretty accurate. But they're long tubes—guns, not howitzers. They fire a flat trajectory, so errors tend to magnify."

"Christ, you artillery numbers assholes are all alike. Talking about long tubes, flat trajectories, and crap like that. You ought to spend some time out in the bush at this end of it. Artillery doesn't hit where I need it, it's not worth a damn to me."

I'd tell Englander how many months I *had* spent at the other end in the bush as an artillery forward observer with an infantry company when I'd first come to Vietnam. I'd tell him how many times artillery had saved us when things began circling the drain while I was out there. I expect he'd smile as if it didn't make any difference for the reason that, to him, no matter how far out in the bush I'd been, I was still a rear echelon motherfucker in his eyes. The war got small and close out here; you relied only on yourselves, and so I was just a REMF to him.

I don't tell him that, and just ask, "Are the Montagnard crews on the four-deuce mortars you've got out here any more accurate than our 175s?"

"Probably not," he sneers. "Sometimes, if the weather's clear and they aren't fucked up from chewing too much betel nut, they can hit the river over there with their mortars. Wouldn't bet my ass on it . . . This, though,"—he reaches down and slips a Ka-Bar out of his boot and sticks the point of the heavy black-bladed survival knife into the table—"this is your best friend here."

"A couple of grenades and a knife between your teeth are more dependable than artillery?" I ask and venture a grin. "Once in a while, you get in shit that calls for a bigger pop than a grenade, though, don't you?"

"That's what napalm is for," he says.

"Yeah, a half-hour wait for pair of Phantoms and about twenty thousand bucks' worth of napalm bombs."

"Man, I don't know what they cost."

"Not the point," I say.

"Here's the point, man," he rejoins. "Why don't you come out here with my team and a platoon of these Yards sometime when we're on an op and show me how good your guns are? Maybe you're right. But this Ka-Bar is still good enough for me."

The bird comes to get me soon after, and I climb on board, simmering. When I get back to San Juan Hill, I tell the infantry commander, LTC Prentice Mattier, about what the đại úy had done and Englander's indifference to that apparent murder. Mattier just blinks at me. When I tell LTC Dolby, my own artillery battalion commander, about it, he grunts and says, "Best thing would be just to shoot 'em." I'm not sure whether he meant shoot the đại úy, Englander, Mattier, or all three.

CHAPTER 2

CPT Englander had acted gung-ho as hell about my coming with him on a mission. So I'd expected a radio message to set it up right away. But nothing. LTC Mattier smirks when I tell him and says something about how the Special Forces "march to their own fiddler."

I try to contact Englander at Téthian. Whoever answers speaks little English.

"This is LT Weisman. Can I speak to CPT Englander?"

"No *bic*," comes the response.

"Captain, Captain?"

"Wait, wait."

Then five minutes or so and another voice. "Cap-tan Englander away. Out somewhere. Get op order. Go. Dark one. Bye-bye." The last, I hope, is them signing off and not a description of Englander's condition.

So I wait while two weeks pass in which all hell intrudes and I have no time to worry about Englander. First, Delta Company's forward observer, Dennis Pines, takes a bullet in his leg. Not life-threatening, but he'll be away to heal maybe half a month. LTC Dolby, hard up for replacements, apologizes but says he can't send anyone to cover for Dennis until he can get back out to the field. That leaves Delta with just a young RTO I have to coach until Pines can return to his post. Next, Bravo Company gets tasked for a short search and destroy mission south to the recon zone where commo is a nightmare. I have to send two of my three men to staff a relay point for them, leaving me and my liaison sergeant Alan Dobbs splitting round-the-clock shifts to make up for their absence. During that, Charlie Company's FO, tour over, heads home, and the company's new FO, a raw butter bar LT, needs me to familiarize him with our area of operations. "Maybe even to hold his hand while he pisses," SGT Dobbs snorts.

Then one gloomy night, the hill gets pasted hard. It starts in the middle of the night, maybe 0200, when a pair of explosions jolt me awake, jarring me out of what might have been a wet dream if the war hadn't interfered. A shock bangs open the door to my sleeping space in the briefing room bunker. Gunfire rattles outside. Another detonation booms close and strong, throwing me half out of my bunk. A gust of smoke blows in through the open door carrying with it the sweet banana odor of dynamite. Another bang. The ceiling of the bunker shakes, and dirt rains down on me. Spooked and dopy with sleep, I pull myself up, hearing other distant concussions. I lurch from my bunk, thinking, *What the hell, what the hell?*

This long in Vietnam, I'd have thought I'm immune to fright, but not, and so, heart racing, hardly thinking, I stumble out into the wrecked briefing room, into blackness lit by the flicker of explosions, into more dust and sweet dynamite smell. Far off, another bang. Not artillery this time; something simpler, satchel charges, sappers!

In the briefing room doorway, the flickers from outside illuminate the body of a dink sapper, dead from his own satchel charge, the detonation of which has blasted apart much of the furniture there and thrown him half into the bunker. His belly is burst, head twisted sideways, face loose and slack on one side as if pared free from the bone. Glimpsing him in the fitful light, I say to myself, "Fool," duck back into my room, and pull the chain hanging from the light in the ceiling. I'm in my boxer shorts and a T-shirt, no weapon! The light is dead, so I grope in the dark for my M16, for a bandoleer, and my helmet. I find my boots and stuff my sockless feet into them. So fortified, I head toward the battle.

A single bulb lights the tunnel between the briefing room bunker and the operations center, dust floating in its light. Bloody footprints lead toward the TOC from a broken and upturned floorboard. I bring my M16 up and step toward the tarp covering the tunnel's far end and on into the operations center. There, but for the dials and telltales of radios, it is almost pitch dark and full of low, urgent whispers. Here, in this bunker too, dust hangs thickly, and the smell of dynamite is strong. A faint glimmer from outside reveals that the front of the bunker part of the sandbagged entrance is down. I can make out the shape of an infantry grunt. His M16 comes up toward me; in the light of a flashlight, he sees who I am and nods in belated recognition. A second man restacks the sandbags. It is dark otherwise, most lights out to try and keep the dinks from seeing inside through the broken wall.

Hearing me come in, the other soldier on guard there turns my way, M16 raised, demanding, "Who?"

"Friendly," I say quickly, "LT Weisman."

"Ah," he says, not knowing me but still letting his rifle muzzle droop a bit, "OK."

"It's OK, he's one of us," I hear MSG Mike Turpin, the TOC's night NCO, say. "Leave the fucking redleg alone. We need him."

At this, there is a nervous laugh from my right, and I realize it comes from LTC Mattier, who is standing just this side of the tunnel's exit. A little bit of light comes through a gap in the tarp, and in it I can see one foot is bleeding. So the bloody footprints leading into the bunker are his. He is leaning unsteadily against the TOC's front wall, wearing only his undershorts, weaponless, barefoot, his right foot raised, blood dripping from a gashed big toe. He looks dazed and muddled. He sees me look at him. Laughs again. His mouth works, and he points to his foot, saying, "Stubbed it in the tunnel, maybe broken." With no time for him, I nod and say, "Sir," and push past.

SGT Dobbs is at the artillery station not far from Mattier, hunched over our map, talking insistently across the landline to the battalion fire direction center. He hangs up and waves me over. "Thank heaven, you're OK, LT," he says, a tremble in his voice the only evidence of his alarm, adding, "A bunch of sappers got through the wire. Bunkers seven and thirteen are gone, number twenty-seven is damaged. We have KIAs there, but we don't know how many. Infantry says there are damned dinks running all over the hill."

Sappers got through? What the hell? I think again. Still feeling only half awake, the phrases keep running through my thoughts. I try to shake it off. "Yeah, must be throwing satchel charges, I smell it," I say. "Got to be sappers."

There is more artillery thunder from all around the hill, distant from us. Another satchel charge blast, very close, shakes the TOC, and everything except a few battery-powered radios dies.

"Fuck," says a voice, "they got the generator."

MSG Turpin also says, "Fuck!" I can just make out his shape in the dark, lit only by the dial lights of the few working radios. He grabs a rifle and moves to the broken door and out around the toppled sandbags. Soon, a sputter comes from outside, and the power comes back on; the sound of radios comes again. They flare and fade on the uneven current of the emergency generator.

Turpin comes back into the TOC as the sounds of a firefight somewhere on the hill surge briefly. "OK, we've got juice," he says. "Damn clusterfuck everywhere out there. Lotta dinks got through the wire." He turns to a couple of PFC radio operators and tells them to grab their weapons and join the two soldiers now guarding the front entrance from outside. "Go with them and help keep the goddamned dinks from getting us, you hear?"

The two PFCs, who are techs more than fighters, look suddenly terrified. They stay sitting in a kind of shocked confusion. "We're RTOs," one laments.

Turpin has none of it and rasps, "Both of you, move! Now! Or you might be dead fucking RTOs!" and with that, they grab their weapons and rush out of the TOC.

Next to me, listening to the exchange, SGT Dobbs gasps. He's been on the hill for eleven months, as fine an artillery liaison sergeant as there is in Vietnam. But I doubt he's seen any actual combat like this. "God!" he says.

"You have a weapon? Alan," I ask to try and calm him.

"Yeah, oh, yeah." He reaches to touch an M16 hanging off the radio stand next to him. He looks from me to the broken door, eyes wide.

"It's OK, man," I say. "Let's do our jobs. Just be ready."

"Yes, sir," he says. He *must* be rattled, calling me sir and all.

Our jobs involve more than our own battle. A call comes in over the battalion artillery push, a choppy voice over a rough, badly broken transmission, call sign unfamiliar. The voice has a barely understandable accent, though not Vietnamese. "Being hit," the caller says, "I say again, being hit, you give support? Over."

I grab the radio. "Say again your call sign. Over."

A pause and then, "This is ... Artful Torre ... uh ... Artful Torrent. Can you help? Over."

SGT Dobbs is flipping through the loose-leaf pages of our call sign register and finds an entry. "It's Téthian, LT," he says, "the Special Forces camp."

A huge *wham* slams us from a short distance to the west outside our TOC bunker. Radios on generator power crackle.

In that brief quiet, I hear MSG Turpin yell into his own radio handset. "Yeah!" he says. "Yeah, I know it's fucking sappers. Yeah, I hear, dinks got through the wire, throwing bang-bangs around like Independence Day. Are you getting some troops out to hunt 'em? ... I know, I know, not much light out there with the big generator down. We've cut the light circuit. The little bastard we're using now hardly puts out enough juice to run the TOC." He sneezes abruptly, a half-dozen snorting staccato gusts because of the dust sifting in from outside. He bellows, "Fuck!" and sneezes again.

Again, around our bunker comes the chatter of small arms fire. "AKs," Turpin says. He grabs for the handset of his radio and starts issuing orders I can't hear over the TOC's clamor.

I key my radio handset and call back to Téthian, "What's your situation. Artful Torrent? What do you need?"

"Being hit, it's mortars. They come from across the river, I think. Can you give help? Over."

I recall that the Téthian camp has its own mortars and should be able to engage, but they've called us for help, so I leave that thought. "Roger, we can shoot for you," I say. "Can you give me a grid for the enemy mortars?"

"What, what? Grid?"

"Location, I need the target location, the grid where the enemy mortars are, understand?"

"Uh ... wait, please wait." The mike stays open, and I hear fast chatter back and forth in a strange, atonal language very different from

Vietnamese. I suspect it is Jarai, spoken by many of the Montagnards. The sound of detonations is in the background.

The delay is maybe half a minute, and then the same thickly accented voice comes back. "Yes, yes, grid is (something sounding like numbers in English but spoken too fast to be clear), big stuff is firing from there. Big, big, you bic?"

"No, no bic," I say. "Say again grid, say slowly this time."

"Yes, yes, I sa' again . . . sa' again . . . grid is three-three-two-zero at four-five-seven-nine." Understandable this time, if still heavily accented.

As I talk to the RTO at Téthian, SGT Dobbs is marking that grid on our map. "You know we can't hit that from here, LT," he says. "It's way beyond our max range. The 175s at LZ Crux can hit it. Maybe their eight-inch howitzers can too."

"Call 'em," I say. "Give them the fire mission."

Back on the radio, I tell Téthian, "We've got guns that can hit that. Wait one for shot on that target."

"Yes, yes," the voice comes back. "Yes, please, quick."

I wait for the firing sequence to play out and shot to be announced, again wondering why it isn't CPT Englander on the radio. Abruptly, an exchange of fire sounds from not far outside our TOC bunker. Turpin barks, "Damn it to hell!" and issues another call over the radio for a squad to get here from the bunkers on the line to secure the TOC.

"You hearing this, Sarge?" I call over to him. "Téthian's being hit."

"Yeah, I hear, LT. Word is a hell of lot of places are being hit right now: us, LZ Bronco, Dottie, Hill 411, Dragon, couple o' Snake-Eater camps too. Dinks are puttin' on a hell of a show tonight."

I get the report of "shot" from the battalion FDC and relay it to Téthian. "Artful Torrent, this is San Juan Hill. We've got shot. That means the guns at LZ Crux have fired. It'll be about thirty seconds before the rounds get there."

"Yes, yes," the soldier at Téthian responds.

"Listen, Artful Torrent, somebody there is going to have to adjust that fire."

"Adjust? Who?"

Christ, I'm thinking, *this guy has no idea what to do.* "Yeah, somebody's going to have to tell me where to move the rounds, how much left or right, how much to add or drop. You bic? Over?"

"Uh, yes, yes, I bic. Wait, wait," comes the voice, accent thickening near to opaqueness. Then silence, and in it I get and relay to Téthian the announcement of splash, five seconds to impact. We get no immediate response from the SF camp.

The soldiers at the TOC entrance have managed to hang the door back in place and revet it with the fallen sandbags, a little protection at least from the battle outside. The door opens, letting in the sounds of small arms fire so sharp that I drop the handset and grab for my rifle. It's not enemy, though, but a grunt in helmet and flak vest, calling out, "Friendly," as he enters.

"Hey, fuckhead," says one of the PFCs on guard, "you've gotta let us know you're a friendly *before* you come in. Guys here damn near shot you."

"Sorry, sorry," the soldier, just a kid really, croaks. "CPT Herman sent me to tell you it's sappers. He says to tell you there are dinks all over the hill!"

At this, LTC Mattier levers himself away from the TOC wall and limps toward the grunt. "What? Sappers?" he says as if this were news. "Get a flying squad out there," he goes on, grabbing the young soldier by the shoulder.

"What?" He looks uncertainly at Mattier, who, in only his boxer shorts, shows no sign of rank or identity.

"Flying squad!"

By now, MAJ Echols, the infantry battalion executive officer, has come into the TOC. He sees what Mattier is doing and tells the soldier to get a medic. "Go get one for the colonel," and pushes him back out the TOC door.

"Sit," Echols says to Mattier, propelling the battalion commander to a folding chair pocked with old shell fragment holes. More bloody footprints mark his path. "Stay here, sir. We'll get someone to fix your foot."

SGT Dobbs leans over to me and whispers, "What's a flying squad, LT?"

"Hell if I know, Alan. Something from another war. Colonel seems to want one, though."

"Jesus," says Dobbs.

We wait another few beats but hear no response from Téthian, and so I grab up the handset and call them back. "Artful Torrent, Artful Torrent, this is artillery liaison on San Juan Hill. Did you see where the round landed? Do you have an adjustment? Over."

This time, there is a different voice, still scratchy with distance but more confident and understandable. "This Artful Torrent," the new voice says. "The round you shot. It too *làm tình* dark to get good look, but maybe is a hundred meters left side of where enemy mortar flashes are coming."

Left side? I stare at the map. Gotta be south. "Roger," I say. "We'll move it a hundred meters to the right and shoot again. Wait one. Out." SGT Dobbs relays the adjustment to the battery, saying, "New voice there."

"Yeah, better, seems to know what to do." I key the mike again and ask if CPT Englander is there.

"No, no, *tôi không*. Can't tell where. He out on job. Somewhere away. Long, long way west. In Laos, I think," the man says. "All Snake-Eaters out on op. Just me and small part soldiers here at camp."

Man! The Yards are in heavy shit, and Englander isn't even there to take charge!

We are caught in twin battles, one virtual over the radio, one real, right outside where we sit in the TOC. Another dull thud of explosion sounds somewhere out on the hill, this one likely over toward where Bravo Battery has its guns, and with it, I'm convinced that firing artillery at targets out there in the night is a waste of time. Waiting for LZ Crux to shoot again, I flick on the mike on my landline headset. "Who's on this line?" I ask.

"It's Red," the voice comes back. Red (from his initials, RED) is the artillery battalion's senior RTO.

"Red," I say, "this is LT Weisman. Give us end of mission on the HE you're shooting on our defensive targets and start putting illumination out north and south of the hill."

"Roger," Red responds. "You got grids for where you want it?"

"Hell, I don't care, no time to plot any, just put 'em close to the hill maybe two hundred meters out north and south."

"Coming now," he responds, and he's off the line again.

I grab the line to the four-deuce mortar unit on the hill and ask them if they have any illume rounds.

"Got about twenty, sir," says their FDC chief.

Not many, I think. "Fire a couple north and south of us, close in as you can. Then call me before you shoot more. I don't want you to use up all your illume now." Being right here on the hill, the four-deuce can be much more responsive than the distant artillery units. So I want to reserve most of their limited illume stock for later if things start going bad fast.

Saying that, I also realize that if this is the run-up to a full-on dink ground attack, we'll need artillery targets closer in to disrupt anyone massing to come up the hill. I grab a map and plot a quartet of them in the valleys north and south, close to the base of the hill. "That's where I'd put my assault troops, Alan," I tell SGT Dobbs. "So let's preempt 'em. Have Red start hitting those targets now too."

He nods and flicks on the landline again to relay that fire mission to battalion.

The battery at Crux announces shot and then splash, and soon the soldier at Téthian comes back with more corrections. "You getting close to target, *ngài*," he says. "This time, shoot all battery."

"Roger," I tell him. "On the way."

For a moment, things are quiet in the TOC, and Mattier, still sitting in the corner like a kid in time out, asks again, a bit timidly, "Flying squad?"

"Being done, Colonel," MAJ Echols tells him. As he says that, a medic from Alpha Company comes in with the same young grunt from before.

"Fix him," Echols says to the medic, pointing at the colonel. "Give him morphine or some damn thing."

I expect Mattier to bellow an objection, but he just sits there, still seeming stunned. "Caught my foot on that broken board," he explains to the medic, who just nods, businesslike, ignoring the colonel's confusion and dosing him with morphine before beginning to treat the gashed toe.

Again, there is shot and then splash from LZ Crux. The soldier at Téthian tells us, "Good, good, yes, getting them. Shoot again."

We roger, while another thump comes out on the hill, and with it, the jury-rigged TOC door rattles again. Outside now and close is the sound of a full-on firefight, the crackle of M16s and AK-47s above the beat of machine guns. Far off to the west from the hill's other peak is the deep growl of the Quad .50 machine gun. The firefight outside dies, and a buck sergeant from Alpha Company pushes into the TOC and up to MAJ Echols. "Sir," he says, "CPT Herman sent me with a security squad to guard you here in the TOC. Had to fight our way up here. Killed two dinks. A lot more of 'em still out there. We're set up around the TOC and the briefing room."

Echols nods and says, "Good." He waves the sergeant back outside and turns toward me. "David!"

"Yes, sir?"

"I don't hear any artillery falling out there now."

"No point for those targets, Major," I say and tell him why and where I've shifted the fires to likely troop massing points.

Echols stares at his own map for a beat or two and nods approval. "Oh, yeah. Good idea. Do it."

Téthian comes on the radio to report, "Got 'em, those rounds got 'em. All dink enemy are gone now, all blown away. Good. Enough shooting for now." He signs off, and we're back to our own mess here on San Juan Hill.

I call the battery at Crux to thank them and call end of mission. "The Yards there say you took out the dink mortars. Nice shooting."

"We live to serve. Out," comes the mordant reply.

That over and with time to consider our situation, it worries me that stuck inside the TOC bunker, I have no direct idea of what is happening out on the hill. I do have a forward observer, Greg Salmi from Alpha Company in their command bunker. "Alan, do we have contact with LT Salmi?" I ask SGT Dobbs.

"I tried before and couldn't get him, sir. Got too busy to try again."

"Yeah, I know. We've got time now." I call over to Echols. "Major, can you get him on the horn for me?"

"Will do," Echols says. He grabs up a radio handset himself, and a moment later, I get a radio call from LT Salmi.

"Greg," I say. "Where are you?"

"Bunker twelve."

"Everybody OK there?"

"Yeah. Dinks didn't get this far."

"Do you have a good view of the valley to our north?"

"Sure."

"OK, then, fire missions to the north are yours. It's a sapper attack, so watch for more dinks coming up the hillside. Do you have commo with the battalion FDC? If so, give your fire missions directly to them. Shoot whatever you need to, even danger close. I'm going to keep the illume coming so you can get a decent view there."

"Roger, yeah, I have commo. Wilco on your orders. Over."

"It's all yours on that side of the hill, Greg. Out."

That still leaves the hill's east, south, and west sides. I call CPT Patterson, the Bravo Battery commander, and he puts Bill Dunphy, his fire direction officer, out on an OP on that side as a forward observer with a good view west and south. Bill's a former FO and will do fine. East? Damn, nobody's there. Nobody to send there either.

"Major," I say to Echols, "can you get me a couple of guys for security? I'm going up on the roof here to set up an OP and watch our east flank."

I'm not sure whether the look I get back from Echols is one of appreciation for my courage or alarm at my recklessness, he finally saying, "Yeah, OK, David, I'll get you some security."

SGT Dobbs looks at me. "I'll go out there with you, sir," he says.

"Nah, man, I'm the FO. You can work these radios better than I can. Stay here and run things."

"Yeah, OK," he says, both regret and relief in his voice.

The east slope of the hill below us is steep and rocky, not an easy way up for an assault. It is dark there too with the main generator blown and the hill's floodlights out. The illumination rounds coming in on the hill's south aren't able to light this flank. So I'm out in it, ensconced with a radio on top of the TOC in a small fighting position of culverts and sandbags just above bunker six. Jammed in here with me are a couple of grunts from Alpha Company's first platoon, both with M16s, one also has an M60 machine gun. The first is a Latino PFC named Francisco (call me Frank) Alvarez; the other, the one with the machine gun, is a black soldier, an SP4 who tells me his name is Amos Bell.

"Bell, you and Alvarez watch my back while I look for artillery targets," I tell him.

"Yeah, sir," he says. He starts as there is the crackle of a small firefight across the hill near the mess tent, which appears to be on fire.

"No hot chow tomorrow," Alvarez snorts with nervous humor.

I have the radio set on battalion artillery's push. I've got binos, compass, and a map (*like old times* comes the thought). I call Red and give him a grid for illumination rounds. The 155 mm battery from LZ Martín, about seventeen klicks northeast, will be shooting for us. A long way off for them, right at the max of their range. Because they're short on ammunition, I'm still not using the four-deuce mortars on our hill, keeping them ready in case of a close-in attack.

A minute or so later, I get the report of "Shot!" from Red, and then after an eternity of waiting (maybe thirty seconds), "Splash!" and four illumination rounds soon pop out high up a hundred meters or so to our east and float down on their parachutes, casting a brilliant flaring yellow light over the hillside. We can hear their empty canisters crash into the valley to the south.

"Man, look down there, LT," Alvarez says. And I see it, a handful of dinks, fewer than a dozen in all, coming up the steep slope, ducking from rock to rock. They are in the ravine in what would be bunker seven's field of fire. But bunker seven is a smoking ruin, and so the dinks can move up the hill's flank safely out of sight of other nearby bunkers. As the parachute flares' light hits them, they scuttle behind boulders. They are only a hundred meters or so from our bunker line, very close for artillery.

"Bunker six, you've got dinks coming up the ravine!" I yell to the grunts below me.

"Thanks, we'll get them," a voice comes back. I see the shapes of men from bunker six move toward the ruined bunker, but without cover, they are being cautious, engaging only briefly when they are able.

I'm not waiting, and I key the radio handset again, telling Red I have another fire mission. "Grid six-three-six-zero, three-eight-four-two. Direction one hundred. Proximity danger damn close. Two guns HE in effect."

"Roger. How close?"

"Maybe two hundred meters from us. I may have to walk it in closer."

"Yipe," Red says. "OK, you want it, you got it. Stand by." I know the four-deuce mortars would be more responsive, but I've rarely used them in close support, and this isn't the time to practice."

I warn the men from Bunker 6 that I've got artillery coming in and watch them scamper back to its shelter. A minute or so later comes, "Shot," from Red and then soon "Splash." The big 155 rounds come wailing in, their shriek a fierce howl this close. They detonate sharply in orange flashes of fire and rolling smoke just down the slope from us. We can feel the shock and hear the whiz of shell fragments flying overhead. In it, I see the dinks go to ground. Then after the shells detonate, the enemy soldiers dart south on the hill's flank away from the incoming artillery.

"Right 50, drop 50, repeat!" I tell Red. "Artillery coming in close. Keep your heads down!" I shout down to the bunker below us.

"Give 'em hell, man!" someone shouts back.

Soon, another pair of the big shells come in, closer to us and more to our right. The dinks are forced further that way, right into the line of fire of an M60 machine gun from bunker six. From where I am, I can't see if any of them are hit, but clearly, they are pulling back down the hill. I tell Red to have the guns repeat that target, same data, four rounds.

"Gone, sir," says Bell, watching and now punching a fist into my shoulder. "Sons o' bitches don't like bein' that close to that big shit. Man, I love watching that artillery slam down."

The third volley comes. The dinks are heading full tilt away from it, down the hillside trying to get out of range of the fire from bunker six. Seeing that, I call, "End of mission, but keep the illumination coming," and get back, "That's affirm," from Red.

"They moving down," Bell tells me, pointing. "Don't look like there was many, sir," he says. "Maybe not a big attack like we thought."

We sit watching for maybe five more minutes. Abruptly, as we are beginning to breathe easier, from the top of a bunker to our south comes the rattle of AK-47 fire. Some of it smacks into the sandbags around our fighting position. Shadows flicker on that bunker; within them are orange muzzle flashes from the enemy's rifles. We duck behind the culverts.

"Yaaaah! Fuckin' dinks over there," SP4 Bell blurts, and he pops up and fires back with the M60. Alvarez and I join with our M16s. I sense movement on top of the bunker on the corner nearest us.

"God, he's got a satchel charge!" I say. I shift my aim and see the face of the dink, a grimace of determination, arm back to throw the charge. I'm not a great shot with anything smaller than a howitzer. But the man is close enough and back lit by one of the illumination flares, so accuracy hardly matters. I fire. The bullet takes him somewhere in the chest. He tumbles back, dropping the satchel charge. "Bomb!" I shout, and the three of us duck below the rim of the culverts around us. There is the shriek of a terrified voice sounding just before the charge's detonation and then the violent smash of debris blown at us from the roof of the bunker. With no time to cover my ears, I'm momentarily deafened by the blast. Up again, I see three bodies up there on the now-torn sandbag roof, the nearest one—the man I'd shot—dismembered as if butchered, dark patches of blood everywhere.

Shadowy forms move away from the other side of the roof, telling us there had been more sappers heading up there. I call the TOC to tell them, and soon, there is a fire team from Alpha Company setting up to occupy that roof.

Not long after that, the sound of enemy fire begins to die all over the hill, mostly fading to an occasional shot here and there, merging into the calls of voices from our troops around the hill's perimeter. The booms of satchel charges have ceased. The urgency abated, I find myself trying to catch my breath, gasping as if I'd just run a mile.

"Looks like they *didi-ing*," says SP4 Bell.

"Yeah, boom and gone," says Alvarez.

I tell the two soldiers with me that we will sit where we are for the moment to be sure no more sappers are coming.

In the quiet, PFC Alvarez suddenly exclaims, "Hey! Look, *ese*, I been hit. Didn't even feel it." And he shows Bell and me his left shoulder where a bullet has creased it.

"Purple Heart time," Bell says.

Alvarez's eyes are big as he pulls back the edges of the tear in his fatigue jacket. "Hurts like a bitch now, though," he says.

"Naw, naw," Bell tells him. "It ain't deep, man, just a scratch. Get you a Purple Heart you can show Jody back home, like I said, but ain't even worth a trip to the rear. Next time you get hit, try to catch a bullet so's you can go home. This ain't nothin'."

"Screw you, man," Alvarez says. "Isn't bad enough to go to the rear but ruined my only good shirt. It don't mean nothing, though, dinks!" He shouts the last toward where the enemy had retreated.

"Ha," Bell says. "Infantry always gets the shit end of the stick. Maybe you oughta come out like the LT here in nothing but your tee and shorts, cock hangin' out like his and all."

"Yeah," says Alvarez, grinning as SP4 Bell tears open the sleeve of the PFC's fatigue jacket and ties a field dressing over the small wound.

"When you get back, you have one of the docs fix that so it don't go all full of puss on you," Bell tells him.

It is dawn before the hill goes off alert, more than three hours since the sapper attack. The two grunts and I continue to sit in our OP until it is fully light, keeping an eye on this slope of the hill. We have only one other event just before sunrise as one of the Viet Cong sappers, looking to have been wounded by fire from the bunker sometime before, decides to break downhill. He's figuring, I expect, that he must move before he is exposed in the light of dawn. I've been having illumination fired periodically, and the dink's movement is exposed in the light of a parachute flare. There is a rattle of M16 fire from the bunker below us, and then, fiercely, an RPG lances back at the bunker from where the dink has again gone to ground. The rocket-propelled grenade arrows into the cyclone fencing of the RPG screen in front of the bunker and is thrown back down the hillside, whirling like a pinwheel. It catches gravel and dirt as it spins along the ground, flinging it back at the bunker. There is a short, loud yelp of pain from one of the soldiers there.

As the flare gutters out, I can see the dink begin to move again. The next flare coming down highlights him on the slope. Fire from the bunker wastes him.

In the full morning light, MAJ Echols, Alpha Company commander CPT Herman, battalion SGM Alberto, and I (but not LTC Mattier, who is in his bunk, foot bandaged, sleeping off a double dose of morphine) stand looking at the burned-out ruin of bunker seven just north of my OP on the TOC. The center of the bunker had blown outward and then collapsed.

"We lost five," Echols says, emotional despite his exhaustion. "Three of them right here. Sappers got through the wire below here and threw a couple of satchel charges into this bunker. The other soldier in it got dusted off to Chu Lai with some nasty burns. They had to dig him out from under all the sandbags. Seven more wounded bad enough to be dusted off. Hell of a night all right."

We walk on to bunker thirteen on a promontory twenty meters west of and just below the level of the burned-out mess tent. Two more grunts from Alpha Company had died there. Two others in the bunker had had blast injuries.

"Only one satchel charge got tossed in here," SMG Alberto says. "So, not as bad. Hell, what am I saying? We lost two guys here."

A dead sapper lies where he died halfway up the ammo box steps to Artillery Hill. I walk over to look. The body is on its back, head downhill, grizzled, and older, unlike the child soldiers the VC usually send on such missions. The dink had been ripped apart by M16 fire as if something wild had torn into him. A cascade of blood had run from the body in a scarlet stream, pooling two steps below. On the dead man's shoulder is a canvas bag holding half a dozen Chicom grenades. A gunner from Bravo Battery had seen the sapper coming up the steps. The dink had already thrown two grenades—one a dud, the other only a fizzle. Before he could toss another, the gunner's fire had hit him, and he'd gone down. The artillery watches out for its own.

Six more dead sappers hang in the concertina wire in the gully below bunker ten. They'd been caught in the flare of the illumination rounds and shredded by machine gun fire from the bunker.

"Including these, that makes the bodies of seventeen sappers in the wire on the perimeter or inside the wire this morning, and that's probably not a third of all that hit us last night," Alberto says. The stocky, rock-solid sergeant major shakes his head. He stops, picks up a battered folding chair from the mess tent, and drops himself onto it. "Goddamned war."

He's a lifer saying that, I think. When lifers talk that way, maybe it's time to pack up and go home.

Later, comparing notes with SGT Dobbs, I learn that the Viet Cong had hit Téthian twice more during the night. One Yard soldier had died, and three were wounded. Word is that the artillery we fired headed off a bigger attack. Not that we will hear any bit of thanks from Englander. Why the American team wasn't there, why the garrison was left with only a few of the Yards to fight off the attack, is unexplained.

CHAPTER 3

The silence from Téthian continues until one afternoon nearly three weeks after my first visit there when I finally get a message from Englander. It comes as I'm on the radio, trying to talk Delta Company's new and terrified forward observer through a nasty firefight. Afterward, with the firefight over and my FO lightly wounded but OK, I pick up the message chit from Englander. It's bluff, just six words, "Grab your balls and come out." It appears his A-Team is going out on a "snoop and poop" mission and he wants me to go with them so I can show off what artillery can do. LTC Mattier, still hobbling on his injured foot, smiles as if he'd thought of it himself and tells me to go out and "teach those apes a thing or two about your guns."

The last time I had been at the camp, Englander had provided me nothing but a canteen cup of water and that only when I'd asked for it. This visit, on the rickety counter in the operations shack is a bowl full of fruit, some small Montagnard-style sweet cakes, and a pot of tea. Hardly largess but a feast compared to the sort of hospitality I had experienced before. I sit, refusing to wonder at this change of mood, enjoying one of the cakes and watching as the captain takes me through the goal and line of march of the mission.

He spreads a topo map of the Sông Re valley out on the counter and points to the depiction of a small stream that enters the Sông Re from the east a klick and a half north of the camp. He traces a route for some five klicks east along the stream and up a narrow valley through a scattered *ville* of Montagnard hooches. There, the trail turns southeast and up a steep defile for another klick or so.

"Except for this last bit, it's an easy march," Englander says. "We're going to head up the valley and then, here,"—pointing to the turn in the trail—"go a couple of hundred meters up the mountain to a little ville too small to be on the map. Hey? A subdistrict chief is living there, a scorpion-mean old bird named Lê Văn Dũng that we want to talk to. We're supposed to grab him and bring him back down the valley to the ville of Tà Ma, where a helicopter will meet us and lift him out." He looks at me and smiles mildly. "If we get contact with the dinks along this route, you can show me how your artillery will keep us out of the shit. It's beyond the range of our mortars. You do have a battery that can hit this stretch, don't you?"

I look. The entire length of the stream itself is an unobstructed target for both the 175 guns and eight-inch howitzers at LZ Crux up in Minh Long. It's even just within range of the 155s there. The final piece of the trail up the canyon is another story, lying perpendicular to the gun-target line from Minh Long, making it a far more difficult target. The canyon part seems shallow enough, though, that I think our guns should be able to hit most of it. I nod and tell Englander I am satisfied there will be plenty of artillery support available if he needs it. We talk almost genially for another hour, going over details of the mission, and then lapse into storytelling. Englander is still pleasant but always one-up about the brutal missions he and his team have carried out. I press him about the operation he'd just been on. As before, he tells me only that it was a black one, adding "in Laos."

"Hairy sort of attack here last week while you were gone," I say. I tell him I'd seen the fresh scars left from that battle when I'd landed, a big shell hole a few meters from the pad, the remains of a smashed sleeping bunker, scorched, tumbled sandbags.

"Yeah," he says. He sits. Finally, as if he's a miser pulling out a coin, he goes on, "Yeah, and your guys did a good job shooting for the Yards here then. Pulled out their bacon, thanks."

My turn to say yeah, nod you're welcome, thinking, *Fuck, yeah.*

We sit for a bit again, neither speaking, the silence abruptly uncomfortable. Finally, I ask him, "You don't want me here, do you, Hugh?"

"No," he admits after a pause. "Higher-ups want me to see what you can do, so I've gotta—"

"Look, I know, I and the rest of the battalion, in fact the whole Americal Division, are just grunts to you. We're OK in big fights, lots of bombs and big guns and heavy-assed air support. You Snake-Eaters like your fights close and personal, you've got a jones for a knife-in-the-gut kind of fight. Our artillery doesn't figure in that. Does it?"

"Fuck," Englander says. He blinks as though I've lanced an old wound. "Tight situations we get into, there's no room for your arty . . . And when it does come half the time, it isn't worth a damn, late or off target or worse. Case in point, we were on one clusterfuck of an operation with the ARVN back a year or so ago. They're worthless SOBs. The damn ARVN FO decided to call in some artillery without coordinating with me. The shit missed its target and cut down a dozen Yard troops and four of my A-Team. Three of 'em were KIA." His grin is hard, no humor in it. "I swore I'd never again get within ten klicks of where artillery was firing. I said then I'd shoot any fucking redleg who got in my line of fire. Still haven't changed my mind. But higher-ups want me to give you a chance. Orders, so I'll give you a fucking chance." The grin softens a bit. But it's still hardly friendly.

My ride arrives to fly me back to San Juan Hill, and Englander walks me out to it, slapping me on the back once again almost as if we're buddies, saying, "Be careful, you hear?"

"Get your shit together," I tell SGT Dobbs when Dolby's order confirming the mission comes down a couple of days later. "I'll need a radio operator if I'm going out with Englander. That'd be you, Sergeant."

Dobbs, two weeks shy of his DEROS day when he is scheduled to leave Vietnam, has not seen action off this firebase for the more than eleven and a half months of his tour. He stares at me with a sloppy smile, eyes wide open, breathing hard.

"But I'm short," he finally blurts.

"Well, here's your chance for some heroics out in the bush before you go home."

His look of astonishment hasn't slipped. "Sir . . . I mean, hell, we've had plenty of stuff here on the hill—rockets, mortars, the ground attack here last month. I've seen enough heroics."

I let him hang there for a moment and then smile. "Nah, Alan, both of us can't go. Alpha Company's going to be here on the hill for the next week. I'm going to have their FO, LT Salmi sub for me up here as liaison officer. But you'll be running things as usual. I've already put Salmi on notice about that."

"Christ, boss, I thought for a second there you were serious. Aren't you going to take an RTO with you?"

"Yeah, I am. The new guy, Private Wilbur, I guess, now that he's back from that relay mission. It's what he gets for being low man on our liaison team's totem pole. He missed the sapper attack. This will give him a taste of real action."

"Pussycat Wilbur? Think he'll know what to do, boss? It's only his first month in Nam."

"Perfect. He hasn't been in-country long enough to develop your impudent attitude. Tell him to go back to LZ Bronco and draw some field gear and a radio. Tell him we're leaving after mess call tomorrow evening."

SGT Dobbs nods and then looks down at the AO map fixed to the table of our liaison station. "A small point, sir, but going out with CPT Englander to show him the value of artillery won't be much of a lesson for him if you're out of range of most all the guns. The line of march for your mission, the way it is laid out now, is within range of everything from Minh Long. But if you go any further west, the only pieces that will hit targets that far are the 175s, and at that range and the way the terrain is laid out, all they're going to hit are mountaintops."

"I know, Alan. That's just what I told Englander, but we'll make it work if we have to. That's what we do. Anyway, COL Dolby tells me that won't be a problem."

I'd met Pussycat Wilbur when he first got to the hill, but I've yet to see much of him, having assigned him to the relay mission and then our late-night liaison shift, the latter meaning he mostly is asleep during daylight hours. Sitting next to him on the Infantry Hill helicopter pad the afternoon he and I are heading to Téthian, it strikes me how young he is, just nineteen, still slightly pimply faced and hardly shaving, his reddish hair in a flattop overdue for trimming but still with a Stateside correctness. He is maybe an inch taller than I am, a bit thin, but scrappy looking, freckle-faced, in fact a lot like the other puppy draftee warriors that fill out our units in Vietnam. I'm just approaching twenty-five, but it seems like a whole generation comes between us.

"Where'd you come by the nickname Pussycat?" I ask him.

He shrugs and offers an embarrassed grin. "My real name is Felix, but *nobody* calls me that, sir." He tells me he is from Rochester, Minnesota, where his father is a chest surgeon at the Mayo Clinic. "He'd been a doctor in a MASH unit in the Korean War," he says, pride in his voice.

"Didn't they just make a movie about one of those units? In fact, I think they *called* it MASH, kind of a black comedy. *Stars and Stripes* had a review, supposed to be funny."

"Haven't seen it, sir. My dad wouldn't think anything about the Korean War was funny."

"So your father being a doctor and all, how'd you end up over here in Nam? Couldn't you get a college deferment or something?"

"Yeah, I did."

"And?"

"Flunked out, sir, my first semester. Screwed around too much and fucking flunked out. Got drafted. Dad was really pissed."

"Damn, that *was* pretty stupid," I say, thinking Pussycat's story sounds a lot like my own.

"That's what Dad said. Told me to watch my butt because he didn't want to see me in his operating room."

"Damn."

He lights a cigarette, and I see his hands are shaking. "You OK, Cat?" A better nickname, no pussy about him. He seems relieved at this renaming.

"Yes, sir, I guess. This is my first time out in the field." He puts a hand on his M16. "Never fired one of these except in training. I couldn't sleep last night, so I spent hours cleaning it. Grunts over in the chow line were telling me these M16s jam real easy if you don't keep 'em clean."

"That's true," I say. I have my own M16 slung over my shoulder. It is also pristine, never fired in anger. I'd carried a different one during my six months as Bravo Company's forward observer and fired it not at all in combat until my last ferocious night in the field. "Maybe you'll need it," I tell him. "But if we get into anything deep, it's the radio I want you to take care of first. Without a radio to call in fire, we'll be in a world of hurt with hardly a fucking reason for us to be out there." I see he is still shaking a bit, and I ask him if he'd eaten dinner.

"No, sir, my stomach was churning, and I couldn't get a thing down."

"Can't go out on an empty stomach, Cat." I pull a chocolate bar out of my fatigue pants pocket, a real Hershey Bar I'd gotten from home and kept in the briefing room fridge, not one of the almost inedible tropical bars that come with C rations. "Chew on this. You'll feel better."

When he unwraps the chocolate, I see it is already soft, hardly a surprise. This late afternoon in Vietnam's dry summer season is uncomfortably hot for us where we sit on the dirt wall by the naked pierced steel plate of the helicopter pad.

I look at the rucksack Cat has buckled atop the PRC-25 radio he has on his pack frame. "What do you have in there?"

"Just some C rations, an extra radio battery, mosquito repellent, a poncho."

"Dump the poncho. You won't need it. It's going to be months before we see any rain. Repellent's good, though. The jungle is nasty with mosquitos."

He tosses the poncho to one of the grunts manning the pad. I don't imagine Cat will see that new poncho again.

"Do you have plenty of water?" I ask. "You'll go through a lot of fluids in this heat."

"A regular canteen plus this big one," he says. "SGT Dobbs made me fill both." He shows me that both the quart- and gallon-sized water containers are full. "That's got to be enough water, won't it be, sir?"

"Yeah, I imagine, but make sure that if it's not, you don't drink from anywhere else, not from the river and especially not from any standing water. Parasites in the water here will eat you whole from the inside out."

He shudders a bit and shakes the smaller canteen on his web belt again. "Yeah," he says, looking happier as he listens to the slosh.

Off in the direction of the coast, moving above the bomb-cratered mountain peak of Núi Tam Cáp, there is a dark dot I can see approaching. From it, I hear the distant beat of helicopter blades. The pad master, a chunky master sergeant with heavy, dark-framed glasses who everybody calls Bilko, sticks his head out of the pad operations shack and calls out to us, "That's your bird inbound, LT." He waits a few beats and then steps out into the middle of the pad and tosses out a beer-can-shaped smoke grenade. It pops and begins spewing a plume of bright-yellow smoke across the corrugated metal. With hardly any wind blowing, the smoke just hangs, directionless, a dense lemon-colored cloud rising only a bit in the heat coming off the pad's surface. Finally, a tug of breeze comes up to push the plume eastward, and I watch the bird flair and settle toward us into the slight wind.

"That's us, Cat," I say. We shoulder our gear and duck under the rotors and onto the bird. PFC Wilbur seems surprised when I tell him to fasten his seat belt.

"They never told us to when we flew to San Juan Hill from the coast," he says. He fishes for the ends of the straps.

"That's a milk run now," I say. "No birds have taken fire on that route for a long time. Six months ago, it was different. But the way west to Téthian is over Indian Country where we might have to dodge some ground fire, and you'll want to be belted in good if the pilot has to grab some quick air."

Cat tries to look unruffled, but I see him steal a hand up to check the tightness of his seat belt.

The pilot pulls pitch, and we rise over the Sông Ba Tơ valley. The bird climbs to an altitude that leaves the river below us looking like a scribble of blue pen running north into the high green-clad mountains of Minh Long Province. For more than a dozen klicks at the western end of our flight, we leave behind all lowlands, and as I've done before, I search in vain for any memorable terrain, any standout landmarks in the vast jumble of high, densely wooded ridges and deep ravines. Down there it *is* Indian Country for real, a territory we rarely patrol, where enemy base camps could be hidden beyond any chance of detection, a landscape of clandestine trails, of enemy supply depots and armories and ammo dumps that have grown there steadily over the years of the war.

Finally, we reach the four-hundred-meter-tall ridge of Ńui Ta Gâm, a rocky, jungle-covered heap to the east of the camp, where the ridge's northern face nestles into a curve of the stream of Núoc Lac. A click further west, the smaller Suôi Nùng joins it, and then the combined streams flow three hundred meters further west to merge into the broad channel of the Sông Re. We sweep around the northern curve of the ridge, past its steep and heavily wooded face, and emerge in the Sông Re's long north-south valley. Light from the lowering sun still honeys the treetops along the ridge crest, but the valley floor is far enough below it that the river's western bank already lies in deepening shadow.

As we fly into the camp, I wonder at the vitality of this river valley, deep green with rice paddies, the bluffs east and west of the river buried in dense jungle canopy. A thin waterfall (a shadow of what it will be when the monsoons come) falls through that canopy from a high slice of the ridge atop the western bluff. The smell here, too, is of a jungle richer and more fecund than that of the dying forest further east I have walked so often, this one less touched by the poisons of war. On the far shore, blocky Montagnard hooches clustered near the river on stilts make up the ville of Téthian. They have a look of thatched gothic houses plucked from some forest of Europe and settled here in the jungle. The homes are dark and solid looking, far different from the flimsier-looking hooches of the Vietnamese over on the coast.

The camp is on a low mound along the river at the south end of the hamlet. What I was told of the camp (wrongly as it turns out) is that its complement is a dozen men of a Special Forces A-Team and a company of a hundred or so CIDG, South Vietnamese Civilian Irregular Defense Force troops. That's a formal name for a ragtag militia of Montagnards whose hatred of war is only outweighed by their hatred of the Viet Cong who raid their rice and steal their young men as fodder for the war of liberation against the South Vietnamese government. Most of the operations they conduct are dark, stealthy, and generally undisclosed.

The bird flares and settles onto the camp's small pad, bucking a bit in the choppier air next to the river. Nobody has bothered to pop smoke, and thus the bird has no indicator of wind direction for its landing. We are down, the blades still spinning, the bird hardly come to rest when the crew chief points to the pad and gestures for me and Cat to jump off. "Let's go, Cat!" I shout over the beat of the blades. "They aren't going to stay down here long." We are barely on the ground with our gear when the pilot pulls pitch and lifts the bird. The dust-filled blast of its ground effect almost blows us over as we duck away.

The Téthian camp smells pungently of *nước mắm* fish sauce and chicken shit, the latter apparently the product of a dozen or so black-and-white speckled Montagnard Cochin hens roaming freely around the hooches and bunkers. The red-headed, puffy-feathered birds are clustered at the helicopter pad, squawking in protest at the blast from the rotor blades as our helicopter lifts off. The hens finally quiet down and move in their jerky fashion out of our way as we walk toward the operations shack.

There is no one to greet us as we debark. In fact, no one is visible at all, neither the team nor any of the Montagnards. No one even appears to be on guard. We walk past more reminders of the recent battle here, bullet holes pocking one sandbag wall, a cistern partially blown down and dry, a man-sized bloodstain deepening the red in the camp's red dirt. Finally, as we come up to the operations shack, I began to hear voices speaking in what I guess is the Montagnards' Jarai dialect: a language flat and atonal, with almost German-type gutterals. But none of the Yards is visible.

Cat and I approach the shack, and a Montagnard whom I recognize as the đại úy I'd seen before steps out of the open door. From behind him, CPT Englander appears. He and the đại úy are both dressed in tiger fatigues, their faces camoed with angular strokes of green and black grease paint. Both also have on tiger-striped boonie hats, a lot like the floppy-brimmed hats some of our regular troops also wear in the field, swearing by them as lighter and less of a burden than the standard steel-pot helmet. The pleasant and genial Englander of my last visit seems gone. He is once again the humorless and arrogant prick I had met on my first visit here.

"About time you got here," he says. "I was beginning to think you'd wimped out."

"You said 1800 hours, Hugh. It's ten minutes shy of that right now."

He makes a show of glancing at his watch, shakes his head, and changes the subject. "Face paint in the hooch on the table, get yourselves greased up." He peers at our helmets and points at a box of boonie hats by the hooch. "Got some *real* soldier's covers here if you want 'em. Steel pots are going to get heavy on this trip."

"Yeah, choice looking, man," I say, "but in my book, cotton boonie hats do a lousy job of deflecting a bullet. Personally, I'm sticking with my steel pot." Cat nods agreement.

Englander's sneer says "Suit yourself," him saying, "Anyway, get set. We leave when it's dark."

"I figured," I say, motioning for Cat to follow me into the ops shack. "Let's go in and get tarted up for this trip," I tell him. "And get me the battalion FDC on the horn. I want to be sure they have our preplotted targets ready for the mission."

"About that," I hear Englander say behind me.

I turn. "About what, Hugh?"

"Mission's going in a different direction from what we laid out last week." His face is blank. I would have expected at least a twist of a smile as he shoots down my artillery preplan.

"What new direction is that?"

"Lê Văn Dũng's not where he was when we sussed this out last week. Not on Núi Mum anymore." He looks at me, but I don't even let myself blink. Finally, seeing I'm not going to comment, Englander says, "Naw, we got new intel that he's in a ville on the other side of the Sông Re, in some ugly country about five klicks over the west side of the ridge."

"Christ, Hugh," I say. "You found out about this when?"

"Day before yesterday."

"And you didn't think to let me know."

"Hell, man, why? You said yourself that the guns you've got, the 175s, can shoot a lot farther than that, maybe another eight or ten klicks farther." Then he does give me a little sneer. The same topo map as before is on the table, and Englander pulls it over and puts a finger on the spot where Lê is supposed to be now.

I am boiling inside at his unconcern. He surely knows that this information will change everything for me. The previous objective had been an easy target for both the eight-inch and 175s at Minh Long. This new objective is below the reverse slope of the long bluff that parallels the Sông Re. I'm sure he also knows it is beyond the range fan for the eight-inch howitzers and, though not at extreme range for the 175s, far enough toward it to cause real problems. The 175s can hit somewhere close to this new objective but not very far down into the deep valley we'll have to traverse to get to Lê. Looking at Englander, it is clear to me that he's fully aware of all this and thinks he has me busted. So with this new obstacle, he can confirm to himself that artillery is not flexible enough to be a benefit to teams like his out here in the woods.

"You knew this two days ago and didn't bother to tell me?" I say again.

"Hell, man, it's the same guns firing from the same firebase. What difference does it make?"

"Listen, Englander—"

"CPT Englander."

"Listen, *Captain* Englander," I say with the respect due a man who outranks me by only about two months, "I carefully plotted defensive targets all along the line of march I *thought* we were taking. I'll have to scratch those now and plot a different set along this new line of march. If you'd let me know of the change, I could have had it done before I even came here."

"We're leaving in an hour or so, soon as it's good and dark, Weisman," he says. "So if you want those targets called in, you'd better get cracking. Hey?"

Cat is looking at me in confusion, getting it that CPT Englander thinks he is leaving us without most of the artillery support that is the prime reason we are here in the first place. But he clearly doesn't see why the captain seems to be trying to screw us.

"Cat!" I say to him. "Bring me the CAC code book and the radio. Let's get a new set of targets to battalion FDC."

Here, in this flourishing jungle, unlike the ravaged and silent woodlands closer to the coast, the air is full of bird calls and the hum of insects. Though it is growing dark, the night is still hot, and this close to the river, the jungle air is humid. I am sweating. My fatigue shirt hangs on me, sodden at the armpits, limply damp everywhere else. I have it buttoned to the throat and at the wrists to fend off Vietnam's vicious strain of mosquitos. They hover around me in the hooch as though reconnoitering a gap through my liberally applied mosquito repellent. Cat is slumped against the wall of the hooch. He looks as miserable as I feel, sweat running down his face. I am going over the route Englander had traced for me on the map.

In this new battle plan, we are to cross the river using shallow-draft wooden boats the Montagnards had obtained from villes north of the base. The boats are like large, wide-gunneled canoes, unlikely to tip in the Sông Re's modest dry season flow. We'll then head west through a narrow valley and climb the steep four-hundred-meter height of the ridge. Once up it, we will pass over the crest of the ridge and then drop down its even steeper western face. All this through triple-canopy jungle in the pitch dark. We'll go on to a stream the map labels Dak Monit, flowing through yet another narrow valley. We will turn south into the valley and make our way a final klick to the ville of Monit where Lê Văn Dũng is now supposed to be staying. Once we have Lê, the plan is to head back to the clearing and—stealth no longer being a concern—call for extraction. On the map, the clearing appears big enough for two birds at a time to come in and lift us out.

"No sweat on this," Englander smirks. "Well, maybe a little."

As I trace our route on the map, what bothers me most is not the steepness of the terrain (hell, I figure I am in as good shape to make a climb as any of the A-Team members), it is that this land beyond the Sông Re is purely wild, owned for all practical purposes by the Viet Cong. In fact, the trail we will be taking over the ridge is likely a supply route for the VC. Who knows what we might run into as we travel on it?

Because the mission is to be stealthy, operating both in heavy jungle and near enemy positions, Englander is taking only half his twelve-man A-Team. The Montagnard company's đại úy has brought a twelve-man rifle squad to augment the split A-Team. Even counting me and Cat and the đại úy, that's just twenty-one soldiers, hardly a potent force if we hit anything heavy. Looking at the map with me, Cat is pale with nervousness beneath the camo grease, and I think seriously for a moment of taking the radio myself and leaving him back at Téthian. He must sense my emotion because as we are getting our gear on, he says, "I'm coming, LT. I'm going to be OK."

It is almost pitch dark on the river; not a light is visible on the far bank. The moon, which will show just a sliver of a crescent, will not rise until an hour after midnight. A faint phosphorescence clings to the water, and above us is another river, this one of stars crossing a cloudless and inky sky. I learn that though the team owns some night-vision devices of the old heavy and bulky generation one type, on a nearly moonless night like this one, they would likely be useless. The A-Team has elected to travel lighter by leaving theirs back at Téthian.

Four Yards paddle our boat, with Englander, Cat, and me in the middle. Ahead of us is a boat with four more paddlers plus the đại úy and two of the A-Team. A third and fourth boat follow ours with the rest of the Yards and the final A-Team members. Only the slight splash of the paddles breaks the silence as we cross the Sông Re.

Surprising myself, I find I'm not much nervous. I suppose I've been in Vietnam too long for that, but entry into such unfamiliar territory always raises a knot of unease in my gut. You don't know. So you fear because death can come in so many shapes, often with no warning sign or token and often when you feel most secure. The Yards seem entirely at ease. I've been in Vietnam nearly a year yet have rarely seen Montagnards up close. I know that the Yards, Vietnam's original people, are ethnically distinct from the Vietnamese who had come more recently from China and Tibet with a different language and culture. Close up, I see they are different physically as well, darker skinned with shorter, narrower noses than the majority Vietnamese and with eyes lacking the Vietnamese's epicanthic folds. Compared to the tonal Vietnamese language, the Yards' speech sounds flat and almost western.[1]

---

[1] The Montagnard Jarai language, though all of one pitch, is thoroughly strange to me. I do know a few words of pidgin Vietnamese, mostly learned from the boy Quan, whom we had rescued on a mountain trail and took in as a ward of the infantry battalion. He had taught me *chào ông* for "good-bye," *cám ơn* for "thank you," *cockadau* for "kill," and *chiêu hồi* (literally "the way back"), which meant to come over to the American side. You heard bits and pieces of Vietnamese in shops and bars in the villes. You got the sense if not the denotation of the language from the posture and attitude of those speaking to you. But everything about the Yards'

The Yards' top sergeant is a tough bird named Ksang. He is short like the Vietnamese but more solid, slightly graying, his face dark and lined. The Yards' đại úy is sour, almost sullen with a constant crackling anger in his eyes. The sergeant's face, by contrast, is constantly alight with humor and apparent joy in the intensity of life.

The river's current is slow but gives us a slight drift to the north, pushing us away from our planned landing on a sandy bank. Instead, we hit the western side of the Sông Re in the middle of a rank and muddy bog. When the first of the four Yards who had been paddling our boat—a lowly teenage *chiến sĩ*—jumps out, he sinks to his knees in the muck and immediately wails in pain. Two of the other Yards pull him back into the boat, and Englander shines the red beam of his flashlight on the boy's leg, which runs dark with blood. The Yard has gashed his leg on something in the mud, and it is bleeding freely. The Yards' medic splashes over from the first boat, which has landed upstream of ours, takes one look, and says something to the đại úy about *kotang drah*, which I learn later is "angry blood" or "bleeding bad" or something similar in Jarai. The đại úy, looking bitter, says something back to his medic and then turns to Englander and says, "Got to take him back and fix this. Ữ'?"

Englander says, "Fuck!" stares at the wounded man for a few beats, and then tells the đại úy, "Yeah, have a couple of your men take him back," says "Fuck!" again, and orders the Yards paddling the boat to move us to a better landing spot.

So not yet on dry land, we are down three men.

The Yards move our boat upstream twenty meters or so to where the landing is more solid, pull it up onto the bank, and let us out. Then two of the Yards begin taking the boat with the injured man back across the Sông Re to the Téthian camp. Almost at once as we debark, clouds of mosquitos descend upon on us. The repellent I had put on keeps them at bay, but their hum—the pitch of a thousand tiny dentist's drills—is

---

Jarai language is new: *ho'dĭp*, "to live"; *huĭ*, "to be fearful"; and *amuaĭh*, "to love." Though the Yards have a term for war, *bla ngă*, their lexicon for its implements and for the titles of warriors is almost all borrowed from the Vietnamese: *đại úy* for "captain," *trung sĩ* for "sergeant," *người lính* for "soldier," and *pháo binh*, "cannon soldiers," for us artillerymen.

maddening. We walk now in almost complete darkness. No sound or light comes from the houses around us, as if the villagers have been warned and either sit silent in the dark or have gone away from our line of march.

In this deep night, what is Montagnard house, what is tree, and what is the distant but looming shoulders of the hills are almost indistinguishable. The only sign of the men in front of me are dime-sized dots of fluorescent paint the Yards and American troops have on the backs of their hats (Englander has dabbed some on my and Cat's helmets too). I am convinced that Englander banked on the darkness confusing me enough that I would screw up and lose my orientation and location. For an artilleryman, that is all you have. If you know where you are, you can know where the enemy is and where the guns are that would shoot for you and you are worth something out in the bush. Lost, turned around, you are worthless, and I sense Englander is counting on that. It is the core of the reason, I suspect, that he changed our destination, hoping it would leave me muddled. It's why I spent time in the ops hooch at the camp studying the map, learning the lay of the land we would walk through.

The flat stretch of it runs for perhaps two hundred paces from the riverbank between the darkened houses of the Yards to the gravel bed of Highway 5B. Past the highway comes the sudden penetration into jungle. The upslope begins gradually between hills closing in steeply on either side. It is clear to me, though, that by the way Englander frequently checks his map, this is a new route for him too and he is hardly more familiar with it than I am.

My own orientation method—essentially dead reckoning honed over months of humping through the bush as the forward observer for Bravo Company—is not much of a trick. I know how many paces (at 1,300 of my paces to the kilometer, about two and a half feet a pace) we expect to walk. So from the river onward, watching our compass direction and sensing the changing lay of the land, I count my steps as we move. Doing so, I am willing to bet Englander I will be able to give him our grid location within ten meters anywhere on our line of march.

We are just beginning that march, just past the graveled surface of Highway 5B, and only three hundred paces in from where we'd left the boats when Englander, who is walking just behind the point man, stops, and I hear the order for the rest of us to stop hissed edgily back down the line.

Cat, right behind me, whispers a worried "What?"

"Wait," I say back. And I hear one of the Yards ahead of us hiss urgently, "Ayăt!" (The enemy!) and then a quick spatter of more Montagnard speech, voices barely audible.

Englander comes back down the trail to me, saying, "The *trung sĩ* thinks there may be some dinks up ahead of us a hundred meters or so."

"Ambush?" I ask.

"Could be. If you got guns pointing this way, get 'em ready."

I hear Cat say, "God!" in a softly awed voice, and I take the radio's handset from him and quietly call, "Glad Pacer One-One, this is Able Footman Two-Niner. Over."

SGT Dobbs's voice comes back almost instantly. "Pacer One-One. Go ahead. Over."

"Roger, action in the three-three, four-six grid square. Point some guns my way. Over."

"Wilco," Alan says. "Do you have a fire mission for me?"

"Negative yet. Maybe some dinks, possible ambush about a hundred mikes on from our position."

At this, Englander holds up a hand, barely visible in the deep dark under the jungle canopy. "Don't shoot. Just have 'em ready, hey? The Yards' trung sĩ is sending two of his guys up to check it out." His voice is crisp as if directing a novice how to act.

I ignore it, just saying, "We're ready."

So we stand, waiting, not moving, breathing as softly as we can until the word comes down the line again, "Nothing!" No ambush ahead, we will move again.

"Man," says Cat behind me, and I know it is relief rather than disappointment I hear in his voice.

"One-One, this is Two-Niner. False alarm, stand down. Over," I say into the handset.

"Roger, Two-Niner. Take care. Out."

We walk further, the path, less used here, softening some under our feet as we press deeper into the jungle past the last of the Montagnard huts and then into a place where I can sense the dark shapes of the hills crowding more closely around us. We halt again just where the path begins its steep climb up the side of the ridge. Englander tells the đại úy to have some of his men reconnoiter the way up to the ridgetop. I stand with nothing to do but wait, itching with the ghost of a desire for a cigarette. I'd stopped smoking after the firefight on Hill 800 nearly six months ago. I'd figured having the dinks trying to kill me was enough. But the urge comes back to me at times when things get tense. I pull out my canteen instead and let a mouthful of water trickle down my throat. There seems to be no air here under this deep jungle canopy, the heat and humidity pressing in on us, drenching me in sweat that won't evaporate, the jungle now mostly quiet except for the omnipresent hum of mosquitos. Cat is hardly two feet from me, and, save for the dot on his helmet when he turns his head, I can't see him at all. I whisper his name, and he responds with a barely audible "Sir?"

"Drink some water, Cat," I tell him. "We're going to be here a few minutes. Englander sent a couple of the Yards up to check out the trail."

I swallow another mouthful. The water is lukewarm but feels good going down. A mosquito hums into my ear, and I brush at it fitfully. In Nam, I learned to hate them then and forever. The war will sweep away from me as I age, its details will blur, edges fraying into a different life and new set of memories, but the needle sound of a mosquito will remain ever fresh and unhinging.

Soon, the call of "Moving" comes down the line, and we begin to walk again, the almost silent pad of footsteps in front of me nearly the only signal of our progress. The slope grows steeper, the climb arduous through the heavy air. I worry for a moment that Cat won't be able to keep up and realize quickly enough that he is younger by more than five years and likely far more agile than I (I feel like an old man at twenty-five). The path grows still more precipitous, and I am glad I had decided to leave my rucksack back at Téthian. The few things I carry, my map, compass and binoculars, my M16 and ammo bandoleer, my canteens, and even the small weight of a chocolate bar and some crackers are by themselves a burden as we climb. I begin to regret that I hadn't traded my steel pot for a boonie hat like the Yards and American troops have. Regardless of its weight, though, the helmet seems a refuge. Maybe it won't stop a bullet, but I have seen more times than I care to remember what rifle fire can do to a man's unprotected head. In this darkness, all I see in front of me are a dozen or so faintly glowing sparks of phosphorescence moving as if levitated above the blackness of the trail.

It gets worse. There is a thud and "oof" from the path above me. The man one up in line goes down, and his feet slide into mine, knocking them out from under me and sending me back almost into Cat. I grab at something I hit, the slender trunk of a sapling, and cling to it for dear life as the man who had slid into me flounders, trying to find purchase on the trail. By the grace of God, I hang on to my rifle with one hand while grasping the bit of tree that is all that keeps me from sliding away down the hill. The man, SSG Tom Hicks—the team's engineer—manages to get his footing again. My face aches. In flailing for purchase, the heel of his hand had hit my chin and his nails had raked my cheek. His elbow had also whacked my steel pot, jolting me, but I suspect he had taken the worst of the blow. Fortunately, Cat, who had better footing, had finally helped stop us.

"Man!" Cat says. "You all right, LT? I thought we were going all the way back down the hill."

I tell him I am fine (not quite true, my face burns from where Hicks's nails scored it.)

SFC Hicks manages to get purchase on the trail again, catch his breath, and say, "Sorry, LT. Don't know why the goddamned CO wanted to come this way. Couple of klicks north the trail goes *around* most of this ridge. This is shorter but fucking steep going, especially when it's too dark to see a man's ass a foot in front of you."

So it seems that in trying to piss me off, Englander has succeeded mostly in pissing off some of his own men. I just grunt, "Yeah," and start forward again when I hear "Moving!" passed back from the line of men in front of us.

Finally, we make it to the crest of the ridge and try to get our breath back, walking on the flat for a couple of hundred meters. Then we head down the reverse slope of the ridge on a trail that, if anything, is steeper than the one we had come up. The men around me, at least the

American troops, are trained well enough to keep most of their thoughts to themselves, but I know nobody is happy about taking this trail. Has Englander taken it before? I don't know but intend to ask him when we get back to the camp. In truth, we make decent time going down, the path here being well-trod, with some steps even cut into it at the steepest points. That it seems well-used gives me the willies, though, because the only ones likely to be using it are the Viet Cong.

We are about halfway down when there comes a rushing, a sense of something big in the air north of us, flying past and then gone, and in a moment from beyond the distant Dak Sêlo river valley comes a muffled detonation. Englander storms back up the steep trail, pushing through the Yards and past his own men, shoving Hicks aside. He gets into my face, close, voice low but barking. "Weisman, I told you not to shoot any fucking artillery without my say so."

I don't like it, not his attitude and not his angry penetration of the bubble of my space.

"What the hell, Englander?"

"That was your arty shooting, wasn't it, 175s going off out there?"

And I get it: to him, because I am artillery, everything artillery that happens out here in his territory is my doing. I know he thinks that, sees in me the personification of all the guns and shells and implements of the big war that others are fighting, while he carries out his own more intimate campaign out here in these pristine western mountains.

"I didn't call for it, Hugh. It's H & I, harassment and interdiction fire, targets out in the woods on trail junctions and the like," I say. "It's supposed to keep the dinks wondering where it is safe out here and where the next rounds will fall. But you know that, you must hear it every night, the shells from the eight-inch and 175s going off somewhere in these mountains. You can't be surprised."

"They're too damn close, Weisman. I don't like them shooting when we are out here."

I put a hand to his shoulder to push him back a step and get him out of my face. "They don't shoot where there are friendly troops like us. They know where we are. But you know that too. I could call and have 'em stop shooting the H & I stuff. But that would be a real tip-off to the dinks that we are out here."

"Well, call and tell your artillery buddies to keep that shit off of us. Got it?"

"They already know, Hugh."

"Call them just the same."

"Will do, Captain."

So I call Alan and tell him, and he laughs and says that, yes, they know where we are planning to be tonight, and that the H & I targets they are shooting this night are some five klicks away to our northwest. We are way out of danger.

"Do you want a change in them?" he asks me.

"Nope," I say. "Actually, they're kind of a comfort out here, kind of a high-explosive teddy bear to cuddle to."

"Screw you too, sir," Alan laughs and says, "Out!"

Down from the ridge at last, we feel the trail began to level out. Over us, the jungle canopy opens enough that even on this yet moonless, solely starlit night, I can make out the shapes of the men around me. We take a quick break at the bottom of the trail to orient ourselves. I swig from my canteen and gnaw on a bit of tropical chocolate and have Cat call Alan again with a sitrep and to get a commo check. Alan's voice comes up Lima Charley (loud and clear) over the handset, lessening one of my worries.

So far, though heavy going, the trek has been a cakewalk with no signs of the enemy. Now, we turn south along the stream the map labels Dak Monit, a tiny tributary of the larger Dak Sélo River that runs somewhat parallel to the Sông Re a few klicks west. It has become very silent in this stretch of jungle, the hum of insects, even the keening of mosquitos gone. I do my best to imitate the team members' stealth, their ability even in this darkness to put their feet down quietly, revealing hardly a whit of their motion. The night is now so quiet that the snap of a broken stick or the whisk of one pant leg against the other seems thunderous.

About half a klick south, things get scary as the little valley briefly narrows into a ravine no more than a dozen paces wide, the stream in it knee deep and moving faster. On either side of us the ravine's walls are sheer rock more than twice a man's height. Above them on both sides of the stream, the map shows the valley rising steeply for a long way. It is a perfect spot for an ambush, and Englander sends one of his sergeants and a couple of the Yards ahead to reconnoiter. They come back, and there is an urgent whispered conference between the captain and the sergeant. At last, Englander grunts, "Nothing here." And we press on through the bottleneck, though not without a lot of neck craning to check out the danger. From there, we walk a bit less than two klicks south along the stream, the towering flanks of the ridges to our east and west sensed more than seen. The sky, which has been visible for much of this stretch, disappears as jungle canopy closes in on us again. It is exactly the sort of country I had expected with only the higher part of the western ridge exposed to fire from the big guns. The rest of the area is just too deep for the flat-trajectory 175 shells to drop into.

All at once, our file comes to a halt at a spot where the Dak Monit forks into two smaller streams, the western branch spilling from a cleft in the ridge that climbs steeply into dense jungle.

I can see nothing except the faintest difference between the darkness of the jungle canopy and the still darker masses of the high hills around us.

Englander walks back down the line to where Cat and I hunker next to a large boulder. He flicks the red masked light of his flash onto his map, tracing a finger along where we are. (It cheers me to see that my dead reckoning is right on and that we are exactly where I have figured us to be.) "Up here about a hundred meters is a good place to settle in," he tells me. "The ville that's our objective—just a handful of Yard hooches really—where Lê Văn Dũng is holed up is a couple of hundred meters further on up. I'm going to take most of my team straight up into the ville. The Yards are going to circle around the back side and set up a block. I'm going to leave Mike Olsson and four of the Yards here with you. Tell me your artillery can do us some good here."

"Yeah, no worries there, Captain. You're going up the east-facing flank of the ridge, so up where the ville is, that entire ridge side is a clear target for the 175s."

"OK," he says. He sounds a little disappointed that artillery will be available. "Don't shoot *anything* without my go-ahead. You hear?"

"Got it, Hugh."

So Cat and I, SSG Olsson, and the four Yard riflemen set in among a bunch of large rocks next to the stream. It is quiet and close, the humid air hanging about us without motion, rich with jungle smells. The only sounds are those of a swarm of mosquitos that rise out of the vegetation. I slap on more repellent, stifling a sneeze as its alcohol reek fills my nose. One of the Yards pulls out a bun filled with a pungent fish paste and begins chewing at it. He senses me watching, pushes the bun toward, me and asks, "Bŏng?" I shake my head, and he returns to eating the bun himself. I call Alan and get confirmation that the guns will be ready if we need them.

"Roger, keep 'em all turned this way," I whisper to him, though I know they will be.

And we sit, ten minutes, fifteen. At just beyond twenty minutes, there is the deep note of a rifle shot from high up on the ridge.

"AK," SSG Olsson says. He chambers a round in his M16, and I hear Cat choke out the word "Oh!" and one of the Yards hiss, "Po'ro'sua!" (Fighting!) and, "Čang!" (Wait!)

We hear the sound of return fire, the fast rattle of several M16s, and the slightly deeper sound of first one, and then a pair of AK-47s. Cat, never before in combat, presses almost lover close against me, whispering repeatedly, "What? What?" and I tell him to just stay down but be ready.

"It's up on the ridge, Cat, far away," I say. "Give me the handset." One of my preplanned targets is about one hundred meters downhill from the little ville, and I call Alan, telling him to get the data ready for that target. "Don't load any rounds yet, but be ready, man," I say.

This is nothing new to me, and I don't think I am even nervous about it, just hunched there behind the boulder, keyed up at the rising sounds of a firefight. Cat, though, is getting his first taste of combat and is right next to me, issuing soft moans at each burst of gunfire from above.

The shooting suddenly dies away, and soon from the direction of the ville comes the rattle of stones down the steep stream bed. Then Englander and his team and the rest of the Yards are back. Between two of the sergeants a few paces away, I can make out the shape of what looks like a dink, trussed up, gagged, hands bound but still struggling against the Yard soldiers holding him. One of the Yards is moaning, and SSG Olsson—who is the team's medic—moves over to him alongside the Yard medic.

"Hit in the leg," he says to Englander. "Not mortal. We can move him, but he can't walk."

"Christ," Englander answers. "OK, get him so we can carry him. Two minutes, that's all. Then we move before the dinks can get their shit together and come after us."

Englander turns to me. "How about getting some arty up on that ville? Can your guns hit it?" He sounds as if he hopes they can't.

I'm not about to paste the ville with artillery fire when I didn't know who all is there. Yeah, it is true we are in a free-fire zone where I needed no permission to shoot at anyone. But I don't relish dropping high explosives where there might be noncombatants.

"I could put some stuff between us and the ville. Put up a barrier to keep them from following us?" I say.

Englander hesitates. I know he really wants me to blow the shit out of the several hooches up there on the ridge face. But he says, "Yeah, do it. Put some big rounds in there to block if they try to follow us."

I call Alan with the fire mission. "Shoot my target number four, reconfirming grid two-niner-zero-zero, four-two-seven-zero. HE on the ground. Platoon two. Use the 175s." Both Alan and I know that target is way too close to us for me to be shooting the initial rounds at it without a mark first, but this is something out of the ordinary, and LTC Dolby has told the fire direction center to give me anything I want on this mission.

"OK," SSG Olsson whispers from where he has been bandaging the wounded Montagnard, "this guy is ready to travel."

"Weisman," Englander says to me, "You got some arty coming or not?"

"Coming," I tell him, and just then, Alan announces, "Shot!"

"On the way now, Captain," I tell Englander. "We ought to *didi*."

"Yeah, let's go," Englander says, and almost in the same instant, Alan announces, "Splash!" to me, meaning impact in ten seconds.

The freight train racket of incoming artillery roars into the little valley, and a pair of 175 mm shells hit in a stunning double burst above us on the slope of the ridge. As the detonation resounds, we didi, hauling along the dink captive and carrying the wounded Yard as quickly as we can safely go back down the stream toward our extraction point.

One of the Yards has come down the mountainside carelessly carrying a ratty-looking backpack slung over his shoulders. The đại úy has twice snapped at him curtly with "Răng, răang, krâo," which a Yard trung sĩ who speaks passable English tells me means to be careful, "poison plants are in the water." I don't know what that means and try to ask him, but all he can say is "Xin lỗi" (So sorry), and stops trying to translate.

Whatever it is, the Yard carrying the bundle steps carelessly among the stream's boulders and slips, a startled "Ô," escaping him. He tumbles back. The backpack hits a rock, and from inside it, we hear sharp hiss.

At this, Englander goes wild, blurting, "Get it off him. Get it off now." He jumps to pull the bundle off the Yard soldier himself, saying, "Fuck, fuck, all we need." He and the đại úy manage to get the bundle free, and Englander flings it away from the stream. "Go, *nao, nao*," Englander orders and begins splashing downstream careless of the noise he's making. All at once, all of us are moving.

"LT?" Cat starts to say to me. I have no idea what this is about and just tell him to move.

We had traveled like ghosts when we came up the Dak Monit. The sound of that movement had been no louder than a sigh of wind or an extra ripple in the soft mumble of the water. Back down the stream, running from the place where we had left the backpack, we go faster but once again cat-silent after that initial alarm, the muted moan of the wounded Yard our only voice. Lê Văn Dũng, gagged, blindfolded, and trussed like a turkey, is in the middle of our file, held between two of the Yards, most of the time carrying him to keep him from making noise.

I move up beside Englander, wondering what the hell that craziness with the backpack back there had been all about. "Better not to ask, Weisman," he says to me. I press, but he just brusquely tells me, "Not here," and won't talk more.

Even with the artillery I've dumped on the mountainside trail, we know that the dinks are following us. Crafty as they are, they apparently don't care to be silent, and the sporadic crack of sticks or the muffled splash of a footstep tells us they are not more than a couple of hundred meters or so behind us. Our biggest objective is to make it through the point where the stream narrows through the ravine. Past there, it will be less than a klick to the extraction point.

Fifty meters from that ravine, Englander calls a quick halt and directs the Yard đại úy to send two of his men forward to look for signs of an ambush. A quick flashlight blink from them tells us they have found nothing, and so we begin to move. We thread our way through the rocks, wading in the knee-deep stream. The first of the Yards are just ahead of us, already into the narrow ravine, when from above to either side, the night erupts with AK-47 fire. The dinks had let the first two Yards pass and then hit the front of our file. Muzzle flashes light the night as a hail of incoming fire blasts into the men there. The rattle and pop of the dinks' weapons is terrifying in those close confines. Immediately, our Yards set up a howl, and all of us began to return fire, but it is too late. The two Yards who had already gone through the ravine are cut off. The next three of the Yards behind them go down instantly.

Englander bellows, "Back and cover!" and the troops of the well-disciplined team have, in an instant, scrambled out of the stream bed and pushed back maybe twenty meters from the ravine, firing as they go and finally ducking behind rocks on either side, below the Dak Monit's steep banks. The dinks in the ambush quickly catch on and aim their fire further back at us. It spangs off the rocks in front of us but does no damage. Several Chicom grenades fly in at us from the dinks' position on the walls of the ravine, only one detonating and that one too far away to do much damage. But we are stuck. We can't go back because of the dinks following us, and we can't go forward into the treacherous passage of the ravine. The banks to our sides are too high and sheer to easily climb. Where did those who ambushed us come from? A relief force, most likely, come from further downstream, where climbing the high banks is easier. If anything, it tells us just how many of the enemy are in the area.

"Dammit, we're pinned," Englander says. The dinks rattle some more AK fire at us, but likely realizing we are under cover and not moving, they let that fire taper off.

MSG Flanagan slides down in the rocks next to Englander. "Bad spot," he says. He shines the red glow of his flashlight onto his map to show Englander where the dinks are. And it is then I realize the captain has been wounded. Some of the flash's glow splashes over Englander's arm, and I can see blood, looking black in that light, soaking the right shoulder of his shirt.

"Shit, Cap, you're hit."

"Yeah," Englander says. "Hurts like a motherfucker. Through the meat of my shoulder. Don't think it got the bone. Anyone else hit?"

The first sergeant calls out for those wounded to report and gets just two replies from the Yards, both hit but nothing serious. Two of the Americans are also wounded, Larry Arguello, the weapons sergeant, with a thigh wound, and Tom Hicks, the engineer sergeant who had crashed into me on the climb up the ridge, with a bullet wound across his ribs. Neither is wounded as seriously as Englander. SSG Olsson, the team medic, slides over and begins working on Englander's shoulder, with Englander growling, "Shit, Olsson, could you be any more ham handed, hey?" He turns to MSG Flanagan, wincing as Olsson works on him but able to ask how bad a situation we are in. "Dinks in front got us pinned?"

"Dinks in front of us ain't the problem, Cap," Flanagan says. "The ones coming up from behind are. Get us in a crossfire pretty soon."

"Top, any idea on what happened to the three Yards down there in the water?"

"Dunno, Cap. Dead, I think. Wait." Flanagan leans across the rock and calls to SSG Owen Dabrowski, "O-man, can you see, are the Yards down there alive?"

Dabrowski, the A-Team member closest to the ravine, says, "Can't tell, Top. Want me to fire a flare?"

"Yeah, go ahead."

There comes a pop and hiss as a hand flare shoots up over the ravine and begins to float down on its small parachute.

"What do you see, O-man?"

"Damn, they're wasted, Top."

"Not just shot up?"

Nah, Top, they're blown to shit."

"What about the other two who were on point?"

"Don't see 'em. They musta didi'd."

So of the dozen-some Montagnard soldiers we'd started with, only the đại úy, his first sergeant, and three Yard soldiers, including the wounded man and the two guarding the captured dink Lê Văn Dũng, are left.

At the first moment of the ambush, I call Alan and tell him to put a marking round on the nearest of the preplanned targets I had set on this line of march.

"Christ," Englander says, hearing my call for fire. "How the hell are you going to get the 175s to shoot here in this valley? Stuff from those guns is going to hit way far up on the ridge behind us, isn't it?"

"175s would," I tell him. "That's not what's shooting for me, though."

At that moment, I could hear Alan announce, "Shot!" over the radio Cat was carrying.

"So who the hell is shooting for you?" the captain asks and then yelps as SSG Olsson pulls the bandage tighter over his wound. "Aaah, aaah, Olsson. That's good enough. Leave it. I'll live . . ."

"105s are shooting for us from Hill 400 about four klicks north of Téthian. Battalion artillery put a battery of 'em up there this morning. Artillery folks don't like to go anywhere we don't have guns to shoot for us."

I hear Alan announce, "Splash!" and seconds later, the bright flash and boing of a white phosphorous marking round goes off above the ravine about a hundred meters out from where we are hunkered. A second marking round I'd called in goes off a hundred meters or so up the stream behind us, near the other dinks.

"Well, I'll be damned," Englander says.

"Not this time," I say. And I say to Alan, "Give me a platoon two on both targets."

"Roger," Alan responds.

"Hell," says Englander. "You aren't going to need them. I don't imagine the dinks figured on artillery being able to get in here. They probably already didi'd when those Willie Pete rounds came in." He twists around and snaps, "Man, finish up," at SSG Olsson, who has been tightening and taping down the bandage.

Alan has already announced, "Shot!" on the two volleys from the battery, and I call for everyone to get their heads down. "Big stuff coming in."

The 105 rounds slam down, us in the eye of their storm, their ripe bursts scouring the ravine and the riverbed behind us. Close, close, it is devastation, rock shards flying, shrapnel whizzing past, so near, the blasts hard and sharp. In their roar, you hear nothing else. I grab the radio handset from Cat and bellow, "Repeat platoon two! Both targets."

The flashes are brilliant in the deep night. In them, someone is shrieking, and I am afraid one of our own or one of the American troops or the Yards has been injured in the razor squall of shell fragments. The second volley comes in, crashing just as powerfully. Then gone. The shelling has been so close that seasoned as they are, even our troops cower behind the rocks, shaking now, momentarily deafened in the blast. And it is clear the dinks are done for, dead or didi'd.

"Son of a bitch!" Englander says.

MSG Flanagan, an old sergeant who has surely endured many such cannonades before, stands, a dark shape against the darker trees, voice steady, asking if anyone else is hurt. None is, and the mystery of the shriek is not explained. Perhaps it was one of the dink ambushers at the ravine, wounded and crying with the pain. So we begin to move, climbing out of the rocks and merging into a unit again.

"Let's go before the dinks can get their shit together and come after us," Flanagan says. No one argues.

I am proud of Cat. The young soldier, his combat cherry popped, stood his ground, making sure I had radio contact with the battery. Bravery is subjective, a mastery of duty over fear. Terrified or not, Cat did his job, and that was bravery to me. I take the handset from him and tell the battery, "End of mission."

"Roger," Alan says and then more softly, "You OK?"

"Yeah," I respond. "We were in the middle of a damned turkey shoot. Got some wounded and KIAs. Cat and I are OK, though. We're headed for the extraction point. Keep the guns pointed our way."

"Wilco. Out."

The two missing Yards, happily unhurt, meet us at the extraction point. We carry out the bodies of the three killed in the ravine and load them on the birds that pull us out. We also carry CPT Englander, who has passed out from pain and loss of blood. Unwilling to wait for a dustoff to medevac him, we push the captain aboard the extraction bird. I have no idea if he is going to live or not. As we fly back, SSG Olsson works on him, putting in an IV of plasma. Englander hadn't let on how badly he had really been hit. He was an asshole but a finely competent one, and nobody wished him dead. The Montagnards are stoic about death of their own, their mourning at the loss of their fellow soldiers contained and measured. The families of the Yard soldiers live in a ville near Téthian half a klick past the north gate of the camp. They come silently for the bodies of their dead, looking resolute. They hold a brief ceremony and then carry the bodies back to the ville.

The đại úy explains to me that the bodies must be buried in their village or their spirits will wander ceaselessly in search of their homes. The father of one of the dead Yards takes a knife and makes a long cut on the dead man's thigh. "Lets bad yang out, so his family have no evil," the đại úy says. I see no tears.

With Englander unconscious, the đại úy takes charge of the interrogation, disappearing into the back room of operations hooch, taking Lê Văn Dũng with him. The bird comes for me and Cat before I can discover what they are planning to do with the prisoner. Nothing good, I figure. We load aboard.

Hours later, back on San Juan Hill, I hear from Englander, who, against SSG Olsson's advice, has stayed at the Téthian camp.

About the artillery that saved the team? "Yeah, quick and accurate" is Englander's sole comment. "You moved a whole battery just to be sure you'd have support?" he asks reproachfully.

"Yeah, man, we did. You really think I'd go out on a mission as an artillery observer without knowing I'd always have guns to shoot for me?" I ask him if he's going to the rear to get his shoulder looked at.

"Nope, Doc Olsson's good as any REMF doctor. I'll stay with my men."

I wonder if it's a good idea not to get treated at a real hospital. His choice, I think.

I try to ask him about the hissing backpack they had retrieved along with Lê Văn Dũng.

"Fucking worst of the worst," he says of it. But as before, he tells me it is not my concern and clams up entirely after that. *What the hell?* I think.

Cat is quiet on the flight back to San Juan Hill. Neither of us was wounded in that mess. It was the sort of battle we mostly fight now at this ratty tail end of the war, a tortured sneak through the night, a quick crazy grab of a supposed VC official, five crazy, shit-storm minutes of combat, and all was over. More than enough for Cat, though, I figure. I ask him if he is OK.

"So you've had your baptism by fire, and you survived," I say.

"Yeah," he says. "I guess. God, you were out in the bush for six months doing stuff like that every day, weren't you, sir?"

"Pretty much, Cat."

"Man!" he says.

Later back on the hill, I hear him telling CPL Mallaby about the mission. "The LT and I came out without a scratch," he says with wonder. "Three of the Montagnards killed, three of the Special Forces guys wounded, but not a scratch for the LT and me."

That is also the last I see of CPT Englander for weeks. I'd half expected to hear he was dead, thinking the shoulder wound had looked a lot more serious than the captain had let on. But he survived. Back at the arty battalion HQ, I ask LTC Dolby if he'd heard whether Englander had gained any respect for artillery from what happened during our mission.

"Not a word," Dolby tells me. "I'm going to figure that means he found it useful. If he hadn't, we would have heard about it all up and down the chain of command."

I had not intended to ask, but curiosity needs to be assuaged. So I say, "Colonel, who are these guys? They wear Special Forces uniforms and talk the talk, but something is off about them." I tell him of my sense of the camp's weirdness, of the team's strangely lax discipline, and of the sense of disconnect with the mainstream of the army.

"They're a Hatchet Team," Dolby says after a moment, after massaging his temples as if conflicted on whether to answer. "Yeah, they run deep operations under direct MACV authority. They act like they're Special Forces, but they're not."

I look at Dolby, mouth open to ask. "No," he says. "I can't tell you what they are or what they're up to. I don't know a whole lot more myself. I've been told to give them all the support they ask for, give them a capable liaison—that's you, Lieutenant—and keep strict secrecy otherwise. You know now because I trust you, but that's all I can say."

That's all of it. But Dolby seems to want to talk of thing less weighty. So we sit, chatting about other matters not so urgent or unnerving. This is the point that I finally tell the colonel something I've been thinking about for a while—that I want to extend my tour in Vietnam.

Dolby looks at me and nods. "I'm not surprised," he says. "You're nuts to do that, you know. But I'm glad you want to stay. Things are going to get ugly as we wind down our part in this damned war. So I'll be happy to have an experienced hand like you stay on. How long do you want to extend for?"

"A second tour, sir, for now."

"Yeah, that should take you to about the end. And I'll see you'll make captain on time. Congratulations."

I thank him, and I stand, staring out his office window in Duc Pho, wondering about Englander and the deep, dark riddle of his Hatchet Team, thinking of what I've just done. Nuts is right, I realize.

The next morning, as I'm waiting for a bird back to San Juan Hill, I get word that Dolby wants to see me again. I get into his office to find him and his sergeant major waiting for me. As if fearing I will change my mind, Dolby has my extension papers ready and sits, smiling slightly as I sign. He also promotes me to captain on the spot, a week early (as if to reinforce the irrevocability of my decision). He pins the double silver bars on my collar, and I salute him. I tell him my bird is waiting, and he smiles a bit. "Let it go, David. Catch one later this morning." He taps the papers. "You've got plenty of time now."

So we talk again, this time of things having absolutely nothing to do with the war—a rare moment of calm. I'm a field officer, and so I don't get to see my commander often in person. Seeing him again now, I realize how little the artillery colonel has changed little since I had first met him in August 1969. There is a fraction more of a slump in the way he sits at the map table; he's a fraction grayer in his fringe of hair, a little bit more of the long-at-war thousand-meter stare we all acquire and in the way he looks more through me than at me. But it would take an expert observer to see it in his still tight-wound intensity. Dolby is the superior officer I respect most. The scuttlebutt is that he will soon have the eagle of a full-bird colonel on his collar, and if so, he'll likely be bumped up to a job at division artillery headquarters in Chu Lai.

"It's true, I'm afraid, David."

"I'm not looking forward to breaking in a new commanding officer."

"I imagine you'll get along."

"What now, sir?" I asked him. "What assignment for me?"

"Unless you want a battery to command, and if so, I can give you Bravo Battery in a month or so, I'm going to leave you as liaison officer with the 7/31. If you are hoping to see more action, I can't promise you much. With more of the U.S. force pulling out and going back to the World, what we'll increasingly have now is a support role."

"I'm happy as LNO, sir. I don't care so much about action. I've seen my share," I say. "I just want to stay to the finish."

"Me too, David. Me too."

"Sir, are you going to send me back out with CPT Englander?"

"I don't know, David, I truly don't know."

CHAPTER 4

It is the winter of 1970–71, nearly six months since our last encounter, before I see CPT Englander again. The battalion is moving to South Vietnam's far north. Around San Juan Hill, bunkers blow apart as we prepare to abandon the firebase. Heavy teak beams are thrown through tattered sandbags, through the meat of the hill itself and the shattering earth. Their detonation sends fine soil raining down. Every particle of it seems entangled with every past shriek of battle here and with every flash and flare of our combat's years. I hear the call of "Fire in the hole!" again and again around the hill's perimeter. Combat engineers have long since pulled up the pierced steel plate deck of the hill's helicopter pad and carted it away to pave the pad of our new hill. We will hardly be clear of the dismantled firebase before enemy soldiers begin scavenging the bones of the hill and carting our castoffs away, leaving little beyond the charred teak beams and the culverts rusting in the cold ashes of the trash dump fire.

North of us near the river, Bravo Company is in a firefight. The crackle of their M16s and the harsher snap of AK-47s carry to us through the monsoon season's chilly air. Corky Thurber, now a first lieutenant, commands Bravo. He could have gone back to the World last October, found an easy billet at Fort Ord near his home in Santa Cruz, and served out the rest of his active-duty time running an advanced infantry training company in the California sun. Instead, Corky had re-upped for another tour, like me, unwilling to leave behind the spirits of our dead comrades in arms still wandering among the ruined teaks, among the elephant grass and bamboo, restless, their blood unsettled in the clay.

We are hit as the dismantling of the hill continues. A sniper picks at us from the low peak to our west. A man from Alpha Company goes down, hit in the thigh, screaming for a medic, who rushes to stanch his blood. I grab our radio and call in a fire mission, but with Bravo Battery readying for the move and the four-deuce mortars already gone north, the artillery fire must come from far away, and by the time it arrives, the dink sniper has vanished as all the enemy seem to vanish. Alpha Company Charlie Oscar CPT Herman details a squad to set up an observation post on the part of the hill overlooking that peak to watch for more snipers. He should have done it before, I think, but it has been quiet here for weeks now. No one expected an attack today. Careless, but that's the direction this disintegrating war is going.

A clutch of dink 122 mm rockets arcs in on us from the broad bare crest of Nui Tam Cap to our east. The wail of their flight and boom of detonation are lost in the blast and shock of our bunkers' demolition so that when an SP4 from the engineers falls, suddenly dismembered in a bloom of fire and dark smoke, nobody knows why for a few beats until another quartet of rockets flies in. CPT Albert Lin, our battalion surgeon, begins urgently searching among the stack of his packed-up aid station gear for an aid bag. I find myself down in a half-demolished revetment, my radio in hand, calling, "Common Spring One-One, this is Common Spring Three-Niner. Fire mission. Over," to the guns at brigade HQ at LZ Bronco.

CPT Lin crouches over the stricken engineer specialist, hands working in the vast wound in the soldier's side, blood everywhere and nothing to do that can save him. SFC Hansen, the aid station chief under CPT Lin, hangs a plasma drip as the doctor clamps shredded arteries. I can see them beyond the tumbled sandbags in front of the hole in which I am sheltering, working on the fallen specialist. But the soldier is dead.

The battalion fire direction center at Bronco announces, "Shot!" over the radio, and I roger the shot and then roger the splash of the sheaf of 155 mm rounds directly atop Nui Tam Cap, watching them through my binos as they burst in a tree line, red hearts flickering in their smoke. The distant rumble of their detonation follows.

"Repeat battery four by four," I tell the FDC.

My liaison sergeant, Malcom Morris, Alan's replacement, slides into the hole next to me, cursing. "Damn dinks. Ah think they killed that engineer. They're going to dust off that guy from Alpha Company, hurt but OK. But, man, oh, man, seems like this war ain't never going to be over." SGT Morris has his M16. I don't have mine. As I've so often done, focused on calling artillery fire, I've left my rifle leaning forgotten against a bunker a dozen meters away. Fortunately, there is no sign the dinks are following the rockets with a ground attack. Heavy fire from the 155s erupts again across the broad ridge of the mountain that is the source of the rockets, a hopscotch pattern of the four by four, sending up a roiling cloak of smoke that covers the peak. We wait, but the rockets have ceased.

"End of mission," I call to the guns at LZ Bronco. I'd like to have a gunship do an aerial recon of the area where the rockets originated. In these days of dwindling air resources, that is a fantasy, and I don't even bother.

We climb out of the dismantled bunker and walk to where Dr. Lin is standing despairingly, his hands and fatigues bloody, the contents of the aid bag tumbled around him. The dead specialist's body has already been carried off by other engineers who are standing with it on the pad waiting for the dustoff bird to arrive and take the wounded man from Alpha and the remains of the young engineer away.

"Nothing! I wasn't able to do a thing," CPT Lin says to me in the soft, almost musical tones of his Hong Kong-learned English. It is the first man Lin has seen killed so close in front of him in this war. Lin had seen the rocket coming in, seen it impact next to the specialist. "It just smashed him," the doctor says, his voice full of wonder.

SFC Hansen is packing up the aid bag again, looking at the blood pooled and already drawing flies. "Christ," he says.

Things are unraveling for us. A year and a half ago, when I had arrived on San Juan Hill, there were still nearly half a million U.S. troops spread from the DMZ to the Mekong Delta and on south, a seamless intertie of combat units, logistics, communications, and support. We fought, and the gunships flew for us; the dustoffs carried off our wounded and our dead; the air strikes came when we called for them; the food and the ammunition reached us; support and reinforcement reached us. We fought the dinks. We fought the weather and the terrain. But our support never flagged. Now in January 1971, our troop strength has dropped by half to barely 280,000, and our support is now touch-and-go at best. This morning, when Bravo Company had called for gunships to rake a ridgeline along the Sông Ba Tơ from where a VC sniper had fired and wounded a grunt from their three-zero platoon, the gunships never showed. Corky raged on the battalion radio push.

"Where is my support?"

"Gone north to Quang Ngai City. An ARVN company is caught in an ambush."

"I've got a wounded man, Private Houston, hit in the leg."

"We'll try to get a dustoff out to you."

"Get one, damn it, get one!"

Bravo Company has a new artillery forward observer, George Hessian, the fourth to succeed me since I left the company a year ago. The stocky, sandy-haired artillery second lieutenant is from the Ozarks. "Pruitt, in Arkansas, a mite bit back in the woods from Jasper, a wide spot in the track nobody ever heard of, sir," he tells me.

"Yeah, that's in Newton County along the Buffalo river, isn't it?" I ask him, and he's wide eyed. "When I was in high school," I tell him, "my friends and I would go down to northern Arkansas from Kansas City to spelunk in Ozark Caves. We used to stop in at the dry-goods store in Pruitt and buy jerky and Kentucky Crook cigars."

"That's Beelers' store. I know it," he responds. He shakes his head at the coincidence.

This day, with a monsoon closing in, LT Hessian can't get communication with the Charlie Battery fire direction center at LZ Crux in Minh Long. SGT Morris and I are forced to set up a temporary relay point on San Juan Hill to maintain a communications link for him and the battalion's other artillery forward observers. We wait here in the remnant of a bunker with a single PRC-25 radio rigged with a long antenna, while Bravo Battery packs up to relocate to the battalion's new firebase far to the north.

"Fire mission," Hessian calls. He's been out in the bush almost a month and calls fire now like a veteran, though in his twang, "fire mission" sounds more like "far mission" and "dinks" to him are "danks." He calls me; I call the battalion FDC at LZ Bronco over by the coast at Duc Pho. The battalion FDC calls the battery of eight-inch howitzers at Minh Long. When the eight-inch battery fires and the battery radio operator announces "Shot," the announcement goes the long way around from the RTO at Minh Long to the radio operator at Duc Pho, and then from Duc Pho to me, and from me to Hessian in a shaky linkage. By the time I can relay the announcement of "Shot" to Hessian, the rounds have already landed, and he is calling back his corrections. So far, in the month he has been with Bravo Company, there have been only brief skirmishes, mostly exchanges of fire with Viet Cong snipers. Today's firefight was Hessian's biggest yet, and it lasted a bare ten minutes. Even so, the communications failings almost did the fire mission in. I fear for how we'll cope if they get in a real fight.

An incoming rocket has blown apart one of the 105 mm howitzers waiting for transport on Artillery Hill, which, limbered up and unlaid, had been of no use in this fight. It stands broken and leaning as a pair of Chinook helicopters take turns lifting the four still intact howitzers from Artillery Hill. The artillery pieces hang below the birds, their packed ammo loads dangling further beneath them, ready to begin their three-hundred-kilometer flight north to our new hill near Khe Sanh and the DMZ. In these days of new austerity, who knows how long it will be before Bravo Battery gets a gun to replace the one they've lost today? And where the battery is headed, they'll need all their guns; a real war is going on up in the north. MSG Michael Stallworth—the chief of firing battery—stares down at the ruined howitzer the way a teamster from the old brown boot army might have looked at a mortally wounded mule. He walks around it, reaches down to run a hand along the broken tube, and then pulls the pin on a thermite grenade and chucks it past the sprung breechblock and into the weapon's breech. Brilliant silver sparks and white smoke gush in an actinic flare from the breech and the muzzle. The dinks will haul the ruined gun away, for what I don't know.

CHAPTER 5

North in Quang Tri Province, our Chinook drops, bucking into a squall of antiaircraft fire from the mountain to our west, tracers rising at us from the jungle-covered peak. The big AA rounds crack by, and with nothing I can do but endure it, I hunch on the bird's web seat, shaking as always. We come down safely onto the nameless four-hundred-meter-high hill that will be the 7/31's new firebase. Here, a battle rages, enemy fire is everywhere, and the bird touches down only long enough to let us off before roaring back up into the sky and gone. I've taken an extra transit day to get the lay of the land and the battle plan for our new area of operations. Both efforts prove unproductive. Nobody has time to explain this northern landscape to me (I'm handed maps and told to study up), and nobody seems to know what we are supposed to be doing up here.

My liaison team is already here from San Juan Hill after a night's stopover in Da Nang. (Hot showers and actual flush toilets! The REMFs there live in luxury.) I get my first look at this new hill four klicks west-southwest of the once abandoned and now reopened base of Khe Sanh. That base last saw real combat in 1968 when the NVA tried to reprise their victory at the battle of Dien Bien Phu and got their butts kicked by the U.S. Marines. Hard won, it was soon abandoned as the war moved away from it in space and time. Our new hill sits north of Highway 9, dominating a six klick stretch of that roadway east and west through the valley. We have set in on the military crest of a scabrous ridge that U.S. units have occupied and abandoned several times during the war.

We have alighted on the long hilltop on a small makeshift helicopter pad onto ground pocked with the fresh and still-smoking craters of one-thousand-pound bombs from a B52 Arc Light strike early yesterday.

Stubs of shattered teak trees cover the hill like a boar's bristles. Here, again, comes the hooting call of "Fire in the hole" as engineers wrap turns of high-explosive det cord around the hardwood stumps and blow them out to open our fields of fire and clear a spot for a paved helicopter pad. The winter sky above us is hazy. Below us, looking southwest, we can follow Highway 9 along the lazy curves of the shallow valley's contours. If we could see west beyond a stretch of low hills, we could view how Highway 9 exits the valley and turns toward the northwest to follow the northern bank of the Xe Pon River, crossing into Laos some eleven klicks further on. Just over those hills, beyond the Xe Pon on the Laotian side, I can just make out the lip of a long, treacherously steep escarpment that rears up and then merges intimately into the still higher mountains of eastern Laos. Rolling further west, serial tranches of those mountains blend into the land's perpetual mist, making sky and hill indistinguishable from one another. East toward the coast, clouds of an early monsoon build over the mountains between us and the South China Sea.

SGT Morris shakes his head at clouds deepening overhead, "Goin' to be a damned beaut of a storm," he says to me. We are watching a CH-54 Skycrane bring in the battalion's makeshift operations center, a war-worn double conex mega cargo container, eight by eight by twenty feet, rust peeking through the remains of olive drab paint. Engineers manhandle it into place, and soon a squad of soldiers from the 7/31 begins to build a sandbag roof and walls around it.

The rain comes heavily while SGT Morris is supervising two riflemen who are sandbagging the bunker he and I will use as our sleeping position. A pair of heavy galvanized culverts rest on top of parallel walls of dirt-filled ammo boxes that are spaced a couple of meters apart, giving our bunker an arched roof that the soldiers also cover with sandbags.

"A danged mansion, isn't it, Captain?" Morris grins, proud of his creation.

"Yeah," I say, thinking of the real bunk I'd had on San Juan Hill and looking at our air mattresses on the raw wood floor, wondering if I'll ever get that bunk back, "a danged mansion for sure."

After eighteen months of working the Sông Ba Tơ valley and the area of operations around San Juan Hill and learning its every nuance, this new AO is as alien to me as the surface of another planet. Along the Sông Ba Tơ, so far to our south now, every path and footprint, every stretch of gravel, elephant grass, and bamboo, every turn of jungle held a memory, held bits of the spirit and essence of the soldiers who had walked there, fought there, and died there. They held particles of those soldiers' blood and sweat, of their breath, of the fabric of their thoughts and the contents of the deepest recesses of their hearts. We knew those turns of the land there as familiarly as if they were the folds and curves of a lover. Bits of ourselves are still there, shed into the ashes of that ruined expanse. Each soldier owns his own piece of the battlefield. It is a universe we will not forget.

It is not that we are ignorant of the terrain of this far north stretch of I Corps. Soldiers cannot afford the luxury of ignorance. It is overcome in the flush of new familiarity every soldier gains as he walks the new territory and learns the rush of the rivers, the sweep of the ground upon which they walk, the cadence of life in the new place, the intimations of battle, the safe havens, and places of danger. It is an instinct to know this. Those who cannot learn it? Their bodies are already fled back to the World.

Up here in our new area of operations, the memories belong to other soldiers, those who fought and endured here, those whose blood washed into this soil, whose sleep is among their own dead, not ours; memories that are part of their own burden, profound to them but spiritless to us. Neither their tears nor their agony attach to us, and we don't know them.

CHAPTER 6

We arrive at this nameless hill with a capable battalion commander. Somebody had shot LTC Mattier. The bullet that killed him, heavy enough to have been from a .45 pistol, had blown bits and pieces of his skull and brain a dozen meters across the parade ground just outside the O Club in Duc Pho.

Though he had been an execrable nobody of a CO, I thought that even Mattier didn't deserve a bullet in his head. Sadly, he was grossly unsuited to a combat command. He had experienced combat only fleetingly as a young lieutenant in the last days of the Korean War. He once told me proudly that he had earned his silver oak leaves in peacetime, Stateside as a National Guard officer in Nebraska. This tattered end of our war in Vietnam was his first taste of real combat in eighteen years.

Incapable of command, Mattier delegated day-to-day operations of the battalion to junior officers, which would have been fine if he'd left it at that. But, time on his hands, he became a cowboy who played at war by patrolling our area of operations in an armed Loach, acting as if he were a gunship commander.

Sadly, Mattier was supremely arrogant in his ignorance, not only usually wrong but also too stubborn and pigheaded to accept advice from any of us working for him. Mostly those failures were just irritations. There came a time, though, that against advice of the battalion operations officer, he had sent Bravo Company up the steep side of four-hundred-meter-high Núi Con Vú chasing a phantom report of a VC base camp at its peak. The day was blazing hot. The mountainside was treacherous, heavily overgrown, and infested with centipedes. Three men were bitten and had to be dusted off in agony. Six more men suffered heat exhaustion—one nearly dying—and had to be dusted off. Reaching the crest of the mountain, Bravo Company had found nothing but a caved-in twenty-year-old bunker left from the French-Indochina War.

Corky, in a fury at the waste of his company's time and damage done to his men, had loosed a salvo of profanity at Mattier.

"You dumb son of a bitch, you sent us up here for nothing! Nothing! Jungle so fucking high that there's no room for an LZ for birds to lift us out of here. Nobody fucking killed, thank God, even if it took a goddamned jungle penetrator to lift out the injured. You dumb son of a bitch!"

Mattier, in the TOC but pretending not to hear, a lieutenant colonel embarrassingly put in his place by a first lieutenant, shrugged and just walked back down the tunnel to the briefing room where his afternoon three pack of chilled beer awaited. Meanwhile, because there was nowhere on that peak for birds to land, Bravo Company had to walk—in one-hundred-degree heat—four hundred meters down the perilous southwest slope of the mountain to an extraction point at Ba Khan creek. Back on San Juan Hill a week later, Corky told me most of the first platoon (which had had five of its grunts dusted off) had talked seriously of fragging the battalion commander.

"They hate his guts, David. But they were idiots for talking like that about fragging, and I told them so," he said to me. "I told them they couldn't say things like that to me. Man, I wish I'd had the balls to just say go ahead and frag the bastard. Do you know they're taking up a collection to reward the man with guts enough to kill him?"

Such command stupidity continued for weeks while the men's anger simmered, and Mattier pretended not to know. Finally, again against advice, Mattier ordered an eight-man squad of the Recon Platoon to set into an observation post on a low hill—more like a rounded mound maybe twenty meters high about a hundred meters from an unoccupied ville eight klicks north of San Juan Hill. In stifling heat, the squad had struggled its way in through dead scrub and thick thorn-covered tangles of underbrush to the hilltop where they set up the OP. Late in the afternoon, the squad leader called the TOC.

"Movement in the old ville on the north side of the path," he said. "Looks like a supply train of maybe a couple of dozen dinks. Moving west to east. Too many for us to engage. I'm calling in an artillery fire mission on it."

Slovenly commander that he was, Mattier's love of playing aerial observer had him already out and flying in the Loach over the valley. SGT Morris and I were sitting at the artillery liaison station in the TOC when the call for fire came in from Recon. We had artillery targets preplotted and preshot along that trail, and as soon as I heard the report from the Recon squad sergeant, I nodded to SGT Morris.

"Mack," I called out to the infantry lieutenant on the operations desk, "tell Recon we have the guns pointed his way. Tell him we will use preplot target four."

LT Mack McFarlane nodded and said, "Will do!" And I was ready to confirm the target to the battery when there came a sudden "Break, break, break. This is Willing Acorn six, negative on the artillery" from the infantry radio. It was LTC Mattier's voice and call sign.

LT McFarlane looked up, incredulous. "Say again, do I understand you say no artillery?"

"Roger," Mattier came back. "Target proximity is too close to the OP."

"Jesus, Mack," I said, "tell the colonel we already shot the target in. We know where it will land. The squad isn't in danger."

McFarlane looked at me, the redheaded lieutenant's ruddy completion reddening further from his frustration. "Yeah, man, will do." He repeated my info to the colonel, who was adamant. "Too damn dangerous. Got a strong north wind off the mountain, maybe fifty knots." (It was maybe eighteen knots, I knew.) "That wind could cause a short round that would hit the OP. Keep your guns quiet. We've got forty mike-mike incendiaries on this bird. We'll go in and light up the dinks. Burn 'em to hell."

"Jesus Christ, sir," the duty sergeant said to LT McFarlane. "It's dry as a desert up there. Incendiaries will likely start a hellacious fire."

SGT Morris was shaking his head in astonishment, saying to McFarlane, "Tell him we know about the wind. We've run the MET on it. Wind speed is already figured into the firing data, LT. Tell the colonel. And tell him we've also got this targeted for air bursts just to be sure we set no fires there."

LT McFarlane relayed this, but it was no use. LTC Mattier wanted to play gunship with incendiaries on a blazing, bone-dry, gusty day. I was half tempted to have the battery fire on the target anyway and might have done so if the damned Loach hadn't been flying around right between the guns and the dinks. What would hit the enemy would likely take the Loach down too. Much as I thought he was an idiot, I wasn't about to face a court-martial for endangering (or even killing) the battalion commander.

Shit, I thought, *there's going to be one hell of a brush fire from the incendiaries.* I told McFarlane this and said, "Mack, tell the squad to move off that hill and run like hell to the west toward the river, ASAP."

LT McFarlane paused not a beat before calling the squad and telling them to do just that. The little valley where this was taking place was beyond a low range of hills that blocked our line of sight. LTC Mattier accepted no blame, putting it all on the wind. What happened next I found out from the squad leader, SGT Pelletier, who was one of four of the squad members that had come back to the aid station on San Juan Hill for Doc Katz to treat their burns. I'd grabbed a couple of six packs of beer from LTC Mattier's private stash and taken them down to the squad.

"Christ, LT," Pelletier had said to me. "Shithead moron is too mild a label for that SOB of a colonel." Doc Katz was applying burn ointment to a raw, scorched patch on the sergeant's cheek and to other burns on his hands. The sergeant looked blown away in body and spirit. He'd just lost one of his squad, a PFC rifleman named Carlos Ramirez, who'd been overcome by smoke, and had three other men with significant burns.

"All because of that bastard colonel." He'd begun shaking with sobs. "Why, sir, why? You and I had artillery preplotted and shot it in this morning when we first went out. But that damn colonel wanted to be a comic book hero, roll in that prick's toy of a Loach, and shoot things up, didn't he?"

I could only nod at that then say, "We could see the smoke from here on the hill, eight klicks away from you. Must have been a hell of a fire."

"Damned inferno, sir. Wind took it right across the creek toward us. All the brush was tinder dry. Weren't any easy paths out. It had taken us half the morning just to push through it to that hill to set up the OP. Things started burning, we couldn't run, just had to push back through. Fire all around us. "He bent over in the chair, a hand on the unscorched side of his face, tears running from smoke-reddened eyes, the salt in his tears, I imagine, stinging his burn. "Goddamn it, sir, goddamn it! I want out of this worthless unit. If I stay, I'm going to kill that asshole of a colonel. I know it!"

1LT Sam Verner, the Recon platoon leader, who'd been a distance south with the rest of the platoon near the II Corps border, had been flown in and came rushing into the aid station. He stood looking at his sergeant and at Doc Katz treating the other three burned squad members. He stood looking. "Carlos?"

"Dead, sir. Smoke got him. Heart stopped and wasn't time to stop to for doc to work on him. Time we got to the river, away from the fire, he was gone."

"Man!"

Verner put a hand on the sergeant's shoulder and stood there next to him as he cried. He looked at me, and I said, "When you want, I'll tell you what happened."

"I expect I know what happened, David . . . Mattier happened. That's all I need to know."

The San Juan Hill aid station was a double conex set on the north side of the hill next to the mess tent, revetted with sandbags. I walked out, choked up myself, cursing. The sky was cloudless, a haze rising from the heat-scorched land, toning it down to a pale blue. From the out-facing wall of the aid station, I could see far north to where the summits of the hills stood out starkly against the hazy sky. Beyond them was a plume of smoke, shapeless, climbing into the turbulent air like the vast slow accretion of a storm, rising and then getting caught in a shear of wind above the peaks, spreading south toward the bigger mountains. In it, I thought I could see bits of flame on the higher flanks of the far hills, the fire burning low as if smothered in the denser, greener jungle there.

PFC Ramirez's memorial service was two days later at battalion HQ at LZ Bronco. LTC Mattier was absent from it, finding a sudden, urgent reason to be at Division HQ in Chu Lai when the service was to take place. I flew out to Bronco for the service and heard much from Recon's grunts about how it was a damn good thing Mattier was staying away.

That next Friday, LTC Mattier, back at Bronco and thoroughly stewed from twice his usual three bottles of beer, stumbled out of the O Club and across the parade ground toward his hooch behind the HQ building. Grunts in the area claimed the gunshot that finished him, as one put it, "sounded like an effing .50 cal." Whatever it was, it was powerful enough to blow his head apart. Generously, the Eleventh Brigade recorded his death as because of "enemy" fire. I didn't want to know who collected, but within a day after Mattier's body was flown off to the graves registration unit in Da Nang, $1,224 in bounty money that had been amassed in a mortar shell container in the four-deuce FDC was gone.

Mattier's replacement, LTC George Linebarger, is as STRAC and squared away as Mattier had been pathetic. Linebarger is crew cut, stone-faced, and hard-assed, but—on his third tour in Vietnam—savvy about ground combat in a theater like ours. The colonel is proudly third-generation West Point; his dad, a retired brigadier general, had commanded a brigade at Normandy in the Second World War. His grandfather, a Marine Corps major, had been the executive officer of a regiment at Belleau Wood in what Linebarger called "the Great War." He was mortally wounded in that battle and buried "over there" in the Marne Cemetery. Linebarger's oldest son is a third-year cadet at West Point.

Linebarger's first act as commander is to ship Mattier's Loach back to Brigade and replace it with a command-and-control bird. He issues a directive that I or another trained aerial observer must accompany him on any observation flights.

CHAPTER 7

LTC Linebarger has named our new firebase on Hill 400 LZ Cadet in honor of his West Point cadet son Christopher. "Good-looking kid," I tell the colonel when he shows me Chris's photo.

"Yeah, takes after his mother, not me for damn sure. I just hope to hell this war is over before he graduates," Linebarger says, the only antiwar sentiment I hear from our new squared-away commander.

We sit on our new firebase with no inkling of our mission up here. The chatter is that we are going to invade North Vietnam. Here at the south end of Quang Tri Province, we are only thirty or so klicks from the DMZ, the supposedly "demilitarized" though highly dangerous zone separating north from south in Vietnam. If true, though, then LZ Cadet, too far from that dividing line to be more than a staging area, is temporary. I ask Linebarger what the mission is up here, and he seems as genuinely in the dark as I a feel.

"Are we going into the north, sir?"

"Damned if I know, David," he says. "Plans for this whole operation are locked down tight at Twenty-Four Corps headquarters in Hue. All I know is that we are to set up this firebase and have the battalion begin sweeping the terrain on either side of us on Highway 9, east as far as Khe Sanh and west to where the Special Forces are at Làng Vei."

I look at him quizzically, and he says, "Really, Captain, all I know is that corps has cobbled together about a division of troops from what remains here in Vietnam for this operation, four brigades heavy with artillery and air. They are reopening Khe Sanh and have sent us replacements to bring the battalion up to strength. All your arty units are getting ammunition loads replenished. Bravo Battery will get a new howitzer to replace the one destroyed on San Juan Hill. Big guns, eight-inchers and 175s from DivArty, are getting new tubes where possible. Lots of birds, especially Hueys, are getting quick maintenance."

"But why sweep Highway 9? That runs into Laos. Do you think they want to do an end run around the DMZ up into North Vietnam?"

"Also above my pay grade, David. I don't know how long we'll be here or where we're going after this. If I were you, though, I'd make my fire plan for this LZ as if we're going to be here a long time. I expect someone will let us in on the ops plan soon enough. Frankly, I doubt we're going into North Vietnam. We'd need three divisions at least for such an invasion, and we don't have even a third of that many troops here."

To me, it's also hard to imagine an invasion of the north. The jagged swath of the demilitarized zone, so I've been told, is a fool's trap of heavily jungled, steep ridgelines rising to one thousand meters at their peaks. The Rao Than River and its tangle of tributaries cut deep channels through them. Further east, the terrain of the DMZ flattens into the coastal plain, easier to cross but heavily populated, making it militarily much more difficult.

What I do know is that this far north, there are big concentrations of NVA and Viet Cong just across the border from us in Laos. I also know that with our force distribution apparently aimed toward North Vietnam, we aren't positioned well to defend against any large enemy units coming at us over Highway 9. Equally unsettling for me, all there are at Khe Sanh are two 155 batteries at to provide us artillery support if our LZ gets hit. I don't know where the rest of the U.S. artillery is deployed up here, but rumor says it is in firebases along the Laotian border.

I have my whole liaison team with me, SGT Morris, CPL Mallaby, and PFC Wilbur. For our liaison station, we have been allotted a small table toward the front (and better-ventilated) end of the TOC conex. On it are fresh 1:50,000-meter topo maps of this part of Vietnam plus the area some forty klicks into Laos. Confusing the issue, the maps also show terrain as far as twenty klicks north past the DMZ. What's immediately clear to me is that with the difficult terrain there and near certainty of heavy NVA fortifications, if we are going into North Vietnam, we will want to leapfrog these and almost certainly have to go in by air. The scary image of an aerial version of the Normandy Invasion comes all too readily to mind.

Meanwhile, while we await a more detailed action plan, all I can do is sit wondering. The infantry has built a fighting position atop the TOC conex. It is a circle composed of two culverts on their sides fortified with a double wall of sandbags around it. 1LT Arthur Gibbons, the infantry's day watch officer, and I sit atop it our second evening on LZ Cadet not long before sunset and watch the most incredible show of force I've seen since I've been in-country. East, a constant stream of birds—Hueys, Chinooks, and Skycranes and various fixed-wing craft—is arriving at Khe Sanh, the once-abandoned base now reanimated, swarming with trucks, tanks, artillery pieces, and troops set in on that plateau in every possible space. Gibbons is my height, stocky, his short curly hair a dirty blond. He'd been a platoon leader with Charlie Company for nine months, enduring the miserable, crazy days under LTC Mattier because he'd had a good CO, CPT Giancana, whom everyone called the Godfather. He had looked after his own men and had stood up unflinchingly to Mattier. Giancana had finally had it with Mattier's dangerous field tactics and had refused to let the company move late one miserable humid night. Mattier had gone into a rage, called for his C & C Loach, and flew out to the field where he had relieved the Godfather on the spot and sent him back to LZ Bronco, threating a court-martial. Mattier had ordered Gibbons to take command of the company and get the troops moving. Then, without waiting to see what happened, he took CPT Giancana with him in his Loach and flew back to the Eleventh Brigade base.

"The colonel would have been happy with the illusion of movement. CPT Giancana knew it but was sick to death of the colonel's asshole ideas. So I had the second platoon put a mechanical ambush out at the grid where Mattier wanted us to move to," Gibbons says, "five claymores on tripwires, a squad set on a hill overlooking it. I kept the rest of the company right where we were when the bastard had come out, reporting *it* as the mechanical ambush site. That way, we didn't have to move at all but seemed on paper to be where Mattier wanted us. Brigade put up with Mattier's shit but wasn't going to send a good officer packing, so they made Giancana S-3 at the 4/3. I commanded Charlie for two weeks before I got pulled in to work in the TOC. Mattier got snuffed the next day. I shed no tears over that."

He's smoking, the smell of it coming strong and coaxing. Though it's been more than a year since I quit during the firefight on Hill 800, I'm tempted. To tamp that temptation down, I ask, "So, Artie, what the hell do you think we are doing up here?" I doubt he knows any more than I do.

"Damned if I can tell you, Captain," he says. "The entire battalion is up here along with most of the rest of the Americal. So's most of DivArty, including the 6/11 Artillery, your unit. The 101st has units here. The Fifth Division does too. There's a bunch more air and artillery and engineers, even MPs and air force. Isn't a square meter of sky that isn't full of aircraft? Every bit of road around here is bumper to bumper with vehicles. It's like a nightmare Friday rush hour on the 405," Gibbons, a native of Los Angeles, adds.

Off to the east, Highway 9 is nothing but headlights as far as we can see past Khe Sanh. West, Highway 9 is taillights as far as we can see toward Laos. The skies around us hum with the engine noise of helicopter turbines and the beat of their blades, like the surge and retreat of an insect swarm, cicadas or grasshoppers or a hive of bees. Distant truck and tank engines cough and growl. But in it I can't hear a sound of combat, not as much as a rifle shot cracks amid the more mechanical noise of the moving army; not a grenade's bang or a mortar's detonation or a machine gun's hammering breaks into the lulling song of military movement.

In this anthill of military operations in southern Quang Tri Province, we sit virtually silent. We have registered our battery of howitzers on a 440-meter hilltop to our west, a funny karst outcropping with a phallic peak that has instantly become known as the Dick. Jungle choking its lower slopes and craggy at its summit, that hill is worthless as a firebase, but the shaft of limestone at its top makes for a perfect registration point. The battalion's four-deuce mortars have registered there too.

Then nothing for the first six days of the month. Bravo Company has hill security during this time, and Corky Thurber, having walked the bunker line until his feet ache, has come up to the TOC to sit with me and shoot the shit about everything and nothing.

"Alpha's first platoon had some contact yesterday," he says. He is a bit shorter than I, still with a hint of pudge, though much less than when I had first met him at our old firebase of San Juan Hill in September 1969. Like most of us officers who have given up trying to look STRAC, his sandy hair is too long. Nor have his jungle boots seen polish in what his first sergeant, MSG Deacon LaCeour, calls a month of Sundays. His face has a perpetually guileless smile. His eyes peer out through thick-lensed, horn-rimmed glasses. Corky is an ace company commander, though, smart, disciplined, slow to anger, respected by his men. He's been with Bravo Company, first as platoon leader and now as its Charlie Oscar for seventeen months.

Regarding Alpha Company's contact, I say, "Yeah, they took half a dozen incoming rounds of AK fire, shot up a wood line with their M16s in response. Nobody hurt, no enemy or blood trails or anything found. It was all over in less than two minutes. Our guns couldn't shoot for them because a constant stream of Hueys and Hooks have been moving from our west coming around to the north side of Khe Sanh to land. They're flying below the max ord of our guns' trajectory, so we'd likely have shot a few of those birds out of the sky if we'd fired the 105s."

"Jesus," says Corky, "what are we *doing* here? Looks like we have half the damn U.S. Army up here in Quang Tri, and except for clearing and patrolling Highway 9, we don't seem to have a goddamn bit of a mission."

He's especially pissed because about the only thing we are getting to eat are C rations. The battalion mess sergeant and most of his crew and gear are up here on LZ Cadet with us. But foodstuff resupply beyond basic combat rations (or occasionally freeze-dried LRRP rations as a change of pace) is impossible because of the complexity of the logistics. A year ago, Corky and I had been the last officers remaining with Bravo Company after we'd been chewed to bits on Hill 800 in a ghastly and horrific all-night battle. All the other Bravo Company officers I had known, CPT Jack, Sam the Sham, and Tom Oberstar, are now gone, dead or back in the World, away from this unraveling war.

"You would know better than me," Corky says. "Are we invading North Vietnam or not? Why the hell else would we be shifting so many troops and equipment up here this close to the DMZ?" He pulls off his glasses and polishes them in a fold of his fatigue shirt. Like everything up here, the glasses are filmed with Vietnam's red dust. The constant movement of trucks and jeeps and armor on Highway 9 below us and in virtually every other cleared space has raised a hurricane of that dust that has settled thickly on everyone. The red dust gets into everything. It hangs in the air like a cloud bank over the lowlands, adding a red tint to the morning mist that gathers these winter days in every dell, depression, and defile of the land around us.

MAJ Echols, the battalion XO, comes up to us, stands listening for a moment, and says, "We'll know more tonight. COL Linebarger's just back from Khe Sanh. He'll brief us at 2000. LT Thurber, have all your officers and platoon sergeants up here at the TOC for it. All the other companies in the battalion are sending up their CO and one other officer."

"You too, Captain," he says to me. "And bring your liaison sergeant." The major looks like he will say more, shakes his head, and walks of toward the TOC conex door.

Over the six days we've been on LZ Cadet, a big bunker annex lightly walled and roofed with sandbags has been added on the sheltered side of the operations center. Crowded into it are two dozen officers and senior noncoms. A double-mantled Coleman lantern hangs from a roof beam. With all of us, it would be close in there, but the weather has been cold this winter and a heavy drizzle falls outside. An open space between the bunker's walls and roof is for ventilation. Still, the air in that bunker is full of our stink, mine as bad as the rest. Nobody's really bathed in the week we've been here in the north. Showers have been promised, but I don't take much stock in that promise. There are worse smells, though— death, putrefaction, burning shit. Camouflage covers a lot, but not an army's stench. Linebarger comes in as somebody, probably MAJ Echols, calls out, "Attention!" at which the talk among us dies and some of the newest lieutenants in the group do snap-to.

"As you were," Linebarger says. He waits a couple of beats until there is full silence in the bunker. A quick space of time, everybody wants to know what comes next. "OK, here it is."

Echols produces a topo map, unrolls it, and pins it to the bunker's back wall and then steps back. I'm in the front row, and I can see it is a pair of maps pasted together, covering our current region and extending into Laos. On it are a pocking of small circles over current U.S. positions as well as more than two dozen of them marking hilltops for maybe twenty klicks along either side of Highway 9 in Laos.

"We're going into Laos?" asks someone I can't see but whose voice sounds like the CO of Alpha Company.

"We can't," says a lieutenant I haven't met before. "It's illegal. Congress passed a law after all the bitching about Cambodia."

"The hell we can't," says a voice from the back; it's gruff, angry, and expressing most of our feelings. *The hell we can't go into Laos,* I'm sure we are all thinking. That's where all the dinks' supply bases along the Ho Chi Minh Trail are, and that's where boocoo enemy troops are holed up. Of course, we want to hit Laos.

LTC Linebarger clears his throat. "OK, enough. Here's what I got from Twenty-Fourth Corps. We are not going to be invading North Vietnam." He pauses and looks around. "Yeah, I was hoping we would too . . . No, the invasion is going to be into Laos along Route 9 all the way into the town of Tchapone. Search and destroy all the way. Take out the dinks' supply depots and the vehicles they use to transport them. Take out all the fuel dumps along the Ho Chi Minh trail up here. Kick their war effort back about five years and give the ARVN a real shot in the arm." He looks around again. "Who said it was illegal for us to go into Laos?"

A pause, and then the lieutenant, a butter bar platoon leader from Delta Company, says, "It was me, sir."

"Well, you're right, son, we can't. After Cambodia, Congress, in its infinite and mystic wisdom, passed the Cooper-Church Amendment making it illegal for us to put U.S. ground troops into Cambodia again or into Laos. It was bipartisan—a Democrat *and* a Republican in the

Senate pushed the bill. So get pissed at both political parties if you want." He grimaces, momentarily pinches his lips with his hand, and continues. "It's not us going into Laos—it's the ARVN. They're sending in about a division of their best troops, marines, Air Cav, their own artillery, most everything but air support. That's going to come from us. Along with logistics and more artillery from us in firebases like this one but right along the border." He shoots a glance at me. "Yeah, I know what you're thinking, David. From where we are on this firebase, most of the locations the ARVN will be occupying or attacking in Laos are out of range for our guns. The incursion starts the day after tomorrow. So tomorrow we are exiting this firebase and moving to a new one here." He points to a four-hundred-meter-high hilltop that's part of a tangled ridgeline a bit more than a klick north of the hamlet of Lao Bao and just east of where Highway 9 crosses into Laos. "We're going to patrol on the southern slopes of this mountain from the border east about four klicks. We're tasked with keeping the dinks from coming down the mountain and cutting off the highway here on the Vietnam side. It's crucial because Highway 9 is going to be the only ground route into Laos on this side of the Xe Pon River." He peers at the map for a moment as if seeking some positive omens and then concludes, "OK, birds will be here to start moving us at 1200 hours tomorrow. That gives us the morning to tear this base down. MAJ Echols has the LZ grids and pickup times for the companies out in the field. Questions? Talk to MAJ Echols."

He looks around for the Bravo Battery commander. "Patterson?"

"Sir?"

"Your arty battalion has the info on when they are coming to transport your guns. But you should have everything packed up and ready to move by 1200 hours."

"Roger," Patterson says. He's looking at the map location of our new firebase, wishing (I know because I'm wishing I could too) that he could get a look at that hill in daylight before bringing in the guns.

"Steve," I say to him, "I'm going to call battalion and try to get a bird for first light. You and I can do a flyover, and we can contact the battalion survey team for a position area survey there to get the guns laid."

"Yup, best way," he says, the quintessential man of few words.

We can fly, but there will be no survey, battalion tells Patterson. Seems the one available survey team is off at another LZ east of Khe Sanh, putting in a battery to help protect LZs Cam Lo and Vandergrift.

"Just go. Get your guns laid and ready to shoot using your best grid location from the map. We'll get you a survey crew as soon as we can" is the word from MAJ Clifton, the artillery battalion operations officer.

Steve Patterson looks at me and says, "Son of a bitch!" knowing we are going in like a half-assed hip shoot with the guns not to be truly registered until we can get the survey done.

Just after dawn, the recon bird, a slick with a command-and-control console and a minigun to supplement the door gunners, comes down on the pad at LZ Cadet, and CPT Patterson and I climb aboard. The pilot pulls pitch, and we lift off into a hazy sunrise, towering clouds to our east streaked with the red of dawn that deepens the pink of the ground fog west along the Xe Pon valley. "You've got us for a half hour," the pilot tells us tersely. I thank him, imagining his crew will have a long day as the ARVN begin their Laotian incursion and U.S. units gear up to support them. Half an hour is just enough time to fly the dozen klicks west to the peak that is to be our new firebase, circle it a few times, and head back to Cadet.

We fly along the Làng Vei valley over a vehicle-choked Highway 9. We can see a long stretch of ARVN units—as usual, refusing to cooperate with U.S. convoy coordinators—already stalled on the single-lane road. We fly past them high above and free of that congestion, among a flotilla of helicopters and fixed-wing craft coming, going, orbiting, and hovering in myriad discordant flight paths. We approach our new firebase location from the south. We see it is a narrow, barren five-hundred-meter-high hilltop with a flat crest hardly fifty meters across and a wider U-shaped ridge surrounding that high ground. The points of the U aim toward Laos. Further east, the ridge gains some patchy jungle cover as it rises steadily toward a series of eight-hundred-meter-high peaks a couple of klicks on. Below it to the west is the broad Xe Pon valley, and beyond that, Laos.

We circle the hilltop; Patterson is not impressed, grousing, "There is no goddamn room to give the battery a normal spread. We're going to have to lay the guns in a sloppy U. And I've heard from battalion that we need to leave room for a couple of 155s that are going to be op-con to us from the 3/16."

I also see that our new hill is less than a klick from the Laotian border, with no intervening high ground, giving us not only maximum reach into the enemy-occupied land but also maximum exposure to any dink antiaircraft or mortar emplacements there. As if to illustrate that danger, a stream of fire from a 12.7 mm antiaircraft gun rises toward us from a wooded peak across the river, purple tracers limning its path. Our pilot banks the bird so hard to the right to dodge the fire, it slams CPT Patterson into me and (save for my seat belt) almost throws me out of the bird entirely. Our pilot yanks on the collective, grabbing for sky, the bird's blades pounding furiously into the air as we climb away from the enemy fire. A Cobra gunship, most likely summoned by a forward air controller riding the air over the border, screams by underneath us, and we can see it loosing rockets and a stream of minigun ammunition to engage the location from which the dink AA gun had fired.

Back over Highway 9, threading our way through oncoming aircraft as we head back toward LZ Cadet, Patterson rattles on about "hilltop's exposed to every kind of dink fire," and I agree with him. I have no wish to be on a firebase so close to enemy-held territory, especially territory that American troops aren't allowed to enter or patrol.

"They could have every goddamn thing imaginable in there, mortars, howitzers, even tanks, and we can't go after them," he says, gesturing back at the dwindling view of our new firebase. "Sitting ducks, goddamned sitting ducks."

Returning to our hill, I see that SGT Morris and the others of our liaison crew have packed our rucks, maps, and radio gear and are ready to move to the new hill, nameless as yet. Morris and the others are eating a breakfast of cold C rations. As I come up to them, he is heating C ration coffee over a flaming ball of C-4, and he offers me a canteen cupful. Bad as it is, I accept it and thank him.

"Not pretty," I say after taking a few sips. "Our new hill is barely a klick from the border, and a few hundred meters past that is the river. There will be high ground behind us and not much room to lay all the guns. But we aren't out here alone. There are batteries at Làng Vei and Lao Bao that can shoot for us if we need support, plus some ARVN batteries will be on firebases not far from us on the other side of the river."

"Fat lot of good those ARVN guns will do for us," says SGT Morris. Cat snorts at the comment. From long experience, nobody trusts the ARVN. They may help if called; they may ignore us. They may even drop artillery right on our heads simply because of slovenly inaccuracy.

I glance around at what remains of our firebase on LZ Cadet, the hill where we have spent the past week. Smoke rises from several burn pits where old ammo boxes and other burnable junk are on fire. Sandbags lie in haphazard piles where bunkers once had been, the culverts they covered already lifted away, as has the double-sized conex that had been our TOC. Where? I don't know. Not to our new base, as no one is on the ground there yet. Morris has had our guys pack up my ruck and tear down the two bunkers we had used. Our radios and map gear and other miscellaneous stuff are stacked neatly near the pad, ready to take aboard our bird when it comes in a couple of hours.

At this point, LTC Linebarger calls me over to where he and MAJ Echols are sitting with their own canteen cups of coffee, going over a map of the terrain around the new hill. Linebarger offers me some, and I wave it off, one cup of that bitter excuse for coffee is enough.

"So, CPT Weisman, you've had a look at our new hill. What do you think?"

"In truth, sir, I don't much like it. Its location gives us good range into the near half of the operations area in Laos. But we will be sitting below a series of higher peaks. I'm not thrilled to have that high ground looking down on us."

"I saw," says Linebarger, "but I don't see any place better on that ridge. Where we are, at least we'll be out at the end of a finger with steep drops on three sides. We would have more room if we located higher, but that would give the dinks more avenues of approach if they tried and come at us up there. The best place would be at the top of the mountain, but that's nearly three klicks east, losing us a lot of range and still exposing us to multiple avenues of attack."

MAJ Echols's comment is a succinct and heartfelt "Crap!"

A flight of slicks, with a pair of Cobra gunships to ride shotgun, begins setting onto LZ Cadet at almost exactly 1200 hours, enough birds to pick up half of Bravo Company in one lift. A second flight will lift out Bravo Battery's 105s, and then the first flight will come back for the rest of Bravo Company and the Recon Platoon. Finally, they will return for the Battalion CP element including my liaison crew. The first ARVN units have already started pushing across the Xe Pon, some units, led by a tank company and other armor, moving by ground, squadrons of slicks and Hooks flying above them carrying other units in by air. Our own lift birds will be gone back to Khe Sanh to refuel and join this aerial assembly line as soon as they drop the last of the battalion. It turns out our other companies will be moved up Highway 9 not by air but by truck and then will have to hump their way up the mountain to get into position. Normally, that would be a twenty-minute trip, but with the highway so jammed, it could take most of the afternoon for our other units to get into position. Were it not for the continuing 12.7 mm AA fire coming at our helicopters from across the river, I'd say that we had the better deal.

It is a cold LZ, Corky announces. He's gone in with the first elements of his company and, by the time we get there, has already established a tight perimeter with the Recon Platoon, reinforcing Bravo's third platoon. Together, they're in position to screen across the dangerous east approach to the hill from the ridge coming down from the mountain. The slicks carrying the battalion CP and my liaison team go down last, me riding with MAJ Echols and LTC Linebarger in the C & C bird. We come in slowly and with care toward the patchy scrub covering on the hill's small peak. SGT Morris and the rest of my team are already off their bird. Ours flares for a landing. I can see SGT Morris suddenly point toward the river, and then he and the rest of my team hit the ground as I make out distant popping sounds over the beat of our bird's blades. We set down. Echols and I jump off the bird and hit the ground.

Linebarger goes off the other side, stepping onto the skid and then down to the hill's raw roiled earth.

A pair of mortar rounds impact on the other side of the bird with a stunning shock as the C & C pilot frantically pulls pitch and begins to lift from the hill. Hit, the bird swings to the right, and I see its other side bashed and blasted, the door gunner there bloody and barely hanging on to his ruined machine gun. The pilot can pull the bird up, and it flies drunkenly away toward Khe Sanh. As it lifts through the smoke and deafening noise of the detonations, I see a man down several meters from me, dust a cyclone around him in the wash of the bird's rotors. My face burns, my ears ring, and I hardly hear anything. Soon, I make out the shrill sound of a human scream and muffled pops from across the river. In the bellow of "Incoming!" I throw myself down flat again as mortars smash into the ground around me, razor fragments of them humming fiercely above. I will never be used to the suffocating sense of terror I feel at such times; my heart pumps in a surge of dread, and I shake my head as if that will clear the ringing in my ears. LTC Linebarger is the man down, half sitting, one leg out in front of him, the other bent, blood splashed everywhere, his entire lower leg shattered. The iron smell of blood is heavy. I'm crying, "Doc!" crawling over to him, pulling off my web belt, reaching down to wrap the belt around the colonel's leg where bright arterial blood has been pulsing. I yank the belt tight, and the blood slows to a seep. A medic with an aid bag comes up beside me and says, "I've got it," and gently pushes me out of the way.

Linebarger was the one screaming, but now the medic has pressed a morphine syrette into the colonel's shoulder, and he has gone quiet. Below me, where Bravo Company has its CP, I can hear LT Hessian calling for fire against the dink mortar position, the smoke of which we can see rising from behind a small hill half a klick beyond the Laotian bank of the river. I watch as a pair of Cobra gunships dive toward that small hill, miniguns roaring their chainsaw rip, rockets smoking away into the hill. The gunships bank and rise, circling for another pass when the battery at the Làng Vei Special Forces camp announces shot, and the Cobras veer south away from the gun-target line. One of the battalion RTOs has already called for a dustoff, which should come in a few minutes from the pad at Làng Vei. LTC Linebarger's war is done, and I think he doesn't deserve this. A decent if strict commander, he had taken charge of a troubled battalion and brought it back to its senses. Weeks later, I will finally hear that he has survived and is at Walter Reed in DC, headed toward a retirement I'm sure he does not want but still learning to live with his right leg a stump. No one else has been hurt seriously. My cheek stings from shattered rock fragments one of the mortars had blown against me. Fearing a major injury, I wipe a hand across the cheek but feel no real wound and find only dots of blood there. It is the cheek still faintly streaked with the marks of SSG Hicks's nails from that mission months ago with Englander's unit. None of my liaison team is hurt. A couple of other men have wounds from mortar fragments, neither serious, but Corky elects to send them back on the dustoff bird to be properly tended to (and to give them a break, I know). During this time, LT Hessian has laid a couple of volleys from the 105s at Làng Vei on the mortar position, and with that fire and another strafing by the Cobras, the mortar shelling ceases.

"Christ," Corky says to me, "what I wouldn't give to send a platoon across the river and bust the chops of that dink mortar crew."

"Can't, Corky," I say. "And, anyway, by now, they've long didi'd."

Corky shakes his head in disgust at the cross-border proscription. "Man, who would know if we just fucking crossed?" But he keeps his own counsel on that and just moves off to check the integrity of his line.

In an instant, MAJ Echols has been effectively promoted to battalion commander, and to his credit, he begins contacting the rest of the 7/31and directing them into strong base areas from which they can do thorough sweeps of the slopes surrounding our hill.

"I'm going to bring Alpha Company up here to reinforce us," he tells me, not asking for permission but for my reassurance that that's the right thing to do. Asked, I'd say I'm an artillery officer, not infantry, and maybe he should ask one of the grunt officers; but with Linebarger suddenly gone, Echols is feeling his way, and I give him all the encouragement I can.

I tell him, "Yeah, good idea, Major," and I actually feel better knowing we will have two and a half companies (including the Recon Platoon) plus Bravo Battery protecting us tonight. Coming back to my own liaison team, I tell SGT Morris to dig in deep. "We've got nothing yet, not sandbags or culverts up here. So, foxholes, good ones. You and Cat and CPL Mallaby be sure to get it done well before dark."

SGT Morris surveys the open terrain around us and just says, "Yeah, Captain, yeah."

It is nearly midnight when we are hit, an hour that has come to epitomize terror to me. With the Hatchet Team, Cat and I had been ambushed at about midnight. A year and a half ago, when I was with Bravo Company, we had gone after a lost artillery platoon at midnight. A year and a month ago, almost to the day, starting at midnight, we had fought the battle of our lives on Hill 800 far south of here on the triple point where the borders of Vietnam, Laos, and Cambodia all meet.

First, as they always seem to do, the dink mortars have come in on us, already registered on the center of our hill from their firing at noon. We have no bunkers yet, but we have wire, a double circling of concertina wire around the whole hill, claymore mines spaced through it. And we have deep foxholes, a zigzag of trench lines really, dug by a bobcat dozer airlifted to the hill in the early afternoon and lifted out at dusk. A Hook delivered several bales of sandbags and a load of culverts. The grunts have slaved to fill the sandbags and build as many fighting positions as they can. The trenches have sandbag berms and tight interlocking fields of fire, machine gunners placed at intervals where their grazing fire can together cover all the key approach routes around us. Before he and the bobcat were lifted out at about 2000 hours, the engineer sergeant driving it also carved out pits for the battalion's four-deuce mortars and for Bravo Battery's howitzers that the gun bunnies from each tube have reinforced with sandbags. With Alpha and Bravo Companies, the Recon Platoon, and the redlegs from Bravo Battery, and adding in the four-deuce mortars and those of us in the battalion operations center, there are nearly four hundred combat troops on this hill. It is a substantial force that would take a truly determined enemy ground and artillery attack to dislodge.

Still, the dinks come. I imagine they would like to have the cover of full darkness, but this midnight, the moon, having risen in late afternoon, is almost full in a starry sky. Despite the moonlight, the dinks send sappers up against our wire, heaving Chicom grenades to keep us in our holes after the mortars stop. We have no operations center bunker yet, just a deep, tarp-covered gouge where the bobcat dozer had cut the earth, with some sandbagged culverts for overhead cover for where the TOC conex—to be brought from LZ Cadet via Khe Sanh—will be dropped in the next day. SGT Morris and I huddle under one culvert at the corner of that tarp, a topo map of our new AO spread in front of us, no lamps but our flashlights for light. Cat and Mallaby are stationed in a fighting position at one end of the big hole; others from the TOC party also stand guard in the event the dinks penetrate this far into the firebase.

The mortars have killed three men from Alpha Company. I don't know them, and in death, they lie under a spread-out poncho, only shapes in the moonlight, unmoving. I've seen too many such dead and feel an emotion somewhere between anger and despair rising in me. *No more*, I think, but that's a foolish hope at best. There are crackles of gunfire from the northeastern curve of the perimeter where the ridge rises into the higher mountain slope. It is the only real avenue of approach that the dinks have, and Corky and Alpha Company's CO, CPT Flynn, under MAJ Echols direction, have reinforced the perimeter there with our heaviest troop concentration. They are behind a solid stretch of sandbagged trenches, RPG screens, a quartet of foo gas barrels, a double line of claymores, and three M60 machine gun emplacements. The deuce-and-a-half truck with the battalion's Quad .50 machine gun is on that side of the perimeter in a wide trench the bobcat had cut for it, further revetted with sandbags. A strong but lesser set of fortifications surrounds the rest of the hill. Each company has a pair of anti-tank fire teams armed with a pile of LAW anti-tank rockets. Nobody expects the dinks to get their armor up onto the mountain we occupy. But as SGM Alberto puts it, "Better safe than clusterfucked."

The words "dinks in the perimeter" echo in my head from that far-off battle a year and a month ago but do not echo on our hill this night. We are too well fortified for the dinks to penetrate. Still, the volume of fire they aim at us from the higher ridge comes with a storm's savagery, mortars, AK-47s, machine guns, even a .51-caliber heavy machine gun. A flurry of RPGs shrieks in at us from the higher ridge, but the RPG screens cut from sections of cyclone fence catch them and throw them back at the dinks, and so the RPG fire quickly stops. Added to the dead, seven, mostly from Alpha Company, have also been wounded, two seriously, requiring dustoffs if they are to keep their limbs intact.

At 0130 hours, I see another soldier I've worked near for months die. SP5 Django Danis, universally called the Gypsy by the TOC crew, is a real Romani, though born and raised in Cleveland. He is voluble, fun-loving, and, at times, fierce. He has been a central character in the TOC almost as long as I have worked there. Tonight, he is in the fighting position near Cat when a mortar round impacts a couple of meters away. Cat is quicker and, at the sound of its falling, has ducked behind the culvert and sandbag wall of his position. Shards of it sing off the culvert above me and Morris. A fraction of a second late in ducking, the Gypsy catches a fragment of mortar shell in his neck. The wound is tiny. It is the way I remember PFC Bradley dying on my first night in the field. A misfired shell from one of our own mortar tubes had come down near the hooch Bradley and SGT Lyons were sharing. I remember that Bradley seemed whole and unhurt except for the tiny puncture in his chest. Hardly visible, hardly any blood. Yet he was dead. And here, the Gypsy has what seems barely more than a pinprick in the side of his neck and, as with Bradley's wound so long ago, barely bleeding. Yet he slumps against the culvert, a moan of pain and wonder escaping him. His dark eyes are wide and uncomprehending; a trickle of blood runs from his nose into his heavy mustache. Animated only a moment before, almost lifeless now, he slides down the corrugated metal into an angle of boneless repose, coughs, and takes a heaving breath. Cat is screaming, "Doc!" and I am pushing past SGT Morris to get there. No help. The young SP5, whom I am ashamed to say I hardly know, though he had worked near me in the TOC for more than eight months, dies, letting out something like a gulp as if trying to swallow. His eyelids flutter. One hand comes up halfway to his neck, not quite finding the wound. It falls. Doc Rodriguez from Alpha Company's CP has come dashing over to us. In coming here, he has ignored everything coming at us, ignored another mortar round that lands at the far west end of our perimeter, ignored an RPG that hisses in with a whoosh and sizzle to bang against the RPG screen, a bang and whoosh as if on a spring, the

RPG thrown back from the cyclone fence screen, a searing torch that sets the underbrush ablaze. Doc Rodriguez takes the Gypsy's hand, a gesture seeming so tender, though I know the medic is feeling for any sign of a pulse.

The medic looks at me. "He's dead, Captain. I'm sorry."

Cat slides down below the lip of the culvert and says, "Goddamn it! Goddamn it to hell!" and does nothing to quench the sobs that erupt from him.

A grunt from Alpha helps Doc Rodriguez lift the dead SP5 and carry him as gently as one might carry a newborn up to a temporary rest with the other three of our dead near the bare ground of our chopper pad.

"Don't make friends," CPT Jack had said to me once. "Don't. They go away, back to the World, alive or dead, broken or fixed, and there is nothing left for you except for how much your heart hurts."

2LT Hessian continues to call fire on the dinks' likely mortar positions across the river. Alpha Company forward observer Grag Salmi (who is my most experienced FO) is on the horn to the Delta Battery guns at Lao Bao, adjusting fire onto the ridge above us from which the heaviest of the enemy fire is coming. Volley after volley of artillery slams into it. I have called for illumination rounds that float down over that ridge, lighting it in stark chiaroscuro. It is not enough to still the incoming fire, though, and I tell MAJ Echols I am going to call for an air strike on the ridge.

"Hell, yeah," he agrees.

"Have our guys mark the perimeter with strobes," I tell him. "We'll drop a Willie Pete round onto the ridge to spot the target for the jets."

"Good idea," Echols says, and he dispatches runners to the Alpha, Bravo, and Recon COs to give them the word.

Stunningly, even with the ARVN pushing into Laos and hell seeming to have broken out over the entire border region, the Air Force Phantoms are on station almost immediately. I tell the forward air controller how we are marking the target and the edge of our perimeter.

"Roger," he responds, "beginning the run now."

From the south comes the roar of the jets dropping from high altitude into a strafing run, and I hear the lead pilot over the AF push announcing, "Here's your snake and nape."

The jets' Gatlings fire in stunning bursts, and then we feel the roaring impact and ignition of the Snakeye bombs and the napalm as the entire ridgetop goes up in a tidal wave of flame, its tremendous heat sending us ducking down behind the sandbag wall of the TOC. The dinks' fire from the ridge stops instantly. The Phantoms turn for a second run, spreading more napalm higher up. They leave, turning high and invisibly in the sky, their roar fading as they head further west along Highway 9 to support the ARVN incursion. With the napalm drop, the battle is instantly over, and we sit feeling the heat of the burning ridge line and listening to the bang and pop of enemy ammunition cooking off in the flames. West, the war is in full throat, a clatter of distant battle as loud as any I have heard in a year and a half in Vietnam. Flashes light the mountains there, powerful detonations resound, the biggest bangs from Air Force B52 Arc Light strikes looking and sounding like chain lightning over the battlefield. Bravo Battery fires nearly continuous missions through the night in support of the incursion. I and my liaison team are supposed to check and approve all targets. But the targets are coming from ARVN FOs who barely keep track of their own positions, and so we have little say on where the guns fire. Our only real job is to post air data so our aircraft know the target direction and maximum height of what we are firing. Whether the ARVN FOs have called in fire on their own men or even have any idea what they are shooting at is nothing we can control. When they call in a fire mission, I just tell the battery to shoot. During the night, supply birds come in five times to replenish our battery's ammo load and to resupply small arms ammunition used up in the battle. I let Cat and SGT Morris sleep, while CPL Mallaby and I run the artillery liaison operation. Finally, at about 0400, SGT Morris wakes and tells me to take a rest.

"Go to sleep, Captain. Cat and I will take it from here."

It is well past dawn before I wake, smelling bad C ration coffee. SGT Morris is shaking me; Cat is already up.

"Coffee, sir," says the sergeant. "Sorry to wake you, but MAJ Echols wants to talk to you."

I take the canteen cup of coffee from him, stand, walk over to a piss tube dug in behind the TOC trench to take a leak, and look around. Below us a klick to the south, in the brightening morning, a steady stream of trucks and armor, headlights still on, shows the ARVN forces continuing their push into Laos. If anything, even more than yesterday, the sky is filled with helicopters and fixed-wing craft carrying supplies to the advancing South Vietnamese units. Across the hill, I can see Bravo Battery's exhausted gun crews, now taking a breather as ARVN batteries on new firebases in Laos take up the burden of direct support for their ground units.

We name our new firebase LZ Linebarger in honor of our wounded colonel. That was MAJ Echols's call, though some in the TOC wanted to name it LZ Django or LZ Gypsy. But the 7/31 has lost their CO, and the battered hill we are on is to be called after him. We've been on the LZ not even a day, and it already has the racking stink of battle and unwashed men, the wolf pussy reek of artillery powder charges, and the ammoniac smell of gunpowder from small arms rounds. The smell of fear is always part of the stench from the latrines and piss tubes, a sort of acid stench, an exudate of our own inchoate terror of the war. The red laterite dust—arisen like the war's ghost from the rusty soil of Quang Tri Province—coats everything. It blows in the wind from birds' rotors as they land, blows beneath our feet in the wind of the river, a wind coursing between the escarpments from the river to our west, fills our mouths and nostrils when we breathe, rasps between our teeth, cakes in the rain like a bloody paste, and soaks into our flesh so that it will not seem to come clean, though miles and decades will someday separate us from this war.

MAJ Echols sits on the sandbag wall of the temporary TOC, looking stunned in the morning sun, face streaked with the red dust, hands on his knees, looking out over the firebase toward the river and the battle going on beyond it.

"You wanted me, Major?"

"David, thanks," he says. "I was OK last night but having an experienced combat officer with me . . . well, thanks."

"Will they be replacing Linebarger?"

"I imagine, but I don't think it'll be right away. I'm the battalion commander for the duration of this incursion, I guess." He sighs, takes a pull of coffee from a canteen cup, and sets it back next to him on the wall. "So what the hell do we do now?"

I know what I would do—I'd get the hell out of here. Word is that on this first day of the Laos incursion, the ARVN are already running into trouble, command breakdowns, misjudgments, disorganizations, things that I already suspect will doom the operation. I'd go back to fighting the same useless but more understandable war in our AO down south. But Echols isn't asking that. He's asking how we are supposed to do our job when we don't even know what the job is beyond supporting the movements of the ARVN.

"My view, sir?" I say. "I wouldn't overthink it. Keep two companies up here on the hill. Looks like the dinks plan to come in force when they come, so we'll need a strong perimeter. Have a couple of companies patrol around the Hill. Let Recon snoop and poop further up the mountain. Meanwhile, get more RPG screens up, get more wire around us, more foo gas. We're not moving anywhere else for the time being. We are here on the Laotian border. The dinks already have our range. So we fortify the hell out of the place. Support and protect the artillery battery here—that's our real job. We will be harassed, but the dinks' real target is all the ARVN units in Laos. They're in for the fight of their life, and we'll have to do what we can to keep them alive."

"Yeah," MAJ Echols says, nodding at what he surely already knows, "yeah. That's good . . . Damn it, David, we lost some good men yesterday—COL Linebarger, Django, and the rest. I'm not stupid, and neither are you. We both know that the ARVN are unlikely to carry this off, get all the way to Tchepone, and knock out all the NVA base camps and supply depots on the way. They aren't capable of it without our direct support, and the damn law won't let us send Americans across the border into Laos. We're in a useless exercise, and I don't want to see any more of our guys killed, not again like last night." He grabs the canteen cup of coffee, takes another swallow, grunts, "Crap!" and splashes the rest into the red dirt. "OK, like you say, let's turn this place into a fortress the dinks will never breach."

CHAPTER 8

Three days later, we get the word that the 7/31 is getting a new commander to replace Linebarger, a LTC Maxwell Bowie.

"Colonel Bowie, like from the Alamo?"

"Yeah," MAJ Echols tells me, his face a portrait of disgust. "I met him this morning. He claims to be descended from *the* Colonel Bowie of Alamo and Bowie knife fame. Nothing like the original Bowie, though (I will learn much later that Bowie was actually unrelated—save in his imagination—to the Alamo hero, who had had no children that lived to adulthood.) We spent an hour drinking goddamned *tea* in the mess hall at Khe Sanh while he filled me in on his brilliant strategy to 'reinvigorate,' as he put it, our effort here on the border."

"Reinvigorate, Major?"

"You haven't heard the half of it, David."

LTC Bowie, as MAJ Echols tells it, had been bitten by the same glory bug as the equally incompetent LTC Mattier (of not-so-blessed memory) and has decided the battalion is doing things all wrong. So without any idea of the consequences, Bowie has changed the battalion's tactics from large unit search and destroy to an untried new scheme of small unit guerilla-like interdiction.

MAJ Echols is an even-tempered man, and the agitation he shows while telling me this can be only the visible surface of a deeper fury at something dangerously wrong. He tells me that "I gather this small unit scheme is a tactic Bowie picked up *conceptually* (Echols puts finger quotes around the word) from some warhorse of a superannuated bird colonel back in the World during a battle strategies refresher at Fort Leavenworth. Man, I imagine that with proper training for our troops, and if we were still operating in our old AO where we rarely ran into large enemy units and where the mission had mostly been interdiction of enemy supply routes, the idea might have some merit. I told him that, here, the tactic has been to have the companies break down to no less than platoon-sized units so to have strength to take on NVA who are moving all around us in force."

But Bowie, says Echols, following the letter of his novel tactic if hardly its intent, is going to order that each six- or eight-man squad will be its own unit, disconnected from its parent platoon and company, set to working by themselves in the messiest parts of the jungle, sleeping in trees by day and setting mini-ambushes by night.

"The plan is to stay out for as much as two weeks at a stretch and then come back up here to the hill for two days of debriefing, clean-up, rest, and resupply. But, damn it, nobody in the battalion has been drilled in this. They're going to be out in squads, scattered all over this hill, hardly ever resupplied, scrounging for food. They're going to get low on ammunition and radio batteries. Or no radios at all since we don't have enough for every squad in the battalion. It is worse than useless. I told him so, and he offered me the chance to go back and find a new unit if I didn't want to cooperate. Christ, David, this small unit thing is worse than useless—it puts our troops in mortal and absolutely unnecessary danger." He stops and blinks in wonder at the idea of it. "So that's the new battalion commander, Captain."

"Man!" is all I can say.

I meet LTC Bowie when he comes into the now-completed TOC just before sundown. With that allegedly illustrious lineage, I've been half expecting to encounter someone like the pictures I'd seen of his supposed ancestor, COL James Bowie, who I gather was a man of medium build with cleft chin and mutton chop whiskers. Our LTC Bowie is tall, long faced and sallow, sort of rickety looking in a stance that is all angles and odd kinks. If there is a smile of greeting on his face, I don't see it.

"Captain," he says as I push through the blackout curtain into the smelly interior of the operations center.

"Colonel."

"You're my artillery liaison officer?"

"Yes, sir."

He stares at me, waiting, as if by a painful silence he expects to draw out more. I say nothing, and finally he says, "Glad to have you here. You get good marks from brigade and your artillery battalion."

We can hear a whistling outside, attenuated through the TOC's sandbags but loud enough to announce that they are incoming mortars. Half a dozen detonations bang in serially off toward the east side of the hill. SGT Morris and CPL Mallaby, whose work area is now at the back wall of the TOC, immediately are talking to an FO (the voice sounds like LT Hessian's but with a newfound quickness and efficiency—the young lieutenant has begun to hone his skills here in this mess of a battle scene). He rattles off the call for a fire mission, a quick exchange between SGT Morris and Bravo Battery's FDC, and little more than a minute later comes the muffled spitting of the guns up the hill from us.

LTC Bowie looks sharply at my liaison sergeant. Clearly, he'd been briefed on fire support protocols, and this is not what he would expect. I step in. "Necessary exigency, Colonel. Division Artillery Command calls it. We don't have to check data with the battalion FDC anymore. Too much happening too fast out here to take time for that."

Bowie shakes his head and finally says, "OK, you're doing fine, Sergeant. Don't let me get in the way." He clears his throat. "Captain, too much a madhouse in here. I'm told you've got a briefing room bunker here. Let's go there and talk."

"Yes, sir," I tell him. It is clear there are no more incoming mortars for the moment, and so we exit the TOC and move the dozen paces to the conex that passes for a briefing room on LZ Linebarger.

Inside is a makeshift table and half a dozen battered metal folding chairs, several riddled with shrapnel holes. A double layer of sandbags revets the bunker, taking the battle noises outside down to a faint clatter. A lit Coleman lantern hangs hissing from the ceiling; its white light is an almost brittle brightness in the little bunker.

"I've been here on LZ Linebarger for at least fifteen minutes, so I'm going to imagine you have already heard what a pigheaded fool I am, how I'm trifling with the lives of the men using an unproved theory of small unit combat." He stops, waits, again staring at me with a half smile.

I have no idea what to say to him. From what MAJ Echols says, there's no point in challenging him either. Finally, I take a breath and tell him, "You just got here, Colonel. My job is artillery. I expect we can work out how I can support whatever tactics you direct."

"Good answer, CPT Weisman. Good answer."

Still, I'm far from sure he's right.

This is still supposed to be the dry season, but the weather is spotty at best, with as many rainy days as dry ones. The split-up squads, ordered to hide during the day and set up small ambushes during the night, don't have the opportunity to find shelter or even engage in the rudiments of hygiene. So it is hardly more than a week into LTC Bowie's small unit concept that the men start talking frag. That's a door that LTC Mattier's death had opened, and it is chilling to think any officer the men dislike is now at risk. That likelihood intensifies after the colonel meets one tired-as-hell squad from Delta Company he'd made walk up the hill in a heavy rainstorm. They are exhausted, and having struggled up the hill's muck, all of them are filthy, soaked, and stinking. I am taking a break from the ordered madness of the TOC and sitting in a poncho-covered fighting position on its south side when the men come walking through the wire, looking like the most miserable bunch of grunts I've seen in a year and a half in Vietnam. It is lunchtime, and they are headed toward the mess tent and likely their first hot meal for more than a week. LTC Bowie steps out of that tent, sees them, does a cartoon double take, and bellows, "Halt, you men. Halt there right now!" He seems mad as hell at how grungy they look. They are standing there, rain running off their steel pots, eyes wide at the smell of hot food hanging in the air. Bowie walks up to them, and SGT Emilio Fortas, their squad leader, sees the look in Bowie's eye and almost whispers, "Attention!" to the men, who, though exhausted, pull themselves erect and stand there as Bowie comes over. The colonel walks from one to the next, looking at their unshaven faces and mud-caked combat fatigues, at their filthy boots and their weapons wrapped in mortar round plastic.

"What in God's name are you?" Bowie says. It seems a rhetorical question, and neither SGT Fortas nor any of the squad answers. "You are the filthiest bunch of army pigs I have ever seen. You *stink*. No, you reek. I know I gave you some latitude with neatness, being out in the woods like you are. But this is miserable, unacceptable, just filth, filth!" He walks to the end of the squad to one poor grunt who is the funkiest.

"Soldier, you look and smell like a pig. Filthy! Worse than any pig. Get down in the mud and root around like the pig you are." The PFC stares at Bowie, uncomprehending. All he wants is lunch and a dry place to sleep. But Bowie is screaming, "Oink, pig, oink!" at the guy. He reaches out to push the grunt down. That soldier has already put up with enough filth and misery this past week for half a dozen tours in Vietnam. He just stares at Bowie, and the way his fist is clenched, I imagine he is about an inch away from taking aim with his plastic-covered M16 and putting a bullet hole dead center in his commanding officer's chest. For what seems forever, the colonel and the PFC stare at each other.

"Christ," Bowie says, "Jesus Christ." He looks at the soldier for a moment more and then shakes his head, pivots abruptly on his heel, and strides away toward the entrance to the TOC. SGT Fortas has seen me watching this scene. He looks over at me, gives me a bare, thin-lipped smile, and motions his squad on to the mess tent. I am thinking that, *God, I hope this is over, that LTC Bowie has realized the stupidity of his actions.* But I doubt it. I do.

We sit for two weeks on LZ Linebarger, shooting for the ARVN units that are getting deeper and deeper into the shit. Around us on the Vietnam side of the border, it is a war of harassment. The battle we fought our first night is the only big one for us. We get incoming mortars sometimes, but few because the dinks have learned we can locate their tubes and respond right away. It is a few rounds fired at us, and then nothing as they break down their tubes and run. A few 122 rockets come in, oddly misaimed and ineffective as if the dinks are only going through the motions. From LZ Vandergrift and the Rockpile to our east all the way here to the border, U.S. units are running into concentrations of enemy, mostly NVA regulars, getting into shoot-outs, losing men and equipment. None of it would you call a major set-piece battle. Those sorts of big planned actions are almost all taking place in Laos between the ARVN and the enemy. In those battles, it is clear the ARVN are outmatched, outgunned, and outled. The incursion has bogged down, and our intel has it that more NVA units are coming into the mix, putting pressure on the ARVN, and moving to roll up the line of ARVN firebases north and south of Highway 9 in Laos.

It is a Sunday morning, raining "cold as a witch's tit in Minneapolis," SGM Alberto says. Rain is turning the red dust into a rusty-colored gunge over everything. LZ Linebarger has acquired the look of a real permanent firebase: line bunkers, a fortified TOC, a mess tent, showers, even a barbershop manned by Freddy "Snipper" Moscone, a real barber from Philadelphia in civilian life, now an infantryman from Delta Company, the lucky bastard borrowed for the duration to cut hair on the hill.

I am sitting with CPT Patterson in the mess tent eating actual hot chow for breakfast, real eggs and bacon that the mess sergeant has scrounged from where I don't plan to ask. Cat comes up to us looking bleary eyed. He'd worked the night shift in the TOC with CPL Mallaby and had gone to sleep only an hour or so ago.

"Captain," he says to me, "battalion arty wants you on the horn now."

"Any idea what it's about, Cat?"

"No, sir, but they said for you to call them ASAP. Sergeant said they told him to get me up too."

I look at Patterson, who looks back at me with a shrug. "Battalion wants you. I guess you ought to talk to them."

"I hope to hell they aren't moving the battery again," I say. "But if they're doing that, wouldn't they have called you too?"

"Probably," Patterson says, "if you're going, can I have your bacon?" He's already reaching for my tray.

"Goddamn it, Steve, leave that. I'll be right back." Patterson filches a piece anyway.

Cat stands there looking confused. "Come on, man," I tell him. "Let's go see what they want now."

It is COL Dolby himself on the horn for me. "I need to talk to you here in Quang Tri," he says to me. "I'm sending a bird for you and Private

Wilbur. Bring your gear with you. You won't be back on that firebase for a while."

What the . . ., I am thinking, starting to say, "Sir, I . . ."

"Nothing more over the radio, David. The bird will be there in an hour or so. So get packed and be ready."

"Roger," I say.

"Out!" And he's off.

I know what Cat wants to ask, looking at me with a wide-eyed question, and I would answer what he would expect, that I have no idea what we're in for and we will have to wait to talk to the colonel before we find out.

Our bird drops out of a hazy sky onto a pad at Quang Tri. The base itself—abutting the ancient, war-battered square citadel city of Quang Tri—is huge, a sea of rectangular buildings, sandbags holding down their peaked corrugated roofs. It is laid out on the flatlands along the broad, shallow Sông Thach Hān River twenty klicks from the coast. The central supply and logistics center for the Laotian incursion, the base is a madhouse of ground and air movement, the latter through which our pilot has to thread to reach our landing site.

This day in midwinter is cold; a fog, now at nearly noon burned to a high mist, rises off the nearby South China Sea. A jeep waits for us as we step off the slick, and the crew chief hands down our rucks and gear. Cat had been silent as we sat in the bird watching the jungle-covered highlands of Quang Tri Province give way to the flat and open expanse of the coastal plain. He had stared out the open bay of the bird, grunting as we flew over Khe Sanh and again as the sprawl of Quang Tri came into view. I knew little enough about what was in store for us. Cat, a PFC, knew next to nothing, and I imagined he was full of worry at what was coming. The jeep driver, also a PFC whose unpressed jungle fatigues and unpolished boots told me this was a rough-and-ready base and not a haven for rear echelon motherfuckers, took off with a jolt the moment we were seated. Our jeep skirted the wide airfield and headed to a pair of sandbagged buildings at the north end of the base near the Quang Tri citadel. He skidded to a stop on the patch of damp gravel that served as a parking area and announced that we were there. "Colonel's waiting for you, Captain. I'll be in the orderly room if you need another ride."

The building is clearly a makeshift headquarters of a cobbled-together artillery brigade comprising the direct support and heavy support artillery units assigned to the operation. In the orderly room, behind a desk piled with stacks of order folders and reports, a buck sergeant sits talking on a field phone to someone who clearly wants details of some ammunition load problem. He sees us enter and waves us toward a couple of folding chairs near a rickety table where a coffeepot steams.

"Be with you in a moment, Captain. Coffee's decent. You and the PFC get some if you like," he says and returns to explaining to someone on the other end of the phone line that he needs the white phosphorous rounds for the 105s *now* or the goddamned battery won't be shooting any close in fire missions. "Yeah, Lieutenant, yeah. I can put COL Dolby on the horn with you now if you like, but do you really want to buck this up to him?" A pause. "OK, thank you, sir. Notify brigade when you're ready to load it." He slams down the receiver, saying, "Son of a *bitch!*" looks at me and Cat and shakes his head. "I don't know what the hell those logistics assholes think we are going to use for marking rounds. Go ahead and have some coffee if you like. It's drinkable. I'll see if the colonel is ready for you."

I haven't even poured a cup when Dolby appears in the doorway of a back office. He is the same as always, rumpled, unmilitary in his bearing, gray eyes behind gold-rimmed specs fastening on me with a suddenly pleased look as if I were an old friend. "David, come in," he says. "You too, Private."

Dolby's office—in reality just the back part of the building sectioned off by a stretch of tarp that was probably once the wall of a tent—is as much as his previous office had been down south at LZ Bronco, with a desk piled with reports, a large table cluttered with maps, and several chairs in only slightly better shape than the two in the outer office.

First thing I notice is the eagle of a full colonel embroidered on Dolby's collar. He had left the 6/11 artillery abruptly for a spot at division, and I had heard that, as expected, he had gotten promoted, but I hadn't seen him since the day he had pinned my new captain's bars on. "Congratulations, sir. I had heard you'd made bird colonel."

"Yeah, yeah." Dolby grins. "I deserve it and all that, I know. Doing a damn fine job and all, I'm told." He waves toward the chairs. "Sit down, David, Private Wilbur. We have to talk, and there's no time for pleasantries."

Cat looks at me, and I nod toward one of the chairs. I take a second one, and Dolby seats himself across the table from us. He unfolds a topo map, moves it so Cat and I can get a good look, and begins to talk with frequent interruptions as intensely noisy aircraft, mostly helicopters, pass overhead. Dolby frowns at the noise, looks at the ceiling as if he can see through it to the irritating passage of the helicopter, shakes his head, and finally says. "I imagine you've seen too much of this map already." He's right. It is of the Dak Mŏt Lop area along the southern Laos/Vietnam border, a place out of my nightmares where, on a high jungle hill a year and a month ago, half of Bravo Company had fought the battle of its life against a sea of North Vietnamese. Remembering, I pull the map over and put a finger on the contour lines that denote that hill, sheer sided on its north and east as the map shows, part of a ridge rising eight hundred meters above the Dak Ho'niang valley and six klicks from the point at which the borders of Vietnam, Laos, and Cambodia meet.

"You're not showing me this for nostalgia's sake are you, sir?"

Dolby shakes his head. "No," he says. "There's going to be an operation near there." He stops and looks at me and then Cat. "This is classified, stamped top secret and all that. You understand, Private? You can't discuss this with *anyone* unless CPT Weisman here says it's OK first."

Cat, looking at the colonel with an earnest expression, says, "Yes, sir. I understand. Yes, sir."

"Good," Dolby says. "And I already figure you do, David."

He bends over the table, pointing to the towering peak that sits right at the triple point where the three countries intersect. "We're putting a firebase in there, two infantry companies, six 155s, and a pair of 175s. Driving *those* two big bastards up there is going to be a feat." He pulls out another map, this one of an area to the west of the first map labeled Ban Phiadouang. "Here," he says, "the ARVN are going to put in another firebase with a battery of 155s on this hill fifteen klicks west of the border. That'll give you 155 and some 175 fires if you need them anywhere in this region."

I'm staring at him because I think I know what's coming.

"I thought it was illegal for U.S. troops to go into Laos, Colonel."

"It is."

"But it looks like we are setting up fire support for exactly that sort of mission across the border."

"Also true."

"Well, Colonel, I'm going to hazard a guess that you're not signing me up to be the liaison officer on that hill on the triple point. So I guess I'm just going to listen now because this plan has me good and baffled." Cat is quiet, staring at the scatter of maps on the table. I don't know if he gets it yet, but I think it is beginning to sink in.

"I expected as much," Dolby says and flashes a quick embarrassed grin as if to say this isn't his idea. "OK, as I'm sure you've figured out, the ARVN offensive into Laos is bogging down. That's a polite way of saying they're getting their asses kicked. A big part of the problem is that the ARVN's message security is as porous as a porcupine's air mattress. The North Vietnamese got wind of the Laos incursion early and beefed up their forces to about sixty thousand troops. That's about twice what the ARVN has there. To take some pressure off them, Twenty-Four Corps wants to create some trouble in south Laos to make it seem as if there is a second invasion beginning there. To respond, we're sending in several CIDG units to tromp around on the other side of the border and make enough noise to get the North Vietnamese's attention and hopefully get them to divert some units to the south. That would ease the burden on the incursion taking place here in the north."

I look at COL Dolby and start to open my mouth, but I suspect I know what he is going to say, so I just shut it and wait.

"Yeah, David, we are sending four units with attached Montagnard companies into Attapu Province in Laos. Each will have an assigned zone. As you found out with CPT Englander, the Hatchet Teams are crack units but not terribly conversant with artillery tactics, so I'm sending an FO with each team. You're going—unless you decline—with the team from Téthian."

"Englander's team, sir? Christ, I would have imagined he couldn't stand the sight of me."

"Not true, David. In fact, Englander specially requested you to be assigned to his team. I'd send a lieutenant—we've got some pretty good ones as FOs. But Englander trusts you, said something about your saving his life."

I snort. "Nothing so big as that, sir."

"Whatever happened, CPT Englander requested you be assigned to his team, and unless you object, I'm going to honor his request." He looks at me through his unmilitary gold-rimmed glasses.

I take a breath. "No, sir, no objection." At that, I see Cat look at me and then at the colonel as if he'd rather be anyplace but here. He knows he's going with me. "I do have a question, though, maybe a quibble. It's illegal for us to send U.S. troops into Laos. So how do we get away with this?"

"I can't answer that, David. It's not for me to say. Twenty-Four Corps is calling you noncombatant observers, as if that will make a difference to any NVA or VC you encounter. If it's any help, the guns supporting you will have all the ammunition they need, and you'll have instant access to them. You'll also have twenty-four-hour air available including a Puff and a flight of extraction birds if you need them."

"And aside from making noise in the jungle, do we have a mission?"

"Yes and no. Making noise is the central mission, throwing worry into the North so they will divert troops in your direction. But there are a number of Viet Cong base camps in that area, lightly defended now that most of their troops have been sent up here to fight the ARVN. So you could have some enemy contact. You'll cross over into Laos here." He points on the map to where Highway 512, which runs past Ben Het west to the border, climbs up a shallow valley and hits the top of the ridge that defines that border. It is the same ridge on which, in January 1970, I had called in artillery and air strikes to take out a long Viet Cong supply train, destroying dozens of trucks and setting more than two klicks of the ridge ablaze. It is the ridge where I had seen what looked to be 1LT Schmidt, the missing Recon platoon leader who many thought had gone over to the enemy side and become one of the (some say mythical) Longshadows. A man looking like him was surely there walking among the dinks on that ridge. But the units that had gone up after to recon that death scene had found no sign of him or any other western soldier.

Dolby stops for a moment, looking at the map. He looks up. "You know about Operation Tailwind last fall, David?"

"I heard a bit about it. It was some op blacker than black in Laos, wasn't it?" I say to the colonel, telling him I know only that it had involved a Hatchet Team from the purposefully misnamed Studies and Observation Group, which had gone in to create a diversion for an offensive by Prince Norodom Sihanouk's Royal Lao Army against the North Vietnamese. The op was a deep dark secret, but grapevine stories said they'd got into a hell of a fight near the Laotian ville of Chavane and had been pulled out with a lot of dead and wounded among the Yards' company troops and with almost all the sixteen U.S. Hatchet Team troops wounded. Got a ton of documents to make it good.

"That was Englander's team, which had been seconded to the SOG for the operation. Englander's biggest bitch was that he had had no artillery support."

"Learned something from me, then, I guess," I say, giving Dolby a bit of a caustic grin. So *that* was the black op Englander had been so secretive about last year.

"OK," the colonel says. "I've got expedited transport for you and Private Wilbur," he stops, looks at Cat for a moment, and then says, "I'm sorry, Private. I'll give you the same choices I've given the captain here. You can go with him or you can decline. If you decline, there will be no repercussions. I'll send you back to your old job on LZ Linebarger and find CPT Weisman another RTO. But I'm told you made a good team on that last op and would be an asset if you go on this one."

Cat doesn't even pause. "I'll go, sir, anything to get out of all that red muck over by the border." He smiles broadly, and I'm thankful; sure Cat will do a workmanlike job out there.

"OK," Dolby says again. "I've got a Caribou sitting on the tarmac waiting to take you to Duc Pho. Supply there with the 6/11 will have gear for you including some sort of beefed-up radio gear, a super PRC-25 with an extended range so you'll always be in com with the firebases. From where you'll be in Laos, it'll reach all the way to Ben Het if you can get an antenna up high enough, I'm told. I haven't a clue if that's true, but I hope so. Any other questions?"

Cat and I look at each other. I nod to Dolby. "No, sir, we're ready."

"Then on your way," he says. "And you two be goddamned careful. That Englander is a bull goose loony for sure."

CHAPTER 9

I've ridden Caribous all over Vietnam and have never come to love them. They are workhorses, the main medium-range transportation between major bases and cities, but they are noisy as hell and vibrate enough to shake your bones apart. The web benches where you strap in have had every iota of comfort designed out of them. Not an hour after we meet with COL Dolby, after a quick meal at a poor excuse for a mess hall, Cat and I are on board the Caribou for what amounts to our own special charter flight to Duc Pho. We're the only passengers amid a big load of tarp-covered pallets, ammunition, foodstuff, and other miscellaneous necessities of war.

"The flight takes about an hour and a half, Captain. You'll want earplugs for it," the crew chief says, offering me a set. He gives a second pack of earplugs to Cat. They are a sort of yellow putty the size of a cigarette filter, and when I stuff them in my ears, the engine noise of the plane drops to a bearably dull rumble. We belt in, and the bird almost immediately begins rolling into an abrupt, high-powered takeoff. Cat is thrown against me as the craft seems to jump up into the sky to present as difficult a target as possible to enemy antiaircraft gunners. This plane has a row of porthole-sized windows down each side (some Caribous don't), and we can watch the landscape roll by, flat plains of rice fields below us, jungle-covered mountains climbing to our west. The view is short-lived, though, as the plane climbs into the low bank of rain clouds that hangs over central Vietnam. We bounce and then bounce more, and I am deciding I am not going to like this flight much when the aircraft manages to climb above the heaviest of the clouds and the air gets smoother.

Despite the noise and vibration of the flight, I drift into a fitful sleep in which I dream of an endless climb up a jungle-covered hillside with mosquitos keening all around me. I awake as the Caribou makes a hard landing at LZ Bronco and rolls to a stop on a rain-swept runway. We debark. Not far away is the row of buildings that are the HQs for the infantry units of the Eleventh Brigade and the guns of the 6/11 Artillery. Once again, a jeep, this time with its canvas top up, waits near where we have landed to take me and Cat to the artillery battalion supply building. It is strangely quiet here, as if the war has seeped out of the land and oozed northward, no sounds of gun or cannon fire, nor any whisper of incoming to break the drumming of rain on the runway's tarmac or its rattle against the canvas of the jeep's roof.

The SP4 who is driving the jeep says, "Captain, I'm supposed to tell you we are going to supply for some special gear they have for you and then right over to the chopper pad for a bird that's waiting to take you where you're supposed to go." He puts the jeep in gear and pops the clutch, and we jolt off toward the artillery battalion supply shed. "Nobody would tell me where you're supposed to be going, sir. Just to make sure to pick you two up, get you what you need, and to your flight."

He gives me a quick glance and then goes back to driving. I say nothing except "Thanks." And Cat, talking my cue, says nothing at all. The specialist driving us gets the hint and shuts up.

The sandbagged supply warehouse is cold inside and seemingly devoid of personnel, another sign of the war's displacement to other parts. Cat and I wander for several minutes past shelves of combat fatigues, rucksacks, canteens, poncho liners, and such (some new and still in their plastic wrap; some gross and grimed from the field) before we find a small office where a master sergeant greets me with a terse "Good afternoon, Captain" and only a nod to Cat.

"Here's the extra gear you're supposed to get, sir. A radio—it's a PRC-77. Not much different from the PRC-25 field radios you're used to. More reliable, has encryption capability, bonus is it's a tad lighter than what you've been used to. Range on these is generally about eight to ten klicks, but this one is amped up to get you about fifteen klicks with the short antenna and maybe twenty-five with the long whip. Also has a long wire antenna that will get you maybe forty klicks' range on a good day. Must be strung horizontally from trees, though. You'll need to be in a secure area to use it."

Cat picks up the radio—strapped to a rigid pack frame—and hefts it. "It is a little lighter," he says. "Extra battery and all the other add-ins are going to make it heavy as lead, though."

"Also supposed to give you these," the supply sergeant says. He holds up bags containing two M17 gas masks. "Each kit also has packs of atropine and pralidoxime auto-injectors."

"Jesus!" I say. "That's for nerve gas. Why the hell are we getting that?" What are we getting into? The memory of the hissing bundle Englander had abandoned on our last op together makes me blink.

"Don't know, Captain. I was ordered to provide you with them. Leave them for all I care. I have no idea what sort of mission you're going on, so I don't know why you'll need these masks."

"No, we'll take them," I say, thinking that this is getting stranger by the minute. The M17 mask is not secret stuff; every new soldier learns how to use the mask and auto-injectors in basic training. Cat looks at the sergeant with the same question. We usually carry a much lighter mask in the field to protect against nonlethal stuff like tear gas.

Cat fixes his rucksack to the radio's pack frame, while the supply sergeant shows me through the clutch of 1:50,000 topo maps of eastern Laos and the border area he is giving me. One, the Dak Mŏt Lop map that COL Dolby had showed us again brings a pang. The contours of that map section are an indelible imprint in my memory. My eye is drawn immediately to that hill in the 7924 grid square in the map's upper-left quadrant. Too many of Bravo Company had died there a year ago for me not to have a lump in my throat. I slip the packet of maps into a pocket of my ruck. We change into tiger-striped jungle fatigues and, despite my better judgment, agree to trade our steel pots in for the sort of boonie hats that CPT Englander had tried to get us to wear on our last op with him. The supply sergeant apologetically explains it is orders from above that we have to wear them to "blend in" with the Yard troops. Cat and I stuff our rucks with a few days' worth of freeze-dried LRRP rations, beg a few boxes of the better-tasting Cs and some warm items—sweaters and poncho liners for the chilly nights—and we are good to go.

Our flight to Téthian on a slick Huey is long and bumpy through low clouds heavy with cold rain that blows into the open cabin of the bird. Here at five thousand feet, the door gunners are wearing warm flight suits, while Cat and I in our tiger-striped jungle fatigues can see our breath. The crew chief has given us poncho liners to wrap up in for warmth, which help a little, warming the body if not the soul. I've been thinking about this "mission" of ours in southeastern Laos. Except for our orders "to raise hell," there is no true battle plan for us beyond targeting several supposed VC base camps. What if there is nothing there? What if there is too much there, a VC battalion- or regiment-sized unit, say, far too big for us to fight off? It is illegal for us to be there despite the flimsy effort to sugarcoat our role as "observers." There is nobody within twenty or more klicks to come to our aid if we get into deep shit, nobody except artillery and air support, which is a comfort of sorts, but that isn't boots on the ground if we need reinforcement. And COL Dolby had made it clear that there will be no rescue units lined up to come for us. "Jesus!" I say and see Cat nod as if he has read my mind. I ask him how he is doing.

"Oh, I'm OK, sir," he says. "I'm trying to see the big idea in this, but it just seems strange. Are we going to be OK?"

"Look, Cat, we are going out with a dozen of the best soldiers in the world, backed up by a full company of butt-kicking Montagnards, with all the artillery and air support we need. Any help?"

"Not much, sir."

"Yeah, I guess I feel some of that myself. But no matter what, you and I will have to watch out for each other. Clear?"

"Clear, Captain." We bump fists in a bit of what the black soldiers call the dap.

It is forty-five klicks from the brigade base at LZ Bronco out to Téthian, half an hour flying time for our bird in this heavy weather. In it, the late afternoon is almost dark as dusk. Wads of gray fog hang among the teak trees on the mountains below us; squalls of rain blow in through the bird's open bay doors. It is after 1830 hours and growing dark when the Sông Re valley comes into view from out of the clouds and we drop down to the pad at the camp. The bird flares for a landing, bucking against a changeable wind, finally settling roughly onto the surface of the pad. This time, CPT Englander is there to meet us along with a couple of Yard troops who take our gear as the bird's crew chief hands it out to them. Reluctantly, Cat and I surrender the poncho liners and step out onto the ground.

Englander comes forward as we move out from under the bird's spinning blades. He reaches out to offer me an awkward handshake, his arm still apparently a bit stiff from the shoulder wound half a year ago. He says something lost in the scream of the helicopter's turbine as the pilot pulls pitch and lifts back up into the clouds. I cock my head at him, and he says again with apparent pleasantness in his voice, "Glad they were able to get you for this mission. I hear you're a captain now. Congratulations. Come on, hot coffee in the ops shack. Warmer there too."

The camp appears little changed from our last visit, none of the Yard soldiers in evidence, none of the black-and-white checked chickens here either, though I suspect they are somewhere out of the weather. The inside of the ops shack is perceptibly warmer from a fire burning on the stone hearth, a coffeepot sitting on a grate over it. To the side of the grate are a pot of rice and another pot with a sort of chopped vegetable along with a platter of what looks like grilled chicken being kept warm there. The same banged-up table is still in the shack. The Montagnard company's đại úy and MSG Flanagan—both still here at the camp, though it has been a long time since I was here last—are seated next to the table, the two of them eating from bowls of rice, chicken, and vegetables. They nod at us as we enter.

"Dinner there if you like Yard food," Englander says. "Has hot-as-Hades peppers in it, but damn good anyway. Or there are some C rats on the shelf there if you want that sort of crap instead."

Cat elects to take a bowl of the Yard food. And though my spice-shunning ancestors from their Eastern European shtetl would groan in warning, I also take a bowl of what the others are eating. One bite, a pepper hits the back of my throat and I can't breathe. The đại úy starts laughing, and then (when I can breathe again) I do too. Damn, I think, we're all suddenly one happy family; though it feels *Heart of Darkness* strange. The đại úy says something with the phrase "Bo mo'ta apui mraih" in it, points at me, and laughs again.

Seeing my look, Flanagan grins, "He says your face is red as fire."

"Feels like it," I say, slugging down some tepid coffee and poking around in the vegetables for more of the curly, dime-size red peppers, pushing them to one side of the rice. Sans peppers, the food is tasty and welcome.

The meal done, CPT Englander pulls out a Dak Mŏt Lop map sheet and puts a finger on the border, reprising the info COL Dolby had given me. "We're going in here where the 512 Highway crosses into Laos. The birds will put us down about a klick to the east on top of the ridge. From there, we will head downhill a klick into the beginning of the Dak Xou valley. We'll head west out of there and make a lot of noise through villes along about ten klicks of that river. Charlie is supposed to have a bunch of base camps and storage depots there where they bring stuff upriver from Attapu."

"How do they get upriver?" I ask. "Looks like a whole series of rapids along the blue line and into the Attapu valley."

"I don't know, man. I guess we'll see when we get there. Doesn't make a hell of a lot of difference anyway, does it? We're just there to cause trouble, whether there are any dink supply dumps or not. You've got plenty of artillery to back you anyway. I expect you'll have a good time."

It's not *my* idea of a good time, but Englander is right in that we don't have any particular objective, and so it doesn't matter what we find as long as we do a good job of riling up the Viet Cong and NVA.

He stands next to me looking at the map for a moment longer and then says, "Finish eating and get your gear ready. A Hook will be here to take us to the Ben Het staging area in about forty-five minutes. I'm going to make sure the Yards are ready to go."

I keep looking at the map and, given my last experience with Englander, wonder if his description of the mission and our route into Laos have any relationship to what we will actually do. *No way to tell, just be on your toes*, I tell myself, thinking that even that doesn't matter, given our free-form mission. Anyway, I've got a load of maps to cover any contingency. We'll just have to see how things shake out.

A Chinook fitted out as a pure passenger bird comes to the Téthian camp to pick us up. In this configuration, Hooks are set up to seat about thirty-six passengers, but those are the American-sized variety of soldier. I'm five feet nine inches, and I still tower over most of the Yards, who are generally as short as Vietnamese men. The fierce gale from the bird's twin rotors seems ready to blow the camp's fortifications apart; the Yards waiting to board duck away, shielding faces, hunched over in its blast. When the bird has settled and the rear door opened, a full fifty of the Yard soldiers—about half the company—pile on, filling the bird until there seems no room to breathe. Cat and I manage to get seats up near the front where the engine noise is the least loud. Adding eight members of Englander's A-Team (the others will remain behind with the rest of the Yards to maintain security at Téthian), in my mind, overloads the big bird. But it lifts off with no trouble in the dense winter air. I stuff in earplugs to cut the noise for the forty-five-minute, 120-klick ride to Ben Het. The smell of the Téthian camp, a sort of wet-dog, dried-fish, soldiers-too-long-without-a-bath fetor stays with us, concentrated and heavy in the bird's passenger cabin. An army may travel on its stomach, but it carries its own stench along for the ride. The crew chief dims the cabin lights; a muted roar growls into my plugged ears. The bird lifts with a lurch, rising into unquiet air, turns toward the west and Ben Het, and begins to climb. Outside, it is now fully night; gusts of wind and rain buffet the bird as we ride through the heavy cloud cover. Cat and I are seated near a window, but on this stormy night, there is nothing but blackness to see outside. Somewhere above the clouds, the moon is full and in full eclipse, rusty colored, already well into the depths of the earth's shadow. Caught in our cocoon of storm, we don't see it. Instead, in the darkness, rain blows in through the open rear door where a tail gunner sits with his M60.

The base at Ben Het, a dozen klicks east of the Vietnam, Cambodia, Laos border triple point, is sodden when we reach it at 2200 hours, the bird settling onto the wide chopper pad. I had expected to see a flight of slick Hueys waiting on the pad to take us on to the border, but the expanse of patched asphalt is empty, and when we alight from the Hook, an SP4 from the base directs us to a mess hall a couple of hundred meters away where we will wait for the lift birds to arrive.

Englander is not in a good mood. "The goddamned lift was supposed to be here to meet us," he says. He kicks open the mess hall door, kicks a chair out of the way, and says, "Shit!" louder and then bellows, "Somebody get me some coffee!"

I'd tell him it's the weather that's holding us up, but he knows that. I wonder why we can't just take the Chinook onto the LZ, but I suppose the landing area is small and suitable only for the smaller and nimbler Hueys.

A sergeant from Ben Het's operations center comes in as a KP serves coffee to me and Englander at our table in the officers' corner. The sergeant looks from one to the other of us and asks, "CPT Englander?"

"Yeah," Englander says, takes a sip of the lukewarm coffee, swallows, and looks at the sergeant.

"Sir, your lift birds are still at Dak To. They were on another CA before yours, and weather has delayed them refueling to get here."

"So when the hell am I going to get some birds?'

"About an hour, sir."

"Man!" He tries another swallow from his mug, spits it out, and shouts, "Damn it, do you call this shit coffee? Make something I can drink." He turns back to look at the sergeant, who, apparently seeing that Englander is not anywhere in his chain of command, seems to care very little about how pissed off the captain is. "An hour?"

"Not much I can do, sir. Pad master at Dak To controls their movement. I'll send a runner to warn you as soon as the birds are airborne."

"Yeah, Sergeant, why don't you do that?" Englander puts the mug down and shoves it away, slopping some of the coffee onto the oilcloth cover of the officers' corner table. "I'm going to take a piss," he says to no one in particular and strides away toward the mess hall door.

A young PFC on KP comes up with a coffeepot in his hand. "Are you an officer too?" he asks me. I realize my tiger-striped jungle fatigues have no mark of rank on them.

"Yeah, a captain," I say. And then, seeing the kid is nervous as hell after Englander's tirade, I add, "I'm not in as bad a mood as he is."

"Uh, OK, sir. Do you want coffee too? This pot is fresh." I nod. He pours me a mugful and walks carefully away without touching Englander's mug.

CHAPTER 10

We don't get our lift birds until 0220 hours, four hours after we landed in Ben Het. By then, CPT Englander is in a perfect rage, and even his top sergeant is reluctant to approach him. In the interval since we arrived here, the storm has intensified, rain coming down in sheets that are wind swirled across Ben Het's pad. When the birds settle, we charge across the PSP and onto the craft. We are soaked in the cold deluge and soaked again by the hurricane of chopper blade whipped water as we board. One of the choppers is a command-and-control bird equipped with a communications console, and Englander motions me to it. I climb in next to him as Englander pulls on a flight helmet and jacks into the bird's com system. There is none such for me, and while I can see him talking to the pilot, I can hear none of it. It is clear, though, that there is a bit of argument back and forth between them, and then the bird lifts.

Suspicious of that debate and untrusting of Englander's commitment to prior-made plans, I pull out my compass. Englander sees, grins inscrutably, and continues talking to the pilot. We lift into the east wind, rising above the rain-swept pad, eight birds in total, enough to CA the entire unit in a single lift. That we'd gotten so many birds when most are far up north supporting Lam Son 719 is a testament to how important some high brass thinks this mission is. We make a hard 180-degree turn and are soon headed toward the border. Soaked, shivering so that I can hardly hold the compass still, I watch as it displays our direction. I expect us to be traveling generally west-northwest on an azimuth somewhere near 5,500 mils (315 degrees for you nonredlegs). That would lead us to the spot where the diminished track of the 512 Highway meets the Laotian border. I have already called in grids and given the fire order for an artillery prep on that location. Sure, we don't want to make excessive noise going in, but we don't want to let any large enemy unit wait there to pounce as we hit the ground either. A four by four of artillery fire on and around our landing zone is a hell of an effective way to disrupt that. But even holding the compass with my rain-chilled hands shaking, I can see our actual heading is to the west-southwest on an azimuth of about 4,400 mils (250 degrees), which, if we continue to the border, will put us a day's march south of where Englander had told me we are landing. He sees me looking at my compass and knows then that I know, and a shit-eating smirk spreads slowly across his face. It is impossible to talk above the roar of the turbine and the howl of the storm, the bird bucking in it like something alive. That's good because I would have words for Englander that even an infantry grunt might think twice about before using.

After about fifteen minutes of flight, Englander again talks to the pilot over the internal com set, pointing down into the pitch darkness of the storm. I can see nothing, and I doubt the pilot sees anything more. Then, below, all at once, I see the pinpoint flare of a strobe begin to flash, Englander pointing again toward it, our pilot shaking his head, having a few more words with Englander, finally nodding, and then we begin a quick spiral descent. The LZ is a tiny one, a clearing in heavy jungle intermittently illuminated by the strobe and then by the bird's landing lights through the rain. It is big enough for only one bird at a time to land and let off passengers. Surprisingly, Englander directs our C & C bird to go in first, barely touching down before he has jumped off, and I follow suit quickly, hardly on the ground when our pilot lifts away. I follow Englander out of the clearing and under the trees where the rain's ferocity is softened to a heavy drip. I look at Englander, and I know he is waiting for me to ask him where the hell we are. The second bird comes down, and Cat is on it. He finds me and Englander under the trees, and I motion to him immediately for the radio handset. The radio is tuned to the push of the artillery battery on Hill 780 that sits like a wen on the ridge just west of the border in Laos.

"Carbon Valley Four-Seven, this is Carbon Valley Niner. Fire mission. Over," I call. Englander looks at me, startled, but says nothing as I call in the mission.

Though it is an ARVN battery, it is an American-sounding voice that responds, "Carbon Valley Niner, this is Carbon Valley Four-Seven. Go ahead. Over."

"Roger, give me a nav round at the seven-four, two-zero grid intersection."

"Roger, on the way. Out."

Less than two minutes later (a quick response, especially for a battery manned by ARVN gunners), I hear the battery RTO announce, "Shot!" and soon after, "Splash!" To our west maybe a half klick off through an opening in the trees, there is the flash and reverberant bang of a white phosphorous marking round going off. I had worried that I wouldn't see it through the jungle canopy, but the six-hundred-meter-high burst hangs there, clear and bright despite the storm, the azimuth to it 4,000 mils. I call for a second nav round on the 74-21 grid intersection, the azimuth to that one I measure as 4,800 mils. Where the two azimuths cross on my map is our location, and though with just two marking rounds the pinpoint of our location might be off by a hundred meters or so, I see clearly enough on the map where we actually are. I look around for Englander to ask him why in hell we have put down nearly seven klicks south of our announced destination and on the border not of Laos but of Cambodia.

Englander, though, is engrossed in a conversation with a Yard (apparently the one with the strobe) who has emerged from the jungle cover at the north edge of the landing zone. The conversation is via Englander's translator, an older Yard sergeant the others call Trung Sĩ Y Aguăt, which I gather from MSG Flanagan means "white scorpion" in the Jarai Yard language. I find it entertaining that, like our own troops, the Yards refer to their fellow soldiers by nicknames. The man meeting us is in civilian dress, not the Yards' intricately embroidered traditional clothing, though, but American-style dungarees and a short-sleeved white dress shirt, as if he were on his way to a business office. Englander looks at me as I come up. "Figure where we are yet, Captain?" he asks, his face in a bit of a smirk; I imagine he knows what I've done in calling in the nav rounds—though I'm not positive, as his acquaintance with artillery practices seems negligible.

"Yeah," I say. "We're about twelve hundred meters east of the Cambodian border, maybe seven klicks south of where you told me we were going to cross into Laos."

"Good, good," he says, still slightly smirking. "Glad to have a redleg aboard who can keep track of our location." The cheeriness drops from his voice as he adds, "I wasn't pleased, though, that you shot those rounds without asking me first. We get into contact, I sure as hell want you to ask permission before calling in fire."

"Roger that, Captain," I say. "No arty until you want it. Nav rounds hardly give us away, though. And it's my job to know our location. We made enough noise with these birds coming in that a couple of 155 rounds aren't going to make much difference."

Now Englander rounds on me, a dark hulk in the night under the trees. "Screw that, Weisman, that's history. It's not the mission we're on now. We're not going to make any noise, not going to raise hell unless we have to. Going to go in quiet as goddamn church mice and do our job. Get it?"

"And our job is?"

"You'll find out soon enough. Just keep the arty silent unless I tell you otherwise."

"Roger that, Captain," I say again.

Englander turns back to the civilian-dressed Yard, asking through the interpreter where "she" is.

"Where *to'bang* is she?"

"Ngai thâo."

"He says don't know, Captain."

"Christ!" Englander kicks the ground in frustration. "Tell him to take us where he last saw her."

The translator repeats Englander's order in Jarai.

"Ŭ!" the Yard responds.

"He say OK."

"Then let's go," says Englander, and the phrase "saddle up" passes quietly around the LZ. Cat is with me, both of us walking behind Englander a few men back from the Yard who's walking point. We move quietly along a trail through the dense jungle. The slight sound of our movement is drowned in the intensity of the storm, and our only connection to the men walking in front of us is the patch of luminescent material on the backs of their boonie hats.

"Should have invaded Cambodia in '67 the way we'd planned," Englander, once again seeming genial, tells me as we walk, "except that dickhead LBJ scotched the whole thing. He bombed Hanoi but didn't have the balls for a real invasion of Cambodia when there was still a chance to put down the Reds there. Went in last year instead, and by then, things had gone to hell and it did no real good."

How wide, I wonder, do we have to make this war? If Englander were in charge, we might already be fighting in Burma or even India or Afghanistan. Spreading, spreading wider forever. I feel a chill and think I would not want to live inside CPT Hugh Englander's mind.

The trail we move down runs along a small north flowing tributary of the Dak Koi. A half a klick of travel and we are at a pair of communal Yard longhouses built on stilts on an upslope above the water. A smell of burning, of the wet reek of charred wood and burned bamboo, rises around us despite the rain. The longhouses are parallel to the river one behind the other. The forward one, burned till it's almost skeletal, is visible only because there is firelight in the second longhouse, flickering behind a screen of fallen poles and burned-away walls of woven bamboo. Some Yards must have lived here until recently, but no longer, and I think I smell what seems to be the odor of cooked meat. A number of folks died here, I realize. The second longhouse is only partially burned, a whole section at its south end still mostly intact. It is there the fire is burning on a stone hearth, its light coming through a window opening the shutters of which have been burned away. Englander calls for a halt, and the well-disciplined Yard troops quickly set into a perimeter around the longhouses.

Englander tells the translator to ask what we will find here. Y Aguăt puts the question to the Yard guiding us.

"Amăng lăm," the Yard responds.

"He says one inside knows, đại úy," the translator explains.

"Well, then let's go in," Englander says. He steps up onto a bamboo porch extending most of the length of the rear longhouse, and I follow.

He looks sharply at me for a moment but says nothing to stop my accompanying him.

In the half-burned building is a small elderly Yard lying on a pallet and partially covered with a richly embroidered blanket. Attending him is a youngish Yard woman who looks up in fear as we enter. Though the man's blanket is pulled up to his chest, his arms are out on top of it, both nearly covered with ointment-smeared burns. He has an ugly oozing burned patch on his left cheek as well, puckering his grimace so that it looks almost to be a smile.

"Where are the others?" Englander asks, looking unfazed at the sight of the burned man.

The translator puts the question to the old man, who opens weepy eyes, blinks for a couple of beats, and says, "Ro'kŭt hang Khmer Rouge po'ro'taih bla ngă." He licks at a raw spot on his lips.

"He say all taken away by Khmer Rouge who fight war."

"Her too?" Englander asks, and the translator almost whispers the question to the old man, who responds softly, "Ǔ' đah yă tha bo'nai ro'kŭt wŏt." A small tear runs down his unburned cheek.

"He say, yes, the white woman of great respect was taken too."

"Oh god!" Englander says. "Where? Where the hell did the soldiers take her?"

With a supreme effort, the old man lifts an ointment-smeared arm and points toward the border to the west and Cambodia. "Ayăt ko'đong thăn čar Kur."

"At enemy camp in Cambodia, he say."

The old man has fallen into a doze, quiet moans of pain escaping him. I have doubts that he will survive here, and I suggest to Englander that we call for a dustoff to get him back to the aid station at Ben Het. Surprisingly, he agrees readily and directs Trung Si Ksang, the Yards' first sergeant, to call in the dustoff and send a fire team back to the LZ with the old man and the woman to wait for the medevac bird. Frankly, given his burns, I doubt he will survive the trip, but I don't want to let him die here.

Englander and I, MSG Flanagan, and the Yard đại úy sit near the hearth in the longhouse. We are looking at the path on the map to the location where "she" has supposedly been taken. I've had Cat come into the longhouse, ostensibly to have my radio near me, but just as much to let the kid get dry. He was shaking and almost blue-lipped when I'd gotten him in near the fire.

"Not far, maybe four klicks from here, tough going, though," MSG Flanagan says, tracing the marked route over the border into Cambodia and then on to the camp's map location about 1,500 meters from the border with Laos to the west. "Ugly terrain with only some low hills, map shows thick bamboo all over it. A tangle of trails in there too."

"Looks like a swamp to me," Englander says, and then to the interpreter, who is sitting across the hearth from us, "Ask him what the ground is like between here and the Khmer Rouge camp."

"Plai biă hlŭ hang kăč," the Yard in the white shirt answers, looking faintly bemused at the question. "He say much mud and mosquitos," says Y Aguăt.

I've taken to thinking of that Yard as Dress Shirt. Englander, though in a sour humor, thinks the nickname is funny. Dress Shirt adds a word I don't catch, nor apparently does the translator. (I learn later his difficulties are that Y Aguăt, the translator, speaks the Jarai dialect, while Dress Shirt speaks the similar but not entirely congruent Rhade dialect.) There is a quick exchange between the two Yards, finally a tonal word that sounds nothing like the Yard speech, "Cây tre," which is Vietnamese, and then the translator adds, "OK, he say, I think, there is much bamboo there. Is hard to get through it, he say."

"Like I said, a goddamn swamp full of bamboo," MSG Flanagan grunts. "We can get lost as hell in it. I say we wait here until dawn when we can see something there."

Englander is clearly reluctant to wait, anxiety about "her" clouding his expression.

"Looks like a mess to navigate through, Hugh," I tell him. "Top is right. Much better if we wait for light. It's only a few hours till dawn now. We could waste that much time stumbling around there in the dark."

Englander stares at the map, tracing the indication of a pathway marked there that should take us to the Khmer Rouge camp. He shakes his head.

I decide it is time to distract him. "Who is this lady you have dragged us out here to see, Hugh?"

"Lady? ... Oh ..." He looks up from the map. "Lady, yeah. Her name is Bridget O'Meara. She's a Franciscan nun." He stops and looks at me. "Have you heard of Tom Dooley?"

"Sure," I say, trying to lighten things, "it's a great Kingston Trio cut."

Englander snorts. "No, no, not that goddamn song. The man, navy officer and doctor. Base was in Luang Namtha Province way up north in Laos. Great man, got out of the navy and lived there with the Hmong and Khmu with the enemy dinks all around him up there. His work was healing the sick up there in the mountains and heavy jungles, a real wilderness there."

The captain stops, pokes at the fire, and stares into the flickers of flame around the coals. After a few beats, he continues, seeming to tell this as much to himself as to me, "Dooley hated the Commies. I gather he was no saint, for sure—believed in kicking butt when necessary. Sister Bridget had carved something he said on the lintel above her door, 'I know of but one meek, humble man who accomplished anything.' That was what she said Dooley was like. I never met him, but he sounded like one amazing son of a bitch. Sister Bridget was with him through it all, worked with the people. She nursed Dooley when he first came down with cancer. He left Laos in '59. Sister Bridget wanted to go with him, but he wouldn't have it. Told her to stay, that he was going to die if the Lord wanted him to or live if that was what the Lord wanted. But he said that she couldn't change that, so she should carry on with the people up there, that they needed her a lot more than he did."

"Isn't Luang Namtha Province up on the border with China, almost a thousand klicks north of here? How'd she get all the way down here next to Cambodia?" I ask.

"She told me the Pathet Lao ran her out," says Englander. "Dooley was a fanatic anti-Communist, maybe even CIA. Reds hated him, and her too. He and Sister Bridget were like that." He raises his right hand, index and middle fingers pressed together. "Those who knew them called them the Irish Twins. Some smartasses made out like they were some kind of lovers. But she was thirty years older than he was and a devout Catholic nun who took her vows seriously, Jesus her husband

and all that. I guess she must be at least seventy-five now. When she got run out in '66, some friendly dinks brought her all the way south on the Ho Chi Minh Trail. It's funny, because she didn't like the Reds any better than Dooley did. But those dinks thought more of her than they did of Uncle Ho and helped her get away and come down here. She lived among the Yards here along this stretch of the border, staying here in Vietnam so she didn't piss off the Pathet Lao or the Khmer Rouge, living here with the permission of the Viet Cong. She'd learned enough medicine from Dooley to be a decent country doc and take care of the Yards, Hmong, and other hill people out here." He shakes his head. "Now she's gone. I was afraid of that when I hadn't heard from her for a couple of weeks." He pounds fist into the palm of his hand, groans, and says, "Fuck, fuck, fuck, the goddamn Khmer Rouge have her now."

"How'd you meet her?"

"A year or so ago, we were doing a long-range recon op, snooping and pooping out here on the border, just the A-Team. Found a little Yard boy, maybe five years old, all alone in the jungle maybe a klick north of here. Was a Yard village nearby, but they didn't want the kid. Said they had enough mouths to feed, or something like that in Jarai. Never did get a straight translation. Maybe they figured they had enough orphans. Anyway, they said there was a *bo'nai ro'kŭt*, a kindly white woman, who would take in the boy. One of the Yards brought us to this ville. Sister Bridget had half a dozen abandoned kids she was taking care of. We spent three days here, and I got to know her. I've been back maybe a dozen times since. She didn't keep the kids long, figured they would be better off in an orphanage where there were other kids. I got a bird to take them to Quang Ngai City, where there was a place that took in Yard kids. I don't think Sister Bridget liked doing it, but she knew she couldn't take care of them all out here."

"So our real mission is to get her back, Hugh?"

"Yeah," he says, "I came here to get her out before the NVA overruns this whole fucking part of 'Nam. But the fucking Rouge or some other enemy troops have her. So, fuck, yeah, I'm going to get her back." He states at me intently, brows furrowed, "Are you going to give me trouble over that? If so, you and your RTO can get on the dustoff bird with the old man and go back to your kind of war."

"No, man," I say. "We've got no actual mission to speak of out here except to raise hell and confuse the enemy. Going after Sister Bridget will do that as well as any other troublemaking." I look down at the lower left quarter of our topo map showing a tongue of Cambodia sticking up to the north between Laos and Vietnam. "What does worry me is that while we've got at least a thin license to be in Laos, being observers for the Yard company and all that, we've got no such license at all to be in Cambodia. It could be a damned mess if we are caught in there."

"Well," says Englander, "let's not get caught."

The rain tails off near dawn. Sunrise is a gray affair with just a little bit of light reaching us, filtered through the jungle canopy and a heavy overcast. Water from the storm is everywhere. In it, the paths around the longhouses are muddy chutes, slippery and unstable. The Dak Koi, marked on the map as just a fingerling of a stream here near the border, is running high, nearly waist deep in some spots and cold. During the night, the Yards had moved the old burned man back to the LZ we had used, and a dustoff from Ben Het had flown in to pick him and the woman up. Later, via artillery channels from that base, I get the word that he will probably survive, burns likely to heal. We pass the word on to three other Yard women who also had been tending him and got a stream of *bo'ni lu's* of gratitude from them along with a thank-you present of a strange-tasting but filling breakfast of dried fish, berries, and rice.

At 0700 hours, with the sun fully risen and the day as bright as it will be, we wade carefully across the rain-engorged stream and struggle our way up the sixty meters to the top of the ridge that marks the border here between Vietnam and Cambodia. Only sixty meters it might be, but the hillside is soggy as a sponge, and the track marked on the map as a footpath is barely more than a rut in the jungle with water running down it. Leeches abound. We pick them off our arms and legs, cursing. The map shows the trail from there into Cambodia winding down a gentle klick-long ridge that soon tails into a morass of tangled streamlets and low hills. It is heavy jungle with towering thickets of bamboo throughout looking to be almost impenetrable. That's what the map shows. The actual ground is about the same as shown except that the jungle tightens suffocatingly around the path, making it impossible to see more than a few meters ahead. The land—once we're down off that ridge on the Cambodian side—is ankle deep or more in heavy mud. The promised mosquitos are few, the rain and our repellent keeping them down. But the profuse bamboo seems home to trillions of fire ants that manage to find their way through every opening in our jungle fatigues.

We have just crossed into Cambodia. There is the crack of a rifle from up ahead, and the Yard point man, a kid named Y Glun, screams and falls. Englander, walking slack, grabs him and drags him off the trail toward where Cat, MSG Flanagan, and I have ducked into the bushes. Heavy fire erupts from the Yards at the front of the file, though nobody seems to have a target.

"Sniper," Englander says, calling, "Doc!" But SSG Olsson is already here, aid bag out, pulling out scissors to cut away the sleeve around where Y Glun has been wounded in his biceps. The entry and exit holes are small, blood just trickling out—no arteries hit. Without even looking at me, Englander adds a terse "No arty, hold off on it." I've already motioned for Cat to hand me our radio's handset. I look at him curiously, but the firing at the front of the file has already died down.

"Just hold off on having your guns fire anything. Rouge may know we're here, but they don't know what kind of firepower we've got. I'd like to leave them in the dark for a while."

The Yard đại úy has come back to tell Englander that the sniper has vanished into the heavy jungle. "Don't see him more," he says. "Gone, *truia*, sprayed lots of bullets then *didi mau, đuaĭ đuaĭ*, very fast."

"Yeah," says Englander, "I figured."

I motion to Cat to put our radio handset away and turn to look at the young Yard who's been wounded. I can't imagine that Y Glun is much more than sixteen (though the Yards' small stature often throws my estimate of their ages off wildly), a dark-eyed boy whose grin seems perpetual. He's not grinning now. He whimpers a bit as Olsson probes the wound. "Through and through," SSG Olsson says. "Good news is that it missed the bone, just went through the meat of the muscle. Going to hurt like a son of a bitch for a while, but no permanent damage." The đại úy translates that for Y Glun, who smiles thinly. All the while,

Olsson is finishing up the bandaging. He presses a compression bandage to the wound, ties it firmly, and tapes it down to the boy's upper arm.

"I'm going to give him morphine," Olsson says to Englander. "That'll knock down the pain. Bandage will keep bleeding down, but he needs a dustoff back to the aid station at Ben Het. Gotta treat this before it turns septic."

"Christ," says Englander. "We're half a klick into Cambodia. Don't know if we can get birds to cross the border... Hell, Y Giao?" he says to the đại úy. "Get a team to take Y Glun back across the border. I'll have a dustoff meet you there."

"Yup!" Y Giao says, looking satisfied that the kid will be getting real care for the wound. "I will have them go now. He ready?"

SSG Olsson finishes squeezing the morphine into the boy's arm and then pins the needle of the empty syrette to his shirt, nodding to say he can be moved. I look at the wounded boy, thinking he looks younger than my youngest brother, Sam. Though clearly in pain even with the morphine, Y Glun barely makes a noise when helped to his feet. He totters off unsteadily between two of the Yard riflemen, four other Yards go with them, heading back to the top of the border ridge. Apparently, our high priority for air support continues. By the time Y Glun and the fire team with him are out of sight to our east, there is already word that a dustoff bird will soon be on the way.

CHAPTER 11

The finger of ridge we head down is humped with rocky crests as if the backbone of some vast fossilized serpent lies just beneath the soil. The finger finally descends into a marshy tangle of narrow, ankle-deep channels that thread among dense stands of bamboo. The bamboo towers over us, bare culms below, a thicket of interlaced branches and grasslike leaves above that looks as tall as a forest of slender redwoods.

The bamboo seems hard as iron and cutting it as near impossible as chopping down Vietnam's teak or mahogany trees by hand. We walk where the narrow channels of water run. Fire ants nesting in the bamboo swarm when we brush by. Cat, walking just behind me, asks if I know where we are. It is a good question. All I see is green. The light through the overcast and through the bamboo is murky, directionless, a universe of emerald and gray. There are no visible landmarks, so I watch my compass and count steps. Our direction, following Dress Shirt, is generally southwest, the going agonizingly slow. The only noises are the continuing patter of light rain through the bamboo leaves above us, the slap of the drops that hit the stream, and the slosh of our feet through the water. Less heard than felt is the omnipresent hum of insects unseen flitting among the bamboo stalks. It is cold but wretchedly humid here; the air doesn't seem to move, the chill of it barely tolerable. I can only imagine the hell this would be in the heat of the dry season.

Up ahead, there is a yelp and the snick of a machete cutting into bamboo. "*Dro'i!*" and "Snake!" are hissed down the line of soldiers in front of us. As we walk, I see just ahead a deep machete cut in a large bamboo cane, a long thread of blood on it, and below, the halves of a bright green snake—maybe two feet long when whole—thrashing fitfully in the water. SSG Olsson, walking behind me, says, "Damn, a bamboo viper!"

"Dangerous?" Cat asks, his voice soft and worried sounding.

"Yeah," says Olsson. "Bite probably won't kill you. But they hide up in the bamboo and go for the head. If it gets you, it'll be painful as hell. Maybe you'll wish you were dead."

"Gaw!" says Cat. He kicks away the head of the bright-green snake and looks around as if there are more lurking in the densely packed bamboo.

"Venom is hemorrhagic," I hear SSG Hicks say, one of the engineer sergeants walking a couple of places behind us. "You'll blow up like a goddamned balloon. Really bad if it gets you in the face, man." He lets go a gleeful laugh.

"Shut up," Englander says. "You're scaring the kid half to death. It's probably the only one of them we'll see on this whole march."

We move no more than fifty meters before there is another shout of pain and another halt. We have yet to see the enemy, yet to engage anyone, and already we have had two casualties. The second one is another of the Yards, an older man named Y Poro, a squad leader with years of combat experience. That experience hasn't served him well here. He'd stepped into a hole to one side of the trail and onto a punji stake, most likely poisoned or shit dipped. We have to wait while a yard medic cleans the wound and gives him a shot of penicillin.

"That's a nasty wound," SSG Olsson says to Englander. "We get to a clear spot, we should have him dusted off before it gets infected bad enough, he loses the leg."

Englander just grunts, clearly not wanting a dustoff to give away our position, and then nods. "Yeah," he says and shakes his head in annoyance. Another Yard soldier gives the wounded man a shoulder to lean on. I know that man will be in trouble, though, if we don't medevac him soon. I also see that the punji stake he stepped on is one of a fresh batch of them along that stretch of trail.

"New ones." I point out to Englander, which elicits another grunt.

We move on. Were it not for my compass, I would have no way of orienting myself. The light filters down directionlessly through the bamboo maze. We walk among the copses in a crazy series of zigzags following Dress Shirt, who seems guided by markers the rest of us miss. But the needle of my compass is unerring in its indication of our direction, and by counting paces, I see we are now perhaps a klick from where the Khmer Rouge camp is supposed to be.

Abruptly, Englander calls, "Whoa!" which echoes back along our file. We stop and hunker down.

He signals the file to wait and goes forward toward the front of our column. There is no way to relax. Squatting, my backside would be in the chilly water. Leaning against the bamboo, I would be a target for a swarm of the ants. Standing still, cold water up to my ankles and sloshing in my jungle boots, I shiver a bit. But soon, word is passed back down the line that CPT Englander wants me to come up to the front of the file.

He has stopped where the wall of bamboo opens to expose a length of stream that emerges from the tangle of canes and continues to the southwest. Several of the Yards are hunched down on its low muddy bank, providing security for Englander, who is standing under a massive clump of bamboo that arches far out over the narrow stretch of stream. Near him are Dress Shirt, the translator, MSG Flanagan, and Đại úy Y Giao. Englander is studying his map, while Dress Shirt points off through the opening to the west, saying something I can't quite hear. As we come up to the front of the file, I see more open water, a channel widening out to the west looking deeper than what we have traversed so far.

"The son of a bitch doesn't know how to read a map," Englander says to me, nodding at Dress Shirt, who grins though he doesn't understand. "But the trung si says he's trying to tell us the Khmer Rouge base is maybe a klick to our southwest."

"Looks deep," I say, pointing to where the channel of the stream spills out from the bamboo labyrinth and begins to flow westward in earnest.

"Yeah," Englander says. He nods to the Yard point man, who is holding a slender cane of bamboo at least half again his height. The point man leans forward a bit and thrusts the cane down into the stream. It disappears unimpeded almost full length into the water.

"Goddamned deep as hell," says Englander, seeing me wince a bit as the cane shows the water's depth. "It's at least up to our necks and over the heads of most of the Yards."

"So we're stuck," I say. "We'd have to cut a way around it all the way along the stream bank. Take days to do it, and that's figuring the Khmer Rouge troops in the camp don't hear us whacking down a couple of klicks worth of bamboo. How does Dress Shirt there get through?"

Dress Shirt listens to Trung Sĩ Y Ro'mŏn, who offers him a whispered translation of our conversation.

"Use *song*," he says, his face lighting up with a knowing grin.

"Boat, he say, he uses boat. *Song* means 'boat' in Jarai," says the trung sĩ.

"Well, damn if that isn't a help," Englander snorts. "We'll just use his boat to get down this stretch of river. But we don't have any goddamn boat, do we?"

"He say no, no, other way," the trung si translates. "Yua glôn," Dress Shirt adds. He points to a dark spot in the bamboo on the north side of the stream. "*Glôn* easy."

"Not *song*, *glôn*, means 'trail.' Says one is on side of stream." The translator turns to Dress Shirt, and they exchange a few quick words of Jarai. "Trail go up there, onto high ground and then around to other side of camp."

Dress Shirt smiles and nods as if he knows what he's hearing as he listens to the translation.

All at once, there are shots in the distance beyond a turn of the stream to our west. Reacting, I find myself almost down in the river reaching for the handset Cat is already holding out to me when Englander snaps, "Wait!"

There is a second volley of shots, short and sharp. Then nothing.

"Target practice," says Englander, "or maybe a firing squad. Not shooting at us anyway." We listen, but the firing doesn't resume. "Yeah, a firing squad, I imagine. Rouge kill everybody. Thick as fleas on an alley cat around here. OK, where is this trail?"

Dress Shirt shows us the way to the barely perceptible opening of a tight trail that takes off to the right, paralleling our line of march about fifty meters back the way we have come. If the twists and turns along the waterway through the bamboo seemed claustrophobic, the new path hacked through a wall of bamboo is positively suffocating. A foot and a half wide at best, sometimes even narrower, it slashes straight northwest through the most towering stands of bamboo so far. The branches and leaves of the canes weave together tightly overhead, leaving us pushing into a malachite gloom that seems endless. Who cut this passage? Was it the Khmer Rouge, or maybe the Khmer Loeu (the indigenous tribesmen of Cambodia) who live in these almost virgin forests of Cambodia's northeast? The narrow path is hard packed, though not proof to bamboo shoots drilling up through it—meaning, it is frequently maintained or would have long since been filled in by new bamboo growth.

The bamboo is not silent. It creaks, rasps, and rattles high above us, the mass of it swaying together, moved in the slight wind blowing down from the Vietnamese highlands behind us. Its leaves whisper as one voice, unearthly and discarnate.

I'm following one of the Yards, a medic named Y Siu. He is slender and short, coming up only to my shoulder. He carries a rifle and a gigantic aid bag but still manages to slip easily through the bamboo. Suddenly, moving forward, Y Siu seems to disappear into what looks to be an impenetrable wall of canes. It's not, but for maybe two meters, the canes close in so much that the path between them is hardly more than a foot wide. For a few terrible seconds, my pulse races as I wonder how to get through. Englander did it, I think, and he's taller and bulkier than I am. I've lost the sound of men moving ahead. I have to move. Nothing to do but press into the space sideways, pulling my ruck after me. Halfway into the choke point, my ruck snags on something and I can't pull it farther. As a teenager, I was a cave explorer in the Ozarks, pushing carelessly and without fear through spaces this tight and worse. Here, though, I feel a heavy jolt of panic, of grabbing for breath and composure, barking, "Goddammit," but Cat, coming up behind me, pulls my ruck away from whatever has snagged it and says, "Got it, Captain." And I yank the awkward rucksack on through. Steps onward, the path widens a few inches, hardly easier going but enough. I get my breath back. Thin and spare as he is, Cat has no trouble negotiating the narrow spot even with his ruck and radio. Several of the A-Team members coming up after us are big men, and I wonder if they will be able to make it. *That's what machetes are for,* I think.

"At least there are no ants in this stretch," I say to Cat.

"Small favors, sir," he says, a boyish and carefree grin once again on his face. That grin bucks me up. Cat has been careful and a bit timid thus far, and I'm glad to see him looking happier and more confident.

We push on. Ten meters, thirty, fifty, the point man in front of us slowing to hack new growths of canes out of the trail. We smell it long before the point man gets to it, corruption, a gagging stench of something lifeless and decayed on the trail. A dead boar piglet or a monkey of some sort, I think. The purulent stink calls up every memory of things old and dead—things, not people, because even human dead in this war are nothing more than stench and corruption when breath has left them, no different from any other snuffed life to us. Finally, getting up close, I see the corpse of a man, small, a soldier by its garb, with a floppy, olive drab fatigue hat pressed into shredding scalp, the tattered uniform also olive colored beneath its glaze of old blood, fallen and left here. Eyes gone, belly bloated, unshod, with foot bones bare of skin and flesh. No weapon or backpack—those, valuable, are taken; only the corpse is left, being of no value in death and not even worth a burial. Blowflies and their maggots swarm over the body. We can't get by without stepping on it, and so one of the Yards has chopped a bamboo cane into lengths to lay over the body in a sort of corduroy road.

After some five hundred meters, the path turns hard west and begins to climb, becoming muddy and slick under our feet.

"Still no ants here, at least," says Cat in a whisper. "I've been bitten a hundred times. Damn things crawling in my shirt somewhere, Captain." Nor are there any more of the bamboo vipers. I know in this light, I wouldn't see one if it were inches in front of me (thinking with stupid humor that if it were a snake, it would have bitten me, and doing my best not to laugh at myself . . .)

A couple of hundred meters further up an increasingly steep slope, the bamboo begins to thin, giving way to jungle almost as heavy, but open and airy by comparison. It is clear we have reached the crest of a ridge that runs upward to our right. Here, Dress Shirt, walking with the point man, must have called for us to halt. The column comes to a stop; Yards and American troops alike drop into a defensive posture, facing alternately left and right on the trail.

Englander motions me to come up with him to the front. We are now about a klick west and a couple of hundred meters higher than where we were when we had looked at the open stretch of the stream. We are on a small rise in the ridge, whose west side drops steeply back down to the bamboo and water. The small crest is open for a space, and we can see down over the stream—more of a narrow lake here—and on several hundred meters to where there is a large opening carved out under a high jungle canopy. There, across the water from us is the hump of a bunker dug into another hillside, and in front of the bunker, still under the arch of massive overhanging teak trees, is a small dock. A boat is tied to it, canoe-like with a pointed prow, a wide bottom, and shallow draft, maybe ten meters long with a battered-looking outboard motor in its stern. As we watch, someone comes out from under the heavy tree cover and walks down to the boat. At this distance, he is barely discernible even through my binoculars. But from what I can make out, he looks to be dressed in dark green, with perhaps a green fatigue hat on, shouldering a rifle, probably an AK-47from the wooden look of its stock—my first view of one of the Khmer Rouge.

"No way across the water here," Englander says, finger tracing terrain on the map. "Looks like the only way into the camp is to go up this finger of ridge and then move along the rim of high ground between us and Laos. We go southwest for about a klick and then back down the next finger of ridge to the camp. Good?" he asks, looking at me.

The circuitous trail Englander has marked will take us through five klicks of thick, tangled jungle, up and down some four hundred meters of elevation, and then back through another stretch of the bamboo forest. The sun is past zenith now, still high but pressing into afternoon.

"Yeah, Hugh, maybe not good, but the only real route," I say. "If we push, we might get there maybe an hour before dark. Or we can go up to the ridge crest, set in for the night, and go in first light in the morning."

I see that Englander is weighing it. I know he wants to go in quickly, but rain looks to be coming again, and we could get lost as hell in that jungle and end up hitting the camp after dark. Tactically better in a perfect world. But hitting the camp in soggy darkness in the tangled jungle could be a fiasco.

"Tomorrow," says Englander finally, clearly feeling reluctant to accept the idea. "We'll set in on the ridge and send a squad in to recon." He looks at me. "Remember, no arty unless I tell you."

"Yeah, you've said that, Hugh. I'll have targets ready if we need them, though."

Turns out it is a hell of a hump just to get up the finger to the main ridgeline via a trail overgrown, rocky, and steep. That alone takes more than three hours. More than once, we hear thrashing sounds on the Laotian side of the ridge. Not human, too noisy and careless for that. Once on the ridge crest, we find a four-klick-long path that drops steeply down and up twice before putting us on a defensible hilltop a couple of hundred meters back inside Cambodia. Below us, a well-used footpath runs back toward the Khmer Rouge camp. I think we are too close to it for comfort on our knob of hill.

Englander, surely thinking the same, orders, "Stay quiet and no fires, not even heat tabs—the Rouge might smell 'em."

Neither the A-Team nor any of the Yards protest it. Weapons sergeant Larry Arguello and engineer sergeant Gary Greenwood take a six-man squad of Yards on a recon down the trail toward the Khmer Rouge camp. The sun is down, and it is raining steadily by the time they are back with the simple report that the camp looks small and poorly defended, but much of it difficult to reconnoiter being back under the jungle canopy behind a lightly manned bunker line.

"Almost an island, Cap," SSG Arguello says. "Looks like a small platoon of Rouge there. Bad noise and light discipline, like they haven't a care in the world anybody is going to hit 'em. Couldn't tell what all weapons they've got, though, and it's got only one way in across a narrow neck, water on each side of it. So maybe not so easy after all."

"Maybe we ought to just nuke 'em with artillery and mop up what's left," says SSG Greenwood.

"Damn good idea . . ." Englander snorts and then snaps, "'Course if Sister Bridget is in there, all we're going to find is her corpse if we hit that camp with arty. Remember what the goddamned mission is, sport!"

"Sorry, Cap," says SSG Arguello, Greenwood echoing it.

"Fine," says Englander. "Go set goddamn security and be ready to move at sunup."

Later, foxholes dug, poncho hooches set up, some chow (a cold, unappetizing meal of freeze-dried LRRP rations moistened with cold water, since, per Englander, we want no fires to give away our presence), Englander and I ponder the map and talk to SGTs Arguello and Greenwood about how we're going to get into the camp.

"Could be suicide to try a direct assault across that bit of land between the camp and this ridgeline, Cap," SSG Arguello says. "Not much sign of a defense set up there, but if they've got anything, there's, for sure, machine guns and mines guarding it. Cleared out too with a good field of fire. We aren't just walking in across that."

SSG Greenwood nods in agreement. "The neck's about fifty meters long but only wide enough for a couple of guys abreast to cross, so no way for a mass assault. I imagine we could push through if we had to, but we're going to lose a lot of guys if we do."

Englander stares at the map, which, at 1:50,000 scale, offers far too little detail to visualize how to use the terrain there. His eyes half close as he seems to gnaw at a thought. "How deep is the water by that neck of land?"

"Y Gian checked," says Arguello, "said it was pretty deep except by the neck but drops off quickly. Why, Cap, you thinking of us swimming across? You know they could have all kinds of warnings, trip wires, submerged punji stakes, and shit."

We sit. A solution comes to me, so simple I run it through my head again for flaws. The animals we'd heard back on the main trail had been big and noisy, grunting and making rooting sounds in the brush. "Pigs," I say, "wild boar."

SSG Arguello looks at me (or at least my shape in the cloud-covered darkness; somewhere above the clouds is that same bright coin of a moon, but it gives no light here.) "Pigs, funny," he says.

"No," I say, "I mean it. We get one of those boars. Shoot it if we have to. Down that side of the ridge, nobody from the camp's going to hear the shot. We put some Yards in the water by the neck of land, have them throw the boar in, and let it splash big time. Then they push it across with a length of bamboo, follow way back so they don't get seen. If anybody puts a light on it or if it sets off a trip flare or something, all they'll see is the boar coming across the water. Maybe they'll shoot, maybe not. But I don't think they'll be looking for any of us to be coming across behind it."

"Damn," says SSG Greenwood, "they teach you that kind of sneaky shit in artillery OCS, Captain?"

I grin. "Nope, it's my own stupid idea."

"It's not so stupid," says Englander. "You may turn out to be a functional grunt yet." He stops for a moment, snaps his fingers, and says, "Yeah, Larry, go find the đại úy. They're Yards, so they're supposed to be expert hunter gatherers. Some of them must have some hunting skills. Tell him to have some of their guys get a boar, big one, and bring it back here. Tell him to have some others get us a long strong bamboo cane. That dead pig will clear out the way across the water, and we can send in a squad after them to slip in and take out any defenses they have guarding the way into the camp. Tell him to get it done fast because we want to send the boar across while it is still good and dark."

It is maybe an hour before sunup when we settle in heavy jungle across from the only dry land entry to the Khmer Rouge's camp. Cat is hunkered next to me under jungle canopy that absorbs most of a moderate rain. I have checked in with the battery and plotted a couple of attack targets on the jut of land where the camp is and several targets for escape and evasion (if it comes to that) to fire behind us if we need to block the path leading back up the ridge from the camp. It is cold, and I find myself shivering in the drip from the saturated tree canopy. There is only the glimmering of morning light in the dense cloud cover visible where the open water breaks the jungle canopy. In it I can just make out six of the Yards as they carry the carcass of a huge wild boar on a heavy length of bamboo thrust through its hog-tied front and rear legs. It must weigh four hundred pounds, and the stocky but small Yard soldiers struggle to get it down to the water.

They cut the ties binding the legs and heave the carcass into the water, making a huge splash. Voices from the camp chatter in surprise. Two of the Yards slip into the water behind the dead boar and push the carcass forward with a bamboo pole, it bobbing up and down so it looks in the first inklings of sunrise as if the boar is swimming toward the opposite bank. A flare suddenly lights the scene. As we'd guessed, there was a tripwire in the water to catch any swimmers coming across. Had we just tried to swim through in the dark, we would have been caught out there exposed in the flare's light. The flare burns a fierce orange on the neck of land, sending stark shadows across the water from the boar and the ripples around it. Can the Khmer Rouge see the Yards lost in flickering light and waves on the water a half a dozen meters behind the moving mass of wild pig? It seems not. The voices come from across the water again, atonal but very different sounding from the Yards' speech. I make out only scattered words, which mean nothing to me except for hearing the *trung si* translator, who, I gather, also speaks some Khmer, whispering their meaning to CPT Englander, "Mee-uhn ha-et uhvuh-ee?" (What was that?) "Méén!" (What?) Weapons clank, a light flicks on, a strong flashlight beam that cuts through the predawn gloom and searches the water. The light finds the huge boar the Yards had shot. In the dimness, it looks perhaps as if it might be swimming.

"Damn," Englander, squatting down next to me and Cat, says softly in surprise at the gambit's success.

We hear, "Thoat tjrouk, haél toek" (A big pig that swims), and a laugh.

"Banye!" (Shoot it!)

"Yoeung noeng" (Arrogant response, "I will"), and a shot rings out. The body of the boar jerks. Next to me, CPT Englander hisses a soft but sharp "Yeah!"

There is more, another round of gunfire, several shots this time. The boar gets pushed further across the water, and a man in fatigues, backlit by the flashlight in the predawn dark, splashes down and reaches out to drag the dead creature over onto the bank. "Lâ-â mohop aahaa!" (Good food!) and another laugh. The second Khmer Rouge soldier comes down and helps drag the heavy boar up onto the bank, and then they haul it laboriously back into the deeper undergrowth. Their voices fade. No more flare's light. There seems to have been only one.

"Nao!" (Go!) I hear the đại úy say softly, and then four more of the Yards, armed only with knives, slip naked into the water and follow the first two almost silently across to the other bank. With the flashlight now off, there is hardly anything visible under the trees that cover the camp, and not a word more is spoken. I sit waiting, by habit holding the radio handset to my ear, though I have no intention of calling for fire unless Englander asks for it or something far worse (say, a major counterattack by the Khmer Rouge) happens. Soon, there is a sound, perhaps a moan from the entrance to the camp, a brief thrashing in the brush. The sound of something man-sized falling. Then one of the Yards appears and beckons us across. "Truh! Ro'năk ră anai" (Come, safe now).

Englander has run up ahead, taking the bulk of the A-Team and most of the rest of our Yard soldiers with him, leaving me and Cat to trail in with Doc Olsson and a rear guard fire team of the Yards. We stop near the bodies of the two Khmer Rouge the Yards have killed. The morning is just bright enough now to make them out, lying in their own blood, throats cut, next to the carcass of the boar. I tell Cat to stay with me. The brightening morning also reveals a pair of PKM light machine guns pulled from a bunker facing the neck that connects the camp to the ridgeline. Long barreled with an open wooden stock and wooden handgrip, they are old-fashioned but nasty guns that can fire the same high velocity 7.62 round as our own M60s and could have done us some real damage had our Yard sappers not cut the two machine gunners down in our first entry into the camp.

In the dimness of early dawn, nothing else beyond moving shapes is discernible under the jungle canopy. I go carefully, having no desire to be mistaken for a Khmer Rouge soldier and shot. The front of our force has moved perhaps fifty meters ahead when I hear the deep bark of an AK-47 and then shouting and a volley of M16 fire in return. Next comes the immense but slightly muffled bang of a fragmentation grenade and another burst of gunfire. A few beats of silence follow until I hear Englander, voice full of disgust, bellow, "Son of a bitch! She's not here!"

Some harsh talk in Khmer, some responses, Englander again bellowing, "Christ!" and more gunshots individual and spaced.

Now it is quiet. SSG Olsson, Cat, and I move toward the center of the camp a few minutes later to find one of our Yards shot dead and the others dragging up the bodies of about a dozen Khmer Rouge. Several of the Rouge show wounds typical of a firefight, in the torso, face, and upper body. One body is shattered, likely from the grenade we'd heard, which I gather was thrown into a bunker at the far side of the small camp. Movement from further out in the undergrowth resolves into two squads of the Yards who are beating the bushes for any more of the Khmer Rouge.

Are they enemy soldiers? We are not at war with Cambodia, but in a libertine daisy chain of combat, the Khmer Rouge are at war with the anti-Communist Lon Nol government. Nol seized power from King Norodom Sihanouk in a messy coup almost a year ago. The Khmer Rouge are loosely allied with the North Vietnamese; Sihanouk has joined them. Who is friend, who enemy, who an ally, who an antagonist is impossible to sort out. Are the friends of our enemy our enemies as well?

But of four of the Khmer Rouge soldiers, I ask, "What the hell happened?" The four are thrown among the other dead, but their wounds, all center chest, seem not from a firefight but more like those from an execution.

"Didn't know a goddamn thing!" Englander says, his voice a moan of unhappiness.

I want to ask him if he killed them. But I realize I don't want to know if it was in combat, dead like they are in such an unlikely way. I'd heard but seen nothing, and we are in the middle of a dangerous hell, a spot of the war in which soldiers strange to us but not in truth our enemies are dead. What to say, what to say?

There is one Khmer Rouge soldier left alive, though. He looks older than the young soldiers who had held this camp; they teens perhaps or early twenties, he maybe thirty. None has any markings of rank on them. Their uniforms are the same, olive drab and cut like the fatigues I had worn when stationed back in the World. Some still have on billed floppy fatigue caps and not boots but sandals much like the tire-treaded

Ho Chi Minh sandals the Viet Cong wear. This last living one of the Khmer Rouge is a rough-looking customer, burly, an acne-scarred face, who spits at the feet of the trung si when he relays Englander's question about where Sister Bridget is.

"Aa kéé tfoeu!" he says, his voice a growl of defiance.

"He say 'fuck you,'" the trung si says.

In response, Englander busts the Rouge soldier in the face with the butt of his M16. Blood runs from the man's nose and broken lip.

"Ask him again," Englander says, and when he gets the same answer, he stops, shrugs off his rucksack, and paws inside, coming up with a rusty pair of pliers. "Hold his goddamn hand," Englander says to one of the Yards, who just looks back as if not comprehending. Englander spins away and snaps, "I said hold his hand," to the Yard đại úy, who does so, returning a smirk. He snaps something in Jarai to the Rouge soldier, which I imagine means 'hold still,' though I don't know if the soldier understands. Englander jams the pliers against the tip of the soldier's index finger and yanks, and then the man screams for a moment, shakes, and then stares viciously at Englander and the đại úy. The nail from that finger is torn away and now clamped in the jaws of the pliers. Englander smirks back at him, flicks away the torn fingernail, and reaches again for the soldier's hand. It is so sudden, so confounding, I have no chance to react. It is, after all, only a fingernail, but the nonchalant brutality is horrid. Still, the Khmer Rouge soldier looks obdurate and fanatical, and I'm expecting this to go on until the man has no nails left. He looks unlikely to spill anything (if he does even know it) about Sister Bridget's whereabouts. But abruptly as Englander is moving to grab the nail off the man's ring finger, the man says, "Tchaâam, khnyom doing" (Wait, I know). Then he launches into a long rap, pointing westward, saying, "Totoeng khnâng phnom," and much more, which I gather is a description of where across the mountains into Laos the nun has been taken.

Listening to the trung si's translation, Englander sags, face a mask that might be fury or might just be exhaustion of the spirit. All this and the camp is nearly empty, only this older man and a couple of dozen young Khmer Rouge soldiers had held it. We had battered our way through jungle and a maze of giant bamboo, torn our way down a jungle ridge, and encountered this.

"She was here!" CPT Englander says, his voice rising in anger. "Ask him how long it's been since she was here," he says to the trung si translator.

"Âtit mun" (A week ago), the man says. "Srèy tchèènye toew" (She was taken away), he adds and then cowers, hands pressed loosely together in a hopeless *sampeah*, saying, "Kom ba-in," which even I can tell means "Don't shoot" as Englander half raises his M16, grins viciously, and lets its muzzle fall again. The Khmer Rouge soldier has clearly realized that there is an insanity about CPT Englander that he should not challenge, not just because of the pulled fingernail, which must ache, but from Englander's whole demeanor, a look so bestial, anyone would recoil.

"A week," Englander says. Then, turning to the trung si, he adds, "You tell him, you damn well tell him to take us where she is. Tell him to take us or pulling out his goddamned fingernails will be the least I will do to him." Any of us can tell the trung si's translation is filled with the same vehemence, an echo of Englander, who, eyes wide and face red as fire, looks just about as crazy with fury as a man can get.

Defiance leaves the Khmer soldier's eyes. He cowers, head down, finally saying, "Aukhe, aukhe, khnhom nung noam anak" (Yes, yes, I'll take you).

"Better," Englander says. "That's a lot better. It would have saved us trouble in the first place if you'd just said that."

★ ★ ★

CHAPTER 12

Englander makes it clear he isn't waiting for more intel. He tells the most banged up that they are going back to Téthian and calls for a Hook to take them there. The rest of us, eleven in all, wait for other birds from Ben Het to carry us back to last night's LZ, where we will head straight west on Bridget's trail.

The Hook comes and lifts out the wounded. A half hour later, two slicks and a gunship arrive, and the rest of us pile on them. Cat, Y Aguăt, the translator, commo sergeant Frank Rosenbaum, and I are in the bird with Englander; a fire team of six Yards is in the second bird. We lift into a still ragged sky, a shaft of sun breaking through a wedge of blue just to our west. The rain has stopped for the moment, but the Dak Koi, far from the placid stream it was the day before, has come out of its banks on both sides and rages below us. The air is still unsettled, and the bird bounces in it, a momentary heart-stopping drop lifting me from the webbing of my seat. Cat, next to me, hangs on, his knuckles white. SSG Rosenbaum lets out an "Oy!" that sounds like my grandmother. The big guy grins when I respond with the Yiddish "Kvetcher!"

As we climb from the Khmer Rouge base camp, I pull out my map and compass. Englander sees and puts out a hand to stop me, shouting over the blade noise and rush of air. "Nah, you won't need those right now. We're going right where I showed you on the map, no diversions or fake-outs this time."

I give him a half-hearted smile but keep my map out anyway, studying the route he says we'll be taking to a ville he has pointed out.

Our LZ will be the same clear spot in the jungle as last time, but this afternoon, when we debark, we will head west for a klick and then turn north with a hundred-meter-high hill a couple of hundred meters to our right and the ridge separating Vietnam from Cambodia just as close to our left. Once we turn north, the ville that is our objective will be another half a klick straight ahead. In his eagerness, Englander seems unconcerned about our making our insertion in daylight with nightfall still hours away.

"If anybody hears us, they'll know we're coming whether it's night or not," he says. "Once we're away from the LZ, we can move under the jungle canopy, and nobody will have any idea which direction we're going. After the birds lift, the gunship will head east for a klick along the Dak Koi and shoot up the jungle there by the river to draw off anybody headed our way." He taps a spot on the map north of the objective, adding, "Going back, we'll head north about eight hundred meters to here where there is this other bit of flat space, and the birds will pick us up."

"Looks like that second LZ is in Cambodia," I say.

"Yeah," he shrugs, "maybe a little. You've got no problem going back there, do you?"

I open my hands in a "who cares" gesture and settle back for the twenty-minute ride to the border. Whether Englander truly expects to find Bridget out there, I don't know.

In the early afternoon light, I see what I'd missed last time in the dark; the little LZ still looks like a shadowed pothole in the deep green of the jungle canopy, but crossing it are the remnants of a once graveled road—now just patches of red dirt studded with small stones—that show among swatches of elephant grass and bamboo. Rags of low white cloud are caught in the treetops. Pooled water flashes on the patches of roadway as our bird circles for a landing, our pilot hunting for the best angle with wind direction only a surmise from the blowing grass and tops of trees as we come down.

The bird bucks as it touches down and then rests for a moment to let us off. Stepping down onto the skids and then the ground, we quickly duck back under the trees to let the second bird land and let off its passengers. It, too, lifts away into the blustery air, and then around us, it is quiet again, only the gusts of the east wind stirring the jungle around us. Englander beckons us off the path and under the canopy, and we sit as silently as we can for perhaps ten minutes, until off beyond the shoulder of a low ridge to our east, there is the sudden racket of the gunship firing from a klick away.

We wait for that noise to cease, and then Englander says quietly, "OK, let's move."

Before we left Téthian, I had plotted a series of targets as reference points along either side of the trail Englander told me we would use in the event we need quick artillery fire along the high ground. Now, as we head out toward the bit of a ville that is our objective, I do a soft commo check to the battery.

"Roger, I've got you five by five," comes the response from the battery's American-accented RTO, and I roger him back, thinking how that little bit of connection, knowing I have good contact with the guns that will shoot for me if I need them, is reassurance enough for me. I pass the handset up to Cat, who nods and hangs it on his rucksack.

When we are about a hundred meters from the border with Cambodia, Englander gives a low hiss and points to where the trail, now just a faint track through high grass, turns sharply north. We walk it cautiously, staying as close under the tree line to our right as we can get. Ahead, in briefly fulgent sunlight, our way is green and speckled with purple wildflowers, a scene seeming so unwarlike. The path is open and quiet; in that calm, there is only a bit of insect hum and a brief trill of a bird. None in our file speaks; our only noise is the soft swish of the elephant grass against our boots and pant legs. The inclination is to accept the soft and quiet path as empty; instinct says different, saying as if as an alarm that we are not alone. Behind me are the muted footsteps of SSG Rosenbaum and the rest of the Yards. In front of me, Cat dabs sweat off his face with a shirtsleeve. Beyond him, Y Aguăt, the translator, seems suddenly sharply alert and looks hard left and right, as if he has seen something, startling me. But I see nothing past the grass and trees and trail. Englander, walking slack behind the Yard point man, stops abruptly and raises a fist for us to halt. The point man, far enough ahead of Englander so he doesn't see the raised fist, senses after a couple of steps that we have ceased moving and stops too as if grabbed. Englander points us to the shadowed undergrowth beneath the trees where we take cover and hunker. He taps the point man on the shoulder, and together they slip forward around the rightward curve of the hill and are quickly lost to our sight.

They are gone barely half a minute when there is the slap-slap of Ho Chi Minh sandals coming toward us on the trail from the north. The man, in VC black pajamas, is running, and as he comes within perhaps twenty meters of us, there is the crackle of small arms fire from the direction that Englander and the point man have taken. Behind me, one of the Yards blurts, "Ayăt, ayăt!" and brings up his M16 and fires. The running VC falls, managing only something that sounds like "Yip!" and lies still on the path.

Again, there is the crackle of fire from in front of us. "Damn it," I say, knowing we are the only help available now to Englander and the point man. "Let's go." I push Y Aguăt forward, wave my arm in a "come along" signal, and run. Cat is next to me, Y Aguăt coming up just behind, and I am hoping to hell that Rosenbaum and the remaining Yards follow us. I would be calling in fire right now, but I have no idea what is happening to our front and even what target to fire on.

We round the side of the hill, keeping under the trees for concealment if not real cover. Here are CPT Englander and the Yard point man lying behind a section of a fallen teak trunk. The tree line ends here, and beyond is an open meadow of short grass. The hill to our right steepens to a high cliff composed mostly of raw earth as if part of it had recently fallen away. Perhaps sixty meters to the front of us—just below the cliff almost halfway across the open meadow—is a tumble of limestone boulders that looks to have sloughed off the cliff. I can see at least a dozen shooters firing from that rock pile, VC apparently from the glimpses I get of black pajamas. We come forward into a crash of incoming fire that snicks and pings into the trees around us. None of us is seriously hurt, though, ahead, blood runs down the face of the Yard point man from a gash across his forehead. Englander himself looks slightly wounded, a stain of blood on his side close below his armpit. The Yards take cover among the trees. Cat and I move forward until I drop next to Englander, while Cat finds cover a couple of feet away behind a stump. The rattle of fire is all small arms, AKs from the sound, I realize, nothing heavier but still a hail of bullets. The rest of the Yards have taken cover in the trees a few meters back, unable to move up because there's no more room with us behind the teak trunk.

The Yard point man says something that sounds like *"Pool abak"* and gestures toward the way we came. With that gesture, I suddenly understand he is saying, "Pull back," to which Englander growls, "I haven't got this far to retreat," looks at me, and says, "Can you get some arty on them?"

"I can," I say. But I'm thinking that the rocks where the VC are closer than danger close range from us, and with the guns directly on the other side, we are right on the gun-target line where a near miss could do us real damage. It means care must be taken, especially since the battery—despite the few Americans attached to it—is made up mostly of ARVN gunners. I know I need to put a marking round up first, maybe two hundred meters back from the target, and adjust closer. Likelihood is the dinks will didi when that first white phosphorus round goes off. Maybe Englander and the others will be able to hit them as they run, maybe not.

Bullets continue to rip into the trees around us; Englander and the point man fire back, more to keep the dinks' heads down than to inflict any real damage. As I'm grabbing the radio handset from Cat, there is a fusillade of fire from the Yards behind us, bullets barely nipping over our heads. Englander bellows, "Cease fire, sons of bitches! You're going to hit us!" and the fire from the rest of our team slacks off.

I break squelch on the radio and call, "Carbon Valley Four-Seven, this is Carbon Valley Niner. Fire mission. Over."

"Niner, this is Four-Seven. Go ahead," comes the immediate response.

"Grid seven-five-zero-zero. Over."

"Roger, seven-five-zero-zero. Out."

"Two-one-seven-five. Over."

"Roger, two-one-seven-five. Out."

"Dinks in the open, proximity danger close, adjust on the gun target line. One round, Willie Peter up two hundred in adjustment, platoon two, HE in effect."

"Roger," the battery RTO repeats my call and adds, "Danger close!"

"Yeah," I respond, "I mean, danger goddamn close, barely sixty meters."

"Wow! OK, wait for it."

"We can maneuver up there to get a line of sight," Rosenbaum calls to Englander.

"No cover here," says Englander. "Stay where you are. We're going to lay some arty on 'em."

The AK fire continues at us from the rocks. Englander and the point man return it, and there is a moan as if one of the dinks there has been hit.

"Got one of 'em," Englander yips. "But this shit is going to bring more of them soon. Where the hell is your arty fire?"

Almost immediately as he asks, there is an announcement of "Shot!" from the radio Cat is carrying, and seconds later, "Splash!" With the round coming directly at us, I see the flash of its burst before the wailing of its approach reaches us, a white bubble of smoke growing and then the gong of the detonating WP round.

"Not close enough," Englander says, and I'm going to tell him I know that, that it was a marking round because we're so close to the target. But nothing breaks up a firefight like the threat of incoming artillery fire. With the burst of the marking round, the fire from the rocks immediately stops, and I see black pajama-clad troops darting away to the north keeping the rocks between them and us. Englander fires his M16 again, and there is more fire from the Yards behind us, several of them standing now but unable to get a clean shot past the rocks. I call for the battery to drop a few rounds on that same grid, hoping the enemy soldiers will be right under the fire when it comes down. But the running dinks elude it and are quickly gone into heavy trees on the other side of the meadow. One of the Yards carrying an aid bag, an older man I've not met before, comes up. The Yard's left hand has a splotch of keloid burn scar, and part of his ring finger on that hand is missing. He kneels next to Englander, indicates the widening stain of blood on the captain's fatigue shirt, and asks, "You hurt, đại úy?"

"Him first," Englander says, pointing to the blood on the point man's face.

"He not bad. You, đại úy, you first," the Yard medic says again and refuses to move until Englander pulls his fatigue shirt off to let the man get at his wound. It looks to be a mean one, probably painful as hell but not serious; the bullet has sliced through flesh and maybe off a rib but hasn't gone deep. Englander fidgets, wincing as the medic squeezes in antibiotic ointment and dresses it. Finally, the captain growls, "Enough!" and pushes the medic toward the point man, whose forehead has been slashed by a shard of wood that AK fire had splintered from the teak trunk. The gash is not deep but, like all facial wounds, is bleeding freely. The medic cleans and medicates the wound and covers it with a field dressing that soon blooms with a rich red flower of blood.

Bandaged, Englander stands, staggering a bit from what must be more than a little pain, saying, "Christ, let's go. The ville we're after is in the jungle just past the bare hillside."

"You know they're going to come back, Hugh, likely with reinforcements," I say to him.

"Yeah, yeah, but not until they can get some support to come back with. We got time. Let's go see if we can find any of the Yards that Bridget was living with."

Maybe a hundred meters on, the cliff curves east into the jungle for a stretch creating a sort of heavily forested box canyon before curving back west and climbing to a higher peak. All the terrain east of the meadow is heavy double and even triple canopy growth. It seems to me a perfect spot to get trapped with no egress except back out the way we've come. But Englander is adamant that we find the ville where Sister Bridget had lived and learn more about what happened to her. This time, the captain himself takes the point, holding his M16 stiffly, left arm pressed firmly against his bandaged wound. He leads us up a path, its entrance almost invisible in the midst of the vines and undergrowth. It travels up from the meadow into the deeper jungle. The firefight over, birds have begun to sing again. Except for that birdsong, the land is quiet, the air here among the trees windless, carrying a rich odor of fertile growth abetting the faint musky fragrance of agarwood that hangs in it. Maybe fifty meters in, we come to a cleared space under the trees with only the highest canopy left covering it. What Englander has been calling a ville is in fact just a single structure: a squat, square version of a Montagnard longhouse on stilts, heavily thatched, its siding fashioned from bamboo. The longhouse occupies the far side of the cleared space backed up against the slope, the steps at its front leading to a small sort of porch. On that porch, sitting placidly as if nothing of the war, no firefight, no bang of incoming artillery had been anywhere near, is a wizened, ancient-looking Yard. He is wearing traditional Montagnard clothing, a long, dark, and richly embroidered shirt over dark trousers, with the incongruity of a faded navy-blue NY Yankees baseball cap on his head over close-cropped gray hair. His hands are working a knife against a stake of teak, shaping a face much like those on the funeral stakes I'd seen at Téthian. As we approach, he looks up amiably as if armed bands of Yards and clandestine operations troops pass this way every day (*Hell, maybe they do*, I think).

"Ask him where Y Nan is," Englander directs our translator.

The old man gazes back at us, shakes his head finally, and says, "VC ngă Y Nan atâo. Hăng dro'i jan."

"He say, Y Nan body dead now, VC kill him. He with spirits."

"Oh, man," Englander says, nonplussed at the news. He looks around at the rest of us as if for support and takes a step forward to lean against the edge of the porch. Finally, he looks up at the old man. What now? Englander had told me that Y Nan was the man he knew here, the one who was most likely to know where Bridget is. He stops and scratches nervously at his cheek. "Tell him we are looking for Sister Bridget," he directs Y Aguăt.

The translator utters a short version of that in Jarai, ending with "Anih yă tha?"

In return, the old man smiles slightly, puts down the stake and knife, and opens his hands in a gesture of ignorance. He offers a long, animated reply.

"What?" Englander asks Y Aguăt when the man is done speaking.

"He say he don't know," the translator tells us.

"He chattered along for about a minute, damn it. Is that all he said?"

"No," says Y Aguăt. He looks quickly from me to Englander, takes a deep breath, and finally says, "He say she with *Mặt trận Thống nhất Đấu tranh của các Sắc tộc bị Áp bức*." He sees Englander's look of perplexity, takes another breath, and translates the Vietnamese haltingly as if reciting a phrase he learned in English by rote. "He say she with united front of struggle of oppressed ethnicity."

"What?"

"She with—"

"I heard . . . son of a bitch . . . I heard. He's saying she's with the OLM, the goddamned Montagnard Liberation Movement. That was . . ." He sits down on the porch. "Oh, damn." He turns to Y Aguăt. "She's not with the OLM. She hates the OLM. They're ruthless, kill women and kids as often as they do men. Tell him we have word she's somewhere around here."

"Do I ask where she is, đại úy?"

Englander explodes, "Ask! I'm goddamn sure he knows."

"Ho'get anih?"

At this, the old man stops and looks blandly at Englander for a few beats, finally turning, waving us into the hooch, and saying, "Truh, kâo po'buh." He goes inside with Y Aguăt. After a surprised pause, Englander, Cat, and I follow.

The interior of the hooch is dim, only a bit of green-tinged light filtering into it through closed woven screens. We walk through a front room with a sleeping pallet rolled in one corner and a low bamboo table, all very neat. Past a partition, there is a second room, brighter, screens pulled open. A framed dirt-filled hearth much like that in the ops shack at Téthian, about four feet on a side, has a charcoal fire going below a patch of thatching in the roof lifted to let the smoke out. A pot bubbling over it gives off a spicy aroma. The old man points to the hearth, makes a lifting motion with his hands, and says, "Yŏng apui."

Englander stares at him, looking as if he is trying to divine meaning from the old man's words. Helpfully, the old man grins and makes the same lifting motion, repeating, "Yŏng, yŏng."

"What the hell is he saying, Y Aguăt?" Englander says.

"He say pick up fire, đại úy."

"Pick up the fire? How the hell are we supposed to do that?"

Y Aguăt repeats the question in Jarai, and the old man calmly walks over to one corner of the room and takes two heavy bamboo poles from behind a mat hanging there. "Anai-nê," he says and offers the poles to Englander. "Tôn kính người phụ nữ cũjing tờ glu'h adih."

"She down there," Aguăt translates.

All at once, I get what this is about. There are slots under the wooden frame of the hearth, one at each side, large enough for the poles to slip into. "Hugh," I say, "I think he means we should use these bamboo poles to lift the whole fireplace up."

"Then he should say so," Englander barks, and he and Y Aguăt slide the poles under the hearth. They each take one corner. Cat and I take the other two corners, and we all lift. The hearth, fashioned from hard-packed dirt and teak timbers, is horribly heavy, maybe a couple of hundred pounds, and I stagger trying to pick up my part.

The old man laughs at this, points to the opposite corner of the room where the floor is clear, and says, "Adih! Adih!" which I take to mean "There" or "Put it down there" or some such. Then "Răng!" laughing again as I almost step into the open space under where the hearth had been.

"God, that's a load," Englander says, dropping his corner of the hearth the last half foot onto the floor. I see that the old man has taken a long pole, closed the first vent, and pushed open a second one in the roof over the space where we have set the hearth. From the front, the longhouse had appeared entirely supported a meter and a half off the ground on stilts. But I'm gathering now that the ground slopes up under the structure so that the back half where we are rests on solid earth. I'd expected a small secret dugout space under the hearth. But moving the hearth away reveals an opening perhaps two feet square that appears to drop through a limestone passage into a deep space below the house. A wooden ladder leads down. The waft of a breeze from it warns me what is there; the air has a familiar chill, like that of the caves I had explored in the Ozarks as a kid, cool, a taint of damp earthiness to it. A faint smell of death rides on the breeze. Immediately, I fear what is coming, and my gut is already twisted in knots at the thought. I can see no more than a couple of meters down into what looks to be a natural cave opening; the rest recedes into darkness. I used to love caves, had been a devoted spelunker as a teen, but no longer. These days, the idea of tight places fills me with panic and dread. Those terrors had had their genesis on a caving trip to Arkansas I'd been on the summer after I graduated from high school. I had been with several friends exploring a mucky sinkhole and had become mired, head downward, in wet clay for a horrible few minutes. There was no purchase in it, and I had come close to dying before my friends had pulled me out. That was the last spelunking trip I had taken for years. Fear of constriction, of being trapped, of suffocation has hijacked me in tight places ever since. Though the entrance to the space below the fire is as wide as those of some of those Ozark caves I'd investigated, I want no part of this. A pang of that old claustrophobia bursts into me, and I step sharply back from the entrance to the hole, breathing hard, my heart hammering. What comes out of my mouth is simply "No!"

Interestingly, Englander is also flatly opposed to going down there. "I'm no tunnel rat," he says. "I don't do caves."

Cat, however, allows that he is willing, though he looks hardly happier about it than Englander or I am. So, mustering bravado, I say, "Dammit, Cat, go ahead if you are OK with it. I'll be right behind you."

Englander nods, looking no happier than I feel. "Y Aguăt," he says, "ask the old man what we are looking for down there. Is that the way Bridget went?"

"Hră mở'ng mặt trận Thống nhất Đấu tranh của các Sắc tộc bị Áp bức," the old man says and points down.

Y Aguăt steps over and peers down the shaft as if looking there for the translation, finally explaining, "He say down there are papers from united front." I realize he's saying that important documents about OLM are in the cave.

"Goddamn it," says Englander, kicking at the frame of the hearth as if to scatter the embers. "That's the second time he's said it. OLM has been a dead movement for two years. They signed a treaty with the South Vietnamese government, gave up their guns, and went back to farming. It's history, old history." He turns on the old man and punches him in the shoulder, shouting the question this time. "Bridget. What about Bridget? Is she down there? Did they take her that way?"

"Ôh thảo! Ôh thảo!" The old man is holding up his hands, waving them in what must be "No."

"Goddammit! I'm not looking for papers. I'm looking for Bridget," says Englander. "Do you smell that? Death. Somebody is dead down there." He stops and shakes his head. "If it is Bridget, I don't want to know."

The decision of whether to go down into the cavern ends up being made for us. One of the Yards we have left in an observation post out toward the meadow has come back to warn that a large group of VC looks to be returning to where we'd had the firefight.

"How many?" Englander asks.

The Yard rifleman says, "*Kĕt keng,* many, many," and flashes opened hands three times, signifying that there are maybe thirty VC coming our way.

"We don't want to get into a damn firefight with a bunch that big, Cap," SSG Rosenbaum says to Englander. "Do we go down, or are we going to take on a whole platoon of dinks, Cap? Isn't any way out of this canyon, cliff walls all around the way they are. We can't fight our way through thirty dinks. We fight, all of us'll be KIA."

"Christ," Englander says. He looks down into the cave entrance, kicks some dirt into it, and listens to it fall a few feet. "Y Aguăt, ask the old man if there is a way out of this cave."

"Adih nao?" Y Aguăt asks.

"Pŏk ataih ƀoi čŭ'," the old man grins as if trying to reassure us and points off toward the north.

"Hiŭ'm ataih?" Y Aguăt asks.

The old man considers, grins again, and says, "Ôh ataih, ai ñu anĕt rôk."

"He say other side of mountain. Maybe short walk."

"What the hell," says Englander. "What's a short walk?"

Y Aguăt shrugs. "Not long. Jarai no word for it."

"Ahhh!" says Englander. "Fuck, fuck, fuck." We all had known there was peril in coming into this blind canyon. But we're not strong enough to take on thirty of the enemy, despite any artillery support I might muster. So, down, stench of death or no.

My heart sinks at the thought. Still, though I may not be much for claustrophobic caverns, this'll be better than a shoot-out with the VC. Truthfully, I'm briefly willing to consider the alternative, as chancing a bullet in a firefight with the dinks and going down that hole seem equally disagreeable options.

Cat volunteers to go first.

Englander sees my hesitation (hell, my agony at this, which is calling up every fear of tight spaces I have), punches my shoulder, and says, "You too, man. We ain't going down there alone, Captain."

"To'gŭ glông adih," the old man says.

"He say man can stand up tall in there," Y Aguăt translates, grinning helpfully.

"Sure, he can say that," I moan. "He's not even five feet. It must seem big as a subway tunnel to him."

"Down," Englander says emphatically, and as Cat climbs down the ladder, he prods me again.

So, half feeling I won't be able to breathe in there, I settle one foot on the ladder, crank my courage up to maximum, and begin climbing gingerly down following Cat.

The ladder squeezes down through a tight meter of water-worn limestone, which then opens into a modest-sized cavern that the light from Cat's flash shows water has carved out of the karst. The Yards, apparently oblivious to the tight space we are entering, climb down after me and then Englander and finally SSG Rosenbaum, who, at six feet six, is by far the largest man among us. He works his way awkwardly down the confines of the opening shaft, saying unhappily, "*Gotenu!* I hope it doesn't get tighter than this or I'm not going to make it."

The group of us, now crowded at the bottom of the ladder, is at close quarters in the limestone room. Light from above illuminates the space directly under the ladder. The rest is a dense, bituminous darkness. Englander, Cat, I, and SSG Rosenbaum all have flashlights, as do a couple of the Yards. Flicking mine on and exposing the closeness of the cavern in the light's red beam almost makes things worse for me. Neither Cat nor the short-statured Yards seem concerned at these narrow quarters. Both Englander and Rosenbaum look agitated as hell over our confines, Englander flashing his light around nervously, apparently looking for the way out or maybe for any sign of Bridget. From above us comes a muffled flurry of small arms fire, shouting, a scream of pain, and a grinding noise, and then the light from above is cut off as someone sets the hearth back down over the cave entrance.

Around me is the clatter of M16s being charged, and Englander says, "Man, that was the damn dinks," his voice tense. He shines his flashlight at the shaft leading back up to the longhouse. It is totally blocked there now, some dirt drifting down. I wonder if the VC have made it inside the longhouse, who is dead up there, and how long it will be before the enemy soldiers figure out that the hearth is covering the way into our escape tunnel.

Our flashlights are not much illumination. The pitted and carved walls of the room are dark and full of shadows cast by our lights, shadows weaving as if living in the moving lights. Everything is wet from rainwater seeping in. In the momentary quiet, we can hear the drip and plink of that water into puddles along the walls. I shine my flashlight around the crowded chamber, trying to locate the passage that the old man had said leads out to the other side of the mountain. I can't begin to say how much I want to just climb back up the ladder and push my way back into the longhouse, VC there or no. I close my eyes for a moment, take a deep breath, and realize that the air seems to be moving slightly against my face. I try to relax my shoulders, which tension has made drum tight. I open my eyes again and move my light to the right across one of the walls, to where there seems to be the beginning of a passage, feeling a pang when I realize that the passage is a dead end barely two meters deep. My light picks out the gleam of a shallow rivulet of water running from a hand's-span-wide crack in that wall, flowing across the cave floor and disappearing into a much narrower crack half a meter on. I'd look further, but at the blunt end of the passage, my light has picked out the shape of a footlocker-sized wooden chest, no hasp or lock on it. I stop, staring at it, thinking that if Bridget's body is down here, it could be in that chest. SSG Rosenbaum, closest to that side of the room, sees it too and approaches it cautiously.

Cat quietly asks, "What's he doing, sir? We ought to find the where the cave leads out and move."

"Keep looking, Cat," I tell him. But I move closer to SSG Rosenbaum, forcing myself to concentrate on what might be in the chest.

The big commo sergeant pushes into the stub of passageway, saying, "Better not be any damn snakes or stuff in this thing." Not saying that there better not be a body in it. Coming from a man his size, the quaver in his voice seems almost comic. He moves to the chest, kneels, carefully pushes up on one corner of the hinged lid, and begins to lift it.

When he has it about a third open from behind me, goddamned Englander gives out a guttural "Boo!" SSG Rosenbaum drops the lid as if he's been bitten. He lurches back into the nearest Yard, half knocking the man over. Englander laughs shrilly at Rosenbaum's show of fear, and the sergeant turns on him angrily, saying, "Captain, people have been shot for less than that." He is not smiling. I realize that this is Englander's way of breaking an impossible tension.

Englander says, "Couldn't help it. You looked like you'd seen a ghost."

"Maybe soon," Rosenbaum says, and Englander just points at the chest, saying, "Open the damn thing, man."

As this goes on, Cat has moved to the far side of the room maybe ten paces away from us, searching among deep shadows where the ceiling drops to hardly a meter high. I see him duck around what had looked to be a jutting of the rock wall, into a cleft and disappear. A beat on, as Rosenbaum is again lifting the lid of the chest, Cat sticks his head back out from the cleft and calls, "Here, this is the way out."

"Wait," says Englander, and then to Rosenbaum, his voice almost breaking, "Frank, anything in that box?"

"Yeah, Cap, got a satchel in it. Looks full of papers."

"Ahhh!" Englander, relief hissing out of him. There comes a thudding from the hearth covering the hole above us. "Take 'em. We've got to go."

At the noise, which sounds like someone probing for an escape hatch, the Yards around us start talking excitedly. I push past two who are standing near the exit passage, move around the rock to the cleft, and look at where Cat has just vanished. A passage a meter or so high and wide continues there, ankle-deep water running on it, its eroded walls chiseled open wide enough for a man to pass. Stumps of stalactites protrude from the ceiling, looking as if someone had broken them off for easier entry. I feel more air moving past me from the passage. Cat is about a dozen steps into it, shining his light further on.

"Looks like it goes, Captain," he says.

The passageway is small and confined, but the solid rock of it—no mud or earth to collapse—seems to make a difference, allaying the worst of my claustrophobia. I stop and close my eyes again and fill my lungs with a few deep breaths. I feel the air that is moving here and think that people have been in here, walked out through here, and broken off obstructions to make it easier to get through. I think that the passage is large enough to walk through and that if it stays this size, I will be OK. I think that the batteries in my flashlight are nearly new and should last for a klick long trip.

"I'm coming, Cat," I say and begin to follow him, hearing as I do so the others coming up after me, footsteps slapping on the stone floor, splashing in the water. *Go, damn it,* I think. And I do.

CHAPTER 13

Telling myself there is no turning back, I gut it out. I've turned my own flashlight off to save batteries and am just following Cat, his light a red bubble in the passage ahead. Still, I'm hunched over, walking carefully. Missing my steel pot now, I have one hand over my head to feel for bumps or projections. Cat's light casts long shadows that jerk and oscillate behind him as he moves. The sound is of our feet padding along on the stony floor; the biggest noise is from splashes in the thin stream running down the passage with us. The floor is slick and worn from many feet before us, telling me this is a well-used highway. No one speaks, and as we progress, we stop each score or so of meters and wait silently to hear if anyone is following us. Here and there in the cave are ragged edges of limestone draperies and broken flowers of gypsum, crimson in the red beams of our flashlights, looking so like those in the caves I remember back home. We come to a slight turn and splitting of the passage, a larger one to the right, the other lower and narrower to the left. I would take the right-hand passage for its headroom and breathing space if nothing else. The roof of it actually widens into a crack that goes up several meters. But there is an arrow someone has marked on the cave wall in the soot of a miner's carbide lamp. To me, it clearly points to the lower, left-hand turn. My need is for the wider way, but my instinct says follow the arrow.

Englander comes up to us. "What the hell's the holdup?" he says. "We go that way, obviously." He points down the larger path.

"Arrow says this way," I tell him.

"Screw that, gonna have to squeeze down just to get in there."

"Air's moving in from this one," I say. "Somebody put that arrow here for a reason. I say this is the way out."

Not happy, Englander snaps, "If we go down this one and there's no out from it, we're screwed if dinks are following us."

"Same for the other one," I say.

"I'm going to see," he says. And with that, he turns toward the larger right-hand passage and begins moving down it. His light disappears as he negotiates a turn, and then I hear an echoed, "Goddammit!"

A moment later, he is back, frustrated. "Doesn't go anywhere at all. Just narrows to a damn crack."

The left-hand route dips to less than a meter high under a shelf of rock and then even lower after a couple of meters. I gladly let Cat go on ahead, figuring that if someone is to get stuck here, it's not going to be me. Soon, I hear him breathing hard as he gets on hands and knees for a moment. Finally, he says, "I'm through, lots of room now. Stink's worse in here, though."

So I gulp, get down on all fours, stare at the floor of the passage, and force myself to move through it, pushing my ruck and M16 ahead of me. A meter or so in, the space between the walls narrows until my shoulders scrape on either side. A surge of panic rises into me from the feeling of that imprisoning rock pressing in around me, and I am almost frozen, stopped, my breath coming in gasps. I let go a moan, fumble my flashlight on, and see that the tight crawlway opens out an arm's length farther. I know that if the tight space had been longer, I would not have continued. I'm sure Cat, his face seeming almost in flames in my lamp's red light beam, sees it too, urging me to move. "Come on, Captain, just a couple more feet and you're through," he says, smiling.

And I move, struggling forward, my shoulders rasping against the rock on either side, my knees in the shallow water, pushing, pushing again until I can drag myself out into a wide space, the passage opening here into a room two or more meters high, maybe four meters across.

"Holy hell," I say. "That was not good."

My breath finally back, I am able to see that this stretch of the cavern is a place of extraordinary beauty. Cat's and my lights shine off of a wall of thumb-sized quartz crystals, off a flowstone drapery wide as a tapestry that has grown from a crack in the ceiling, extending all along the right side of the space, at a crystal-clear pool a few inches deep, rimmed in flowstone, soda straws hanging from a low ceiling above the pool, globular pebbles of calcium carbonate cluster across the pool's bottom.

The death smell, though, is stronger here, brought by air moving from the passage beyond us.

Englander follows me cautiously but gets through with no trouble. Small as they are, the Yards easily get through the low passage and into the room with us. SSG Rosenbaum is another story. He takes one look at the bottleneck in the passage and declares firmly that he is not going through it.

"What the hell you going to do, then, Frank?" Englander says, kneeling down to peer under the low ceiling behind us.

"Going back and take my chances with the dinks, man. This is a nightmare here."

"No, you're coming with us, Frank. Everybody else made it. You aren't that much bigger."

"Am so," says SSG Rosenbaum. "Hell, just my butt is bigger than any of the Yards with us." Y Aguăt laughs at this and shares Rosenbaum's joke with the other Yards, whose laughter seems to shame the commo sergeant into moving. So he gets down on hands and knees and looks through the narrow bit of cave to where we all are. For a few beats, he still can't seem to move forward at all, griping at the confines, and then he just stops. "Did you hear that?" he asks.

"Shhhhh," says Englander, and in the ensuing silence, we can hear the faint noise of movement from far back where we have come through the cave.

"Damn dinks are coming," says Englander. "You sure aren't going back to them, man."

Rosenbaum moans again, pulls of his ruck and shoves it and his M16 through to us, and begins to creep forward. I feel for him, projecting my own irrational anxiety onto him. He is doing fine until the narrowest spot just before the passage opens into the room we are. His bulk and broad shoulders jam him tight as a cork into the space. He struggles to move forward and gasping wordless grunts of frustration. He heaves forward but can't get past it, and I see the beginning of pure horror come into his expression.

It is Cat that comes to the commo sergeant's rescue. "Get onto your side, Sarge," Cat tells him, "that way your shoulders won't be wedged."

Rosenbaum, in his blooming panic, doesn't seem to hear Cat, who pushes past me, gets down next to the sergeant, and starts whispering something to him.

"Yeah? OK, yeah," Rosenbaum says, levers himself up sideways, heaves a huge sigh, and slides on his side through the narrow space and into the room with us.

"Son of a bitch," SSG Rosenbaum says. "This isn't any place for someone big as me to get through."

Watching the big commo sergeant's struggles, my own panic has subsided. I imagine, though, that if my expression looks anything like his (sweat running in rivulets, eyes wide and unfocused, cheeks flaming in the red light of the flashlights), I must be the image of fear. Seeing SSG Rosenbaum's full-on fear makes me, for the first time since we've come down here, feel as if I can breathe easy.

Now it is Englander who looks as unsettled as anyone. "Let's go. We've gotta move before the dinks catch up to us," he says. His voice cracks with his own strain.

It is the now calmer Rosenbaum who tells him, "No, wait! Let's leave the dinks a little surprise here." He paws into his ruck sack and pulls out a fragmentation grenade. "Let's set this sucker in this narrow space and set a tripwire across it. The dinks try to come through here and trip it, it's going to blow a big bunch of them away."

"Man!" says Englander. He studies the space for a few beats. "I don't know, Frank. Enclosed space like this, shockwave will propagate through it like it's in a gun barrel. Maybe do us as much damage as it does the dinks."

"We can hide it in the passage back there, Cap. Blast should mostly travel the other way. Only thing is, I'm not going to be the one who goes back there to set it up." SSG Rosenbaum says that so seriously that Cat and I and soon even Englander just start laughing.

"Man!" says the commo sergeant. "What a war!"

In the end, it is Cat who goes back. He ties the grenade's pin to a bit of commo wire Rosenbaum gives him and places the grenade in a niche in the rock. He strings the wire back down the side of the passage and behind a hook of rock near the bottom. Working with great care for the small force needed to pop the pin out, Cat threads the wire across at head height, weighting it with a chunk broken from the flowstone in our chamber (I actually feel a bit of regret over damaging this beautiful piece of stone drapery), and pulls the pin out just enough to leave it on a hair trigger. It is jury-rigged, and whether it will go off is a good question. Setting the tripwire without setting the grenade off puts Cat almost into a fit of his own panic. He says, "Captains, with due respect, get the hell away from me. So if this thing goes off, it won't get you too."

Englander just watches impassively, and when Cat is done, he nods and says, "Good. Now let's get the fuck out of here."

We are about a hundred meters down the passage (I've been counting my paces mostly as a distraction from my claustrophobia) when the grenade detonates. There is a distant flare of light, a shock. The bang, though throttled through the narrow opening to the passageway we are in, is deafening, the entire cavern seeming to ring, gong-like. Heartbreaking screams follow. We have done some real damage to the VC chasing us. I doubt it will put them off our trail but surely will make them slower and more careful. We may get out of this cave and into concealment in the jungle beyond it yet.

We have progressed another 150 paces along the passage when Cat says, "We're going down."

Lost in my own funk, my first thought is he is saying we are "going down" as in "dying," but I almost immediately realize he means the main part of the cavern is angling downward. The whole character of the cave here is changing, branching off into numerous side passages much too small for us to take. A crack in the floor we have been following has now begun to widen, the sound in it a sough of moving water from below. A soft breeze, cool and moist but smelling more strongly than ever of something ripely dead, is now blowing at us from the passage to our front. We are nearing the outfall from the cave, the way back into the aboveground world. Not good, though, is that the roof of the passage is getting steadily lower as we progress. No help to me. I want out, my heart starting to race again with the sense of the walls tightening around me. Cat's flashlight has dimmed to almost nothing, and I give him mine, anything to help us move out of here! He snaps it on, and there I see, calming me, another arrow drawn in soot on the passage wall, pointing in the direction we are going. We have stopped, because while the arrow points one way, there is another passage almost as wide and far taller going off to the right.

"Which way?" Englander asks.

"There," says Cat, pointing the way the arrow indicates.

"Looks better that way," Englander says, and I'm about to tell him to follow the damn arrow like last time when there is a series of soft thuds from a ways up the tunnel behind us.

"Jesus," SSG Rosenbaum says. "That's footsteps. The damn dinks are still following us."

"Screw it, let's go," Englander says.

Cat asks, "Which way?"

"Whatever way you want, man. Just go!" comes as almost a groan from the captain.

"That way, then," says Cat, and again we move in the direction the arrow points.

We are another fifty paces on when we get to a place where the ceiling dips sharply down. Behind we can hear footsteps more clearly and what seems to be a voice, almost a hiss, saying, "Hãy cẩn thận. Tôi nghe người Mỹ trước chúng tôi."

"He say, 'Be careful, Americans ahead of us,'" Y Aguăt translates.

"Goddamn it," says Englander. "Move. Last thing we want is a firefight in here."

Cat has been examining the passage ahead and tells us, "It gets lower, but it goes. Looks like the ceiling is high enough to get through. I think I see light ahead, maybe the way out."

"OK, then move," Englander says again.

Cat is down on the floor, his rucksack and radio off, pushing them ahead. The last thing I want to do is follow him, though he says, "It's OK, Captain, maybe a foot and a half high here. You can get through no trouble." And he's past it telling me that he can see the way out now, sunlight there. And I get down, my ruck and rifle off, pushing them ahead. The length of this low piece of the passage is maybe two meters. "Plenty of room, plenty of room," I am telling myself. Forward over the crack in the passage floor, which is several inches wide, dropping a meter or more underneath me, and the sound of water below in it stronger now. I wriggle forward, my knee smacking into rock as I push, my butt bumping the low ceiling.

"Almost through now, Captain," Cat tells me. There is the sharp crack of rifle fire from back along the cave, the sound of it ricocheting from the stone of the passage's walls. At that, a numbness washes over me. My heart races.

Englander says sharply, "Go, man. They're shooting at us."

I hear the rattle of AK fire, a muffled crackle from the cavern walls, and the higher-pitched, almost deafening reply of M16s from the Yards at the back of our file. I want the hell out of this narrow place, my panic rapidly rising further. I'm struggling in a way that only makes the going harder. For an instant as I push forward, I feel something catch at my web belt, a projection of rock briefly holding me fast as all the agony of remembered terror, of being caught again in that clay-filled sinkhole in Arkansas floods into me. But I push forward and feel the web belt come free of what was holding it, and now I am through. Beyond is a space more than head high and wide enough for me to stand next to Cat. I clamber out, worthless for the moment for any fight, shaking, breathing hard.

There is another sharp rattle of gunfire, a yelp from one of the Yards, a grunt as Englander tugs his way through the bottleneck behind me, and then the three of us are standing up in the large chamber that leads out to the real green world. Almost as soon as CPT Englander gets out, all the Yards come, sliding through the narrow passage as if it is no obstruction at all.

Last is SSG Rosenbaum, he of the solid, massive girth, and he is pushing his own way into the narrow space of the bottleneck, cursing, grunting. His rucksack and radio come through. He pushes his rifle through to us. But he lets out a curse and a "Damn it." And he is stuck. Whatever projection of stone that hid caught my web belt has him caught solidly now.

"I can't get out. I can't."

"Push through, man!" Englander tells him.

But the commo sergeant says, "God! No, I'm wedged. Butt's too damn big."

"Reach a hand out here. We'll pull you through."

Cat is kneeling at Rosenbaum's head, hands under his shoulders, trying to pull the big man out. But his 260 pounds are wedged unbreakably there. All Cat is doing is jamming him more tightly. Still, he says, "Come on, Sarge, come on," pulling.

It is SSG Rosenbaum who pushes Cat away. "God, no! Can't get through. I'm good and stuck. God, god, I'm going back."

"Man, Sarge, the dinks are there," Cat says. "You've got to come to where we are."

"Can't!" and there is a rattle of gunfire. Rosenbaum shrieks, "*Oy, god, hit, I'm hit.* Gotta go back." The big man is hit again in the legs as he is thrashing, trying to pull back away from us into the larger chamber behind him when there are more shots. Then I see him—tears of pain and fury running down his face, dripping off his nose—yank a grenade off his belt, strain with his other hand to reach it and pull the pin, and shout at us, "Grenade. Get the hell away!" And he chucks the fragmentation grenade back behind him. I can hear it rattle off the stone of the passageway and hear alarmed voices shrieking excitedly in Vietnamese, "Xem ra, quả lựu đạn!" All of us push back in the chamber where we are standing, away from the commo sergeant. There comes a massive, though muffled detonation, the sound of screaming also muffled by the SSG Rosenbaum's bulk. His whole body jerks and writhes there. "Man, I think I killed myself," he says. A slosh of blood runs across the floor of the passage past him and into the chamber where we are standing and then down the crack into the gush of the stream below. SSG Rosenbaum's eyes go dim, lifeless, and unfocused, and he is dead.

Tears are in my eyes. He was a good man. We had talked of it once about how hard it was to be here, so far from other Jews. I'd told him the story of how CPT Sol Katz and I had ordered a delivery of kosher delicacies from the Jewish Welfare Board. "Herring?" he'd asked me. "Did they have herring?" I'd said yes, and the sergeant had grinned. Now he's dead, and I can only smile at that memory as a few words of the mourner's kaddish come to me. I begin to whisper them. But there is noise from the other side of his body, angry cursing in Vietnamese.

"Chết người đàn ông chặn đường của chúng tôi!" (Dead man is blocking our way!)

"Kéo anh ta ra!" (Pull him out!)

"Tôi có thể không! Tôi có thể không." (I can't! He's too heavy.)

They are furious because they can't get past the body.

"Let's go," Englander says. He looks back at the dead sergeant, and I know he's thinking what I am—that we don't want to leave our dead behind. But there's no way to pull the corpse of the big man through, and the fact is that even in death, he is protecting us, blocking the opening and keeping the dinks away from us.

So Englander kneels and reaches under SSG Rosenbaum, pulling off the big man's dog tags, and we move, going on down the now roomy passageway out of the cave, into soft green, into warmer air and the last of the light from a setting sun and a lowering sky. We emerge in a cleft between two cheeks of the mountain onto a rock channel tumbling down into broken jungle. Maybe a dozen meters beneath us, blood-tinged water spills from a pool in the rock and showers down the mountainside into a stream below.

In that pool is a body, small and thin, looking almost childlike in the way it lies cuddled facedown against the rocks. Snarled gray hair covers the body's neck. It is clad in black pajamas. Its arms and legs are angled unnaturally against the bank. Here is where the stink of death originates, the stench so strong, I can hardly breathe without choking.

Englander sees it as soon as I do. "Ahhh!" he says, seeming to be fighting for a word and finding none. He climbs down and steps forward into the pool's bloody water, moving until he is a couple of feet away from the one lying dead there. "Ahhh!" he says again. He kneels, reaches forward to grasp at the body's shoulder, pulls his hand back, and then reaches out again. The corpse bobs in the water and flips over, suddenly faceup. Silt from the pool's floor washes momentarily around it and then clears. We see a beard, the toothless face of an old man. Englander stares, lets the body go, and collapses onto the rocks at the edge of the falls.

"Oh, god!" he says. "I was afraid it was . . . afraid it was . . ." He shakes himself as if an animal shaking off water or anger or fear and stands. "Oh, man, it's not Bridget. Oh, man."

Down from there and once again under open sky, I call in a pair of nav rounds that confirm my estimate of our location. We are on the northeast side of the mountain, almost a full klick from where we went into the cavern below the longhouse. The stream that runs from the cave and down the foot of the mountain is a trickling tributary of the Dak Koi. The remainder of the trip, a klick down the rest of the mountain, another klick northwest along a second arm of the stream to where it begins just at the foot of the border ridge, the climb across the ridge to the soft open field of the pickup zone just inside Cambodia—all that we traverse almost in silence and in a gloom that is only partly sunset. CPT Englander walks it in a double dose of pain, the hurt from his wounded side, now stiff and aching, and the far more intolerable hurt from the loss of SSG Rosenbaum, who was as much Englander's friend as he would allow anyone to be. Englander walks it with a sob now and again escaping him, no real tears, but his eyes wet and red, tears of loss and relief blended. We limp up the slope to the border ridge, exhausted, Cat and I leading as if Englander and the Yards are too spent to care, me carrying the satchel of papers I had taken from Rosenbaum. We cross the border into the grassy open space beneath a dark sky in the last of the twilight, a gentle rain falling on us. There we call in for extraction and wait.

The long flight back to Téthian is somber, Englander silent, the noise of the bird's rotors precluding talk. Our bird and the second slick settle one at a time on the camp's pad, letting us off, lifting away into the deepening evening. At another time, I would expect Englander's temper to explode over this mission, which failed to find the nun and seems to have gained us nothing but a good man's death. Englander, Cat, and I settle into the operations shack. We've not eaten since this morning, and we dig into bowls of vegetables, rice, and meat a Yard woman brings us, subduing our hunger if not our pain.

Finally, Englander sets his bowl aside, grunts, shakes his head, and says, "I'm done."

Cat looks at him quizzically, but I understand right away. "We're not going back after Bridget?" I ask.

"No. We've been out there twice now and only got men killed. I know she's out there. But I'm done. I'm not exposing my team or the Yard troops to this danger again. I . . ." He stops and puts his hand to his forehead as if to stifle tears. "I'm not . . . I'm just not," he finishes, blinks, and looks away for a beat. "I guess we don't need you and your RTO anymore. Why don't you stay the night, and tomorrow morning I'll get you a bird to take you back to Bronco? You can go back to the real war. Forget this craziness."

"You're not going to keep looking for Bridget? If you are, we can stay and help if you want. We brought back all the documents from the cave. You're going to want to go through them for intel on her, aren't you?"

"Yeah, but it's all in Jarai, and I'm going to have to send it back to higher-higher to get a good translation. Going to take a few days, I expect."

"Listen, Hugh, I'm sorry about losing Frank and the others before. You're right. If you're not going back into Laos right away, there is no need for me or Cat here. Get us a bird in the morning to take us back to LZ Bronco tomorrow. I'll call COL Dolby from there and see what he wants us to do. Probably go back up north. But I imagine that anytime you want to start this mission up again, he'll make me available to you."

"That's good," Englander says with the faintest turn of a smile, and he seems to mean it.

CHAPTER 14

But the issue doesn't end there. We get an augmentation of Yard troops from a Special Forces camp on the Song Re north of Téthian. With that influx, Englander's resolve to end the hunt fades, and he determines to make one more try to find the nun.

"Our best lead was in Laos, on the other side of the border from the Khmer Rouge camp. I'm going to take a couple of squads of Yards up there and see if we can pick up the trail," he says. "If you don't mind taking one mare stab at this, I could use your big guns."

Do I want this? It is not the war I know. It is heart-stoppingly crazy, insanity from a crazed man. We should go back to Quang Tri, back to the war we are familiar with. But regardless of what I decide, Englander is going back, and I just can't leave him without the support I can provide.

"You're nuts, man," I say. "But maybe I am too. I guess if you're going back into Laos, I'm going too."

Englander's solemn look flickers into a brief grin. "I think you like this Snake-Eater shit, no matter what you say."

Half a day later, we are back on the ridge overlooking Laos. The unit, with the added Yard troops, is almost up to full strength, and we've brought most of them with us. It is a strong, disciplined force, ready for anything. We think. We had landed stealthily on a peak a click north and walked south down the ridge on the Cambodian side. But our stealth is wasted. We are hit almost as soon as we cross the border westward into

Laos. We have come through a stand of spike-covered silk cotton trees onto an open place on a side ridge jutting down into eastern Attapu. Here, the trail is bare of cover for perhaps fifty meters. The rain is gone, but the air is wet and chilly, the sky clothed in lowering clouds. As our point element crosses the open space, spurts of mud track across the clearing, carrying the beat of a heavy machine gun. It suddenly pounds, and its fire rakes us from a low knob two hundred meters to our west. I am almost to the edge of the open space, and I drop without conscious thought, warning Cat to get down and ducking into the concealment (though no true cover, no real safety or protection) of a stand of elephant grass rimming the open side of the finger. I am already turning to reach for the radio handset from Cat. Things impalpable, bullets from the machine gun and small arms that sound like AKs, crack through the undergrowth, their motion indifferent to the hindrance either the grass or our flesh might cause them. As I watch, the fire slams into the point man, a Yard in his late twenties named Y Beo. It stuns him and sends him staggering back to where he tumbles onto the stony ground, limp and torn. He dies before he can even scream. Also dead in that fire is another young Yard, Y Phor, an M60 machine gunner walking slack behind the point man, who dies without getting off a shot. SSG Pike, one of our A-Team's weapons sergeants, walking third, is also down, and I can see his bulky form fallen behind a high stand of the grass, wounded though still alive and kicking. The enemy machine gun throws gouts of mud across the open space; in its fire, none of our guys is able even to try and get to the wounded. At least three other Yard troops are dead and half a dozen bleeding from wounds, lying barely concealed in the knots of elephant grass that cover much of the open space. I gasp at the machine gun's sound, a slow, clattering *rackety-rack* filling the saddle between us and the enemy from the low knob of hill where the gun is placed. Only a .30-caliber M1919 sounds that way, a weapon long gone from most of the U.S. arsenal (except for the brown water navy's river gunboats), but any of the insurgent forces in these troubled highlands could be using such a decades-old relic of war. No matter. A .30-caliber round from that old gun will kill just as effectively as one from a modern weapon. The cascade of enemy fire continues, our troops answering, waves of crackling small arms fire overlapping.

SSG Pike carries an M60. He and the boyish-looking Yard who is his assistant gunner have pulled themselves back from the open area and are lying in the grass off to the right of the trail about halfway to the space's west side. Englander calls for Pike to shoot, but with only grass for cover, firing would give away his position and likely bring killing fire on him from the M1919. From where he is comes the sound of digging as his assistant gunner begins burrowing them a foxhole.

"How bad are you hit?" Englander calls to Pike.

His voice is strong but hoarse with pain. "Creased my side, Cap, maybe broke a rib or two, hurts like a bastard but not bleeding much," he replies.

From where I am—still sheltered in the grass just inside the tree line—I can see the shapes that are SSG Pike and his AG. I see no way to get to them where they have gone to ground just out of reach.

The old reflexes do not die. The moment the firing starts, I am pressed flat on the muddy ground, binos to my eyes, pushing the tall grass in front of me aside just enough to gauge the likely spot for the target. I feel Cat already slapping the radio handset into my hand.

No one has to tell our Yards or the members of the A-Team to pull back into a defensible position. Though they appear ragtag, I've come to see that they are disciplined, experienced, now giving as good as they get. We have nowhere to go, though. Judging from the volume of fire we are receiving, the force on the knob to our west is large, a company or maybe even more, and likely dug in. Our Yard mortar crew has set up and has been dropping rounds on the likely locations of the enemy, but their fire seems ineffective, the enemy firing on us as heavily as before. Still, Englander has them keeping hanging mortar rounds, figuring it may be suppressing at least some of the potential incoming.

My map shows caves and sinkholes near the knob. If the map's depiction is correct, the terrain will be giving the enemy troops secure cover against most incoming, a significant advantage with us barely dug in here. Seeing our way blocked by that force, CPT Englander immediately orders a retreat east up the finger to the main border ridge, but our rear guard gets no more than a couple of dozen meters before it reaches a clearing we had previously crossed and begins taking fire from the higher border crest behind us. Another force is now blocking our way back into Cambodia. We are hunkered in a thin patch of jungle between those large open spaces. With no way to move east or west, we will eventually be caught between the walls of enemy fire and cut apart.

"Trapped," Englander says, his voice a yawp of frustration.

"What the hell, Hugh?" I ask. "Somebody had to be tracking us all the way to know we would be headed this direction."

Englander looks at me, blinking a couple of times, but saying nothing. Bloops from the knob to our front tell us that whoever the enemy are, they have the wherewithal to hang mortar rounds. The mortars' whistle soon follows, most of the shells falling off the downslope on the north side of our ridge, none doing us any damage. But I know the ambushers will quickly have our range and are certain to correct their aim. It doesn't take Englander's order to get our troops to dig in, half shoveling at the wet, gravely red earth, the other half of our unit keeping up a stream of fire both toward the knob and toward the border ridge behind us.

During the astounding roar of the battle around me, one component of the noise of battle is absent. I hear no soldier of ours screaming or calling from pain or shock or anger. The Yards and the A-Team are almost hushed, a superbly coordinated unit. It is something so strange to try and fathom given all the bad-mouthing I have heard from others about the supposedly cowardly nature of Yard CIDG troops.

Trying to be silent too, I confirm the grid of the target I'd preplanned for this point in our line of march. It is almost exactly on the knob from which the enemy fire is coming. Instinct wrought from past battles had me call in the precise grid of this target earlier this morning along with others that are also obvious ambush points. Whatever, it saves me precious seconds as I pull the radio handset to me, squeeze the transmit trigger, and call, "Carbon Valley Four-Seven, this is Carbon Valley Zero-Niner. Fire mission. Over."

The American-sounding RTO from the battery responds almost instantly, "Carbon Valley Zero-Niner, this is Carbon Valley Four-Seven. Go ahead. Over."

"Roger Valley Four-Seven, shoot my delta tango three, direction five-six-zero-zero, proximity three hundred, Willie Pete up two hundred for a mark, battery two, HE in effect." The RTO repeats the fire call to me. (The proximity is a fudge; we are far closer than that to the target, not even two hundred meters from the knob and perilously close to the eighty-meter bursting radius of the big 155 mm shells.) I look at Englander, who surely knows how close in I am calling the heavy artillery rounds but says nothing, though I have not asked his permission before calling in the fire mission.

"I'm shooting, Hugh," I say. "You mind?"

He shakes his head. "Just do it, man."

Cat is digging us a hole and has it maybe a foot deep in the gravelly soil when a second volley of mortar fire comes in on us, this more accurate than the last. Shallow though the hole is, it offers some cover, and Cat and I are tight together in it as the mortars whistle in. Shell fragments fizz through the grass, and there is a scream from the north flank of our position where one mortar round bursts. That scream and then a fierce wail of "Doc!" break the disciplined silence, an American voice, one of the A-Team calling out, telling me someone has been badly hurt or he would not have shouted.

A third shattering volley of mortar rounds follows, and then over the radio, I hear, "Valley Niner, shot. Over."

I roger shot and bring my binos up to see just where the marking round will go. "Splash!" I hear over the radio, and coincident with it is the sound of an incoming 155 round, a descending howl, the booming *pong* of the white phosphorous round detonating in a huge blossom of pure white smoke exactly above the knob where the enemy are dug in. I squeeze the handset and say, "Target, fire for effect. Over."

"Roger, firing for effect. Out," comes the response.

I don't wait. We are taking fire from above and behind us as well. On my map, the most likely firing point for the other enemy troops is on the peak of the ridge behind us.

"Hugh," I call over to Englander. "I'm going to put some fire on the ridge up there."

The captain is on the radio talking to SSG Hicks, who is working with the rearward platoon of our Yards digging in among the big trees on the upslope leading to the main ridge behind us. He stops and shakes his head as if refocusing. "Yeah, OK, put whatever the hell you can up there. I'm going to get some guys headed back up the trail to open an escape route, but laying some arty on the enemy up there first would be a hell of a help."

I hear, "Shot!" and as I'm calling in my new target up the hill, I hear, "Splash!" and the tremendous roar of half a dozen big 155 mm shells, and the even louder note of the incoming 175s builds, and then detonations erupt on the knob to our west, their bursts enfolding bright hearts of flame, gray smoke boiling over it all. A moment later, a white phosphorous marking round whines in and detonates over the ridge crest behind us. Hicks tells me it is where I want it, and so I call, "Fire for effect," to the battery. Soon, a similar volume of 155 and 175 mm fire wails through to that target, the crash of their impacts echoing down the finger toward us.

We are caught, though. The enemy to our west seem solidly dug in, hidden in the caverns and deep cenotes of the karst topography, so that the artillery I am dropping on them brings only momentary quiet followed by a renewed rattle of machine gun and small arms fire. The two mortars they have been firing at us have gone briefly silent, though, so our artillery seems to have degraded their firepower at least a bit.

MSG Flanagan, who has been with Hicks organizing a defense on the uphill side of our position, comes down the slope and slides down next to Englander into the fresh foxhole one of the Yards had dug.

"We're set in, sir," he says. "Guys are in holes now. We're OK for the moment. But the goddamn pukes shooting at us are going to figure out eventually that we've got nowhere to go and will come down at us. Must be more'n a couple of companies of them, adding up what's up above us and the ones out on that little hill on our west."

Englander is beside himself with frustration because we're stuck, unable to move and even at some risk of being overrun: too many of the enemy up and downhill from us. He's aggrieved enough to consider trying an escape and evasion down the sheer north or south flanks of the finger we're on, hoping maybe to make it out despite how steeply the ground drops off into deep ravines to either side. But the open space is part of a larger open area that wraps all the way across our finger of ridge from north to south. Trying to get down it would expose our troops to fire from the dug-in enemy now shooting at us. *Stuck,* I think again.

Hunched down into the little bit of foxhole that one of the Yards is widening for him, the captain rages about the impossibility of our situation. "We can't get down the ridge to chase the ones that got Sister Bridget," he tells me, saying that if we can't move, we are likely going to have to call for air support and birds to extract us, giving up that chase. "Son of a bitch!" he bellows. "Can't somebody find us a way down this ridge?"

MSG Flanagan calls up from near the edge of the open area, "No chance, Captain. Bastards are dug in good. Enough so even arty isn't able to root 'em out. We aren't going nowhere down there. We need a dustoff to pull out the wounded and the dead Yards. Might as well call for extraction while you're at it."

I'm expecting an exasperated railing about the uselessness of artillery from Englander. In response, though, he just lets out an incoherent moan and fires a long maddened air burst from his M16, bringing a taunting fusillade of return fire from the enemy down the ridge. "Damn it, Oren," Englander calls to the commo sergeant. "Get a hold of Flycatcher (the call sign for the forward air controller the air force has orbiting half a dozen klicks east of us over Vietnamese territory) and get some jets in to drop some snake and nape on the bastards shooting at us from down there. And tell him to get us a dustoff for the wounded."

"Yup, will do, Cap," the commo sergeant responds, and I hear him relay that message to the FAC. Meanwhile, I've been working with the battery to adjust the artillery fire closer in to us a couple of dozen meters at a time to block the enemy from pushing nearer from either side. It gets hairier. At the call of the FAC, a pair of Air Force F-4 Phantom jets soon come rolling from the east. They heel to the south and then swing toward where the FAC has already dived to mark the enemy position west of us with a red geyser of smoke. I hear the tinny radio voice of one of the jet pilots affirm the red smoke, calling, "Roger, got your little girl's cherry." Then, engines booming, both jets swoop north across the ridge, laying down clutches of Snakeye bombs and twin bursts of napalm. The bombs detonate in a "Crump!" that sends multiple overlapping bursts of napalm splashing onto the finger. The jets fire starbursts of white phosphorous with the napalm to ignite it. Their bombs released, they pull into a high fast climb and turn and come around to repeat their play on the high ridge to our east. In the forest on both sides of us, the napalm goes up in a roar, enfolding us in a back and front embrace of fire, the flames licking thirty meters or more into the air. Its heat drives us down into our holes, and in it the enemy small arms fire quickly goes silent. The burning napalm snaps and chuckles in the jungle. Following it come volleys of artillery fire I have called for, dropping right into the heart of the flame.

It seems that the air strikes have silenced the enemy, and our own troops have ceased firing as well. Englander, who moments before had been calling for extraction, is now all for pushing on west down the finger. Cat looks at Englander as he voices that idea and then looks at me, saying warily, "He won't do that, will he, Captain? It's going to be a long time before that napalm dies down enough for us to get through it, isn't it?"

I'm thinking the same thing, wanting to say that we're going to have to affirm our call for extraction, that if we wait for the napalm to burn out, it will give time for the enemy to reinforce their positions.

"It buys us time for extraction," I say to Englander. "Right, Hugh?" With clear reluctance, he nods.

We soon get the call that a dustoff is inbound, flying with the cover of a pair of Cobra gunships. The slap of the birds' blades rises and falls in volume to the tremolo of a beat frequency as their sounds clash and merge. All at once, the first of the Cobras clears the ridge behind us and aims its angular prow at the burning jungle to our west, diving to lick the flaming tree line with rockets and minigun fire as the slick dustoff bird rides down behind it. MSG Flanagan is calling out to the Yards to get their wounded onto the incoming bird. He wants SSG Pike to join them, but the Yards are already adding six of their wounded and another three of their dead to the bird's load. We'll need a second dustoff anyway to take away Pike and two more wounded Yards. Pike and his AG pull back into the elephant grass to hide and wait for that new dustoff.

The slick with the red crosses painted on its nose and flanks pulls pitch into the heavy air and begins to lift. It is maybe two hundred meters into the sky when from the west (from exactly where the napalm had struck) comes the rattle and clatter of a 12.7 mm heavy antiaircraft machine gun. Streaks of purple tracers mark the path of its fire. The stream of big 12.7 mm rounds tracks south toward the dustoff bird. Their paths intersect; there are moans of misery from around us as the machine gun eats away chunks of the bird's hull and gnaws into the engine housing. The bird shudders; its broken blades lose lift. Around me, the moans descend into a gulf of horrified silence. Our troops watch the bird come apart in midair, watch it fall, flame spouting from its turbine, its ruined tail rotor flying apart so that the bird begins a fierce spin, a precession that throws it back down. In that spin, three bodies (whether those of Yards dead or alive, I can't tell) fly away from the crashing bird. From the elephant grass to our front, an anguished Yard voice calls out, "O'i adai!" (Father of spirits!) and others just moan. The sundered dustoff bird tumbles into the deep ravine north of our ridge, billows of flame exploding from its hulk as it smacks the ground, and tumbles over into the depths. I see no way that anyone could live through that crash. Behind the fallen dustoff bird comes one of the gunships, roaring in a steep dive, twin miniguns blazing to try and take out that heavy machine gun, until a second burst from the 12.7 mm gun knocks the Cobra down too. From the ravine north of our finger, there is now a pair of smoke columns, black and stinking of burning oil, rising to merge with the high ceiling of clouds and napalm smoke above us.

Any thought of a further rescue try evaporates as the FAC calls the Phantoms back for another snake-and-nape run, and the second Cobra gunship pulls into an orbit above us, high enough from the battle to avoid more 12.7 mm fire. The Soviets call the 12.7 mm machine gun a *Dushka* (sweetie), but its temperament here seems anything but sweet.

"They're not going to lift us out until they get any survivors from the downed birds out," SSG Dabrowski says. He gets on the radio to the FAC and shouts that our guys need extraction now.

"Roger," the FAC comes back. "No worries. Extraction is on the way. You stay covered until we can see if any of the crews from the downed birds are alive and we can get them out if they are."

"Man," says Englander, listening to the exchange. "Taking care of their own first."

For almost a half hour, we are pinned there between the two enemy units. The Phantom jets are gone, leaving to refuel, but are then deflected to another battle closer to the coast.

It is now in this lull that we realize the captured Khmer Rouge soldier has vanished. Not wounded or dead, just gone. "Fuck!" Englander screams at the news. "Wasn't someone watching him?" But not. He had been walking number four in our file and had gone to ground when the enemy fire started. Now in the sudden quiet, we look. Had he slipped over the side of the ridge and down its steep face somehow? Had the enemy fire been diversion enough to allow him to go forward? Unknown. But without him to show the way, further pursuit into Laos seems pointless. Yeah, let somebody else tell CPT Englander that.

I lie thinking that and watching another brattle of enemy fire come through the trees and watching one of the Yards, wounded in the leg, his pant leg soaked red, rest there stoically, making no noise at all as one of the Yard medics bandages it. The ridge has the stench of heavy battle about it, gunpowder, the sour reek of blood, the fear stink of sweat overlaying a conjoined smell of burning napalm and steaming jungle. Reflexively, I duck into my foxhole again as one of the big rounds from the enemy machine gun whacks into the tree just above my head, wooden shards exploding. I press myself down as if trying to squeeze right into the damp earth, the bullet's crack and vibration seeming to hang in the air. Cat has widened and deepened our hole so that nothing but a direct hit from one of the mortars will do us in, and he crouches now in it, hanging on white knuckled to his M16, his ruck and the radio still on his back, ready in his mind to react fast if needed. He comes up until he can get his rifle out over the berm of our hole and sights it. Around us, our artillery continues to pound.

"Can't see a damn thing, Captain," Cat says to me. "Not a damn thing." None of us can see. The enemy are hidden in the smoke from the napalm and from the bursting artillery shells, invisible to us, though we think we know where they are dug in.

After a while, a second dustoff approaches us from the east, the sound of its coming a distant drone, a bleat in the clouds growing louder as it rides down to us from the sky. I call a check fire to the guns. The bird slips low to the jungle canopy and then drops suddenly to the open space to pick up the other wounded. Somebody once told me that you must be certifiably crazy before they let you be a dustoff pilot. "They go *everywhere*, man, into shit nobody else will fly through," he'd said.

This pilot may *be* crazy, but he is also goddamned good, settling onto the landing place fast, blades still in a powered spin so that he is actually hovering, riding on the ground effect a few inches from the red dirt. SSG Pike and the other two wounded Yards are quickly helped on, and the pilot yanks the dustoff up into the sky and swings hard to the left following the slope of the finger and then straight ahead, dipping down over its northern slope and gone. Seconds later, I hear it *down* below the crest of the ridge, and then its blades blatt in a heavy beat as it grabs air and slips north away from that 12.7 mm machine gun.

"Man, that's some flying," MSG Flanagan says. But I also know the dustoff pilot had been lucky as much as smart, and we are unlikely to be that lucky again if a bigger flight of birds tries to come in and pull us off this killing field of a ridge. As if in response to the dustoff's successful rescue sortie, heavy small arms fire mixed with the plonks of mortar shells erupts again from the dug in enemy west of us.

Hunkered in my foxhole, it occurs to me that I could die here in Laos, die and disappear, chewed up by the war's indifferent maw. I would marvel that there is wonder but no terror in the thought. One day, free of the war, I may well marvel. Today, though, nothing, stripped of all but instinct, all I can do is fight.

It's a standoff. The artillery and air cover keep the enemy from advancing on us, but they are well dug in and have us caught where we can't move their way without getting cut apart. Night would give us cover, but it is barely noon, and dusk is a good six hours away.

"We ain't holding out until nighttime," MSG Flanagan says.

"You've got ideas, let me hear them," says Englander. He's studying his map fiercely, as if he could burn a hole through the enemy emplacements with the heat of his vision alone.

The incoming enemy fire has died away and—save for still ferociously burning stretches of napalm—it seems almost as if we could stroll out onto the trail and head down the ridge away from the battle. If there is incongruity in this, it is that the napalm has kept the enemy from closing with us but has equally ensnared us here. Cat, still deepening our foxhole, looks as if he'd like to dig straight to the center of the earth, perhaps tunnel our way to freedom.

"Once the napalm burns out, I could have the battery drop a pretty good screen of smoke rounds to cover our move, Hugh," I say. "Way that stuff is burning, though, I expect it will be a good hour before the ground is cool enough to cross."

"Damn it," says Flanagan. He peers over the berm of the hole a Yard PFC is still working on. "If we use smoke, it'll tell 'em we're coming. They've got a few mortars still working and can just keep dropping shells on us as we try to cross. And we'd still have to get over that knob where they're dug in. It's worse up top where the dinks have got a good field of fire and easy shots downhill at us."

I know he's right about the smoke as I look at the stretch we'd have to cross to even get to the knob with no idea if there are more of the enemy troops dug in further down the ridge. We've been here long enough for them to start bringing in more troops and mortars to reinforce them.

"Top's right that the smoke isn't likely to be a decent screen, Hugh," I say. "You know, it's no perfect solution, but maybe we just ought to call in every bit of air and artillery we can on the knob and hope it suppresses their fire enough to get birds in to extract us."

Englander looks at his map again. He holds it clenched so tightly in his fist that it is crumpled and damp with his sweat. I know he hates the idea of pulling out from here and abandoning the hunt for Sister Bridget. I suspect he'd like to chance what we might meet if we press on, using smoke and air and artillery, take the risk that we can get through. Damn the risk, damn the possible casualties, just push through, and follow those who have taken her. If we still had the Rouge soldier to guide us, it might be worth a try. What decides him is a pair of mortar rounds that bloop up from the knob and whistle down among us in the patch of jungle. One detonates in the higher branches of a silk cotton tree, sending shards of the tree's spiky bark down on us like a burst of shrapnel. A bark of pain comes from one of the Yards uphill from us, followed by a call for "Bác sĩ!" (I've heard the word enough from ARVN troops to know it means "doctor" in Vietnamese. I wonder if the Yards even have a word in Jarai for that.)

"Fuck," Englander says, "just fuck! OK, Weisman's right. Best chance is extraction. Oren, call in whatever air we can get. Get the goddamn jets if they're around or a Puff if you can get one. Get the battery ready to shoot, and we'll bring in birds to extract us."

Englander is looking at the map again, at how the trace of the landscape on it rises from the south steeply up the side of the ridge where we are and then has a sheer drop-off again to the north, looking at how the dustoff bird had come in low and then skimmed down and away when it took off. It *is* possible. But if the 12.7 catches the birds as it did with the dustoff slick and the gunship, then there are going to be many of us joining the men who had died when those birds had gone down into the ravine.

I tell Cat to call the battery and tell them to get a shitload of rounds ready to support us, same two targets as before, ready to fire at my command. I tell Cat to do it because I want him to have something to do. He's looked better, tougher, the longer we've been out on this mission, but fear is an enemy that can infiltrate anytime, and Cat is still too much an FNG to have hardened himself to it.

He is on the radio for a couple of minutes and then looks at me, maybe a bit proud of himself for this small accomplishment. "They're ready, Captain. They say just give the word."

Englander shakes his head as if clearing his thoughts. He pushes the map toward me, saying, "We're going to have the extraction on our west again. I'm looking at the terrain up the ridge to our east, and the only clear space for an LZ is just two damn close to where those dinks or whoever are dug in." He looks at me as if asking for my confirmation. He rattles the map, pokes his finger at our location, and looks at me again.

I tell him I suspect he is right but that I want to have a look for myself, saying, "It's going to be twenty, thirty minutes before they can get birds in here to pull us out. I want to get to the east a bit and see for myself what possible LZs there are, Hugh. Come with me."

He still looks dopy, angry, and uncertain. "Come on, Hugh," I say.

Finally, Englander rallies himself and grabs his M16, and we slide out of our foxholes and into the space among the trunks of the silk cotton trees. Not wanting to be out of contact for any time in this situation, I motion Cat to come along and bring the radio. The path we had traversed coming down the finger winds through the tightly spaced trees, their gray bark thick with sharp, inch-long conic spikes like large rose thorns. The grove of trees is only about fifty meters across, and we are soon through it to where the rest of the Yards are dug in. SSG Larry Arguello, the other weapons sergeant, engineer staff sergeant Tom Hicks, and medical staff sergeant Michael Olsson are dug in there with them. The open area is as I'd remembered it, a tight twenty-meter space bounded east and west by towering silk cotton trees, open north and south but only to the steeply falling sides of the finger. Up to the east, where the finger intersects the main ridge, is the still burning jungle and the dug-in enemy troops. How dangerous they are is clear when, as SSG Arguello moves to join us, a shot from an AK-47 snaps at him and into one of the trees barely a foot above his head.

Arguello drops down behind the big tree, and Englander and I hunch next to SSG Hicks nearby behind the trunk and thorns of a still larger tree. Hicks asks, "What's the plan, Cap? We going to push these bastards back or what?"

Englander shakes his head. "Nah, I'm going to get a flight of slicks in to extract us while Weisman here calls all hell of artillery down on the dinks either side of us and air hits 'em with everything they've got."

"Going to have to hurry for that, Cap," says SSG Arguello. "Clouds coming in thick now. Pretty soon, we won't have the ceiling for them to fly."

"Dustoffs fly in anything," SSG Olsson calls from his hole a few trees over on the north flank of the finger.

"Man," says Arguello, "extraction pilots ain't got the balls dustoff pilots have. We have maybe a half hour before it gets too bad to fly." He turns to Englander. "You ain't bringin' the extraction birds in on this side, are you? Ain't space enough for more than one bird at a time. Effing dinks will chop them apart if the birds try to come in here."

Englander looks at me as I nod, nods himself, and says, "Nope. We're not bringing them into this place. It's tight as a virgin's twat. Our best bet is the open space on the west. Dinks have a clear field of fire to it, but if we can put enough air and arty on 'em, we can get birds in and out safely."

I know what it costs CPT Englander to say this. His heart is with trying to push on through to the west, to break through and pick up the trail of those who have taken Sister O'Mara. He shakes himself again and tells Arguello and Hicks to get their guys ready to move to the LZ. "When it happens, it's going to be goddamn quick."

Everything is ready, waiting on the flight of six slicks that are coming with gunship escort from Ben Het eighteen klicks to our east. There will be no jets or napalm. The two that had flown for us earlier are working up north and on the coast far to the east near Chu Lai, and with so many dispatched to the battle in the north, no others are available. The real wait is for an AC-47 Spooky/Puff the Magic Dragon gunship with its three miniguns capable of firing a combined eighteen thousand rounds a minute. It's now refueling in Dak To after flying down from Chu Lai.

"Puff will work the shit out of the dinks" is MSG Flanagan's terse comment when he hears the gunship is coming. The real problem is the weather, with still more clouds rolling in from Vietnam to the east and the ceiling dropping. If it stays clear of our ridge, the slicks should have no trouble getting in; but if not, the Cobra gunships and Puff will have a difficult time targeting the enemy with us so close to them.

"Better goddamn hurry," Englander says.

We have been trading sporadic fire with the enemy on the knob now for nearly a half hour when the deep drone of the AC-47's big twin-prop engines becomes audible to the east.

"That's it," says MSG Flanagan. "That's Puff coming in." And we get word from the forward air controller to get ready, that he will hit the knob with a smoke rocket to mark where the big gunship should fire. The Spooky and the two Cobras will then work the area with their miniguns and 20 mm cannon. I will have artillery already hitting the knob and will lift and shift the fire to our east side as a block to the enemy there, creating a space in the air clear of artillery for the aircraft to work.

"Coming now," announces SSG Dabrowski, who continues to be our contact with the FAC controlling the air operation.

I've already given the order to the battery to fire, and we hear a series of booms from our north as the big shells from the 155s and 175s come roaring in. Their fire erupts on and around the knob, and the enemy fire from that location abruptly stops.

"Yeah, pullin' their goddamn heads in away from that arty," Flanagan approves.

There are forty-three of us left including the Yards, me and Cat, and all the Hatchet Team. SSG Greenwood, who was moderately wounded when a mortar round hit one of the silk cotton trees, has been able to work his way back into the trees with us, his wound more serious than he'd allowed, but he's still able to move. Englander has organized us into half a dozen groups for extraction.

SSG Dabrowski passes the word that Puff is ready to make a run, and I grab my handset and tell the battery to lift and shift its fires as planned. "Tell me when rounds are complete on the current target and you have shifted," I tell the battery's RTO.

"Roger, wait one," he comes back.

Everyone is watching me as I hold my right hand up in a wait-for-my-command pose. One final volley of artillery blasts the knob, the battery RTO announces, "Rounds complete, lifting and shifting now," and I drop my hand, signaling SSG Dabrowski to tell Puff and the Cobras it is safe to make their runs.

The noise of it is stunning. From the ridge to our east comes the sudden impact of the shifted artillery fire. God knows how much ammunition they are expending. I'd gotten the word early this morning that the battery has a huge ammo load stocked and can fire all day without running through it. "Shoot the shit out of 'em," the RTO had said. "We got enough ammo to fire forever." With hardly a beat between the end of the artillery on the knob and the start of the fire from Puff, the sound of incoming against the knob is intense. I know the enemy are deeply dug in so that even the napalm on their position had not rooted them out. But I can only imagine what they are feeling as what remains of the jungle there flies apart under the combined hail of minigun fire from Puff and the Cobras.

From the south, we can hear the first of the slick Hueys coming to pick up group one for extraction. It is a lovely display of aerial choreography, the big AC-47 Spooky gunship orbiting high, passing the knob, raining a torrent of fire on it, the Cobras sliding in underneath and just outside the wall of the AC-47s fire, slicing the knob with their own miniguns and with rockets.

One of the troops in the first group tosses out a smoke grenade that blossoms bright purple against the green and char of the ridge, and the first slick slides down toward it, its left door gunner adding his bit of M60 machine gun fire to the storm of rounds impacting the knob. The bird touches down. Almost immediately, the eight men in that group dash out from the trees, across the open space, and begin piling into the bird's open bay doors. I can already hear the beat of the second slick's blades coming from the south when the first bird rises, slides across low as the dustoff bird did before, and heads toward where the side of the finger drops sharply into the ravine. That's when Englander gives out a moan of misery, because, as if there had been no fire to suppress it at all, the 12.7 mm antiaircraft gun begins firing from somewhere on the knob. Its heavy rounds tear right into the first bird's side and blades, and the whole helicopter does a sudden flip forward and tumbles off the ridge and down into the ravine.

"Abort, abort!" SSG Dabrowski is bellowing into his handset, and the second slick, maybe fifty meters from our ridge, abruptly pulls pitch, blades pounding the air like a trip-hammer as it pulls hard left and just avoids getting caught by the 12.7 gun's stream of fire.

"Jesus, Jesus!" Englander screams. "Where the hell is that dink gun? Everybody, back, back."

We know that two Americans were on that first bird, Gary Greenwood and Tom Hicks, along with six of the Yards and the helicopter crew; in all a dozen almost certainly dead. It is impossible to see down into the ravine between our finger of ridge and the one to our north. Runnels of thick fog and now smoke from the crashed Huey fill it. One of the Cobras breaks off from its orbit, goes around to the west of the knob, and dives into the ravine out of the 12.7's line of fire. Whatever its pilot tells the FAC, it is apparently nothing good because there is not even an attempt to get birds down and try to pull out survivors.

The remaining five slicks have pulled high and are orbiting up a couple of klicks of altitude and at least that far to our east over Cambodia. Englander, furious, shakes his head at the horror of the situation. MSG Flanagan, hunched down next to him, says, "We ain't going to get out by air with that 12.7 in action, Cap."

"I know," says Englander. "Looks like we're going to have to go down and get that gun. That's our only way out."

"Gonna be a slaughter," says Flanagan.

"I know," Englander says again.

Hating the idea of it, I tell Englander that I'll have the battery shift fires back to the knob while he plans the maneuver to get over to it.

As we talk, I hear the đại úy on his own radio, shouting sharply in Jarai, "Ră anai, ră anai, ră anai!"

I'm already on the horn ready to give the command to shift fires when, with the đại úy's shout, there comes a hissing detonation from behind the knob, and an oily mist grows just above it. Half a dozen sharp pops follow it. As the hissing dies, I can hear voices from the knob calling in Jarai, "Nao! Nao! Nao! Nao! Nao!" All fire from the knob has ceased, small arms as well as the 12.7. In that sudden silence, the Yard đại úy stands, points to where the slicks are orbiting off to our east, and calls to Englander, "It OK. We can go now, đại úy!"

"What the hell?" SSG Dabrowski asks.

"No, no, trung sĩ, enemy all done. We can go now."

Once again comes the call of "Nao! Nao! Nao! Đuaĭ ră anai!" from the knob.

"Son of a bitch," Dabrowski says in wonder as Englander, seemingly unfazed, tells him to have the FAC send one of the Cobras in to recon the knob. Soon, the angular black shape of the gunship rides down the air above our ridge and slides for a quick moment into view over the knob. "Nothing," the FAC says to us, relaying the description from the Cobra's pilot. "Looks to be clear now."

"Well, fuck me," says Englander, though he looks more impressed than surprised, and he orders the extraction to resume, this time without any enemy interference.

The two Cobras orbit low and warily over the knob. The AC-47 circles higher above but not firing as the remaining five slicks slide in one at a time to pick up our unit. Cat, Englander, and I and the last of the Yards pile onto the final slick, and we lift over the finger. Below, the ruins of jungle are still burning east and west of where we had been pinned. Fog and smoke too heavy to show anything fill the ravine north of the ridge, the graveyard of more than twenty Americans and

Montagnards. I know we or someone will have to come back for those bodies, for the Americans whom, though dead, we will not leave behind and for the Yard soldiers who had walked the jungle with us and died defending us and themselves.

As our bird rises, I see a man in black pants and a green fatigue jacket come staggering out of the jungle near the knob, dragging a rifle. The rifle drops, the man's hand goes to his chest, and he jerks as if shot, jerks again, and falls.

I ask Englander what the hell happened there at the end. What *deus ex machina* had rescued us?

"The worst of the worst," he says. "Goddamn war. The worst of the worst."

"The voices at the last—shouting from behind the knob—sounded just like the Yards with us," Cat says. "Sounded just like them."

Damned if they didn't, I think. *Damned if they didn't.*

CHAPTER 15

The worst of the worst? I want to ask Englander what that is, the question and what I fear is the answer are bubbling inside me. Englander is busy with his team, though, with the wounded as we fly from Laos to Ben Het and then on to the Téthian camp. We arrive in the dark, nearly at midnight, and there is much wailing from wives and family of the Yards as it becomes clear how many of them were left dead in that ravine in Laos and how many more are wounded.

I watch a Montagnard woman leave the shadows by one of the hooches and walk toward the gathered soldiers. The searing light of a propane lantern hanging off the corner of the hooch illuminates her. In that light, her age is hard to gauge, though her lined face and gray-shot hair suggest one who is no longer young. She pulls at the blue kerchief binding her hair, her long skirt swishing, and her arms out as if asking where her man is. One of the Yard soldiers, an older man, his face as lined as the woman's, steps from a group that has just debarked from one of the slicks, sees her and holds out his hand, saying something lost in the roar of the helicopter's turbine as it lifts. Abruptly, I can hear her moaning, standing there, her hands clutching the soldier's.

Behind me, I hear Y Aguăt, the translator, a catch in his voice, say, "*Ñu ron'guă*, she very sad, *gŏ đah ro'ko'I atâo*, her man dead."

It is far from the only such encounter as a dozen other women are told of their husband's or brother's or son's death in Laos. Almost worse, it seems, is the misery of those told their man is gone to the hospital in Chu Lai. They stand and beg the pilots of the birds to take them there, staring in frustration as the birds lift without them. It is, I will learn, the biggest loss of life the unit has had in nearly six months.

"Hugh," I say, "can't you do something? Get a Hook out here to take them to the division hospital . . . something?"

Englander, the rest of the A-Team and Yard soldiers gathered around him, closes his eyes for a moment—maybe there are tears in them—and finally says, "Oh, yeah, Oren, get Bronco on the horn and tell them we need birds or a Hook to do that." Then, looking at no one, he stalks off to the operations shed and disappears inside.

I stand looking around, not really knowing what to do next. Is this mission over? We accomplished nothing except to take out a small Khmer Rouge base in the jungle and to join in a firefight with an undefined enemy, having a batch of our own killed and killing an unknown number of an unidentified enemy just across the border in Laos.

"Are we done, Captain? Are we going back to the battalion now?" Cat asks me.

I just shake my head, not knowing what we are going to do. "Stay here," I say to him, pointing to a bench outside the shack. "I think I heard the Yards are going to bring some food. You can wait and eat that or heat up an LRRP ration. I'll be back. I want to talk to CPT Englander first."

"OK," Cat says. He drops his ruck and radio, settles onto the bench, looks at me for a moment and then leans back against the wall of the shack, heaves a sigh, and closes his eyes. I'm wishing a bit that I could do the same. Instead, I drop my own ruck and weapon next to Cat and head where Englander has gone into the shack.

It is chilly there and dim, the fire down to coals and nothing illuminating the interior of the shack but the lantern light coming in through the open door. Englander is sitting on one of the rickety chairs near the hearth, hunched over, half illuminated, half in shadow, head in his hands. He raises his head toward me as I come in.

"What a mess," he says. "In and out of Cambodia and Laos, nothing accomplished. Bridget still gone, a bunch of ours wounded or KIA. What a damn mess." He picks up a stick that's lying on the hearth, pokes at the ashes, grunts, drops the stick, and looks up at me. "What are you going to do, Weisman? You and your RTO going to catch a bird back to Duc Pho and go back up to where the real war is now?"

He's moved from fury to anguish to depression in a heartbeat. He picks up the stick again, worries at a splinter of the frayed makeshift poker, pulls the shred off, studies it for a beat, and drops it onto the hearth where it smokes, curls, and bursts into flame. I'm tempted to say, "Yeah, I'm done here." But COL Dolby had entrusted this mission to me, and I expect he would want me to stick with it until it is clearly good and over. This doesn't look good, and it sure doesn't look over.

"What's your plan, Hugh?"

"Plan? Nothing so solid. I've left dead back there, and we're going to have to go back and get their bodies. The invasion of Laos is still going on up north, and we've hardly done anything to attract any of the dink forces down here. And Bridget is gone." He stops as there is a sudden swell of chatter outside, and I can hear SSG Dabrowski saying to the translator, "OK, tell the women that a Hook is coming out and will take any of 'em who want to go to Chu Lai. Going to be here in an hour or so." I hear what must be the translation repeated in Jarai, and then the chatter swells again.

"What a crappy war," Englander says.

"Look," I say to him, "I'm in no hurry to go back north. We've still got plenty to do in Laos. I'm going to call COL Dolby and get his confirmation, but I imagine he's going to tell me and Cat to keep on with you, raise some more hell. That suit you?"

He stops and reaches his hand over to knead the shoulder he'd had wounded in our last mission together months ago. He winces at what must still be stiffness and finally nods, "Yeah, that suits me."

"Tomorrow?" I ask.

"I'd rather, but we've got to get our shit together again. If we want to go out at strength, we'll need to take most of the Yards we'd left here for security. But we still need security, so I'm going to ask Chuck Griffin down at the Ba To camp to lend us a platoon and a couple of his team to ride herd on this place while we go back out. I don't imagine we can get all that done and be ready to move before the day after tomorrow." He nods his head as if listening to some private words of confirmation and finally says, "Yeah, we'll do it that way." He stands. "Come on, let's get some chow. Should be something good to eat. Everything's an excuse for the Yards to have a feast, even the news that a bunch of them bought it in battle." He gets up and starts to walk to the door and then pauses. "You know," he says, "you and your RTO did a hell of a good job out there. I'm far from convinced that artillery is the be all and end all you redlegs say it is, but you know your shit and sure put some hurt on the dinks."

"You're welcome, Hugh" is all I can say.

In the morning, the dead come home. The Yards dance them from the birds to the chime of gongs, an achingly sad *di-dong-dii-dong*, men and women of the tribe lined up with hands clasped, man-woman, man-woman step and step to the chime of the gongs. The bodies are lifted so gently from the helicopter, out of a war they never wanted, out of a death so sudden. How do the Yards cope? Before the war, even a single death to them was a tragedy, one so potent that they dissipated it only with the sacrifice of the water buffalo, which are their most valued creatures.

Y Aguăt tells me that such rare death is mourned for years. Buried, the bodies of the dead are surrounded with icons of the spirit demons that Yards believe inhabit all, carved like hardly formed faces into poles thrust into the earth around the graves. How do they cope now when it is not one death but a dozen and when those dead fell far away, their blood part of a distant land, not touching their ancestral soil at all? We Americans, in mourning, etch the signatures of our dead on walls and monuments, weep, say our requiems and our kaddishes, and are done. We relegate our dead to their place, remembered in ritual and tales. The spirits of the Jarai dead remain, they believe, with the Jarai for long stretches, their hearts embossed into the land. With so many gone all at once, no number of sacrificed water buffalo or iconic carved faces is enough, no song of mourning sufficient. The dance goes on all day as the dead find their rest in quiet graves in the jungle, the icons carved and pounded, the fallen committed to the land to live within that new existence into which their spirits pass. The sound and song and dance and world of the living become wise shepherds of their spirits into the breathing soul within the living world.

Tears are lost to the ground. There is a song lying on top of the music and clap of the dance, a song that streams down M Mere's cheeks with her tears. She grieves for her son Y Mor. His body is so burned, she recognizes him only by the little finger of his left hand, broken and never healed straight. She holds that hand and says, "Ho'get? Ho'get?" (Why? Why?) as if it's a prayer. I look at her, but she doesn't see me. She sees only his spirit, the real core of him that cannot be killed or burned, his body a husk, but his spirit everywhere. Music comes from a drum hung on a bamboo pole, a soft plunk of it mixed with the tones of brightly, intricately painted gongs hung on bamboo poles carried between swaying groups of Yard women. Overlaying the music is the scrape of an instrument like a washboard carried by women in long dark dresses fringed with horizontal stripes of color. Men in knee-length robes also with stripes and with long white cords dangling from their shoulders sing, their song almost a chant. Their dance is stately as they bounce from foot to foot, slowly forward and back in time to the gongs and drum. I am also in tears by the time I can no longer stand to stay and watch.

"What the hell happened there, Hugh?"

He looks at me with a bare smile.

I say again softly, "Somebody hit the enemy while we were still searching for how to get out of the trap. It was some unit strong enough to get behind the Rouge or the Pathet Lao or whoever the hell had us pinned down there. Strong enough to smack them so hard that they couldn't do anything to keep us from lifting out of there. Hugh, I thought we were done for. So what happened?"

Englander pokes chopsticks into the noodles and vegetables we are eating, puts a bite of it into his mouth, and chews and swallows. There is a little white fleck of something left in the corner of his mouth that sticks to one lip and then the other as he answers.

"Damned if I know, David," he says. "I thought we'd bought it, caught between those two bunches of dinks. Then, boom, and they are gone, and we can fly out of there."

"Hugh, I'd say we were followed from the beginning. The sniper over by the Vietnamese border, one shot and then gone. Not like he quit but more like somebody took him out. The dead soldier on that tight trail in the bamboo. All those fresh punji stakes. Then that rescue like gods came out of the sky and took out our enemy. I'd say we had a shadow since we left Ben Het."

Englander says nothing, but I see the quick eye widening that denotes sudden concern. I push the last fact back at him, the one that most perplexes me. "You saw that your Yard company commander wasn't surprised at all when whoever it was took out the enemy on that ridge. He called out something and then the bang, and then he just stood there with a smile on his face and said, 'We can go now.' He knew something, Hugh. He's part of your command. Ask him."

At that, Englander sits, pokes his chopsticks into the almost untouched bowl of noodles, stirs them, finally lets them go, and says, "Damned if I won't ask him." He stands, looks around sharply as if expecting the Yard đại úy to be in the hut with us, and then strides outside. Cat peers at me as if to ask why I don't go with him, but this is Englander's show, and I just give Cat a quick smile and headshake. If there is something to tell, I expect to hear it from Englander soon enough.

Englander doesn't come right back, and MSG Flanagan comes over and tells me and Cat that we can bunk in one of the sandbagged hooches the A-Team stays in on the other end of the hill. Rain, which had been fitful thorough the day, begins to come down harder, though even at a torrent does little to diminish the Yards' funeral observance as Cat and I grab our gear and head to our sleeping quarters. No one from the Ba To camp has showed up to reinforce us here in Téthian, and MSG Flanagan tells me it is because of the storm, which isn't going to die down for another day or more, telling me that CPT Englander is not happy about the delay.

"Your captain is wound pretty tight," I say to him.

"Tell me about it, sir. He wants to head out right now, reinforcements or no, but COL Deschenes told him no, told him to wait for the troops from Ba To." He sees my questioning look.

"LTC Deschanes commands the C Detachment in Da Nang we're attached to. Don't know that he and CPT Englander agree on much, but he ain't really our commander, and so Englander can mostly do what he wants. There have been too many KIA in this op already for Deschenes to ignore it, though."

"So tomorrow, then, Top?"

"No, sir. Weather isn't supposed to calm enough to get the Ba To Yards and Snake-Eaters up here until the day after tomorrow."

We sit watching the rain come down in barrels and the Sông Re rise to bank full. It will not take much more water for the river to come up out of its banks and turn our hill into an island. I get a hold of COL Dolby by radio. He sounds genuinely saddened to hear of the deaths our unit has sustained but happy that Cat and I are not among them. As to what Cat and I are to do?

"You're the man on the ground there, Captain," he says. "It's your choice—stay with the Hatchet Team if you think there is enough of a mission left for you to help, come back up here if you prefer. I'll back you either way. The ARVN are getting their heads handed to them up here in Laos, and our artillery units are straining to support them. So we could use you here. But word from G2 is that the NVA know your unit is down there causing trouble and may divert some troops down there to counter you. That would take a bit of pressure off the ARVN up here, which seems a good reason for you to continue the mission. Just let me know what you decide."

I don't have to think about it. If Englander's team is going back out, I'd do best by going out with them again. "If it's OK with you, sir, Private Wilbur and I will stay for a while."

"Sure, good. How's young Pussycat doing?"

"Uh . . ."

"Yeah, David, I know his nickname. Is he holding up OK?"

"He's a tough kid, sir, and is doing really well out here."

"Good, tell him I'm impressed. Look, this was a nasty assignment from the beginning, and at any point you think the danger exceeds the benefit, then you are free to get the hell out."

"Thank you, sir," I say, adding that the ARVN 155 battery supporting us is doing a fine job.

"Ought to be. I've put an American chief of firing battery in there to oversee the guns and a couple of our best FDC troops in there to compute firing data for you." That, I think, explains the American voice on the radio when I communicate with the battery. At that, Dolby is off, having more to contend with than just my mission. He wishes me good luck and tells me and Cat to see him when we get back.

I tell Cat that COL Dolby is impressed with him and watch a big smile spread as he hears it. "Wow, sir!" he says. "Wow."

Everybody but Englander seems content to rest at Téthian while the storm continues to pound. The Yards bring endless meals of fruit, salt fish, rice, and barbecued meat, and pots of a lush noodle and chicken dish that Y Aguăt tells me is called *bahn cahn*, a Yard favorite. We watch the river continue its rise, until by noon of the second day, it spills over its banks and begins a slow spread across the Rome-plowed flats between the Téthian camp and the river's usual bed. The new breadth of river seethes beneath the torrent of rain. In early afternoon, though, there looks to be a slight break in the storm, the sky lightening a bit and the rain slacking off. Englander, whom I haven't seen for nearly a day, comes into the A-Team hooch and sits down on the bunk across from mine.

There is something fever bright in his face, a look of hope-tinctured anguish. "I've got to go back out there," he says. "Will you come?"

"Out where, Hugh, to the ridge to pick up the rest of the dead?"

"No, no, screw that. Top's going to take a squad out for that. There's some intel . . . some intel . . ." He stops. His hands are shaking.

"Yeah?"

"Man, word is Bridget is out there. Maybe not far from the burned Yard hooches. Been there all along. Not in Laos after all. I'm taking a few Yards and some of my team and going out to get her." His hand is still shaking. His look at me now is a plea. "Will you come?"

"Yes, of course, Hugh."

Not so much as a smile from him, but his eyes widen with something like gratitude. "Thanks," he says.

"When are we going?"

"Now, man. Now. Word is we'll have an hour or two with not much rain this afternoon. I've got a couple of birds to take us plus Y Aguăt and a fire team of Yards back to the border ville."

"Jesus, Hugh, I'd think I'd be the last person you'd want along."

"Nah, redleg, you've proved you can earn your keep. We get into heavy shit, I'll be happy to have somebody who knows how to call down the big stuff. Given what's going on, she's probably gone to ground, so we're going to have to hunt around for where she's hiding. Another Yard ville is about a half klick north from where we talked to the old man. Some indigs there may know more about where Bridget is."

"You think Sister O'Meara is still somewhere we can find her? I'd say she's more likely to be in cahoots with them than to be their prisoner."

"Who knows, David? She was damn good to me and to a lot of kids out here in the woods. I know you think I'm an asshole. Most of my own men think the same, and there's a lot of good reasons for them to think that. But I know Bridget. She's on our side. If she's out there, we've got to go and get her. You in for this or not?"

"In, Hugh, no worse than sitting here in the rain. Do we have room for my RTO?"

"Yeah, I'll have them send two birds for us, so we can take your RTO and a couple of more Yards. With two slicks, we'll have room to spare. You could even bring a howitzer along if you want." He gives me a rare grin.

"I'll have one sent out," I say and grin back in an uncommon moment of comity between us.

But in the unpredictability of war, this changes and Cat and I are called back north.

★ ★ ★

CHAPTER 16

In no hurry to get back north to where the real combat now is, Cat and I take a day at what is left of the Eleventh Brigade base at LZ Bronco, going into the adjoining ville of Duc Pho for lunch. For lunch, we find a hole-in-the-wall noodle place called Pho Hoa Nhà Hàng on a tree-covered side street just off Highway 1. It is a strange interlude; Cat and I are sitting at an outdoor table under an overhanging thatched roof, both with bottles of Ba Moui Ba Beer and bowls of rice noodles, vegetables, and chicken in broth. Cat keeps looking around the quiet street at Vietnamese going about their business, peering at half a dozen small shops, his eyes wide.

"We OK here, Captain?"

"I suppose, Cat. VC are unlikely to be out in daytime in this ville right next to the brigade base. Wouldn't want to be out here after dark, though." In the diffuse light from the overcast sky, Cat's red hair looks like a rusty mop overdue for a haircut, but mine is overdue too. Sometimes you get away with such things in war, and sometimes you bump into a by-the-book senior officer who will chew you out royally for hair a millimeter too long or for the merest scuff on a polished boot. Frontline troops like us get away with more than the REMFs, though. We've already been to the Steam and Cream, the steam bath and soft-core whorehouse right outside the gate to Bronco. There we were showered and massaged, and I won't ask Cat what else for him or tell what for me. Rid of the tiger fatigues, we're back in clean uniforms, Cat's from the supply shed, mine from a stock in my locker at arty HQ battery, my name and camo captain's bars, crossed cannons, and brigade and division patches embroidered on the laundered, though wrinkled, shirt. I've kept the boonie cap, leaving my steep pot at HQ. I'll retrieve it and my rucksack tomorrow before taking the bird back up to Chu Lai and then Quang Tri.

Cat turns his attention from the street back to me. "Think she's real, Captain?"

"Real? Who?"

"Sister Bridget," Cat says. He takes a swig of the Ba Moui Ba Beer, grimaces at its sourness, and asks, "I mean, do you think she exists, or is it just something, some fantasy that Captain has? Maybe she's dead. Maybe she's been gone a long time or never really existed."

"I don't know, Cat. Englander is a strange man. Most of the time he acts like an asshole, talking down to everybody not part of his team. But you saw how he acted when he lost men, especially when he lost SSG Rosenbaum. He was stunned, miserable. I think he really cared."

Cat is watching an older Vietnamese man cross the street near us. The man sees us at the restaurant table and just stares, face a mask, but his eyes showing ill will and an undisguised resentment. "The Yards seemed to like us," Cat says. "People here in this ville don't. I think I get why CPT Englander likes being with the Yards, and they seem to like having him and the other Americans around."

"Yeah," I say. I swig the last of my beer. Now silent, Cat seems withdrawn, for the first time wearing the thousand-meter stare of those the war has beaten up. He seems to be looking at nothing now, all sense focused inward. I know the feeling all too well, the sense of danger and misery so great you don't allow yourself to feel it anymore. I nudge him. "Drink up, son, you may never again get a chance to swill down bear this crappy." He smiles weakly. His eyes flick across the street scene around us. He shakes himself as if waking. He says, "Yeah," shakes again, and seems to be back.

Cat and I sit for another half hour on the quiet street, half willing to relax. We pay with MPC (military payment certificates), which the waitress seems happy to accept even though the certificates are not supposed to be used as currency in dealing with the Vietnamese. It has been a quick stretch of time outside the war, sitting watching the street scene. But I am getting a bit of Cat's feeling of nervousness here, just the two of us American soldiers among Vietnamese that likely do not hold any good will for us. We get up, pick up, and sling our weapons (though we've left the rest of our gear at battalion HQ, our M16s go with us everywhere) and take the several block walk back to the gate at Bronco. We walk past a sentry box where the gate guard gives me a desultory salute, feeling the sense of danger lift a bit, though to be honest, we are hardly safer here than on that street in Duc Pho.

Back in Quang Tri the next afternoon, after a pair of long and unpleasant flights through deteriorating weather, I leave Cat at an EM club and go to find COL Dolby.

I walk into the colonel's office, still makeshift, still a shambles of stacked paper and piles of map sheets. It has not changed noticeably in the week Cat and I have been down south. The colonel stands, brushes off my salute, and grabs my hand, a civilian but personal greeting. "Rumors are you did a damn good job down there, David," he says. "Even that bug nuts CPT Englander said so."

"Wasn't much of a mission, sir. We went out to the border, took out a runty Khmer Rouge base camp in the jungle, fought off an ambush, and got flown back to Englander's camp. Went back out to the border with a squad-sized element and got chased down a corkscrew mess of a cave halfway through a mountain. Lost a bunch of good men. Didn't get a dick's worth of intelligence out of it."

"I'm told you got a satchel full of papers in that cave."

"Yes, sir. Stuff from the Montagnard resistance. That's a bunch I hadn't heard about before. It was all in the Yards' Jarai language and still needs to be translated. Hardly worth the pain unless the issues of our mission in Laos and the Montagnard resistance are linked. Are they, sir?"

COL Dolby grimaces and shakes his head.

"Sir, I know we were supposed to be out stirring up trouble to try and draw some of the dinks away from the battle here in Quang Tri. But this turned out to be mostly a personal campaign for Englander to find this nun, Bridget O'Mara."

"I heard about that," Dolby says. He busies himself with straightening some papers and finally looks me in the eye. "Yeah, David, I suspected all along that might be part of what Englander would be doing. Higher command figured that while Englander is a loose cannon, having that as one of the goals of the mission might goad him into action."

"So this hunt for the nun was no secret, except maybe to me and Cat?"

"Yeah, I'm sorry, David. But I don't think your knowing it would have changed things. Would it?"

I admit he is right. "Uh, no, sir, I suppose not. Still, Colonel, I am fascinated at how emphatic Englander was about this Montagnard liberation movement it appears Sister Bridget is tied up with. What I'd gathered from an earlier talk with him is that the OLM had never been a big deal, except maybe for a few bunches of affiliated Yards fighting alongside VC near the border. Still, it appears the evidence that she is closely tied with them is piling up and that the movement is still alive and well. Frankly, it seems inconsistent with her supposedly anti-Communist efforts that had got her kicked out of northern Laos."

"Yeah, I know." Belatedly, he thinks to offer me coffee from the pot brewing in the antechamber to his office. I say yes, and the desk sergeant brings in some, with real cream, a perk for those in higher command.

"So what now, sir?" I ask. "Are you going to want us back down there with CPT Englander?"

"Not as of now, though it remains a possibility. For the moment, I want you and CPL Wilbur to head back to your battalion's firebase on the border. I don't have to tell you the ARVN are getting the stuffing royally kicked out of them. Our bases along the border are about the only thing keeping the NVA from crashing through the ARVN lines and into Quang Tri."

"Yes, sir, and it's Private Wilbur."

"No, it's corporal. What I hear, he did a great job. His time for promotion is close anyway."

"He'll be happy, sir. This was stressful as hell for a kid like him. The last part, he was right next to SGT Rosenbaum when he was killed. Shook Cat up a lot."

"Well, David, leave him here for a couple of days of decompression if you want. And I'll let you tell him about the promotion. I'd like to give you a few days back here too. But the battalion needs you. They're in some deep stuff right now."

"Got it, sir."

"No need to rush out for a bird, though, Captain. The O Club here in Quang Tri cooks up a damn good steak. Have lunch before you head out."

Cat is bemused. "Corporal, huh? Man, I hadn't expected! Wow, corporal."

"Stick here in Quang Tri today and tomorrow, Cat. Get your new stripes sewn on your uniform. I'll see you at the firebase on Friday. Just check in at the ops shack on the pad for a flight."

Later, just before heading to LZ Linebarger, I see Cat coming out of the tailor shop in Quang Tri. Cat smiles and salutes as I pass by. He twists to look at the corporal's stripes newly sewn to the sleeves of his fatigue shirt with mixed pride and wonder. I imagine a promotion to general wouldn't have surprised or pleased him more.

CHAPTER 17

When Cat and I left on our temporary assignment to the south, there had been a large scrap of tarp hanging on the side of the TOC declaring the hill to be LZ Linebarger. Over the time we were gone, I see that someone had added in parens (LZ Gypsy) in honor of SP5 Django Danis' dying here too. Me? I'd prefer that. Django is dead; LTC Linebarger is reportedly recovering reasonably well back in the World. Regardless, I expect we won't be here very long, and Django Danis is far from the only person likely KIA in this mess on the Laotian border. Cat and I had left with the hill raw but well defended. The hill we return to after a couple of weeks is battered squalor, mortar shell holes everywhere, red muck everywhere. Sandbagged cover is over most of the trench lines around the hill; the pervasive smells of shit and gunpowder lie over all. When we'd left, Bravo Battery's guns were out in the open, lightly protected by sandbagged berms. In our absence, the gun crews had put in steeply banked defenses around each gun and dug bunkers into the uphill side of all the gun positions. It makes for good cover but a difficulty in spinning the guns that direction and depressing them for direct fire.

"Comes to that and we need the guns for final defense if we get overrun, a few cratering charges will take the bunkers down," says CPT Patterson with an air of resignation at our situation. "Overrun us, don't overrun us, all the same to the artillery. It may be the grunts' job to keep the dinks off us while we fire in support of others. But we'll damn well protect ourselves if we have to and the infantry can't." It's not so simple as that, as we are learning, with the NVA threatening to roll up the ARVN firebases in Laos and maybe cross the border after us.

I see that gun 4's position is empty. Patterson tells me that it had sustained significant damage from a direct hit with an 82 mm mortar round almost a week ago, blowing its left equilibrator assembly apart and rendering it unusable. It has been lifted out to Quang Tri on the doubtful possibility it can be brought back to health anytime soon. The crew for gun 4 has been parceled out to the other guns. That still leaves four 105s and two 155s, a pretty healthy number of big guns. That's good because there is no replacement for the damaged 105 in all of I Corps. Every available operational gun is already in use somewhere in this mess of an incursion, fulfilling the adage that artillery is never held in reserve. Such are the shortages we are enduring at this ragged end of the war that no replacement for the gun is likely soon.

SGT Morris and 1LT Burke come up to the pad to meet me. Burke, who has been doing double duty as Delta Company FO and temporary liaison officer in my place, is relieved as hell to see me. "Man, Captain, I have to apologize," he says. "I had pictured the liaison crew sitting on its ass all day drinking coffee and moving pins on the map. Your job is real goddamn work. Glad you're back."

He and Morris bring me up to date on the operation and the horror stories about the kind of commander LTC Bowie has been.

"A stupid high-and-mighty type," SGT Morris adds. "Exactly what we don't need around here. Half the battalion is looking to frag him."

"Jesus, what's he done to piss off so many people so fast?"

"It's this small unit bullshit," the sergeant says. "Things only got worse after you left. Look around, sir. You see the perimeter is thin on the hill. COL Bowie has most of the battalion out in the woods around our AO, implementing this crazy notion out of some strategy book that the companies should break up into squad-sized units and conduct nighttime ambushes all over the goddamned place. This isn't ambush territory. We're in a full-scale shooting war here."

"Looked that way when I flew in here," I say.

"Yes, sir, and, worse, because of the crappy way they are outfitted, we have no easy way of keeping track of where all the squads are set in. Most of them don't have any commo. Infantry doesn't even know exactly where all the squads are all the time. Makes it damned near impossible to call in fire close to the hill for fear of hitting one of them. A week ago, LT Hessian got the word to call in a fire mission down on the hillside just this side of the border. Had word there were dinks massing there to come up the hill at us. He called in the marking round and then got nervous because he thought one of the squads might be there. Did the smart thing and called off the mission. Turned out there *was* one of the squads set in an ambush there, no radio, no commo, nothing. They saw the marking round go off up two hundred; that terrified them, and they pulled up stakes and ran like hell up the hill. One guy in the squad broke his ankle, steep as it is there, making it impossible to run. If Hessian had gone ahead and shot the mission, we might have had six to eight guys KIA. Damn nightmare."

The men, he says, are outraged, and LT Burke tells me they brazenly mock the small unit scheme and LTC Bowie. "Hell, Captain, I've been tempted to drop a short round on his bunker myself."

I grab my gear, and we head down toward the TOC, passing a latrine out of which the sharp stench of shit rolls. "Smell that," says Burke. "COL Bowie has so many men out on those patrols that there's no one left to do sanitation like burning the shit. Shit burning may be bad duty but necessary. Out there and up here both, we've got men getting hurt because of his ideas, and we're living in crap up here while it happens."

SGT Morris shows me to the bunker that he and CPL Mallaby and some of the grunts have built for our liaison crew. It is a dugout on the inner flank of a rock outcropping that gives us heavy cover from anything coming at us from downhill. Dirt-filled artillery ammo boxes make up the uphill side, banked with a double wall of sandbags on the outside. Doubled culverts revetted with sandbags form a roof. A Z-shaped wall with its own overhead cover wraps around the ammo box wood door. More artillery ammo boxes make a floor. Below them, brass shell casings from the 105s, their ends hacksawed off, make a drainpipe to move out any rainwater that gets in. There are four cots that CPL Mallaby has scrounged from somewhere (I don't ask). There is even a lamp plugged into an extension cord from the TOC hanging in the center of our bunker. Another piece of cutoff shell casing rises out of the sandbagged roof as a ventilator.

"A regular *palatz*," my Yiddish great-grandfather would have said of it.

Though I'm told the hill gets mortared frequently, thus far today (and in fact, I gather, for the two days before I got back), it has been quiet up here. The skies, though, especially to our west, are swarming with helicopters and fixed-wing craft, and Highway 9 below us running into Laos is an impossible mire. The gridlock is especially heavy where the highway crosses into Laos just north of the point at which the Xe Pon River makes a curve east and then north before turning back west at the border. Somewhere in the encyclopedia of war's article on stupidity, a picture of this mess surely illustrates the word "clusterfuck." Nobody is shooting at us right now, but Bravo Battery has been firing one mission after the other since I arrived back on the hill.

I leave my gear in our bunker and make my way to the TOC up a path heavily strewn with sand to cover the muck. As I walk in, all four of Bravo Battery's operational 105s fire directly over the TOC with a ringing blast. It is dulled by the double layer of sandbags atop the bunker but still is as pleasant as a sharp kick in the head. Inside the TOC are MAJ Echols and CPT Bill de la Croix (the S-3 operations officer). LT Mack McFarlane, only two weeks away from his DEROS when he can, as he says it, "get the hell out of Dodge and back to real food, real women, and no bullshit from bull goose loony colonels," is sitting with a staff sergeant I don't know (his nametag says "Hamlin") at the operations desk. CPL Mallaby is manning our liaison desk. Mallaby is giving what must be one of a string of helicopters the Sav-a-Plane data of where and at what maximum ordinate our artillery is firing. He looks up at me tiredly and tips me a half salute.

"Thanks for covering, Mallaby," I tell him. "Word is you did a fine job."

He grins a bit self-consciously. "Thank you, sir. Say, is it true Pussycat made corporal?"

"Yeah," I say. "But he was due for a promotion anyway. You aren't jealous. I gather you're up for sergeant pretty soon."

"Fuck, Captain. I don't care. Corporal or sergeant, it don't matter. I take the freedom bird back to the World in a couple of weeks."

"Wow, man. I hadn't been keeping track. Good for you. We'll get you out of here before you get stuck on some fucked-up firebase on the edge of nowhere." I grin.

"Never happen," Mallaby says. The guns fire over our heads again, and he seems not to notice. "Nope, sir, never happen."

There is no sign of LTC Bowie, so I look for MAJ Echols to report in. Echols waves me over.

"Major," I say to Echols, "good to see you all survived our absence."

Echols looks up from a log entry he is typing. "Barely," he says. "Things have been rough here. Welcome back, Captain."

"Happy to be back. We'll talk, lunch will be on me," I say, and Echols and de la Croix both laugh. "Where is the CO? I guess I ought to let him know I've returned."

"Hiding in his bunker, I imagine," LT McFarlane grunts. "Probably won't see you. But if you want to try, it's the one used to be the briefing room before the colonel moved in there. Right next to the senior-officers-only latrine."

"Again, Mack?" I say. The first thing I'd encountered when I had landed on San Juan Hill back in August '69 was the one-holer colonels-and-above-only latrine that now-disgraced LTC Flores had had near his sleeping bunker. I'd been warned then that I risked Flores kicking me off that hill if I used it. Some things never change. Maybe I'd even welcome having Bowie kick me off this hill.

Just outside the entry to what is now LTC Bowie's sleeping bunker is a recently built fighting position. A bare-headed PFC I do not recognize is stationed in it, leaning diffidently against the bunker's sandbagged wall, smoking. A fitful wind from the river carries the cigarette smoke away. The fighting position is not oriented to do much good in the event of an enemy attack. It seems constructed more to protect the bunker's doorway.

"You need something, Captain?" the PFC asks as I walk up.

"Just coming to see the colonel. He in there?"

"He's not seeing anyone right now."

"He having a meeting or something in there?"

"No. Just not seeing anybody."

"OK, tell him his artillery LNO CPT Weisman is back on the hill and would like to talk to him."

"You didn't hear me. I said he's not seeing anybody. You ought to go away."

The conversation seems to be a sort of comic nonsense in which the 7/31's commanding officer is not talking to his staff officers and a PFC is able to tell a captain to go away, no "sir," just "go away."

Half of me is tempted to grab the PFC by the scruff of the neck and move him bodily out of the way (surely a bad move as he's got about four inches of height and maybe forty pounds on me). Another part of me is tempted to bellow, "I'm here!" toward the bunker's closed door. But the entire structure is double walled in sandbags, and I doubt he would even hear me. So I look the PFC in the eye and say to him, "Listen, Private, I am CPT Weisman, the artillery liaison officer assigned to this firebase. I want to talk to the infantry CO, LTC Bowie, and let him know I am back from my assignment. So when he comes out, *if* he comes out, please tell him that. Got it?"

"Yeah, yeah!" the PFC says.

And knowing it is not worth the trouble, I say, "When you are addressing an officer, try to look interested and throw in a 'sir' now and then."

"Yeah, yeah," he says, "sir."

It seems a lost cause. Where are they going to send that PFC, Vietnam? He's already here. I head back down to the TOC to the head shaking of most everybody there when I tell the story.

"Been like that for most of a week," MAJ Echols says.

I shake my head back at him, grab a chair, and send CPL Mallaby back to get some rest. I settle in for an afternoon that, except for the uncomplicated task of warning aircraft away from the gun-target lines of artillery in this area, has nothing of substance for me to do.

CHAPTER 18

At dusk, just before evening mess call, LTC Bowie appears in the door to the TOC. Somehow, in this hellhole of a firebase with nothing but supply essentials coming in, Bowie is in crisp, starched, and ironed jungle fatigues; he's freshly shaved, his boots spit shined. For a dozen beats or so, he stands in the doorway watching the operation center's action.

I offer him a quick "Evening, Colonel."

He seems not to notice. He is looking around the TOC as if trying to understand what we are doing here. His gaze passes over me, but I'm not sure he really sees me. "Good," he says. "Good." He turns on his heel and leaves. The blackout-cloth-covered door whaps shut behind him, and the colonel is gone.

"*That* was strange," I say.

"Does that every night about this time," 1LT McFarlane says. "The man has no recent combat experience or smarts. Doesn't belong out here."

"Does brigade know?" I ask.

"Man, look at what is going on outside. You think brigade cares?"

It is maybe an hour later; most of the TOC crew are eating a crappy hot meal at their workstations. The last of the day has been preternaturally quiet, no incoming fire, no reports of action from any of the battalion's companies, and squads scattered around the hill. Only the infrequent spitting of Bravo Battery's howitzers and the faraway sound of automatic weapons fire along the highway below us break the calm of the evening.

The detonation is strange, deep, a growl more than the jangly crash of a mortar shell. The shock of it seems to drive all the air out of the TOC.

"God!" 1LT McFarlane yelps. "What the hell was that?" He jumps toward one of the firing ports cut into the top of the conex's walls.

"Are we being mortared again?" asks SSG Hamlin, who's been seated next to McFarlane.

"I don't know," MAJ Echols says. "Whatever it was, that was no mortar round. More like a satchel charge or something."

"Can't see shit out there," McFarlane announces, standing on sandbag steps and trying to look out through the port.

But with all the officers in the TOC, it is SSG Hamlin who acts. "Maybe sappers, got through the wire or something." He turns to the SP4 seated at the hill's internal radio net station at the back of the TOC conex. "Toby, get a security squad up here from Alpha Company. I'm going to recon outside." He grabs an M16 from a hook on the wall next to him. I pick up my own and head out the front door with him.

The light outside is fading into true night, but it is still bright enough to see that everything outside the TOC is quiet. SSG Hamlin ducks into the sandbagged culvert that is the fighting position next to the TOC's door. I slide around the side of the bunker, my own rifle ready, set on semiautomatic, a round chambered. Still, I am thinking that if dink sappers are out here, this is a terrible idea. MAJ Echols has come out behind us and has slipped around the other side of the bunker. We meet at the back, calling "friendly" at intervals to let anyone seeing us know not to fire.

"Nothing," Echols says.

"Same," I say back.

From a few meters to our right, I hear LTC Bowie's voice, raspy with agitation. "Major, what the hell was that? Are we being mortared again? Is that you, CPT Weisman? You're artillery. Do a shell hole analysis. I want to know where that mortar round came from." Startled at Bowie's sudden appearance, it takes me a beat or two to realize what he has just asked me, the ignorance of it. "Sir," I say, "I'll check it out. But if it is from a mortar, the round was coming pretty much straight down when it impacted, so there is no easy way to determine any more than a general direction."

"Do it anyway, Captain. I'd hoped the mortaring was over. I want to know if they have another tube set up to hit us."

There is another noise, the sound of running feet, and I am raising my rifle when I realize it is the six men of the security squad coming up from the line. Seeing Echols first, the sergeant who's the squad leader asks, "Major, whatcha got?"

"Some sort of boom," says Echols. "Out here, maybe on the north side of the TOC. The colonel here thinks it was an incoming mortar round."

"We'll check it out, sir. You stay put," says the sergeant. The squad moves off, and a few minutes later, I hear the sergeant exclaim, "Goddamn, look at this!"

"This" turns out to be LTC Bowie's senior-officers-only latrine, that part of it that is left anyway. Something has blasted half the back of it off, and the rest has fallen over. The sergeant has his flashlight aimed at the wreckage, and he walks over to it and reaches out gingerly to pull open the remains of the door. He aims the flashlight beam into what is left of the structure. "Nobody in there, thank God," he reports.

Echols and I walk up to join the squad. From the way the latrine seems almost chewed apart, it is instantly clear to me what has happened. "Claymore," I say. "It looks like it was set up with this tripwire to go off when somebody walked up to the latrine." I point to the shredded mud in front of the blasted latrine and the sad and bloody remains of what had been a yellow dink dog, one of several half-tame dogs wandering the hill. "Looks like this pup set it off."

"Man," MAJ Echols says. "Somebody had this set to frag whoever went into the latrine. Colonel, since you have this off-limits to everyone not a colonel or above, it looks like it was set up to frag you. Might have got you too if the dog hadn't tripped it."

I expect Bowie to fly into a rage at the idea of someone trying to kill him, but he seems stoic about it, maybe resigned, saying, "Damn, get somebody up here to tear this thing down and cart off that dead dog. Damn." He walks off toward his bunker, ignoring us. I look at

MAJ Echols, who stares back at me and raises his hands in a gesture of "Who, me?"

This is crazy. I follow LTC Bowie back to his bunker. There, the PFC in the fighting position (who doesn't seem to have moved despite the claymore going off just on the other side of the bunker) raises a hand as if to stop me.

"Leave it alone, Private," I say. "I'm going in, guard or no guard."

The PFC's eyes widen as if not sure what to do. "Let him pass," Bowie says. The PFC shrugs and steps back. I follow the colonel into his bunker.

Inside, it is like a monk's cell: a cot with blanket and pillow, a footlocker without a lock, a small table with a single chair, and a coat rack where half a dozen sharply pressed uniforms hang, a helmet, web gear, and an M16 are stacked in a corner. A bare lightbulb, its cord running toward the TOC's generator, hangs from the ceiling. There is nothing else here, no personal photos, none of the mementos of home or trinkets a military man usually accumulates.

The colonel walks in before me, pulls out the chair, and sags into it. The cot, precisely made, seems not a place to sit, so I stand.

"Somebody tried to kill me, didn't they?" Bowie asks.

No point in varnishing it, I think. I'm burning inside to tell him a sharper truth, but I say only, "I have no doubt, Colonel."

He flounders, waves a hand, and looks down at the tabletop. I realize that he truly doesn't know what has brought things to this head. Though I am seething at what has likely caused this, I am thinking I should keep my mouth shut. No matter, I'm not part of Bowie's battalion but an advisor from an artillery unit, out of a different hierarchy. Everybody else on the hill from MAJ Echols down is in LTC Bowie's chain of command. That leaves only me, an artillery captain, to tell this lieutenant colonel why every grunt in his battalion, from major to buck private, hates him. I decide I'm not going to, that it will do no good, when Bowie raises his head and looks at me with a miserable sense of bewilderment. I realize it has to be said.

"Colonel," I say, "what we're in here on the border is a combat shitstorm. Nobody who's in this battalion now has been in a fight this big lasting this long. The war has been winding down. People have been thinking about home, about freedom birds lifting off from these shores headed back to the World. Then this."

Bowie starts to say something, gives his head a shake instead, and just frowns.

"Sir, they are, to a man, scared as hell. We've seen far more casualties in the past month than the battalion saw altogether in the six months before." I stop. He watches me. Am I going to tell him? One turning of it would be to say that the men need some relief, some easing of the tactic, some leeway. That would be enough. I think he would accept that grudgingly. But it is not the truth and would only stave off disaster. The truth is that the men hate this colonel because he is an armchair warrior, applying a dubious, untried tactical theory to a practical situation with troops not ready for it. They want him done and gone. The blown-apart latrine says at least some want him dead. I have to say it because no one else will.

"Sir, when I stepped back onto this hill this morning, I knew something was different. It only took my talking to a few of the men here to get what it is."

Bowie starts forward at that. "Talking to . . . to whom?"

"Sir, that's beside the point. Names won't help. This needs to change. The small unit tactic isn't working. It's not wrong. In another place and time, with opportunity to train in it and equip the men for it and organize your command structure for it, I suspect it would be a major contribution to the war. But not here."

"What the hell does an artillery officer like you know of infantry tactics?" the colonel demands, suddenly alert, trying to divert the conversation. I won't let him.

"Yes, sir, that's right. I'm artillery, not infantry, but I've spent enough time in the bush and on forward firebases and out in the field with the infantry to know when something is going to blow up on us. From what I see here, things are only deteriorating. The ARVN are getting whipped. Their advance into Laos is at a dead stop. I imagine it won't be long before they turn tail and run back into Vietnam. On this hill, the 7/31 is right at the danger point where the NVA are most likely to try to punch through into Vietnam and chase down the ARVN. We need this battalion in top form, ready to stand our ground when that NVA push comes. But chopped into these squad-sized units, scattered helter-skelter on this mountainside, they are only positioned to get chewed up if the NVA come through."

"It's that pig thing, isn't it?" Bowie asks. "It's that time I made that slovenly soldier get down and crawl like a pig. They hate me for that."

"Yeah, that royally pissed them off, Colonel. They wouldn't like you much for just that, but dignity was the only thing hurt there, and they would have gotten over it. This is much bigger. The men are afraid you're using a tactic that puts them in jeopardy without the wherewithal to really fight. My advice, captain to colonel, sir, is change things now." I am afraid I have said more than Bowie is willing to hear and that he will order me off the hill. That's nothing that will cause me any harm with my artillery commanders. I haven't been insubordinate; I'm just doing my job. The colonel—in attitude, if not in so many words—asked for my opinion. But off the hook for that or not, I still don't want to leave people here. If I leave, I'll be parting company with the 7/31 at a truly bad time.

LTC Bowie is quiet. He rubs his hands across the rough tabletop as if smoothing a nonexistent tablecloth. "Oh, man," he finally says. "That's right, isn't it? That's right. Oh, man." His look is of surprise, even amazement as it sinks in, and in it he is not seeing me anymore. I pick up my M16 and say, "Good night, Colonel." (He doesn't acknowledge me.) And I go out. It is almost fully night, the TOC a darker shape against the cloudy sky as I make my way back to it, wondering what happens next. I look back once more at LTC Bowie's bunker, closed, silent, impregnable.

CHAPTER 19

The voice on the radio—2LT Archie Hollingsworth, my forward observer from Charlie Company—is frantic. "Harsh Angle Two-Seven, this is Harsh Angle Three-Niner. I don't know what to do. I've got a squad that's trapped. I can't see to shoot for them. They're in heavy stuff, getting hit. We've got no commo with them. I think they're across the border in Laos. I want to get them some arty. I can't see to shoot. Can you help? Over."

CPL Mallaby, sitting at the artillery station in the TOC with me, grabs the handset. "Angle Two-Seven, roger, can you give me a grid for the squad?"

"Angle Three-Niner, my best estimate of their grid is six-seven-zero-zero, four-one-two-five."

"Jesus," I say; a quick glance at the map confirms what I don't really want to know. "Oh, man, if that grid's right, the squad, as Archie said, is across the border into Laos by almost half a klick. Let me talk to him, Scott." I take the handset from the corporal. *Not good, not good,* I'm thinking. I call him back, "Angle Three-Niner, this is Angle Two-Seven Actual. Is that grid confirmed? That would put them five hundred meters into Laos. Over."

There is silence on the other end for a few beats, and then Hollingsworth comes back apologetically. "Three-Niner, I believe that's affirm."

"Roger, Three-Niner, wait one." I see MAJ Echols watching. "Major, are you hearing this?"

"Yeah, they've got a squad that somehow got across the border. Wow!" He and SSG Hamlin quickly huddle over their map. "Dammit, if that's the grid, they *are* in Laos. Charlie Company's got squads scattered all over east of there. That one must have pushed too far west." He grabs the infantry com handset and calls the Charlie Company CO. I hear only MAJ Echols's end of the conversation as he works with CPT Griffin, trying to see if there is a quick way to get to the trapped squad. "Nobody near?" Echols says, more a confirmation than a question. "Can you talk to them? . . . Goddamn, no radio, no commo with them at all? . . . If they don't have commo, how do you know they're in trouble? . . . Squad of the Second Platoon's got a visual from a hill to the east? . . . Ah, Christ . . . Yeah, get somebody moving to try and pull them out. I don't care if it is in Laos or not. Get them the hell out of there." There's a break of a couple of beats, and then Echols tells SSG Hamlin to get him the battalion C & C bird from Khe Sanh. "Right now! I'm going up. Gotta see what kind of shit they are in," he says. He is already up and heading for the TOC door.

"Me too, Major," I say. "I can't see to shoot for them from here." I tell Mallaby to have Bravo Battery put a marking round up over the grid where we think the squad is. "Just a Willie Peter up two hundred as a mark. Nothing on the ground. Just one for now until you hear from me again. Maybe that'll shake up the dinks enough for them to break contact."

"The C & C bird is cranking up now, sirs. ETA ten minutes," SSG Hamlin tells us.

"Good," I say. "Angle Three-Niner, this is Angle Two-Seven Actual. We're going to observe from the air. I'm going to put a marking round over that grid to get the dinks' attention."

"Roger," Hollingsworth comes back, relief in his voice.

I grab my flight helmet, my web belt with canteen, my M16, and a bandoleer from where they are hanging on a hook near the TOC entrance and start to follow MAJ Echols out. (Time was I'd have carried only a .45 for aerial observation. I'd done that until the time the damn pistol had jammed on me at a critical moment. I'd learned my lesson. Now, on every flight, I take the kind of gear I'd want with me on the ground. I even have a heavy damn PRC-25 radio on a pack frame waiting at the pad for me to take along, so I'll have commo to shoot regardless of the situation.) I turn long enough to tell CPL Mallaby to get a runner to go find SGT Morris and have him take my place at the arty station. My intuition is that this is going to be a super clusterfuck with a squad stuck where it shouldn't be in Laos on a hard to get to piece of high ground, without any commo and under attack by an apparently large unit of the enemy. Worse, there's only been a quick visual report from another squad of Charlie Company; nobody has had direct contact with the squad since the firefight started.

That's news straight out of a combat freak show, but the strangest is that standing at the TOC entrance—hand out to stop me and MAJ Echols—is LTC Bowie, whom we haven't seen in a full day, an extraordinary apparition in a starched and pressed uniform, like a figure out of a recruiting poster for anther war entirely, one neither mad nor dangerous. "I'm going," he tells us.

MAJ Echols stops cold and stands looking at his commander with an expression approaching wonder or just plain stupefaction. "Sir?"

"Yes?"

"Uh," says Echols, grinning unhappily, finally saying, "Uh, you have gear, sir? You'll need your flight helmet and a weapon."

"I'll be OK," says Bowie. He pats the .45 on his hip. "This will do."

"Helmet, sir?"

"They'll have one on board for me," Bowie says.

I know no such thing. But he is still the commander.

"The bird's cranking up over at Khe Sanh. You should get up to the pad," SSG Hamlin calls over to us.

"Yeah, let's go," Echols says to me, ignoring the colonel.

LTC Bowie keeps up with me and MAJ Echols as we run up the trampled red-mud path toward the helicopter pad on the summit of our hill. One of Bravo Battery's 105s, pointed toward the west-northwest, spits right over our heads with a ringing bang. I see Bowie start at the report of the gun's firing.

"The target's only three klicks from us," I tell him. "The bang should be now!" Off over the distant jungle, I just make out the puff of a white phosphorous round detonating. Unbidden except by habit, the count between flash and bang comes into my head, nine seconds, three klicks away almost exactly.

A Shepherd to Fools

We have only a few minutes to wait in a sheltered fighting position near the pad before the pad master, a bear of a sergeant first class, comes out to tell us, "The Charlie Charlie bird is inbound, sirs, coming in from the east, about two minutes out."

The sky around LZ Linebarger is unusually quiet this early morning. Though lots of birds are overhead, they all seem to be high up, heading well into Laos to support the unraveling ARVN units. Also, far off and hollow sounding are the rattles of small arms and heavier concussions of fire from armored units, the rips of minigun and rocket fire from our supporting gunships in the air where over we are not supposed to go on the ground. There is a strange sense of desperation about the battle noises, the feeling of one last titanic push west before all energy gives out and the ARVN troops come back, tails between legs in hell-bent retreat.

The approaching beat of helicopter blades sounds above the higher hill to our east, and soon our bird appears. It is not the usual slick tricked out as a command-and-control vehicle but a much smaller observation helicopter, the note of its blades pitched higher, a bumblebee buzz rather than the louder blat of the Huey we had expected.

"It's a damned Loach," MAJ Echols says. "Sergeant, where's our regular C & C bird?" he asks the pad master.

"I don't know, sir," the sergeant replies. "Brigade's been short on birds. They lost a couple already this morning. This is what they've got for you, I guess."

The little helicopter comes skittering out of the sky, dropping toward us quickly across our perimeter and into the revetted space of the pad. The noise of its blades fizzes in that space as the little OH-6 Loach flares for a landing into a ripe streamer from a red smoke grenade the pad master has tossed out. The bird settles fitfully, not quite setting down, bobbing almost into a hover, ready for a quick getaway.

"Just three seats," says Echols—meaning, two plus the pilot's. He starts to climb into the front seat next to the pilot. I have grabbed my radio from the pad master's shack and come around to the bird's right side to board. I prepare to slide into the rear seat beside the mounting frame and ammunition can for a minigun that hangs next to the bird's left skid. I realize Bowie is standing there watching, evidently expecting to have one of the seats. The principal reason for us taking to the air is for me to have a view from the sky of the battle scene to be able to call in artillery fire if possible. I'll be damned if I'm staying on the ground. MAJ Echols is already in the left front seat and buckling in when I hear over the noise of the rotors the colonel say loudly, "Get down, Major. I'm going." Stunned, Echols turns to look at me.

"Out," Bowie says again, but Echols, acting as if he doesn't hear the colonel, tells the pilot to "just fly."

LTC Bowie is standing on the left skid so that the bird can't take off without dumping him off, possibly to his death, so the pilot just hangs the bird there anxiously, looking to see who will be getting in. Bowie leans across MAJ Echols and grins smugly at the pilot, a young warrant officer named Riggs according to his name tag, who just looks confused. "I'm flying here," Bowie tells the pilot. "Major, get out."

Echols looks at me again, shrugs, and blurts, "Dammit, fly, then, Colonel," and climbs down to give Bowie his seat. Bowie, that strange half grin still on his face, clambers up into the front seat next to the pilot, straps in, and then says, "OK, go."

There is a small command console jury-rigged between the front and back seats, and I reach for the cord to jack my flight helmet into it. It is a moment before I realize that MAJ Echols has taken his flight helmet with him, leaving the colonel without one. Somehow, it seems better this way, as if LTC Bowie, though in the C & C bird with me, will still have no say in what we do up here. But the pilot has a spare helmet to offer Bowie, one battered, greasy looking inside, and well-used. I see the colonel eye my helmet for a beat, quickly get the message from me that I have no intention of giving it up, and fussily pull on the one the pilot offers him. We rise quickly, hopping up and grabbing the air in an almost frantic climb away from the dangers of the ground. The sky this morning is full of heavy white cumulous billows shouldering aside the blue. In the angled light of the recently risen sun, the battered trunks of teak trees cast long shadows across the hills. We fly well up over the trees, the pilot carrying us to a significant altitude, maybe three thousand meters, trying to avoid the ground fire that has taken down several other birds in the past week. Our flight path to the northwest parallels a low ridge that delineates the border here. We are east of it over heavily forested hills climbing into Vietnam. West is the broken landscape of Laos, a tangle of small hillocks overgrown with jungle running north from the Xe Pon River, another tangle, this of little rivulets, running through the hillocks. The ridge where the squad of Charlie Company is apparently in contact is a klick and a half further north on the flank of yet another heavily jungled mountainside.

As we fly, I have my helmet switched into the multiband connection, listening to CPT Griffin, clearly thinking he is talking to MAJ Echols, saying, ". . . asshole Bowie's fault I've got squads scattered to hell and gone. Most with no commo. It was only a matter of time before one strayed across into Laos. Goddamn asshole colonel. I'm sorry he wasn't in that latrine they blew, scattered an extra big pile of shit there. I lose these guys, I may just kill the son of a bitch myself." I see Bowie, clearly already jacked into the battalion push, stiffen at that. I can't see his face, but his neck reddens at CPT Griffin's profane assessment. I half expect Bowie to break in and ream his Charlie Company commander, but nothing. I click over to the artillery push so I can talk to 2LT Hollingsworth without all the other back jabber that's on the multiband. Doing so, I try to get my bearings and obtain a fix on exactly where the squad is located. "The jungle canopy is heavy from above, Archie," I tell him. "I see the ridge where you say the fight is, but no sign of troops on the ground. Over."

"Roger, I am about two klicks away to the east and have no visual of it either," Hollingsworth tells me. "A squad of the Second Platoon with a radio is on a peak about twelve hundred meters east of the squad's position. They say they see movement on the ridge and what looks like two of our guys. There's still no commo with the squad that's in contact."

"Ah!" says Bowie, apparently listening in. He clicks over to the infantry push on the bird's com console and calls CPT Griffin, his voice gruff, but more resigned than angry, as if what Griffin had said about him has sunk in. "Do you have people moving toward there to pull them out of this situation?" he asks.

I've put myself back onto the multiband connection so that I can hear both the artillery and infantry conversations. I hear CPT Griffin say, "Roger, two of my squads from the First Platoon and a squad of the Second are moving that way. The terrain is really treacherous there, though, with another steep ridge and a big swampy canyon between them and the ridge on the border. Then another canyon before they can get to the squad that's in contact. Ground to the south is also a nasty swamp."

"Swamp or treacherous terrain, hell," says Bowie. "You get them in and pull that squad out. Do it now, whatever it takes, you understand, Captain?"

I believe it is only then CPT Griffin realizes he is talking to LTC Bowie rather than MAJ Echols. There comes a significant pause as the Charlie Company commander must be thinking that Bowie had overheard his earlier diatribe, finally Griffin says, "Roger, understand. My elements are moving that way as fast as practicable."

"See that they do," says Bowie curtly. "Out!"

We are maintaining about three thousand meters of altitude, orbiting just inside the Vietnam side of the border over green deeply wrinkled hills. Though I still can't see the actual firefight below us, I have a good fix on the ridge where the embattled squad appears to be located, and I've been scanning the nearby jungle for any possible openings big enough for us to insert troops for a rescue. But nothing. The jungle is heavy and deep for klicks around, a canopy too thick to see through. The nearest open space big enough to set down birds is nearly two thousand meters further west on the rocky reverse slope of a towering peak. Given the harshness of the terrain, that's a good couple of hours trek for anyone put down there. A bigger problem for me is that I have absolutely no visuals on any combat on the ridgeline where the squad of Charlie Company is supposed to be in contact. I have no idea if the marking round I had called in earlier had had any effect on the battle. The flaws of Bowie's scheme to put individual squads out by themselves, mostly without a way to contact either their parent company or the battalion TOC, are a disturbing reality here. Maybe the colonel sees it the way CPT Griffin had described it, and if he does, I half hope he feels the same panic the troops down on the ground must feel. No matter: troops are in jeopardy and we need to get them out.

"Mr. Riggs, let's go east a bit and down and see if we can get a lower angle with a clearer view of the ridge from there," I tell the pilot.

"Will do," Riggs says, and we start a turn to our right, flying further away from Laos and closer to the grid location we have for Charlie

Company's command post. They are set in on a lightly wooded knob about two klicks east of the border, and we are less than halfway there when LTC Bowie, mostly silent up to now, abruptly barks, "Down, I think I see them. Turn and go down. That way, that way to the west! There, across the ridge, don't you see them?"

I don't know *what* the colonel sees. We are well over Vietnam now and not in a position yet to see the ridge from the same good angle the unit on the ground has.

"What?" I say. "I don't . . ."

But Bowie is insistent, punching Riggs on the shoulder and pointing west toward a ridge across the border that may be where the unit is in contact. We bobble in a briefly unsettling lurch as the warrant officer loses a bit of his grip on the collective. He looks at the colonel with open astonishment, shoves the offending hand away from his, and regains control of the bird's pitch, making a long turn to the west across the border.

Whatever the colonel is pointing at, though, seems to me to be well north of the location 2LT Hollingsworth had given me for the squad and several hundred meters further into Laos. Incredibly bleating, "Go down, Mr. Riggs. That's them. I see them," the colonel again grabs at Riggs in a wild gesture, this time knocking the pilot's hand entirely off the collective. I shout, "Colonel, no!" as Riggs grabs for control again, but the brief lapse of pitch has dropped us a couple of hundred meters and caused us to slew across the border and over Laos. As the pilot begins to pull up again, a stream of tracers rises toward us from a high spot in the jungle, purple blots marking the path of heavy rounds from a dink 12.7 mm AA gun.

LTC Bowie is screeching, "No! No! No!" as Riggs yanks on the cyclic to power us away from the stream of projectiles. If the blare of Bowie's panic alone could carry us out of danger, we would be fine. But a heavy 12.7 mm round catches the windscreen in front of the pilot with a snap like breaking bone. A sharp spider's web of a shatter pattern crazes it. Whether hit or just stunned, Riggs sags and lets go of the controls entirely. We pitch over, begin to spin, and go down.

I can see little but green, blue, and white whirled together in my vision, overlaying it the sickening sensation of the Loach gyrating out of control and dropping toward the jungle. There's again a babbling of "No, no, no-no-no-no-no-no!" probably from LTC Bowie. I can't see if the pilot is conscious; his hands have fallen away from the bird's controls, the bird's engine losing power. We tip sideways, the view outside the door to my right is not of sky but of hills and a stream rushing at us. And unstoppably down. The bird's rotors rattle and blatt into tree branches, a storm of leaves flies around us, a tilt, a jolt, a crunch and shudder, my helmet slams the com console. One of the console's supports lashes across my faceplate with that blow, with it an image briefly still, bright, green, and unfocused. Down, the bird's engine roars and dies, the bird settles, the stanchions beneath its metal skin moan. The little bird settles further. We are down.

★ ★ ★

CHAPTER 20

You sit. At first, it is dim, and it seems you cannot move, and you listen to metal creaking and the sounds of the hot engine dying. You are quiet, listening, breathing, numb, head full of a dull pounding of pain, ears still ringing with the crash's final sounds, the slap of branches and the crack of trees splintering. You sit. The world has grown so small, shrunk to just the throb of a raw ache swelling in your left wrist and side. A breath scalds you. You sit. You move just so, raising your left hand, and the burn in your wrist is fierce. You come back from dizziness that boils away, come to light, thought beginning again, realization. We've crashed. When the creaking of the bird stops, the crackle of its cooling engine stops; it is so quiet.

I am still strapped into the back seat. A sharp sting tells me my left wrist is injured, maybe broken; the pain when I move it is nauseatingly fierce. When I take more than a shallow breath, my left side also shrieks with pain, and I am certain that means I have broken ribs too. The blur of my vision is from the cracked faceplate of my flight helmet. Yet the helmet itself has done its intended job, keeping my head intact. The pain in my head is thankfully subsiding. I grope down with my right hand to find the seat belt latch. I pop it and feel a sudden release of pressure. It is a moment before I remember LTC Bowie and WO Riggs.

"Colonel?"

A moan, wordless.

"Mr. Riggs?" Not even that.

I realize that I'm not thinking well, that the dinks must be aware our bird has gone down, that we have to move. At that, I wonder if I can even move, fearing that motion will reveal injuries even more serious. But nothing hurts in my legs or back, only the left wrist and my ribs on that side (*Both wrist and ribs broken,* I think fearfully again). So, gingerly resting my weight on my right arm, holding my left wrist carefully away from the seat and the bent ammunition container for the minigun (it is probably that that injured me as I bashed into it), I maneuver myself out.

The colonel moans again. Inside, past my own blaze of pain, I am raging at the colonel, the idiotic, ignorant, thoughtless colonel who had been so stupid as to grab the pilot's hand away from the collective. The 12.7 mm AA gun had sent us down, but we wouldn't have even been in its sights if the colonel hadn't distracted the pilot.

We have smashed through the jungle canopy and down onto the undergrowth, likely invisible from above. Canted as we are, it seems we are on a precipitous hillside, the left flank of the bird half buried in red dirt and jammed into the underlying limestone. The ground on the right falls away into a wooded gulch, just how deep I cannot tell. The door on the colonel's side has been sheared away, the minigun gone with it. The colonel himself is partly covered in dirt and debris. I don't know if anyone is even aware that we have gone down, and if there will be any search soon enough to be of help. Certainly, nobody close knows we are down or there would already be the beat of rotor blades above us, the sense of somebody searching. Looking up, I can see nothing but branches and leaves. We are well below the jungle canopy, which seems to have closed over us as if healing the wound of our entry.

"Shit," I say, just to hear a voice, "shit, shit, shit, gotta get away from here." And I look over at WO Riggs, who seems unconscious but alive. I see he is breathing. His helmet was knocked off somewhere in the crash, though, and the left side of his head and parts of his face are bruised and swelling, his cheek battered and pocked with blood. Past him, I see LTC Bowie coming out of a swoon, the faceplate of his crappy helmet completely shattered, a bloody slash on his forehead, more blood flowing down across his face, soaking into his shirt. Another gash much deeper has torn open his chin. What little I can see of his left leg looks to be jammed unnaturally beneath him, pinned against shattered limestone, almost certainly broken. I listen again, suddenly aware that there are no radio sounds in my helmet headset; it is agonizingly quiet, though the cord from my helmet is still jacked in, nothing broken there. It is the bird's radio that is dead. Painfully I reach back behind me in the bird and rescue my M16 and ammunition bandolier. Plenty of that, seven magazines of twenty rounds each, another full magazine in the rifle. Suddenly shivering, I grab up the rifle, chamber a round, and snap on the safety.

"What the hell?" the colonel says. "What did we . . . ? Did we crash?" His voice is mushy, his jaw probably broken.

"Yeah, dink AA gun hit us when you yanked the pilot's arm." I say it uncaring. He needs to know what his doltish action had caused. "Can you move, Colonel?"

Bowie does barely more than try. "No, my leg is bad . . . hurts . . . hurts," he says. "Caught on something. I can't move."

I am looking for my radio, the PRC-25 that I carry on flights. It will be our salvation. I can call the TOC with it; get them to send a unit to rescue us. I find it, jammed beneath the minigun's ammo canister, tuning dials shattered, one side deeply dented. The radio squawks with broken squelch when I squeeze the transmit button. *Working*, I think, I hope. I try to remember the TOC's infantry call sign and frequency—can't; my head muzzy. I stare dimly at the tuning knobs and slowly remember the frequency for the artillery push, click the broken dials to what I think is that push, counting the clicks, using only my right hand. "Harsh Angle Two-Seven, this is Harsh Angle Two-Seven Actual. Over," I call. Squelch breaks again as it should, but I hear nothing over the radio from my team in the TOC. I try again. "Harsh Angle Two-Seven, this is Harsh Angle Two-Seven Actual. Over." And this time, there is a voice coming back, a clash of sounds utterly unintelligible. I try to talk more, hoping that the problem is only at my end and that they can hear me.

"Harsh Angle Two-Seven, this is Harsh Angle Two-Seven Actual. If you can hear me, break squelch twice. Over." Nothing. I click around the dial near where I think the TOC's frequency is, calling, "Harsh Angle Two-Seven, this is Harsh Angle Two-Seven Actual. I say again, if you can hear me, break squelch twice. Over." A gabble. Then cut off. Goddamn radio, damn radio. The first time I need it in the field and it is broken. I bang it against the side of the fallen bird, bang, bang. Try again, this time nothing at all. Stupid, now it's dead. LTC Bowie is watching me sleepily from his open eye, the other entirely swollen shut, drying blood caked on his face, and soaked like a bib into the weft of his once-crisp fatigue shirt. I am more worried about WO Riggs, who breathes and even moans a bit when I try to shift him but is otherwise unresponsive. What is clear to me, though, is that we dare not stay here. I don't know if any of our side had seen us go down, but this area is surely swarming with dinks, and I have no idea if they saw the crash and, if so, are coming to see who or what they can get from our crash site.

"Colonel, we have to move," I say to Bowie. "I can't get us up the hill, and the way going down just drops into a steep ravine. It looks a little more open up ahead, so I'm going to try and get you and Mr. Riggs out and into cover somewhere ahead."

Bowie seems to have fallen into a sort of trance and looks up only when I am talking to him. "I don't think I can move," he says.

"Sir, we've got to get you out of here. We are in Laos, and dinks will be along pretty soon to check out this crash. We can't be here."

"I can't move. My leg is caught, jammed between . . . can't . . ."

In crashing, the bird seems to have dug itself deeply into the hill, rock snaring it. I am able to move up around the craft's nose, inching along, my side complaining fiercely, finally wedging myself between the hillside and the bird. Pushing with my left leg only results in screaming pain, but my right leg gets purchase, and I shove hard as I can against the side of the bird. Nothing. Try again. No movement. The bird is seized as if in a vise of stone and will not give at all. In that vise, Bowie is caught but good.

"That's a waste of time, Captain. Get the pilot out and go. I'm not going anywhere."

I should stay and defend him from the dinks who are doubtlessly coming, but that would not save the colonel and leave both me and WO Riggs captured. "God, Colonel. I've got to move the pilot. I'm going to try and carry Riggs around the hill to someplace safer. I'll come back for you as fast as I can."

"Uh!"

"Colonel, I'm pretty banged up myself, and I don't think I can carry either of you very far. I just want to get you both under cover, and then I'm going to try and go for help. We stay here and we're good as dead or captured."

Bowie shakes his head a bit as if to clear his thoughts. "Yeah, yeah . . . go . . . take the pilot. I'm not going anywhere," he says again.

I make my way back to the downhill side of the bird and lean in over Riggs, each move an agony. It seems almost impossible, using only my right arm, to lever Riggs up and out of his seat, but the slant of the hillside works for me. I pop his seat restraint and manage to pull his legs around so they're dangling past the broken frame of the bird's door. Leaning in so that I can pull him out, I get my uninjured right shoulder under him and manage a sort of fireman's carry. I want my M16, but I can't handle it and Riggs at the same time.

The pain of holding him sears. I stop, shudder, and try to catch my breath. "Give me your .45, Colonel. I'll leave you my rifle." I realize I am whispering, barely audible, something telling me that I shouldn't let my voice carry no matter how thick the jungle seems.

With Riggs on my shoulder, each step along the hillside sends bursts of agony through my ribs. I move perhaps fifty meters along the hillside, stopping when I discover an overhang where a bit of a stream has undercut a stretch of the hillside, jungle covering it from above and the side. I find it mostly by chance, almost stumbling into the shallow, cave-like space, which burrows a meter or more in from surface of the slope, the thin stream trickles at its bottom. The shade of the jungle canopy, added to the undergrowth's cover, leaves us hidden in a deep gloom, invisible to anybody not looking closely.

"Riggs?"

A moan but with something like recognition in it. I lay him down, which means leaning in to the left, and that brings a stab of torment so intense that I let go of Riggs and he falls the last few inches. His response is another muffled moan as if from an immense distance. I see that the unbruised side of his face—in the light seeping into the space around us—is pale, shocky, and though he seems mostly intact, I am imagining there must a serious concussion and maybe internal injuries as well. I doubt he will last if I don't get him help soon. Eerily, the pilot's eyes are partly open, and the pupils seem reactive to the change in light, though it may only be my hope that makes me see them so.

I want to get up and go back for the colonel, but my side is not letting me, and I have to kneel there for a moment, breathing shallowly and willing the pain to ebb. Finally, grabbing a fortunately placed root, I pull myself up and start back for LTC Bowie. I should be terrified, I tell myself, injured and on foot on the forbidden side of the border. I should be heart-poundingly alarmed. I'm not, though. Perhaps it's the pain, but I feel focused, alert, intent upon getting the three of us away from the downed bird. Every slightest sound is alive with meaning to me, the buzz and flit of insects, the softness of wind through the trees far above, the soft settling of my footsteps onto the jungle floor.

Back at the wrecked bird, it seems evident that Bowie is not getting out without more help than I am capable of. With Riggs safely out, I can slide partially into the pilot's seat and get a better view of the colonel's predicament. His good eye is closed, tears leaking out, mixing with the dried blood on his face. I can see now that left leg is caught between the crushed shell of the bird and the rocky substrate of the hillside, pinned there in a way that I, with my injured side, cannot free.

"Colonel?" I say.

"Wha . . . ?"

"Can you hear me?"

"Yeah."

"I can't get you out, not the way your leg is caught."

"Can't?"

"No, sir."

"Try. Hell with the pain. Try."

I manage to work myself in so that I am lying across the pilot's seat and across Bowie, reaching down with my good hand to attempt to work him free. It will do no good. I can see the shattered end of bone sticking through the lower pant leg of his fatigues. A compound fracture. His left foot is caught as if in a bear trap. Lacking any way to lever it out, my only recourse would be to amputate it, crudely, hacking away at it. The pain alone would send the colonel into shock and likely death. Further up, his thigh seems unnaturally bent, the femur apparently also broken. I can tell him only that I'm helpless to do anything. There is nothing to help in the bird, not even a first aid kit with morphine to deaden his pain.

He is looking at me now with that one open eye. "It's no use is it, Captain?"

"I can try to get up the rock again, see if I can push hard enough to lever the thing off with my legs."

He doesn't seem to hear, saying, "If you leave me, the enemy will find me here, won't they?"

"I'm going to try and get behind it and kick it away from you, Colonel."

"You tried that already. No go. I asked what will happen if you leave me here. Will the enemy find me?

There is no other way up the rock than the one I had already tried; the bird is rammed deeply into the hillside. That spot didn't offer enough leverage. Elsewhere, there is even less purchase and none for me if I do get up on top. Still, I've been trying to climb it one handed.

"Will they?" the colonel asks again.

"Yeah, likely, sir," I have to tell him.

"Then kill me. I don't want to be captured."

"Sir, best would be to leave you here and go for help. We haven't seen any sign of the dinks who are supposed to be around here. Maybe there aren't any. The squad we were looking for doesn't seem to be here either. Maybe it's all been a goose chase. The best I can do is to get away from here as quickly as I can. Parts of Charlie Company are already headed this way. CPT Griffin is only a klick or so to our east. He may get here before the dinks do."

"Damn it, Weisman, it's not just my leg. I can't move at all. I'm losing all feeling in anything below my waist. Something's broken in my back. Who the hell wants to live like that? My fault, my fault we are here . . . This small unit concept is bullshit, I get it . . . We're in a mess of my own creation. If I could, I would go back and fix it. But I can't. Kill me!"

It's a maddening moment; something sour backs up in my throat as I contemplate picking up the pistol and shooting him. It might be a mercy to him. His good eye closes again; more tears leak from it. I rest a moment, sprawled there across the nose of the bird. I'm not moving as much because of the physical pain that makes my own movement so hard as from the mental anguish of the idea of killing another soldier, the CO of the battalion.

"No, sir," I finally say. "I'm going to take Riggs across the border and then come back with Charlie Company for you. You'll need this. I wish you would wait until I can get back with help." I pull the .45 from my web belt and put it into his lap. I take hold of the M16 and use it as a crutch to slowly work my way down off the little helicopter.

The colonel slightly opens his eye, mouth working, and looks down at the .45, saying what I think is "Thank you."

Ominously, out of the quiet of the jungle, there are voices off toward the southwest slope of the ridge. We both hear them: voices saying something like, "Máy bay trực thăng bị rơi ở đâu đó gần đây." I know *máy bay trực thăng* means "helicopter" in Vietnamese. The voices are small with distance, a couple of hundred meters or so away. I can do nothing more, and I back away from the downed bird, refusing to look at LTC Bowie, who mouths "Go!" at me.

As I move away from the bird, there is again noise in the jungle to our south, the sound of men pushing their way through the trees. Carefully, I limp back into the undergrowth and am some ways along the slope, nearly to where I'd left WO Riggs when I hear what I'd feared: the resounding bang of the .45, a single shot—the end, it seems, for Bowie, a sad end to a poor commander. He doesn't deserve this, though, and a rush of shame runs through me as I think I should have stayed, defended him, fought them. Why? We both would have died, and so would WO Riggs left here alone and incapable of moving on his own. But now there is another bang as loud as the first, the .45 fired again, and then the sound of AK-47 fire. Then another few shots from the .45, and then silence, the .45's ammo expended. I find Riggs, seeming almost comatose in the hidden space, giving a hiss as if understanding it. Finally, there is the distance-attenuated voice of one of the dinks, "Không giết ông, một sĩ quan, cấp bậc có thể cao" (Do not kill him, an officer, maybe rank high). There's a final shot from the .45 and the sound of an AK-47 on full automatic, the fast rattle of its firing. Then nothing.

I squat next to Riggs in the small space of the overhang listening to the dinks move past, my M16 ready, expecting every instant that one of them will discover our hiding place. Whether they'd kill or capture us, I don't know. I am an officer, and so my jungle fatigue shirt has markings of rank. I'd never wear captain's bars out in the bush where I would want to look like the scruffiest of low-ranking grunts. But this shirt I wear on the hill has captain's bars and crossed cannons embroidered on it. An officer, I'd be a prize for the dinks to capture. Softly, I unbutton the fatigue shirt, ease it off one-handed, careful of my battered ribs and wrist—leaving on my sweat-soaked OD T-shirt—and push the fatigue shirt into a litter of dead branches and soft dirt at the back of the overhang. The dinks may see it, but not immediately and hopefully not until we are long gone from here. On the collar of Riggs's flight suit is the bar of a warrant officer 1 with its single black square. I don't know if it will mark Riggs to the North Vietnamese as a sort of officer or as a senior technician. I try to pull it off him, but my every touch brings a moan. I give up and leave it on him. I crouch, M16 up, and pointed toward the brush-covered side of our hideaway, a round chambered, selector lever clicked over to full automatic. Riggs's and my deaths won't come without a price. Light enters our hide through a dozen gaps in the undergrowth that covers it, dappling the dark space around us. It shifts and flickers as the enemy pass, their shadows plugging the gaps, their steps moving the branches, moving the light. In it, I find myself holding my breath until I want to gasp, let it out, and grab more air. In it, Riggs's breath is like a baby's soft snore. I've had my hand poised to muffle it if he moans or cries out as the enemy go by. He doesn't, and I let my hand drop, shaking, into my lap.

Thankfully, the dinks pass us by, talking lowly; one voice gruff, older, another sounding very young. I speak no Vietnamese, but the inflections suggest they are talking about finding us.

"Họ đã đi theo cách này?" (They went this way?)
"Tôi không biết!" (I do not know!)
"Vâng, cái nhìn, bạn đánh lừa." (Well, look, you fool.)
"Xin lỗi, trung sĩ, tôi sẽ làm tốt hơn." (Excuse me, Sergeant, I will do better.)

There's a grunt from the older-sounding voice, and then quiet again. The footsteps fade as the dinks move north in their search.

"Riggs, if I am going to carry you, I don't want you to look like any sort of officer, so we've got to get this warrant officer bar off you," I say. He's not hearing me, but the sound of my own voice helps break me out of a chill of fear and confusion. I talk to myself, I listen, and maybe something will come of it. "What the hell are these, Riggs? Not fatigues. Some sort of flight suit. How does it come off?" I sit, staring, hurting everywhere so that I can't seem to think. The flight suit is a tough fire-resistant thing with the insignia of his rank embroidered on the collar. The damn thing seems all zippers and snaps, and I wonder how I am going to get him out of it. There is a zipper down the front, his blood caked in it, and it is all I can do to hang on with my brutally painful left hand while working the zipper down. "Gotta get this off you, Riggs. Gotta."

I work it over his arms and down. As I do, he gives a low moan, and his eyes flicker. But he's out. The damn thing is one piece, though. Some ripstop material I can't tear. "Hell, Riggs, hell. I can't get this off you. If the dinks catch us, they'll see you're a warrant officer, and there's nothing I can do about it." Except there is after all. There's a zipped pocket on one pant leg with something hard inside that turns out to be a survival knife. I see it is sharp when I unfold it. I stab the point of the blade through the waist of his suit and saw through the tough material.

"God! Off! You look like a derelict, this thing hacked half away." I stuff the top of the suit into the back of the overhang, under leaves next to my shirt. Now we're a pair in OD T-shirts. His is bloody from a deep cut on his cheek. Rankless, we could be any grunts, no sign we are officers of any sort.

It is alarming to me that Riggs is so comatose, he does not even whimper at this manhandling. Done, I sit for a few beats, trying to breathe through the pain of my battered side, my mind a sudden and agonizing blank, just breathing, and trying to think what to do next. Next, I'm looking up blinking, realizing I must have zoned out for a few beats in a haze of exertion. I come to slowly, the chill in the overhang shivering me awake, and I jerk my head up. *Move!* I think. *Just move.* Get back into Vietnam before the dinks come back in force to strip the downed bird. I fumble at the pocket of my fatigue pants where I have stuffed my map, spread it across my knees, and, in the dim light of the overhang, force myself to study the terrain depicted there. I am almost sure our bird crashed on a hillside half a klick or so west of the ridge where the firefight supposedly was taking place. The map depiction of the terrain to the east looks so daunting that the temptation is great to just stay in this overhang with Riggs until he either dies and I can leave him, or he comes to his senses and is able to walk out of here under his own power. But I know I can't wait. I must go while it is still light and before my side stiffens to the point I can't move with or without Riggs. I try to still my jitters, quiet my breathing, quiet the pounding of my heart as I listen for any sound of the dinks who had passed by. Nothing. Only an insect hum and the call and rejoinder of birds in the jungle around us.

In my numbness, I lose myself again in an ugly though unprofitable thought: was it cowardly to leave LTC Bowie at the wreck? I tell myself it would have been stupid to go back for him; that he was inextricably trapped in the downed bird; that I could not have saved him, and by going back, I would have put WO Riggs in jeopardy and risked my own death or capture too. One should never confuse heroism with foolhardiness, I tell myself unconvincingly. I despised Bowie for his reckless indifference, and now I wonder if I'd been just as indifferent to him. No, if I'd gone back, Bowie *and* Riggs and I would have been lost. So why do I feel like such a shit?

Nothing, though. I have to move. I lever myself up, bringing a hiss at the pain that shoots down my side as I do. I put my head gingerly out of the brush covering the overhang to where I can study the lay of the land. North, the jungle-canopied hill curves up and away into another finger of ridge. South past the crashed Loach, the hillside we are on becomes a nearly sheer drop into a deep and rocky ravine. There is the precarious path along that way that the dinks took coming up here. But in my condition, carrying Riggs, it's a long shot that I could make it that way. West would take us further into Laos with no easy path back out. The best way looks to be due east, where the land slopes more gradually down into the ravine, a much longer route out but far less steep. Even this route is chancy. On my own, I might get there relatively easily, despite my injuries, but carrying even one as scrawny as Riggs, it will be hell getting down into the ravine and back up its eastern side.

Through a thin spot in the jungle growth, I can see the far side of the ravine, which climbs a steep wooded slope onto a second ridge. The lay of the land seems to correspond to the map image of it, and if so, I know where we are: inside Laos about three hundred meters west of the Vietnamese border and maybe a klick away from C Company. "We can't wait here, Mr. Riggs," I say, saying it aloud, though I have no idea if Riggs is conscious enough to hear and understand. No matter, speaking calms my nerves a bit. I sling my M16 onto my shoulder and torture myself further by dragging Riggs out of the overhang. Strangely, while I can hear the faint sounds of helicopters passing far overhead, there is no sign any birds are down low looking for us. We could wait for rescue, but in this deep jungle, help may never come. Just north of our overhang, I see, is a shallow drop-off of perhaps a meter onto a wide ledge, and I think that if I can drag Riggs over there, I can get beneath him and pull him onto my shoulder in a fireman's carry.

As I begin to do it, I hear him say something almost intelligible, a sort of "Wha . . . ? Where go . . . n?" and I see that his eyes have fluttered open a bit. "Riggs?" I say, "Can you hear me? Do you know what happened?"

"N . . . o." More a hum than actual speech. His eyes flutter again.

He's alive and in a state at least approaching consciousness, although he seems unable to understand what I am doing or even able to help.

So I'm doomed to carry him. The slope in front of us is steep but manageable, descending perhaps a hundred meters to where, through the trees, I can see the floor of the ravine level out. I have pulled Riggs onto the shoulder on my bad side, supporting him with my left arm, broken wrist held high and away. Moving like this hurts like a bastard, every footstep down a jolt from leg to aching side to wrist. But this way, my right hand is free to grab roots and branches like living guywires. It is not hot, perhaps in the sixties, though the air is still and humid under the cover of the jungle, humming insects everywhere, the sweat of exertion pouring off me. I struggle over the rough jungle floor to the ravine's bottom where a shallow creek runs through a bed of fist-sized rocks interspersed with a few boulders. The light here below the canopy is a muted green. The purl of the water through the rocks is soft. A dragonfly hums nearby, a sudden deep throb of wings by me so close, I flail at it with my good arm. Breathless now and aching, I have to rest. I stop and bend down with exquisite care to lay Riggs against a large rock so that he is partially sitting up. He is still rag-doll limp but breathing, eyes unfocused but seemingly tracking things around him. A good sign, perhaps.

"I've got to put you down, Riggs, got to rest," I say. I doubt he hears me, lost as he is in his own oblivious cocoon, but I tell him I will get him up this ridge and across into Vietnam where Charlie Company is spread out over the ridge beyond. "If we get there, we're safe," I say. I free the canteen from my belt and let a little of the water dribble down my throat. There is a tempting plentitude of water in the little stream, but even in this wild part of the terrain, one never knows what parasites lurk in it. I try to drip a bit of water into Riggs's mouth, asking him if he can swallow it. Some runs out over his lips, but it seems some stays, and maybe his throat has moved a bit in a swallow. Here at the bottom of the ravine, there is only the soft lap of the stream and a dozen interlaced thrums of dragonfly wings. It seems so peaceful and far from combat that I am pulled to stay here, maybe for an hour or so, just resting. But I have the sense the dinks are searching for us, or at least for Riggs (not knowing I am with him). Staying here is crazy, high ground all around, no place to hide. By my watch, it has barely been two hours since we crashed, hardly more than 1000 hours in the morning, too long a time until dark to lie low here.

High on the slope behind me, I hear a thrashing in the undergrowth, and I panic, grabbing my M16 and looking for cover. Except for the boulder that props up Riggs, there is no place to hide, no other rocks big enough, without leaving him and ducking into the trees across the creek on the uphill slope. But then the noise fades. It is clearly dinks, their voices coming thinly to me through the trees.

"Bạn có thấy họ đi đâu?" (Did you see them go?)

"Không đây. Chúng ta hãy đi xung quanh đồi." (Not here. Let's go around the hill.)

There is more but too muffled to hear. They don't seem to be coming down this way, and my heart, a drumfire in my chest, eases. I look at

Riggs. His feet have moved a fraction, enough to make me think he is not paralyzed. His eyes remain half closed and unfocused, tracking nothing once again. I suspect he's suffered at least a bad concussion, and maybe worse, possibly a fractured skull, maybe his brain swelling (I'm no medic and have no skill to tell). So I again sling the M16 behind me and squat in front of Riggs, trying to ignore the growing stiffness in my side, aching all over. I lean into him, head under his left armpit, and wrestle him onto my shoulder again. The stab in my side as I lift him is deep but not as sharp as it was at first, and I wonder if that is a good sign or one of deeper injury, a warning that damaged nerves have given up screaming their pain. This upslope is steeper but a shade more open with less undergrowth than the one I came down. It looks to be at least a hundred meters to the top of the border ridge, but the openness means I can traverse the ridge at an angle rather than straight up, trading distance for angle of slope. It is suddenly strikingly funny to me how such mathematical concepts as slope rise up in my thoughts from my long-ago OCS gunnery classes. In a flash of hallucination, everything I look at on the hill seems momentarily embedded with numbers denoting distance, direction, and elevation. It seems I can almost read the elevation and deflection of the best uphill trajectory as my heart again pounds. I stop, take a breath, subdue something of a hysterical laugh, and let things come back into focus before starting to climb again. The jolting appears to rouse Riggs a fraction, and a slight moan escapes him. I step up, force myself forward, and step up again, inching up the slope, stopping every few steps to catch my breath. I keep Riggs on my shoulder because I don't know if I can get him back up there if I set him down.

"Man, Riggs, I hear flies." In fact, I hear a swarm of them humming through the trees, a faster, higher note than the dragonflies. And I smell death—the sour iron stink of blood, the reek of shit, of scorched wood, burned leaves, and cooked meat. I stop just below the crest. Ever so carefully, favoring my left side, I let Riggs slide down against the rocket-fin-looking bolsters of an immense teak tree. He slips between two of the bolsters as if enfolded there, eyes closed now, breathing raggedly. There is nothing more I can do for him here. I unsling my M16 and move carefully up the slope into the buzz of the flies and deeper into the stench of fresh death. I stop; bile comes into my throat. What I step onto where the ridge levels out is a killing floor on which are the remains of half a dozen men in torn and bloody U.S. combat fatigues, stripped except for that, boots missing; rucks and rifles, steel pots, and web gear gone. Here, a man whose head took a bullet, lies heaped upon himself, eyes half closed beneath a lace of his eyelashes, his brows below a gaping space of nothing. A man disassembled rests next to him, his legs gone from what was surely a grenade. Others are scattered in unseemly repose, arms akimbo, bodies scorched and unraveled. Everywhere is blood and shattered branches. One man had shit himself, whence the smell of it, and who *wouldn't* have let go his bowels in the disorder of dying, grasping that you are done for.

I've no doubt that it is the squad from Charlie Company, blasted into a ruin of carcasses, stripped of everything useful and left here. Did they give as good as they got? There is no knowing. There are no dead dinks here because they cart away their dead. Still, heavy blood trails wind away through the trees up the north slope of the ridge, whispering that this squad of Charlie Company fought ferociously, whispering of some or even many enemy wounded and dead, but without corpses, they are a force ghostly and uncountable. Bile is back in my throat, and I grab for my canteen, take a deep swallow, and stand breathing shallowly, the scene almost too grim to take in. If the squad had had a radio, it is gone with the rest of their gear.

By my map, where I stand now is precisely on the border, my left boot in Laos, my right boot in Vietnam, looking north along a ridge whose crest is as clear of brush as if some Olympian hand had rubbed it away before drawing the boundary here. Along it, a trail leads north and south. On the north lead, the terrain climbs steeply, heading up onto a ridge that the map shows will eventually ascend to the 1,100-meter-high peak of Yaaw Phuu (Long Mountain in the Lao language), six klicks to the northwest, the angle of the mountain's slope growing more acute and the way more heavily wooded as it goes. East—the way I want to go—the ridge drops precipitously for at least a hundred meters into Vietnam. Perhaps, even with my injuries, I might make it down that climb alone, but not while carrying Riggs. South, the narrowing ridge slopes gradually down for a klick into a trough between two high points, the map symbols showing the trough to be an overgrown karst basin full of sinkholes and channels: a swamp.

   Shouldering Riggs again, my rifle at the ready, a round chambered, I turn south, avoiding the death scene, limping down along the ridgetop trail, looking for an accessible way east into Vietnam before my strength gives out.

★ ★ ★

CHAPTER 21

I can hear voices arguing shrilly in the jungle behind me, loudly enough that they can be only a few dozen meters back.

"Đường này. Thấy, dấu chân?" (This way. See, footprints?)

"Nhanh chóng đi xuống đó. Những dấu chân được gần nhau. Ông bị thương, mệt mỏi. Chúng tôi sẽ bắt anh ta." (Quickly go down there. The footprints are close together. He is wounded, tired. We will catch him.)

"Cẩn thận, chúng tôi không biết nếu anh ta chỉ có một mình" (Careful, we don't know if he is alone), comes a third voice, differently accented and hardly as musical as the first two, a western-sounding voice startlingly strange here deep in the Laotian jungle.

When I hear it, I am nearly at the south end of the ridge, down to a nose of broken boulders close to the beginning of the swamp. The comatose WO Riggs slung over my aching shoulder, I am slowly traversing a narrow stretch of broken rock north of the boulders that is open and clear of the jungle for a space of some thirty meters. Past the boulders maybe fifty meters further on, the last trace of the ridge toes into the wetland.

The boulders make a nest of a sort, cover that I struggle toward, dismayed at how close behind us the enemy has now come. Heaving Riggs along, I work my way over a large rock and into that stony nest, yipping softly at the pain in my ribs and trying to set him down as gently as I can; not so gently as I would hope with every breath an agony. Around us, the nose of the ridge is narrow, a bridge between the higher slope and the swamp further on, constricted enough that it leaves no way for the dinks to flank me. To get at me, they will have to come over the rocks directly toward me. It is a perfect spot to make a stand, if I have to, though I think that making a stand here will almost certainly end badly.

I hear those voices again out of a fuzzy incomprehension, waking as if from a short sleep, coming to realize that I must have passed out again and slipped down among the rocks. How long? I can pop my head up just enough to look back up the ridge to the tree line. Nothing. I'm sure the Vietnamese voices are not phantoms arisen from my exhaustion and pain. But the sounds of speech are loud, the dinks surely near. So my blackout can't have been for long. Still wooly, though, I sit without moving to try and let the world come back into focus. I tell myself to calm down, that though dinks may be coming for me, I'm in a hard-to-breach stronghold. I have a nearly full canteen and a chocolate bar stuffed into a pocket of my fatigue pants. Not good for long, but if I can hold the dinks off for a while, it may be long enough for some of the grunts from Charlie Company to get here. The dinks can try to wait me out or even drop mortar shells on me if they have a tube with them. But if they want me alive, they are going to have to come across the open area, a space of rock bare of any cover or concealment. I'm decently armed with four grenades and 160 rounds of ammunition for my M16. By my watch, it is not quite 1300; there are five hours or more until dusk. God willing, I can outlast them and hope that friendlies get here before it is dark and this all goes to hell.

Riggs is my chief worry, though. He is not breathing well, his inhalations are choked and sometimes gasping, and I worry that he has begun a slide into death.

"Riggs," I whisper. Earlier, he had responded with some disconnected but conscious speech. This time, he doesn't answer at all. Just before I apparently blacked out, I had laid him down in a narrow space between two upended slabs of rock, well out of any danger of dink fire hitting him. As I faded, I must have half fallen across him onto my injured left side and now am playing hell levering myself upright. I get a handhold on a rock spur, pull myself up to where my legs are under me, and manage to get to my feet. Up, I look at Riggs and see his lips seem parched, a fleck of white spittle dried on his lower lip. I screw off the top of my canteen and try again to dribble some water into his him, having to pull his lips open to do it. The water drips in and then just trickles back out. His eyes are half closed, his face pale, almost gray. I take a mouthful of water myself, and as I am putting the top back on the canteen, I see him all at once take a deep, shuddering breath like a sigh, and shake as if he is going to awaken, shake again, and then just lie there, still unconscious, breathing unevenly.

"Damn it, Riggs, are you in there?" I say, leaning over him, saying it softly into his ear. Still nothing. He's failing, and for a beat or two, I panic, realizing that if I want him to live, I have to get him away from here and up to where Charlie Company is.

A meter or so from me, at the uphill end of the rock pile, two massive boulders abut each other, leaving a V of open space between them that is a natural firing position. Favoring my sore side, I carefully pull myself around and squat, leaning forward against the stone. I push my M16's barrel just into the point of the V, where it is at the ready but, I hope, impossible to see from the front. Here, I can look across the gentle upslope of stone that gives me a full field of grazing fire. Nobody will find it easy getting across here. It is all I can do, and now I just must wait. For a fragment of an instant in the tree line, I see the many-fingered leaves of a philodendron bush shake. Wind? No, nothing else is moving like that. I watch, hardly daring to breathe as the leaves part again, and I get a flash glimpse of a face and dark hair beneath a pith helmet peering my way warily through the leaves. The dink patrol is here! Voices:

"Xấu tại chỗ, trung sĩ, không bao gồm đối với chúng tôi. Nhiều đá ở dưới đó nơi ông có thể được ẩn." (Bad spot, Sergeant, no cover for us. Lots of rocks down there where he could be hiding.)

"Không có cách nào khác để có thể đi qua dễ dàng. Nếu anh ta là có, chúng tôi sẽ phải hút anh ta ra." (There is no other way to get across easily. If he is there, we will have to smoke him out.)

"Ahhh!"

I have no idea what they are saying, but it is terrifying to think enemy soldiers are hardly a stone's throw away from me. They seem unconcerned that I might hear them. I suspect they must think I am alone, a natural assumption because, carrying Riggs, I have left only a single set of footprints. Truly, for fighting them—if it comes to that—it doesn't matter. Riggs has the knife and a .45 holstered on his belt, but comatose, he is *hors de combat*. There is only my M16 ready to answer enemy fire. Waiting for the dinks to come, I get the unbidden and black thought that I could just leave Riggs here for the dinks and move on now. Heartless, but chances are that if I take him with me, he will slow me enough that both of us will die. Left behind, the dinks would soon find and capture but hopefully not kill him. They already appear to think that there is only one American come through here and, finding Riggs, might figure they have the one they've been pursuing, take him, and go. He is dying anyway, I tell myself; it would not hurt to leave him. But how coldhearted am I? I've already left LTC Bowie to die. I'm not leaving Riggs.

Minutes pass. I hear the dinks argue again, voices now carefully soft enough that I get no clear sense of their speech.

Then, suddenly, as if one has lost his temper, comes, "Lỗ đít, đi, làm như tôi nói! Đi hoặc tôi sẽ bắn bạn bản thân mình." (Asshole, do as I say! Go or I'll shoot you myself.) Accompanying this outburst, there's a thrashing noise in the undergrowth on the ridge, and now, "Vâng, thưa ngài, tôi sẽ đi." (Yes, sir, I will go.) The same young face as before looks out from among the green philodendron leaves. I hear, "Đi!" and, as if pushed, the young soldier lurches out of the undergrowth and stands, looking wildly about. He is wearing a regular soldier's green fatigues, not the black pajamas of the Viet Cong, and not Ho Chi Minh sandals but real boots, once probably black but now dirty and scuffed almost to a gray (not so different from ours I would think if I weren't riveted, watching the enemy come toward me). He holds his AK-47 at the ready as he pushes out a meter or so further onto the open space of the ridge. He stops, crouching as if it will give him cover, and looks around again, eyes fearful.

"Di chuyển!" (Move!) I hear the older voice bark from the bushes behind him.

"Có! Có, trung sĩ!" (Yes! Yes, Sergeant!) the young NVA soldier says. He half stands and takes another step in my direction.

Can he see the muzzle of my M16? I have him in my sights, finger on the trigger. Sweat runs off my forehead and into my eyes. I duck down to blot it away and rise again to see a second much older man (the trung sĩ?) coming out of the undergrowth behind the young soldier. He pushes the reluctant young one further forward, looking around sharply as he does so, eyes experienced and probing. His rifle is up, and his view is fixed in my direction; almost instantly I'm sure he sees me. His eyes go wide, and he shoves the younger soldier aside, sending toward me a well-aimed burp of fire from his AK. His rifle blats, bullets hiss and ricochet, and rock chips sing from the stone around me. I yelp (the trung sĩ surely hears me) and drop back, tumbling onto my side. More fire comes, and I know I have to get up and return fire.

"Đi! Chạy!" I hear the older man bark as I struggle back up to the firing position. The young dink has come forward a couple of meters, not running as the older soldier wants but slowly and then accelerating as the trung sĩ shouts, "*Chạy!*" (Run!) again and shoves him.

Up, I level my M16 and fire a wild burst back at them. It is hardly aimed, but my fire still manages to rake the younger dink, and he goes down, voicelessly, flailing back into the trung sĩ, who catches a round in his shoulder and spins. I fire another more controlled burst, this one into the trung sĩ and the bushes behind him. One of my rounds tears open his throat. He lets go of his weapon; both arms fly up as if in surrender. He reaches for the wound with one hand and staggers, and he, too, is down.

All together with the fall of the stricken trung sĩ, there is a shriek, the word "What?" in clear English, and another soldier tumbles forward out of the bushes. This one falls, stretches, gropes for his dropped AK, and goes still. This third man half out of the undergrowth—struck by some of my fire into the trees—lies fallen behind the trung sĩ. I wait, tense, hanging on hard to my M16 and watching the line of undergrowth for more dinks. One beat, two, a dozen, and all stays quiet. Is this the lot of them, a little patrol, all dead now? Watching them for any indication of life, I begin to realize the third fallen soldier is different from the other two, taller, broader shouldered. From my concealment, I can't see his face, only the back of his head and neck, his right arm lying across the trung sĩ, that hand in plain view. What catches my attention so startlingly is that the man's hair is much lighter than that of other two enemy soldiers, gingery rather than black. What I can make out of the skin of his neck, though deeply tanned, seems still lighter than that of either the young soldier or the trung si. It is the hand that I fix on, though. There's a dark blot like a stain on its back, clear and bold even against the hand's tanned skin. It could be a smear of dirt or a scar or shadow cast by the way the hand lies. But it looks most like a tattoo, hard to make out at this distance. I wish for my binoculars, lost back on the downed bird, but even without them, I'd swear the mark is the parachute and circling wings icon of an Army Ranger.

A Longshadow? One of the American turncoats? I'm staggered. Desperately, I want to climb out of my lair of boulders and get close enough to see. But I don't trust that there are no more dinks behind these three. So I wait. Their bodies lie inert; flies are already coming to the blood spreading around them. There's no motion or sound from the jungle behind them or from further up the ridge. I want to climb out of this nest and cross the thirty meters that separate us, get close enough to see who this soldier really is, and see if he is anything other than a taller, lighter-skinned dink. Too far to risk in my shambling condition. Still, that tattoo! I watch to see if all three are dead and watch for breath or any twitch or motion. Ten minutes, fifteen now, and nothing. The jungle behind them is still but for the rising hum of flies gathering on the blood and seeping wounds. I would go to look if not for Riggs, who is still breathing and even twitching in his stupor. The dead man seems to be at least as tall as I am. The gingery hair; the pale shade of his skin. Not a dink? A Caucasian? The mark on his hand revelatory if I could see it clearly. I don't dare go. Perhaps I hear motion in the jungle up the ridge from the fallen three, maybe a dink or a patrol of dinks coming down to investigate, maybe just jungle critters: an antelope-like saola or hog badger or cat. So, caution. Yet I would go and look if not for Riggs. I wish for a camera; mine is far away in my footlocker at LZ Bronco. I know I have to go now and take Riggs away from here. No time for expeditions to examine the enemy dead.

As Riggs and I have hidden here in this tumble of boulders, the day has grown dimmer under gathering clouds. Spatters of rain now begin to hit the back of my neck. It hits Riggs too, and, wondrously, in it he lets go a soft groan. As I've waited, my side has stiffened so that now just sitting up sends sharp spasms through it. My left wrist has become badly swollen and feels hot to the touch. Brutal pain accompanies any quick movement of the arm. I can't wait here any longer.

"Riggs?"

Nothing, or maybe a sigh.

"Riggs, we have to move. I'm going to pick you up now."

Fat chance, though. He is down where, to lift him up, I have to straddle him and hunch over. The agony of that sets me reeling, dizziness manifesting again. I shake it off and try again, leaning across and reaching down with my right hand to grasp his T-shirt to pull him up. It seems no use, the thin material starting to tear. God, god, god, I can't do it. Go find help? Where? I can't leave him, not while he's still breathing, not after I've brought him this far. But I'm at a loss for what to do until—out of nowhere as I pull one last time—Riggs stirs and puts his hands down at his sides, grunts like a stalled engine coughing to life, and lifts himself as I pull him up. Is he conscious? I exult in the idea.

"Riggs?" I say. "Can you hear me?"

"Huh?"

"Do you know who I am and what happened?"

"I . . . uh . . ."

"We crashed."

"Yeah . . . I . . . know . . ."

"Can you walk?"

"Uh . . . maybe . . ."

I try harder to lift him, my side stiff and my injured ribs fiercely protesting. Riggs gets a leg under himself, grabs a knob of rock, and manages to stand without my help for a moment before wobbling. Abruptly, just as I'm thinking he will be able to move on his own, he fades and falls back against the rock. His eyes roll back, and I am just able to catch him before he passes out again.

"Riggs?"

Not a sound, he's out, muscles slack, though breathing more evenly. Was that a final flare of energy before death? I don't know.

On its downhill side, the nest of boulders opens out into a slim passage that leads to the last bit of ridge and on into land swampy and overgrown. Riggs, though unconscious again, with my support, is still standing, sagging against the rock, my right arm against him to hold him up. Moving carefully, I find I can lean forward to put my left shoulder into his midriff and lever him aboard. I begin to carry him again, hurting worse than ever, but buoyed by the evidence that WO Riggs might not be dying after all.

The ridge ends in a shallow and stagnant mire thickly layered with algae, hummocked with low thorny bushes and almost certainly teeming with leeches. Happily, with the light rain coming down, there are no mosquitoes evident. Still, I don't want to be this near the water when they are likely to come out at dusk.

"No place to go but in, Riggs," I say softly, ruefully, setting him down as gently as I'm able. I pull the ankle drawstrings on my fatigue pants down over my boots and tighten them (not well, my left hand barely holds on to the string). This, I hope, will keep the leeches out, though I shake my head at that certain futility. Before I move on, I stop to swig from my canteen, which is thankfully still more than half full, and then try with little success to get some water into Riggs.

There is a drift of dead tree branches tumbled together at the bottom of the ridge, and I pull out a staff-like one, my height, fungus-blackened teak mostly bare of bark. Now, after hoisting Riggs up again, it is just push forward through the swamp, rifle slung, feeling ahead with the branch over a bottom uneven and in places deeply holed. With Riggs on my shoulder and my footing precarious, if I step into one, I'm likely to drown before I can struggle out. By the map, this stretch of wetland is not quite a klick across. After that, the map shows the land rising again onto the skirt of the 880-meter-tall mountain marked as Dông Hai. Up on the mountain's first low military crest, I should find elements of Charlie Company, safety, and access to a dustoff for WO Riggs (and for me with my bunged-up ribs and wrist).

Longshadows? To calm myself as I struggle across the swamp, I mull the memory of the dead redheaded enemy soldier. Longshadows was what 1SGT Schlagel had once called the supposed American deserters for casting a longer shadow than the short-statured Vietnamese. I also heard them called White Cong, a more vicious-sounding name, evocative of bad guys, angry psychos, self-hating Americans gone over to the other side. And a misportrayal, the legends of the Longshadows were larded with a particular claim of a pair of them called Salt and Pepper—one shorter, Caucasian, and fair-haired; the other, taller and black. In the tale's telling, race or height didn't seem to matter as much as did their status as turncoats. Their base of operations seemed to shift with the teller, anywhere from the DMZ down to the Mekong Delta and beyond.

Such was the flight of fancy that had plagued the dreams of 1SGT Schlagel so many months ago, a belief in U.S. deserters turned coat to fight alongside the enemy. A myth, a rumor, a legend of war, though Schlagel had maintained he'd seen and fired at one of these deserters on the night we had been attacked near the ugly tree. Long-since-dead major Connelly had believed *he'd* seen a tall, blond Longshadow (maybe I had seen him too) among a column of VC escorting a supply train along the Laotian border also months ago and miles south of here. Out in the field one evening over chow, I'd listened to Schlagel and a young black troop named Marcus talk about the Longshadows. Schlagel had told Marcus how the Longshadows were behind "every screwed-up mission of ours, every accident, every blown ambush, booby trap, and dud." Schlagel had gone to check the perimeter of our defensive position, and Marcus had seen me standing listening and asked me what I thought. "This stuff real and all, Fox Oscar? Do there really be turncoats and all out there wanting to mess with our shit?"

I was going to say it was all a fragranced lie, like the scare stories about gremlins in WWII who were blamed for all sorts of aircraft failures. But Marcus was a here-and-now kind of guy who knew nothing at all about WWII except that his daddy had fought there in Italy in the all black Ninety-Second Division.

"Was in some nasty shit over there, that man was," he'd told me. Marcus, carrying an M60, had often walked slack behind point man Mad-Dog when the Two-Zero Platoon was in the front of the file. Point men don't give a damn about mythology; their eyes, ears, and perceptions are tuned to the real and immediate. The job of a slack man like Marcus was to walk next behind the point man, have his back, and watch for action just ahead and to either the side so that the point man could observe the bigger picture. Slack men gave no more of a damn about mythology like the Longshadows than point men did. "It ain't shootin', I ain't carin'," Marcus had once said to me.

I had told Marcus I didn't disbelieve in Longshadows. I'd just never figured I'd see one (until now at least). "There might be army deserters out there in the bush. Maybe working for the other side, God forbid. Maybe Salt and Pepper are real. But this is a big war, and still there is no evidence there have been many U.S. soldiers gone missing. So even if there are some Longshadows, I don't think they could do us much damage."

"That's what I'm talkin' about, Lieutenant. Ain't no point in worrying over what you can't see. Is there?" he'd asked, grinning.

"Ain't," I'd said, grinning back. Marcus had been a good guy until the day he'd decided he'd had enough of the white man's war, had sat down, and told anybody who asked, "I ain't going . . . Mr. Charlie ain't called any of us a nigger. I don't have no argument with him." Enough black troops sat down with him that it threatened a mutiny likely to spread throughout Vietnam. Even though he'd blustered about killing the battalion commander—in fact, had held a Ka-Bar knife to his neck—he ended up getting an early out from Vietnam and had gone back to the World. No punishment, even an honorable discharge, if he agreed to keep his mouth shut about the incident.

It is late afternoon. I'm fried. I'd been barely able to pull myself along the last stretch. The traverse of a single klick of swamp has taken nearly three hours. I've rested with Riggs on my back at just about every hummock I've come to, rested, aching, bending half over, afraid to drop the pilot for fear I will never get him back up again, for fear I will let him slip into the water and not be able to pull him out before he drowns. At one point, I wade across a dozen meters of open knee-deep swamp. The bottom is just muck that grabs at my boots. Halfway across, it feels like I can't take another step, and I bend over to try to keep Riggs on my back. My boots have kicked up silt from the bottom that hangs in an unmoving cloud in the still water. Around me, a light rain dimples the water's surface. Riggs slips, and I groan, knowing I am going to lose him and knowing that if I do, I will not get him back up out of the water again.

Then, "No . . .," he says softly. His hands grab at my web belt.

"Riggs?"

"Yeah?"

"Can you . . . ?"

Nothing except a muffled reply, but he is hanging on, and I struggle across the rest of the open water to a fragment of island where I stand, listening to the rain, listening to Riggs breathe, him again unresponsive as if that little moment of wakefulness again exhausted him. I let go a low moan of misery, bend to pull Riggs a trifle more securely onto my shoulder, and step off again. It would be so easy to give up and just sit here. Finally, I move.

A hundred paces or so beyond that little island is the eastern shore of the swamp, a grassy bank below a tree line. Further east, a brushy slope climbs toward a ridge, this slope headed into Vietnam.

"I'm not going any farther, Riggs. I'm going to put you down here."

I ease him down onto the bank, too tired to try and make it under the trees out of the rain, too tired to do more than let him slip off my shoulder and drop until he is resting on his side. My stomach is a knot, so tight I can't even straighten up, my left side a searing burn, my wrist throbbing. Kneeling, I catch the bank under my right hand and lower myself to it, knees hitting, and then I fall onto my side and back.

"Riggs?"

Nothing.

"Goddamn, I hope there are no dinks following us, because I can't move a damn inch more." I lie back and look up into the uniform gray of the late afternoon sky, letting the soft rain hit my face. "Every inch of me is soaked, Riggs. I don't even want to pull off my pants and see how many hundred leeches I've got on me."

I can hear him breathing—a good sign, I suppose. He's had fits of consciousness, but mostly he's been inert like this. After a bit, I am able to get my right hand behind me and push myself up into a sitting position and get my M16 unslung and across my knees. There is no movement across the water to the west, no sign of any dinks following. There are a couple of cans of C rations in one of my pants pockets, an emergency stash I've learned to always carry. I've got a P38 can opener on my dog tag chain. But it's a two-hand task, and with my injured wrist, I can't get a grip on the can of ham and lima beans. Hardly my favorite combat meal, the thought of it (something we call ham and motherfuckers) normally would be distaste. But knowing the meal is right here, only a sealed can away, is agony. I try to grip it between my knees but can't keep it still enough for the little opener to catch the can's rim. I've also got a C ration tropical Hershey bar in the left top hip pocket, though, and I can't reach it with my right hand, and, suddenly, the ridiculousness of it all hits me, and I start laughing, expecting any moment for Riggs to join me.

No.

But gently, gently, heedless of the ache, I manage to work my left thumb and forefinger into the pocket and stretch that leg out to let the pocket come open a bit. I am shaking with how much it hurts just to reach in and pull out that chocolate bar, just barely grasp it. It slips out, and I can get it with my right hand, tear away the wrapper with my teeth, and gnaw at the hard chocolate as if I'm some sort of ravenous rodent.

"Man, Riggs, that's better. Riggs, are you hungry?"

A bit of ragged breathing, nothing else.

I get my canteen out. "Plenty of water. Dinks will probably blow my ass away before I run out." I hold the canteen between my knees and work the screw cap open. For one frightening instant as the cap comes off, my aching legs give way and the canteen starts to slip. I grab it in time, breathe, and take a wonderful cool swallow.

The swamp we'd passed through had the ripe sulfurous excremental smell of rotting vegetation. Here, at its far end, a stronger deathlike stench hangs among the trees, one as potent as if a decomposing body lies hidden in the undergrowth. Somewhat restored by the chocolate and back on my feet, I push through the bushes into the stink where I gasp and—heart hammering—search frenziedly for a corpse. There is none, and I stop, breathing hard until, looking up, I see one tree decked with scores of spiky football-sized fruit. It dawns on me that these are durians, a fruit both delicious and potent with the fragrance of decay. The deathlike funk that comes from them makes them war's perfect condiment. Neither Riggs nor I are dead, yet our small piece of the world here already reeks of it. I take a durian back to Riggs and get the survival knife out of his pocket. I use it to cut into the pale-green football-sized fruit covered with inch-long spikes.

"These are supposed to be good to eat, Riggs,' I say, hacking at the fruit's thick rind. Eventually, I am able to cut a wedge of it. Inside is a rusty-colored, custard-like pulp imbedded with one of several large seeds. "God, it stinks!" but I scoop out some of the flesh with two fingers, and hungry as I am, the taste is a wondrous surprise, rich like almond-flavored custard. "Little bit oniony too," I call back to Riggs, who just snores on. The rich flavor overwhelms the smell, and I eat the whole damned but delicious thing.

A while later, rested a bit after sitting under the trees, I manage to pull the unconscious Riggs up under the cover of these durians, lay myself back against a pile of leaf litter full of god-knows-what crawlies, lie for what seems moments amid the god-awful durian stink listening to the drone of mosquitos begin, and almost instantly I am out.

It is dawn. Off somewhere in the overcast sky is the blatt of a helicopter fading to the east. Far to the west also is the tumult of renewed battle, the attenuated crackle of a dozen firefights, the distant crash of ordnance, bombs, and artillery, so soft as to seem like hushed thunder. Close, there is nothing but an insect hum and the faint splash and wash of the water I crossed the night before. WO Riggs lies next to me under the cover of the durian trees. He is quiet and so still, I look twice to see that he is breathing. His right eye is badly swollen; face a dark contusion beneath it. I won't attempt to wake him yet. Putting my right arm behind me, I try guardedly to lever myself upright, stopping to wait for pain to come and subside. Thankfully, the pain in my side seems not as sharp, though I am so stiff, I can barely stand. My left wrist is swollen and useless, throbbing when I let it fall to my side. Oh god! Spots of blood decorate my fatigue pant legs. What? I'm not wounded. There are no tears or punctures in the cloth. Using only my right hand, I manage to release my web belt and work the button and the zipper loose. Pulling the pants down, I find a dozen or more bloody spots on my legs, mostly down below my knees, and then, suddenly, I spot handfuls of swollen leeches in the pant legs; they fall off as I stand. I yelp and work the ankle drawstrings loose. The rest of the leeches fall away. I'd leap up if I could and dance to shake them off. But all I can do is pluck the remaining blood-filled creatures off and fling them away and yank down my boxers to see if any have climbed that high. (They have not, thank God.) With some pleasure, I relieve myself into the water, work my pants back up, flicking away a final two leeches, and stand, trying to think what the hell I am going to do next. Despite the night's sleep, I am done in, going no further. If the dinks come, they come.

"Riggs," I say, "we aren't going anywhere. I'm too goddamn stiff and sore to pick you up again. Riggs?"

He is still out, and I am terrified that, while still alive in a sense, he has no life left in him.

"Christ," I say and manage to kneel and pull his left eyelids open. The eye moves! Half focuses for a beat, and I think that is evidence that Riggs is still inside there.

"But we're not going anywhere, man," I say again.

I look to breakfast off another durian, but now, far off across the swamp toward the Laotian side of the border, I imagine I hear voices.

"God!" Dinks searching for me. Are they really? I stop. I hold my breath to try and listen for those faint voices. My pounding heart seems loud enough to drown them out and give me away. Again, coming from the east is the beat of another helicopter, and I want to drag myself out from under the trees and flag it down, wave to the high and faraway speck. But it crosses north and falls away from me. I sit. The splashing out in the water beyond seems louder. Dinks? In the bushes, I sit down on my right butt cheek, left knee up, left arm across it on which my M16 rests. Are there voices? If so, they are still far away.

"Damn, Riggs, I wish I could see. Binos are still in the bird, doing our dead colonel no damn good. I didn't think . . . I didn't . . ."

I peer out across the water, leaden, reflecting the leaden sky.

Voices? Yes. A few hundred meters away. Clearly dinks, though I make out only their tonal rise and fall, words blurred into the distance. I would crawl into the deeper trees, dragging Riggs, but I am frozen here, every muscle aching when I try to move.

"They will have to get close to see us, Riggs. This is pretty good cover."

Nothing. I'm frozen as beats of time bleed away until, perhaps a hundred meters away, they round a big scrub-covered hummock rising out of the water. One . . . two . . . three . . . four . . . five, I count, coming across toward us, all in green fatigues and pith helmets, AK-47s at the ready, a patrol of North Vietnamese Army regulars. As they get closer, I see that three of them look young, one maybe my age, the fifth one—their trung sî?—much older, wading carefully through the knee-deep water.

"*Có!*" one points and shouts. A bolt of panic hits me as all fire at once. They aren't pointing at me. I had expected the mass of their fire to catch me and Riggs in the trees and cut us down. The dinks point at something behind me, the rattle of their fire aimed off to my right and up at the lowest slope of the ridge. There comes the sound of fire from behind me, and one of the young dinks goes down in the water. The other four dodge back, splashing toward the cover of the hummock. I hear it, separating the sounds of the dinks' fire from what is coming at them, sleeting the water around them. The firefight lasts eternal seconds. The dead dink drifts slowly in the slight current in water reddened with his blood. The four other dinks are behind the hummock now, trading fire with someone on the ridge. The dull drumbeat of an M60 pulses from that ridge, its voice deeper than the high crackle of M16s. Shouts (English?) from the ridge. And now comes a racketing whine overhead, a plume of white phosphorous blossoms and twangs directly above the dinks, and they scatter from the spot where the next artillery round will be HE. In a fragment of time, they are gone back into the swamp; only the dead one, floating in the bloody open water, remains. The HE round whines in and impacts on the deserted hummock in a fountain of smoke and water.

I am too stunned to speak. All in can do is suck in breath and let the pounding of my heart subside.

"There, the dink in the water. Dead, man."

"Get him. We can show the brass we got a body count today."

"Be careful, man. Maybe some dinks still watching, shoot your ass when you get out there."

"I ain't goin', be mofo leeches in that water."

"Go, man, you owe it to yourself."

And, suddenly, there are half a dozen U.S. troops walking past the copse where I am hidden. They step down to the bank and stand looking across a couple of dozen meters of water to the dead dink. They are filthy, in T-shirts, helmets, two with OD green towels around their necks, one with an M60, muzzle still smoking a little, the rest with M16s. Their collective funk rivals the stink of the durians around me and Riggs.

I'm choked up. "Hey!" I manage to say.

They turn in an instant, weapons coming up.

"Friendly!" I call. "Friendly, friendly!"

"Who?"

"CPT Weisman. We got shot down. Got the pilot of the bird with me."

"Captain! We've been looking for you. Where the hell are you?" one asks.

"Here, in the trees. I'm kind of banged up. Moving is hard."

Two of the grunts come toward me; others still wary, watching the trees around me and Riggs for movement. Soon, they have pressed into the bushes where we are hidden.

"What the hell, Captain, you all right?"

"Sort of, banged up, though. No don't grab that arm. I think the wrist is broken. Maybe a couple of cracked ribs too. Mr. Riggs here is a lot worse off. Concussion maybe, or more."

From the ridge, I can hear a man calling, a familiarly hoarse voice, Archie Hollingsworth, my FO for Charlie Company, who's apparently been traveling with this squad on their search. It is funny that during all this, I am thinking about how Archie had once explained he'd been a heavy smoker since his early teens.

"Screwed my voice up, Captain."

"Cigarettes will kill you, Archie," I'd said. "I quit, man."

"Man, this war'll kill you. I'll worry about cigarettes later."

It is Archie calling down, and the grunts quickly tell him they've found me.

"CPT Weisman is here, Fox Oscar. Kinda dinged up from the crash. We ought to call a dustoff."

Now it is Archie, a week or more of dirty-blond beard on his face, a filthy green T-shirt, stinking as much as any of the grunts.

"Nice shooting on those dinks, Archie. Pretty god-danger damn close to me, though." I manage a grin.

"Nice to see you too, Captain. Where's COL Bowie? He make you walk out carrying the pilot by yourself."

"Bowie's dead, Archie."

"Shit!'

"Yeah, we went down on a ridge near where you'd reported that firefight. Hit by a dink AA gun. Bowie got trapped in the bird. I couldn't get him out. I carried the pilot to cover. Dinks found Bowie in the bird. He stood 'em off with just a .45. Dinks finished him." I can't tell him I couldn't bring myself to go back and see for sure he was dead.

"Man," says LT Hollingsworth, "at least he went out a hero. Doesn't make up for all the shit he put the battalion through, though." He steps closer and reaches out a hand. "Can you walk, sir?"

"Yeah, I guess. I carried Riggs here over from Laos. Feels like I'm beat to hell, though."

"Did you find the patrol?"

"Yeah," I say. Through the pain and the relief of rescue, I manage to get out the story of how I had found them all dead. "Hell of a firefight, man," I tell Hollingsworth. "Lot of blood trails going away. They must have done in a lot of dinks before they bought it." I give him the coordinates of the bodies and listen while he calls it in, his voice heavy with the bad news.

One of Charlie Company's medics has come down the ridge and is kneeling in front of Riggs, looking at him with concern. He turns and looks at me and Archie. "I got a dustoff coming, ETA about ten minutes. I think your pilot here's got a skull fracture, maybe brain swelling, way he is looking." He moves to me and feels my arm carefully. "Let me get a splint on that wrist, Captain, maybe not broken but swollen up like a king-sized salami for sure."

It is hardly ten minutes until the slick Huey with the red cross on white on its nose drops down over the ridge. One of the Charlie Company grunts pops a yellow smoke grenade that plumes out to the east, and the dustoff bird flares and grounds itself near it about ten meters from the water's edge.

"Glad you made it, sir," Hollingsworth says and slaps me lightly on the back as the bird's crew helps me onto the bird and into a seat next to where they have laid WO Riggs. A moment later, the pilot pulls pitch, and the bird bucks in the slight wind, rises carefully along the upslope of the ridge, catches open air at its top, and turns east, headed toward the triage and aid station at Khe Sanh. If you asked me about that fifteen-minute flight, about what we saw or what anybody said to me during it, I couldn't say a thing. I remember a corpsman on the bird looking at the splint the Charlie Company medic had put on, nodding, and saying, "OK." I think I remember asking him how Riggs was, though I don't remember the answer.

I must have dozed because I only remember waking up in the Khe Sanh aid station, a nurse cutting my T-shirt off and exclaiming at the ugly blue-green bruise that covered my whole left side from armpit to hip. They must have given me a sedative because I remember nothing more until I come to on an X-ray table at the hospital in Quang Tri, the tech's voice fading in.

"They want me to take another picture, Captain," he says. "First one shows two bruised ribs, not broken, though, but the one of your wrist was inconclusive, maybe broken, maybe not. Just sit still while I get another picture of it."

And I doze off again.

I guess it is several hours later when I wake in a bed. A nurse sees me, and, soon, a young captain in surgical scrubs comes in and sits down near the bed.

"So, Captain," he says, "you've got two badly bruised ribs and a sprained wrist. Nothing broken. You were fortunate. I want you to stay here for a couple of days, so we can keep the ribs iced. There may be a bit of a separation that will take a while to heal. It would be best if you didn't have any field duty for a month or so. We can put a rib belt on you to limit movement. But it would be better, since this is not a break, that you don't wear one. It's important for you to breathe deeply a lot to help keep your lungs clear. A belt would restrict that. We've got your wrist sprain wrapped. I suspect it will be a week before you will feel like using it for much again. Let the swelling go down first at least. Now that you're awake, I'm going to have you moved into a ward. Two, maybe three days and you should be ready to get out of here." All terse and business like and abruptly, he gets up to go. With Lam Son kicking hell out of our troops and the ARVN, I imagine our med facilities are taxed to the breaking point. Stress on medical personnel must be horrendous.

"Doctor?"

"Huh?"

"One thing, I was brought in with a warrant officer, guy named Riggs. Looked like a head injury. Any word on his condition?"

"Sure, Captain. I'll check." And he's gone.

I doze again and wake to find an orderly ready to help me walk into the ward down the hall. "You was asking about a warrant officer, what happened to him and all, sir?"

"Yeah."

The orderly's eyes are sad, and I expect the worst. He studies a piece of paper. "We checked. Says here that WO Riggs has a skull fracture, brain swelling. He been shipped off to the big hospital in Japan."

"How is he? Is he going to pull through?"

"It don't say, sir. But they don't ship no dead men off to Japan. Got body bags for them. So I suppose he got a chance." He gives me a wry smile. "Come on, Captain. Let's get you into a real bed. Get you a bath too. You smell about half dead yourself."

It will be weeks after this all is over that I will get a letter from Riggs from Camp Drake in Japan. It will be short. "You saved my life, Captain Weisman. I will owe you forever, Bill Riggs." Short but in my heart for all time. Riggs will offer no back-in-the-World address, and there will be no response to the much longer note I send back to him. Intentions fade, I have wanted to contact him again over the years but never have, though. Like my old RTO, Cisco, he has slipped through the cracks of the war and gone.

CHAPTER 22

It ends up being six days before they let me out, a nurse warning me not to do any heavy lifting, particularly with my sprained left wrist.

"How long?"

"Your body will tell you. If it doesn't hurt much when you try it, you're probably OK. I imagine your ribs will be sore some for several weeks. Stuff like that heals slow," she says as she touches my wrist gently. To her, I'm in good shape, all four limbs intact, no bullet wounds, nothing broken. I get care, quick and good, but I'm not their priority.

The nurse is a fine-looking brunette, and I'm a normal twenty-five-year-old male who's been in-country for a year and a half and almost all of that out in the bush, far away from round-eyed women. I smile, and she smiles back, but I suspect I would be at least the ten thousandth soldier to hit on her. She is pleasant and genial to me, but that's it. Thick hide, no interest. I don't even bother to try. That wrist touch is a fantasy for me by myself in the dark of night, and my only other positive when relieving it is that my side doesn't hurt so much anymore.

The hospital is a sprawling compound of big tin-roofed shanties, sandbags on top to hold down the roofing, the dilapidated structures surrounded by walls of sandbags and dirt-filled ammo boxes. Its wards smell of blood and urine and disinfectant. A revetted mess hall serves decent food and excellent coffee, reason enough to stay an extra day or two. By day four, I'm up and moving on my own, walking around in hospital pajamas with no sign of rank—from general to private, in the hospital, you are a casualty and exist somewhere outside the chain of command. I've longed for peace and quiet and should appreciate this rest, but all I want is out, back to the war, back to the World, back to somewhere where I am involved in my own life. The supply sergeant at LZ Bronco has sent up a fresh uniform for me to replace fatigue pants torn in the crash and the shirt left under the bank where I'd concealed WO Riggs. On day five, I slip into the new uniform, into my jungle boots, pull on the shirt with the embroidered cannons and captain's bars, and, suddenly, it is as if the war has come back into focus. An orderly calls me sir. A PFC outside the hospital's mini PX snaps me a salute (When was the last time? I'm almost too startled to return it.)

Day six, drinking some of that good coffee in the mess hall, I spot a rangy blond guy that can only be one man.

"Olsson, that you?" I call.

He turns and looks around the crowded dining area, missing me where I am in the officers' mess area. "Olsson, over here." I stand, putting up my good hand in a wave that he spots, and then breaks out in a big smile.

"Captain!"

"SGT Olsson, good to see you."

"Man, Captain," he says, eyeing my still heavily wrapped wrist. "You a patient here?"

"My last day. The bird I was in got shot down."

He gives me the standard look of sympathy and relief you give to anyone who has survived something ugly, lifting his eyebrows at the end in a what-happened query.

"Idiocy happened. We were in a Loach doing aerial observation on the border. A 12.7 hit us. The battalion commander and I were up in it. He died after the crash. I got banged up, sprained wrist, badly bruised ribs. I carried the pilot out. He had a fractured skull."

"Man! You back with your unit?"

"Yeah, over on the border just north of the Lao Bao crossing." I look at Olsson, who shows no signs of a wound or injury. "What are you doing in Quang Tri? Are you OK? Did your A-Team get sent up to work with the Snake-Eaters here?"

He looks glum. "No, sir. We're still at the Téthian camp. I'm fine, but a buddy of mine, Sam Hofstetler, is a medical sergeant with an SF team over at Lang Vei. He took some mortar shrapnel a few days ago and is here recovering. He's going to make it, but we don't know if he will be sent back into the field or get a ticket back to the World. We did our medic training together. CPT Englander gave me a few days to come up and see him."

"Hell, I'm sorry, Sergeant. You have time to sit down and talk for a bit?"

He looks around at the tables in officers' country. "Uh . . ."

"Yeah, I know, you want to sit with the real soldiers, not us brass. How about outside? There are tables out there in the shade, no hotter there and some breeze?"

His smile breaks out a bit. He nods. "I'll get some chow and be right out."

He comes outside with a battered metal tray. I have had one of the Vietnamese mess hall guys bring a full pitcher of iced tea. SSG Olsson and I talk: a little bit about our backgrounds (mine from Kansas City, his from Duluth), families (neither of us has a wife or kids), about what an asshole CPT Englander is (though a damn fine commander), and how much longer this damn war is going to last. After three glasses of tea (and one pee break), I get to the question I want to ask SSG Olsson.

"Sergeant, what the hell happened on that ridge in Laos? There at the end, I mean."

"You mean, who pulled our nuts out of that fire?" He scratches his close-cropped head.

"I mean, we were in a real jam there, caught on that ridge between two units of the enemy, no way off except through them. Birds were going down from their AA fire. Then, wham! Somebody takes out the entire force to our west so that birds can get in to extract us. Who were they? That's what I mean."

"The OLM."

"Huh?"

"The OLM, the United Front for the Liberation of Oppressed Races. Rebel Yards. Hell, half of our own Yards are part of that bunch or fellow travelers. A bunch of them followed us the whole way. You wouldn't know, but when you've been out there as long as I have, you see signs.

I knew. They were the ones who cleared out most of the Khmer Rouge camp before we got there. I'm pretty sure they had been watching us since the birds set us down on the border."

I play with the iced tea glass, sweated with moisture on the outside. A drop breaks free and runs down the side. I don't know what more to say. Finally, I ask Olsson, "Englander said it was the worst of the worst. What'd he mean?"

"He said that?"

"Yeah, there was a big bang and then a series of pops like smoke grenades going off. He said it was the worst of the worst."

"There are things we know in this fucked-up war, things we ought to know but don't and things nobody ought to know. If it'd do any good, I'd ask Cap myself. I've got an idea, but I'm keeping mum about it. This is one question it's better not to ask." Abruptly, the sergeant stands up. "Good seein' you, Captain. You're a hell of a fine artilleryman. Everybody on our team knows and respects that. Nothing about that day I could say would make a difference. Let's leave it at that." He stands, pops me a smart salute, shakes his head, and just walks away.

What the hell was that all about? *The worst of the worst?*

✭ ✭ ✭

CHAPTER 23

LZ Linebarger reeks with the stench of gunpowder and burning shit, of the stink of unwashed soldiers, of the ammoniac smell of overflowing piss tubes, of the fumes of burning garbage in the hill's trash dump midden (sheltered for security in a bomb crater inside the east perimeter), and of the smell of the churned red earth's filth and must. Even at a thousand meters, coming in on the bird from Quang Tri, I can smell it. Stinking smoke rises from the hill in a dozen places, into the still air and filthy gray cloud cover hanging above it and above the Xe Pon river valley in Laos to the southwest. Fires and columns of smoke are everywhere there too, all along Highway 9 where the broken ARVN army flees headlong back home to Vietnam. Gunships flank us as we drop toward the hill, firing rockets and minigun bursts at the jungle across the border to suppress enemy AA fire. The bird flares and drops into the shelter of the pad in more of a hover than a landing. Its blade sound is fierce in the revetted pad's confines. A shirtless cargo crew rushes forward to yank ammo and rations and precious bags of mail off the bird. The bird's crew chief gives me a hand down.

"Thanks," I say, though my gratitude is lost in the turbine roar and blatt of blades. I move away gingerly, my left wrist still wrapped and my side still tender.

In the six days since I've been gone, the hill has transformed into a real fortress. Everywhere are fresh dozer cuts in the red earth and bunkers piled with sandbags. The TOC bunker is deeply bulwarked, sides and top. Facing west on either side of the hill's central high point are Quad .50 machine guns mounted on sandbagged deuce and a half trucks. Between them on the highest point of the perimeter's west side is the unmistakable domed turret of an M48 Patton tank, so dug in and sandbagged that its main deck is level with the ground. One of the Quad .50s is firing, and the two 155 howitzers in pits to the right and left of the pad also fire as the bird that brought me here lifts away over the mountaintop to the east. As the bird's engine noise fades, I can hear over the firing of the Quad .50s and 155s, the stunning, though distance-attenuated volume of fire from the other side of the border near and far, from small arms and artillery, and from the rips of miniguns and the rattles and detonations of indefinite origin—a mean and likely futile battle.

The pad master nods a greeting at me. "Good to see you, sir. Watch when you head to the TOC. These days, we seem to be gettin' mortared about every ten minutes."

No mortar rounds fall as I make my way down the path to the operations center and push through its door. It is SSG Hamlin at the infantry station who first sees me enter and calls out, "Welcome back, sir." The S3, CPT de la Croix, is seated next to him, engrossed in a conversation with a lieutenant I haven't seen before. He raises a hand in greeting. That new LT, I realize, must be the replacement for that lucky bastard Mack McFarlane, who, whose tour up, had flown back to the World. I don't see MAJ Echols, whose command station up and behind CPT de la Croix is unoccupied. (I learn he's over in LTC Bowie's former bunker meeting with a major from Brigade S2. *Didn't take long for the dead colonel's space to be put to something useful,* I think.)

At the artillery station are SGT Morris and Cat. Both stand as I approach; Morris with a grin, Cat with a look of relief on his face.

"Cat here thought the dinks killed you, Cap," SGT Morris says. "I told him it couldn't be allowed to happen because it would take too damn long to break in a new liaison officer."

Cat gives me a half grin. He's seen a lot in his few weeks in Vietnam and looks like a veteran soldier now. He offers me his chair at the arty station.

"Nah," I tell Cat. "I want to get settled, talk to MAJ Echols and such before I sit down here."

"Did you hear what happened to CPL Mallaby, sir?" Cat asks.

"What?" I see SGT Morris's face shift to a serious look.

"Wounded," Morris says. "A mortar fragment got him in his shoulder. Not too bad, only the meat there, not the joint. Happened early on the day before yesterday. He got taken to Quang Tri hospital. That's where you were, wasn't it, sir?"

CPL Mallaby was at the same hospital where I was, and I didn't see him or even know!

"Yeah, that left just two of us to handle this station for the past couple of days. I had LT Pringle in here last night to spell us." Pringle is the FO for Alpha Company, which I gather is up here with Bravo as a beefed-up hill security force. George Hessian, the FO for Bravo Company, is also here on the hill, and I expect I'll also call on him to help relieve us if things get tight. I tell SGT Morris that I might try to get back to Quang Tri to see how Mallaby is if things quiet down enough for me to go.

"He isn't there anymore, Cap. He needed some specialized surgery, so he can keep full use of the arm. They sent him to Japan for it and then probably back to the World. I expect Mallaby's done with Vietnam." (I will write to Mallaby and receive a friendly note in response from where he is recovering in a hospital in Minneapolis near his home. "I never thought I would miss Vietnam, especially not the weather," he writes. "But witches' tits are warmer than it is here this winter. It was good working for you, Captain. I hope you get home safely.")

The tension here in the TOC is the highest I have yet experienced. Smiles are few and fleeting. Voices of the infantry and artillery duty teams are hushed but taught. The artillery map board near SGT Morris is marked with half a dozen Save-A-Plane designators indicating six simultaneous fire missions from Bravo Battery (the data for them include altitude, direction, and the grid squares of the start and end points of fire) to alert aircraft—that's as many Save-A-Planes as I've ever seen marked at one time.

Cat yawns and shakes his head, and I look at him, his face drawn, eyes bagged with exhaustion. "How long have you been at this, Cat?"

"I dunno, sir, maybe twelve hours?"

"You, Sarge?"

"Same, I guess."

"I'll take the rest of this shift. I'll talk to Echols later. You two go get some sleep. Send LT Pringle up here to me first, would you?"

Both liaison team members, looking tired but grateful, push out of the TOC. I drop into the seat SGT Morris has vacated, stare down at the topo map of our AO, and shake my head at the masses of green grease-penciled dots demarcating the likely positions of friendly units on the Laotian side of the border. (I say likely because in this fog of battle, nobody knows for sure where the ARVN units are.) The map also has a haze of orange marks indicating likely enemy positions. There's also a long corridor prominently marked in red over Highway 9 itself, boldly labeled "No fire!"—the escape route for the wildly didi mauing ARVN units.

"Crap!" I say again, and as a new forward air controller checks in, I grab the radio handset and begin to read off the long list of Save-A-Plane designators, already feeling tension climb up my still sore and once again stiffening side.

Darkness is no balm. It finds me and MAJ Echols in a sheltered fighting position atop a bunker near the Patton tank, watching a pattern of 12.7 mm tracers rise toward the hill from across the river and slapped by the shock and roar of outgoing fire as the tank responds with its 90 mm gun. The howitzers behind us fire with a stunning crack. The tank's gun is a softer bang, resounding in its low-angle fire, dust and smoke billowing. The dug-in tank rocks with the recoil. Far across the valley at the apparent source of the 12.7 AA fire, there is a flare of orange and a soft boom coming a few seconds later as the tank shell impacts.

"The tank's done a good job of suppressing the AA fire," MAJ Echols tells me. "Direct fire artillery from the battery is effective too, but this is what these track asses are trained for. Sad to say, when we leave here, we're going to have to blow the tank to hell. Running it up the steep side of this hill did the engine in. We were barely able to maneuver it into the dugout it is in now."

I try to tell Echols about LTC Bowie and how he died, how responsible I feel. But he apparently already knows. "It's not worth the worry, David, or even a second thought," he says when I start to explain why I hadn't stayed to protect the trapped colonel. "Bowie knew what he was doing, knew all of you were sure to die in a fight with the dinks if you stayed and didn't get that pilot out of there. He was a colonel, for Christ's sake, and knew the risks."

I'm shaking, eyes damp, telling the major I should have stayed anyway. "COL Bowie is dead because I left him, sir. If I'd stayed, maybe—"

"Maybe hell . . . if you stayed, you would have faced an NVA patrol by yourself. You wouldn't have been able to fight them off. Bowie would still have been killed for sure. You couldn't have gotten him out of the downed bird. We had to blow the whole bird off his body to get it out. You and the warrant officer would have been killed or possibly captured, and we would have lost three officers. You did the right thing, David. Don't ever think otherwise."

He's right, I know, though in the dreams of it far after this raggedy mess at the end of the war, far along the years when it is only a memory, I still think I should have stayed, should have tried. Nobody can tell me otherwise.

In the valley below, the ARVN trucks and tracks dash our way from the rout in Laos, their vehicles running with full lights as if light discipline has no currency and the disaster they are running from no refuge in darkness. The sound of distant battle is a tattoo of fire along that road. Even in the dark, a stream of helicopters tears through the sky overhead back and forth across the border, pulling out the chicken-with-their-heads-off, crazy-running South Vietnamese troops. Earlier, with the descending sun behind it, I had watched through my binos as a Huey a klick or so beyond the border tried to lift ARVN troops from a burning laager of abandoned armored personnel carriers. I could see the agony of men jumping for the skids as the bird rose, see the bird's crew chief kicking at the hanging ARVN troops dangling from the bird's open door, see some fall from perhaps fifty meters in the air, the bird droop toward the ground again overloaded, and see it half spin to the right, and then three more clinging ARVN fall, and the finally lightened bird ascend, rising over our hill and on to the east. God help the ARVN who had fallen, surely either dead from the drop or injured past caring.

"The ARVN gave as good as they could. They're not cowards. But this was a tragedy from the get-go," Echols tells me, his tone bitter.

"Their higher command couldn't keep their mouths shut, and so the North Vietnamese knew everything even before we did. The NVA knew where to put their troops to defend, where the ARVN line of attack would be to counterattack. What the whole damn battle plan was. What a monster clusterfuck!"

Echols makes no claim to military genius, no Alexander, Pershing, or Lee. But he is a solid commander, tactically able and uninterested in sophisticated tricks. He has the hill well-fortified, two infantry companies set in on its perimeter, two more plus the Recon Platoon drawn in and patrolling the surrounding mountain, moving in strength to interdict and turn any possible enemy assault. It is not a fancy plan, not aimed at honor or glory, but simply a firm defense. The hill has not been hit significantly since he put this system in place. My sense is that commanders above him in the chain recognize this. Though just a major, Echols will remain CO of the 7/31 for the remainder of his tour.

For the next week, our danger, fortified as the hill is, is minimal. We take some 12.7 AA fire that the Patton and the Quad .50s quickly suppress; some mortars come in, hasty and mostly misaimed. There are occasional enemy sorties against the hill's defenses, mostly at night, mostly leaving shreds of dinks and tatters of uniforms in the wire next morning. Adding up the infantry and artillery on the hill, we have more than three hundred troops here, solidly revetted. Thus, well dug in and heavy with firepower and with all the air support we need, we are not likely to be dislodged. Our location, though, at the choke point where the border and Highway 9 come together in the tight space between the Xe Pon River south and the hills north, makes us the cork against the soaring pressure of battle.

CHAPTER 24

Four weeks into the Laos incursion, the ARVN have given up. Their battered units, most abandoning everything, are pouring out of Laos. Some come headlong on foot along the ruin that Highway 9 has become. Others grab for spots on anything that moves, land or air. From the sandbagged fighting position on that forward bunker on LZ Linebarger, I can see on that highway an uncountable number of out-of-fuel, damaged, or abandoned ARVN trucks, tracks, howitzers, and even tanks, many purposely destroyed by our own Phantom jets to deny them to the enemy. The wreckage makes Highway 9 passable only in a single muddy, vehicle-choked lane heading east toward us. Supported by the Recon Platoon, Charlie Company has been tasked with fatally damaging any abandoned vehicles and heavy weaponry the jets have missed in our AO. From the border southeast to where Highway 9 adjoins the Xe Pon River, troops of those two units are moving among the abandoned vehicles, setting off cratering charges or laying thermite grenades on engines. It is agonizing to watch the destruction of all these vehicles, but the truth is the ARVN will not come back for them and they would fall into the hands of the NVA if left intact.

West of the border in Laos are at least as many abandoned ARVN combat vehicles, but because U.S. troops cannot legally cross into Laos, we are helpless to deal with them on the ground. Not so from the air, though. With the ARVN retreat (stampede is a better word for it) winding down, our jets and gunships have been turning their attention to destruction of these vehicles. Phantom jets roar in low across the border dropping napalm and HE to blow the vehicles in place. Others, where possible, we target with destruction fire missions from the guns on LZ Linebarger. But destruction missions require observers to conduct them, and none of us is willing to spend the necessary but dangerous observation time flying over Laos. So the only destruction missions we shoot are those we can observe from our side of the border. The two FOs on the hill have been tasked with this duty. Here, we have a bird's-eye view of all this action, and so I watch the blooming fireballs and the gray smoke bursts of high explosive along the highway west almost a third of the way to the Laotian town of Tchepone. That town, centered on the northern terminus of the Ho Chi Minh trail in Laos, had been the declared objective of this entire Lam Son 719 campaign.

I don't fault the ARVN troops for their flight from this defeat. Fierce but undisciplined, unruly and ill-led, naïfs in allegiance to a foundering regime, they now have only themselves to depend upon. That gone, hope lost, they run.

A helmeted PFC wearing a flak jacket comes charging across the hill toward me. Half breathless, he manages to get out, "CPT Weisman, MAJ Echols wants to see you right away."

"Briefing bunker?" I ask.

"Yes, sir. He says it's urgent."

That's not much of an explanation; everything is urgent these days. Still, I grab the M16 I carry everywhere with me now and hurry back along the path to the briefing bunker. Inside are MAJ Echols, 1LT Matt Dieffenbach, who recently took command of the Recon Platoon, and the S3 CPT Bill de la Croix. Echols nods as I enter. The map sheet covering our location and the one covering the adjacent area to the west are spread out on the ammo box wood table.

"This is LZ Bão (Vietnamese for "storm"), about sixteen klicks from us in Laos," Echols says, tapping the 53-37 grid intersection to our west. I see it is on a hilltop southwest of the Xe Pon and likely blocked from any easy road access from the now impassible highway a klick north across the river. "Two hundred of the Eighth ARVN Marines—one infantry company and one battery of heavy artillery—have been occupying it during this campaign. This morning, getting the word that an NVA armored brigade was moving to overrun the firebase, they began pulling up stakes and didi mauing for Vietnam. They're better disciplined than some of the other ARVN units, but it's still more of a scramble than a retreat. They've been commandeering whatever air transport they can get and running like hell back across the border. Our birds have already pulled some of them out—maybe an infantry platoon and most of the gun crews so far—and dropping them at the Special Forces camp at Lang Vei."

I stare at the map, fearing I know what's coming.

Echols continues. "As solid fighters as these marines are compared to the rest of the ARVN, even they are terrified, grabbing onto any birds coming in. One overloaded slick already nearly went down. Its crew chief threatened to shoot 'em all if most didn't get off. The fuckers have been leaving everything there at LZ Bão, including a battery of six eight-inch towed howitzers and at least a thousand rounds of eight-inch ammo."

"No way do we want the NVA getting a hold of that kind of heavy artillery. If they do, they've got the range and the ammo to plaster this hill and a lot farther," CPT de la Croix adds.

"David, how much farther past us could those guns shoot from LZ Bão?" Echols asks.

"The max range for those guns is seventeen klicks, sir," I tell him, pondering the map. "Where they are, they could hit this hill and cover the highway for probably two klicks past us into Vietnam. See here, along the Xe Pon valley, the land is generally flat or at least just low hills between us and LZ Bão. There's nothing to obstruct those eight-inchers from firing at that maximum range."

"Shit," says Echols, "so they could do us some damage."

"With a thousand or so HE rounds, they could do a hell of a lot of damage," I say. "The towed versions of the eight-inch are old, World War II vintage, but still as accurate as anything on the battlefield. The projectiles they fire are monsters, more than two hundred pounds each, with a bursting radius of eighty meters. They get those guns zeroed onto this hill and we're dead meat."

"Yeah, I figured," says Echols. He slaps his hand onto the map. "I hate it, but we've got to go in there and take out those guns."

"We can't send Phantoms in with snake and nape to blow them up?" I ask, but Echols is already shaking his head.

"Too far into Laos. The dinks have boocoo AA all along the highway. Two Phantoms have already gone down near there trying to take down NVA units. Brigade is dispatching birds and gunships to pull out the ARVN marines. They'll go low along the river and pop up onto the hill, touch down just long enough to grab the friendly dinks, and then didi back here."

"The Phantoms can't take that route?"

"They could try *if* brigade is willing. But we can't have them drop napalm on that hill until every friendly is off. If we miss coordination timing on that, the NVA will have those guns off that hill and gone. The ARVN have abandoned plenty of prime movers there in Laos—deuce and a halfs and larger—big enough to do the job. So we're going in during the extraction and to make sure the guns are spiked."

I suspect the next question already has a bad answer, but I ask it anyway. "Jesus, Major, can't the ARVN marines spike those guns themselves on the way out? All it would take is a thermite grenade down each tube and they'd be done."

"You'd think," says Echols. "But the ARVN are like headless chickens. Out is their only thought. Brigade doesn't want to trust that they'll do those guns in before they leave. They want us to have a platoon go in on the extraction birds, spike the guns while the ARVN are being pulled out, and then come out again with the last of the marines."

Man! Going into Laos once again where the law says we can't, into a shitstorm on purpose!

Echols reads it on my face. "Hell, if I could, David, I'd wait for the air force to put in an Arc Light strike and plaster them with five-hundred-pound bombs to blow the whole hill to hell. But by the time the B-52s get there, the dinks could have those guns hitched up and gone. Brigade says get them, law or no law. So I'm sending the Recon Platoon to do the deed. I'll need one of your FOs to go in with them and make sure the guns get spiked for good and certain. Whom do you want to send?"

Frankly, I don't want to send in anybody. It's an impossible task, with batshit crazy ARVN marines and gunners panicked to get out of there, NVA units closing in. AA fire everywhere. No choice, no damn choice at all. "I'm going, Major," I tell Echols. "No point in risking one of the FOs. My responsibility, so my job."

The fact that MAJ Echols doesn't argue with me just jams me more. What am I letting myself in for?

"OK," says CPT de la Croix. "We've got birds inbound in about fifteen. Recon is already assembling on the highway for a combat assault. The birds will pick them up, and one will come up here to pick you up. The pad master has a couple of cases of thermite grenades." De la Croix smiles more than a little ruefully. "So grab whatever gear you need and get up to the pad."

I consider taking Cat to carry a radio. But Recon will have radios aplenty, and we'll be out of range of any guns to shoot for me—meaning I won't have use for my own radio anyway. I see no benefit to putting Cat at risk just to stand there and watch things go to hell on LZ Bão. I've got what I need: a map, my M16 and a full bandoleer, my steel pot, and what fragments of courage I've got left to muster. Back into Laos, back into Laos. The very thought chills me.

I join 1LT Dieffenbach on the third of the five birds taking Recon across the border. It swoops in just long enough to pick up me and the cases of thermite and join the CA. We are, for certain, in agreement on one thing: we don't want to be on the ground there for more than an hour, tops, a lot less than that if possible. Our bird lifts and turns to the south, and I watch our hill drop away below us. Its mottled green skirts merge into the wooded plain north of the river pocked with a muddle of low hills. Down there, at the ruined and now-abandoned ville of Lao Bao, the border crossing looks impassible, blocked by a littered monster of a junkyard of dead trucks and tracks right where Highway 9 crosses into Laos. The river's banks, once rife with rich jungle green, are shattered, blackened stretches of well-churned muck. The river here is broad, perhaps fifty meters across and at least six or eight meters deep. I have no idea if its water is ever clear, but now, in the rage of this conflict, its stream is dark, oily, chunky, and filthy as a sewer pumping the slop of war eastward to the sea. Still, though bank full from the rains in the mountains of Laos to the west, the river is docile compared to the wet season torrents of the Sông Ba To' and the Sông Re I had worked along with Bravo Company far to the south in Quang Ngai Province so many months ago. Battles may be raging along Highway 9, but from our altitude, the sense of what is below is of funereal peace, a miraculous calm masking desperate and unseen fights.

Dropping almost to the water, we turn to follow the river, skimming it so low, it seems we could, if we wished, dangle our feet into the stream. We move apparently unmarked by the enemy troops that concentrate mostly along Highway 9. Within a few minutes, the river makes a sweep several klicks to the south, splitting from the highway, taking us away from the heart of the combat. Here, the Xe Pon's course meanders. It leads us above stretches of black-speckled green reeds along its banks and past dead rice paddies. Beyond the rotor noise, it seems quiet here, though we pass over the wreckage of dead villes as tattered and tortured as any I have seen on the Vietnam side of the border. Beyond us north and south, the river valley spreads serenely without a sign of the titanic battle boiling along the nearby Highway 9.

"No AA so far, that's good!" Dieffenbach shouts to me over the bird's turbine roar. I nod, not even trying to answer through the noise. We are seated in the open left door of the bird, feet hanging above the skids, a wet and chilly wind whipping at us. Next to me, the door gunner leans on his M60, staring at the passing terrain, fiercely vigilant. No one has to be reminded that we are over Laos, where U.S. troops are not supposed to go. In and out, this is to be quick, no extra chances: spike the guns and didi mau boocoo fast. With me and the Recon platoon leader on our bird are four others from the platoon we'd swooped to pick up before joining the flight. They are half a squad of some of the battalion's toughest soldiers, hardly a crease of worry on their faces as we take them into yet another battle. Though, I know, that mask of calm is a lie; everybody worries all the time. It never leaves you, will not now or ever, we know.

Ahead of us are two slicks packed with six each of Dieffenbach's Recon Platoon. Cobra gunships flank them, all riding as if on cushions of air barely above water riffled and whipped beneath their passing. Behind us as we follow a curve of the river around to the north are the other two birds, wagging the tail of our armada. Now we have come to where the hills to our left begin to close in. Still following the river, we make another turn, heading us almost due west. Far off in front of us past another bend of the river, past maybe four klicks of low hills, beyond the streaks of a pair of ruined highways, I can make out the sharp demarcation of a soaring cliff. It is perhaps three hundred meters high from base to rim, cut down by what had been the river's course millennia ago. Ahead the river turns sharply north and then west again after another couple of klicks. Where the river turns hard west, the cliff stops at a sort of beak overlooking the water. South of us, it runs like a towering wall for several klicks before its face bends at a new angle and, there too, runs away toward the west along a tributary stream. We are close now, but it still seems calm around us, the noise of our bird's turbine overwhelming any sound of battle. Now, where the river turns sharply away from us toward the north, we leave it, passing over its bank and up toward a prominence that rises above the other hills—LZ Bão. Dots that are men move across its crest; others, of the foe's army, move in the bamboo and low brush that fur the hill from its base to the wire near its peak.

Now it starts.

As we approach the hilltop, we can see tracers rise from its base in purple flashes. Streaks of RPG fire arrow toward the firebase's perimeter. Pocks of gray mortar and grenade smoke bloom on the slopes and even inside what we can see of a bunker line and a hash of trenches around the hillcrest. Coils and arcs of wire loop around it, as black and defined against the bare red dirt as if scrawled by a fine ink pen. Tracers from ARVN machine guns pour back down the slopes, and other gray puffs, the marks of impacting mortar rounds, touch here and there along the bottom of the slope. This close, the intensity of the fire overwhelms the sound of the bird's engine, fire rattling, detonations rocking us.

Hot LZ? Hot as fire!

"Jesus Christ," LT Dieffenbach yips, and he leans backward to talk to our pilot, pointing first at the hill and then at the Cobra gunships. The pilot says something over his radio, and the two gunships, their miniguns at full rip, dive toward the eastern face of the hill, tearing up the brush and bamboo there and adding half a dozen rockets each to their fire. Under their cover, our flight of slicks slides up the along the hill's face and pops over the crest. The birds flare and nervously settle one by one to the pad to drop off the squads of Recon.

Almost as soon as our bird touches down, shouting ARVN marines rush it, pushing past me and the Recon lieutenant and the other four of us climbing off the bird. More, abandoning their posts (and most of their gear) along the bunker line, come scrambling in toward the pad. Almost as soon as I am off, I push through them, dart ten meters or so away from the bird, and hit the ground beneath the incoming fire sleeting around us.

Three of the Recon troops are immediately hit by AK fire. Two are killed just that quickly; another one with a leg wound is down whimpering with the pain of it and screaming, "Doc! Doc!" I see no medic coming right away, work my own way over to the fallen soldier, grab him by the scruff of his fatigue shirt, and pull him away from the scrum near the bird. He lies there, doubled up on his side, calling, "Doc!" again, arms around the wounded leg, a picture of pain and misery. But there is little blood, and the wound looks to be in the meat of his calf. A Recon medic with an aid bag—bypassing the two dead troopers with only a look to be certain they are past help—pushes over to us, nods a thank you to me, and begins to work on the wounded man. I look for a beat or two at the two dead men. A year and a half in-country and I am still shocked by the casual suddenness of death.

The rest are down OK. But I see the bird we left is in trouble, swarmed by ARVN marines as it tries to lift off. Full and then some with frantic Vietnamese, the bird's blades hammer as the pilot pulls pitch, and I can see the crew chief kicking at the hands of the marines who are clinging desperately to every hand hold, to the skids especially.

"Get the hell off!" the crew chief is shouting. He steps on fingers and kicks at desperate hands.

I hear one of the ARVN marines shout back, "Không, không, không. Đưa chúng ta với bạn!" I expect that means something like "Get us the hell out of here!"

Though the bird's turbine strains, the bird does not want to lift with all that weight and begins to founder as it fights up a few feet off the ground. It chills me that it has gained only a dozen meters or so above the hill when the crew chief manages to kick away perhaps six more marines, finally lightening the load enough for the laden helicopter to climb into the air. Out from the hill a hundred meters or so high, two more ARVN marines lose their hold and tumble, kicking down into the underbrush. Dead or alive, I don't know.

As we debarked, one of Recon's sergeants had managed to grab the wooden cases of thermite grenades and drag them off the bird with him. Hunkered on the battle-torn hillside above the pad, Matt Dieffenbach is calling to his men, pointing to where the six eight-inch howitzers are laid across the hill's crest. "SGT Martin, first squad," he shouts, "one grenade down each barrel! The rest of you, make a tight perimeter and lay down some suppressive fire. We want to be done with this and gone by the time the next lift comes in."

I'm used to big guns, but these eight-inch towed howitzers are antique monsters, WWII vintage grabbed from God only knows what mothballed store of battle relics. Massive, the howitzers are absolutely unsuited to Vietnam's 360-degree war; they are ponderously mounted on eight-tired carriages and braced by substantial split trails dug in behind them. Their maximum traverse left to right is only sixty degrees, hardly a sixth of a circle. To shoot the opposite direction, the crew must dig out and jack up its heavy trails, manhandle the heavyweight gun's sixteen tons around, dig it in, and likely lay it all over again. Their tubes can depress barely two degrees below level, making them useless for direct fire down the slope of the hill. The guns, likely not fired for hours or even days, point haphazardly, some aimed high, some at their lowest elevation. No two are aimed in the same direction. None looks ready to shoot.

I watch one of the Recon troops pull the pin on a thermite grenade and chuck it down the throat of one howitzer whose tube is almost at its lowest point, though still head high for the soldier. There is a hiss and a gush of gray smoke from the tube's muzzle, a gush of hot sparks following it, and, suddenly, the hiss of thermite combustion that rises to a roar and then dwindles within a minute. The crack of heating metal sounds from the gun's breach, now welded shut. Two more of the guns also have their barrels down nearly at the horizontal, and I watch other Recon soldiers chuck thermite grenades down them as well. A fourth gun's tube is raised to its maximum elevation, and one of the Recon troops pulls the pin on another thermite grenade and tries to toss it into the mouth of that raised tube as if trying a basketball layup. He misses.

The smoking grenade bounces down onto the ground, spouting sparks, while the soldier who threw it and half a dozen other Recon troops dodge back away from the searing 4,500-degree heat of the ignited grenade, which burns on the red mud with an eye-dazzling white light.

"Man, man!" I find myself shouting at them. "Crank it down first so you can reach the muzzle." They, not being redlegs, have no idea what I am talking about, and so I get up into a crouch and push past them and the sputtering remains of the grenade on the ground, climb aboard the gun's heavy trail, grab the elevation wheel, and crank the tube toward the ground. It grinds down slowly, and I imagine the ARVN have not taken good care of this piece, leaving the gear unlubricated and tough to maneuver. I manage to get it low enough for one of the Recon troops to drop a grenade in, and I jump away as the thermite reaction ignites inside it.

Two tubes are yet untouched, both raised to maximum elevation. Off in the distance over the river east, I can see the growing specks of a second flight of birds inbound. I don't know if there are gun crews for the howitzers left on the hill. I see none, but frankly couldn't tell the difference between them and the marine infantrymen here anyway. There is at least one ARVN redleg, a trung sĩ wearing on his sleeves the three upturned chevrons of a senior sergeant. He comes running as one of the Recon troops approaches the next to the last howitzer.

The trung sĩ waves him off, shouting urgently, "Không, không, vẫn còn là một đạn pháotrong ống!" and desperately pushing aside the Recon soldier with the grenade. Seeing none of us understand him, the Vietnamese sergeant points toward the large store of eight-inch artillery rounds under an open-faced bunker nearby and points then to the tube, and, suddenly, I know.

"Damn, Dieffenbach," I tell the Recon commander. "I think he's telling us there is still an artillery projo in that tube. If we put a thermite grenade in there, the whole damn thing is likely to go off and blow away everybody up here."

"You just want to leave it, Captain?"

"No, no, for sure, no! We're either going to have to wait until they are ready to pull us off here and then spike it, hope we have time before the damn thing goes off, or fire the gun and then spike the thing." I turn to the trung sĩ, point to the gun, and make a motion as if I was pulling a lanyard to fire it.

"Shoot it," I say. "You bic?"

"Vâng, vâng tôi bic." He nods, smiles a bit desperately, and says, "*Chúng ta cần bột.* Need powdah. *You* bic?"

"Powder? Where?"

"*Có!*" he says and points twenty or so meters past the store of artillery rounds to a stack of powder cans.

By now, the incoming fire, which had been moderately heavy, has increased substantially. Most of Recon have moved into positions in the hill's inner trench, sheltering from a deluge of small arms fire, responding with fire of their own. I find my own spot there as several mortar rounds whistle in and detonate forty meters or so on the other side of the peak. Mud blown up from their blasts spatters down around us. We've already been up here longer than intended, and while the last thing I want to do is spend more time on this hill, I have no intention of leaving with howitzers still here in working order. Waiting until the last minute to spike this gun with a round still in the chamber is a colossal risk. The safer choice: we are going to have to fire the loaded howitzer and then spike it and the other remaining gun. With that, we'll get on our birds to fly out of there after setting a demo charge with timer on the ammo and powder stores so that they will detonate when everybody is off the hill. "You don't want to be there when that stuff goes off," I had told Dieffenbach. "An A-bomb may be more potent, but all those shells detonating at once will seem as big as one. Anyone still on this hill will likely be dead meat."

The trung sĩ, seemingly the only ARVN trooper on the hill not in a panic, has gone to the powder store and come back with a canister of green bag powder. He levers the howitzer's huge breechblock open, slides in the powder, and slams the thing shut. He pulls a primer cartridge from his pocket, inserts it, and looks at me. The gun is pointed almost true north toward the mountains of Laos. The tube is at its highest angle. I have no idea where the shell, once fired, will impact and, frankly, don't much care. I doubt there are any ARVN troops left up north, and the gun has to fire before we can exit the hill.

"Fire in the hole!" I scream at the top of my lungs, stuff my fingers in my ears, look over at the trung sĩ, and shout, "Fire!"

The deflagration of the huge artillery piece is titanic. Smoke jets from the gun's muzzle, mud from the hill rises and rattles in the sharpness of the shock as the piece fires, and, with it, the entire huge weapon bucks back a few inches on its dug-in trails, rocks forward again, settles, and is still. Hardly anything is as monstrously loud or sharp as the firing of a truly large bore howitzer when you are up close to it. I pull my fingers from my ears, wondering if I can still hear and wondering also where in the hilly jungle sixteen klicks to the north the shell from that gun will impact. "Shot!" I whisper and let go a quick laugh. I watch almost sadly as the trung sĩ himself, frowning, takes up a thermite grenade, pulls the pin, and tosses the can expertly up and into the gun's upturned muzzle, turning away unhappily as the flash and heat of the thermite reaction gush out with the last of the smoke from the gun's firing. The stern trung sĩ's look seems full of tears.

One gun is left. Most of the ARVN marines have been lifted from the hill. East of us, the birds returning for us are already in sight. The last of the eight-inch howitzers is on an outcropping on the west side of the hill, off away from the other five and more exposed to enemy fire from the area below the hill there. A parapet protects the gun from much of the incoming, but one RPG has already blown away a chunk of the bulwark there. Another would leave it entirely exposed. A trench line leads that way, but the ten meters or so between it and the gun are relatively open and exposed to enemy fire.

One of the Recon troops has already tried to get to the gun with a thermite grenade and found himself slightly wounded and pinned behind a tumble of sandbags and used powder canisters.

LT Dieffenbach directs a sergeant. "Maxwell, take a couple of squads over to the trench on that side and give him cover to get back."

"Right, LT, what about the howitzer?"

"Forget the damn howitzer for now. Spiking it isn't worth getting him killed. We gotta suppress the incoming first."

The man he called SGT Maxwell grabs a dozen of the Recon troops and points them to the trench on that flank of the hill. "Keep the bastards from firing while we get a man over to disable that artillery piece," he tells them.

Meanwhile, behind us, a gaggle of maybe twenty-five ARVN marines—the last of them on the hill?—is shoulder-to-shoulder near the hill's helicopter pad, fighting for position to be first to board the incoming birds. The lead helicopter pops up over the hill's east face about a hundred meters out and begins to flare for a landing.

Bang. Bang. Bang. A beat of heavy-caliber AA fire comes from the west, smacking into the oncoming bird. It takes out the bird's windscreen and the pilot and copilot in a ringing impact. The bird yaws, skitters right, and smacks down on the north slope of the hill twenty meters or so below the hillcrest. It bursts instantly into flame, sending a rolling pillar of black smoke into the overcast sky. I feel a woeful plummet in the pit of my stomach and duck below the lip of the trench. From there, I can see a second bird coming in behind it also get hit and veer left to slide down just above the south slope, the whole machine shuddering, its turbine smoking and sounding a terrible clatter, apparently having suffered fatal engine damage. In this disarray, the remaining ARVN marines have gone nuts, scattering from the pad, and taking any cover they can find. The shouting in Vietnamese is incoherent and untranslatable. The rest of the flight of slick helicopters, including the Cobra gunships, has broken off their approach and turned back east along the river.

"Jesus!" somebody shouts.

"Incoming AA," says another.

"God, what did that?" LT Dieffenbach asks me. "Something big assed came from the west, didn't it?"

"From that way, LT, I think," one of the Recon troops calls out, pointing off toward the cliff face four klicks to our west. He indicates a spot just behind a low hill at the base of the cliff. From there, the white sparks of tracers rise and stream in an arc toward where one of the Cobras accompanying the flight of slicks is making a diving turn behind our hill. "There, there, LT, see it?"

"Yeah, it's in defilade," Dieffenbach says. "Its fire is coming from just behind that little bump of a hill. Man, that's a lot bigger than any AA they were shooting at us back on Linebarger."

Which is trouble. The enemy AA gun—so far into Laos—is far out of range of the guns we have at LZ Linebarger. The only longer-range guns are the 175s at Khe Sanh, but they as well are too far east to be of any help. And Dieffenbach is right: this is something big, most likely a Russian ZPU 14.5 mm from the sound and the range it is firing at. Dual barrels, I suspect, maybe even a quad from its volume of fire. I've never seen one before, remembering only a long-ago conversation with some LRRP troops at Chu Lai about how the dinks have some pretty heavy weaponry in their more secure bases across the border. ("Armor, big trucks, heavy Russian AA guns, Captain. Much worse than the light-assed stuff they throw at us here on the Nam side.")

Dieffenbach is on the horn to our operations center asking for an air strike. "Man, we're stuck here," he tells CPT de la Croix. "You've got to get something in to knock out that dink AA."

"Roger," de la Croix comes back. "Wait one."

Waiting, we are taking steadily heavier incoming fire from the NVA elements at the base of our hill. We're not a hefty unit up here. Recon had come with only twenty-five men, mostly with small arms including four M60 machine guns whose 1,100-meter effective range is only a third the distance to the dink AA gun. Two are now dead, and another three have been wounded—none severely, thank God, though they are pretty much out of action.

"Digger Six, this is Foundation Two-One. Over." It is CPT de la Croix coming back onto the radio. His voice is apologetic. "Higher-higher says negative on an air strike. Jets are fully occupied elsewhere for at least an hour. Even if we could get them, the only safe route for Phantoms is along the river the way you went. Dinks are said to have the rest of the ingress to Laos covered with heavy AA. Once past your hill, the jets would have to cover at least four klicks right into the teeth of the AA gun there. Brigade says no, too dangerous for the aircraft and unlikely to do you any good."

"So what the hell are we supposed to do here, man?" LT Dieffenbach asks with rising anger, voice hard and unmilitary. "We're surrounded, you know."

"Roger, Digger Six, your best bet is to walk off that hill to the east. The high ground behind you should shield you from the AA fire. We can task the Cobra gunships to hit the dinks on that side of the hill and give you a clear route down. The map shows open space once you get to the river where the birds can come in safely to extract you."

"Roger, Foundation Two-One, wait while we look at the options."

"Don't take too long. Intel says more NVA units are moving your way."

"Roger, wait. Out." LT Dieffenbach looks at me. "Rock and a hard place, man," he says. "We can't stay up here because the dinks are coming from every which way. We wait, and they'll overrun us. We can't get a lift in to extract us because of that AA gun. Can we go down the hill to the river? Hell, I don't know. What do you see, Captain?"

I've been studying escape and evasion routes off the hill, thinking, *Didi mau, hell!* That's no answer. There must be a full regiment of dinks down there by now that we'll have to face if we try that route. The other E & E routes look at least as bad. Of them all, only a run down the east flank offers any chance of escape. *Small chance,* I think, though realizing that our only choice may be to try and didi that way down to the river. The bottom of the hill there is infested with dinks, and we are sure to take heavy casualties if we try it. I look at the scattered ARVN troops around us, supposedly the best the ARVN have, but none seems to be an officer or in any position of command, and no one seems to be organizing them into any defense. It is clear more NVA are engaging our hill now, coming from the west, moving around the base into positions that will eventually enable an assault. As they gather, the volume of small arms directed at us rises. Mortar shells pop here and there across the hill, coming every ten or fifteen seconds now. And every minute or so, another RPG snarls in at us, tearing apart more of the hill's sandbag battlements.

"One way or another," I tell Dieffenbach as an RPG shrieks in and impacts on a bunker a dozen meters to our left, "one way or another, LT, we've got to get off here soon."

"That AA gun will take out any birds that try to get in and extract us. We've got nothing heavy enough to hit that gun, probably four thousand meters away."

But we do have artillery! I've been looking at the remaining functional eight-inch howitzer. "We've still got one gun that will shoot,"

I say, pointing to it. "Range is easy. I don't know, though, if it can traverse far enough left to put that AA gun on the gun target line. I've got to get up to it and have a look. Can you get me some cover so I can?"

"Yeah," he says. "SGT Maxwell, have the squad put down enough fire that the captain here can get over and look at that gun."

"Will do, LT." And the pace of outgoing small arms fire picks up. I can see the pops of dirt going up where the M16 and M60 rounds hit. Under that covering fire, I low crawl over to the howitzer. Immediately, I see that center traverse on the gun aims it to the north of where the AA gun is. Cursing, I crank the gun around to the left, looking to see if I can aim it directly at the enemy gun.

"Damn it, Dieffenbach, I can't tell if we can get it close enough on a line to the AA gun to do damage. These things weren't designed for a 360-degree war. They only fire one general direction. If it won't traverse that far, we'd have to dig up the whole thing, jack the trails back up, and turn the damn thing a quarter of a circle to the left to get it exactly on line. That isn't happening now and would take too long anyway. The dinks would have us all buried by then."

"Shit! Maybe we should just didi off now before another shitload of dinks gets here."

But the artillery trung sĩ has already figured out what I want to do and has grabbed four of the Recon troopers to go with him and get shells from the store of eight-inch ammo. Thinking this is worth one try, I do my best to crank the balky piece around to point as close to the AA gun's line of fire as possible. The old gun creaks and moans as it moves, jams for an instant as I swear and heave at the wheel, and then breaks free and slides the rest of the way to the left end of its traverse. As I'm finishing that up, the trung sĩ comes up with the four men carrying one of the two-hundred-pound shells on a metal rack. He taps me, points to the howitzer's breech block, and asks, "Mở nó?" making a pulling motion.

"Yes, open it, *vâng, vâng!*" I tell him.

Meanwhile, how to set proper firing elevation on the gun. Except for the trung sĩ, all the ARVN redlegs have gone. I know that, at one time, the battery had a fire direction center up here. No more. The bunker that held it, at some recent point, had taken the brunt of an NVA RPG and blown and had fallen in on itself, burying sticks, range protractor, and chart table beneath tons of sandbags. Maybe LT Dieffenbach is right and we should didi and risk the casualties. But the artillery must always be ready to shoot, no matter what the condition of the battery, no matter if there is not a working fire direction center, no matter how primitive its condition is. One whole artillery field manual deals with emergency firing procedures when all you have is a map and a few instruments to convert target range and direction into settings for the guns. There is also a last-resort emergency procedure called black magic that can be used to make the gun settings when you have nothing at all to calculate them. CPT Nathan, my gunnery instructor at Officer Candidate School at Fort Sill, had given us one lesson in firing black magic. At the time, it had seemed more of a history lesson than something useful. How did it come to be called black magic? I expect it was because with no gear to calculate settings, you could use this method to pull settings out of the air, as if by magic. Now, on this hill, hoping to take out that AA gun, I'm trying to remember any of it. I imagine Bravo Battery's FDC back on LZ Linebarger could do the calculations for me. But this eight-inch howitzer is not laid, and in the time it would take to convert adjustments into firing data, I think I can just crank the howitzer around, put some standard settings onto the gun, and fire it.

"Trung sĩ, powder, *thuốc nổ!*" I call.

The Vietnamese sergeant nods and calls out, "*Tôi sẽ giúp bạn có được thuốc sung,*" and comes back to me with a powder canister.

Surprised at myself, I do remember. Enough anyway. In black magic, I remember, the firing charge for an eight-inch howitzer is the distance to target in thousands minus one. "The map says about four klicks, minus one is charge three." I pull the powder from the canister, pull off the extra charges to get to charge three, stuff the powder bag in behind the already loaded shell, and nod for the trung sĩ to close the breech. I am looking for a primer when the Vietnamese sergeant produces one with a grin, slams the breechblock closed, and puts the little cartridge into place.

Quadrant 240, I think that's the standard, and I crank the gun up to it. I shout, "Firing!" at the top of my lungs, stick my fingers in my ears, and nod to the trung sĩ, who yanks the lanyard. Like the first one, this bang is titanic. I'm close enough to the gun that its firing feels as if a wrecking ball has punched me everywhere at once. At this range, the shell takes hardly five seconds to reach the target.

It is high. The smoke of the detonation blooms on the cliff face behind and well to the right of where I think the AA gun is. As if taunting me, the enemy gun picks up firing again, sending a fusillade of rounds in a traverse across the hill face below us. The trung sĩ has seen and has already had the Recon troopers bring me more shells. He has brought up several more powder canisters himself.

"Tốt," the old sergeant says. He nods seriously, waves at the elevation wheel, and tells me, "Bạn làm tốt. Sửa chữa mục tiêu, bắn một lần nữa," telling me, I think, to drop the aim and fire again.

What the hell do I do now? One black magic lesson three and a half years ago with different guns. Call the battery? No need, it comes to me. "What the hell, trung sĩ, we have to drop a hundred meters, left fifty. How does that compute? It's . . ." doing the calculation in my head, "damn, it's twenty-five mils left." I grab the wheel and begin to crank. But there are only ten mils of play to the left remaining. I do the same for quadrant, cranking the gun down five mils.

Bang!

Our elevation is on line with it now, but we're maybe sixty meters to the right. We can't crank the damn gun over more. Damn it!

"Fire again anyway. Maybe we'll hit something close."

Bang!

I see the smoke of the detonating round bloom. With it, there comes a break in the incoming AA fire. Did we get the damn thing? I'm not confident, but with that two-hundred-pound HE round detonating close by, the AA gunners must be shaken to the core. Just to be safe, I help the Recon grunts prep another shell. The swab is barely wet, and I slosh some of my canteen water on it, hoping it is enough to swab out the tube and damp any remaining sparks that might set off the powder before we're ready to fire. "Premature deflagration," the sergeant who had been our old firing battery instructor jokingly called it: "Premature deflagration brings on heavy defecation, candidates, so be goddamned careful."

I slam home the breech. The trung sĩ inserts another primer, and bang! This round wails away to detonate near where the AA gun is. I've been watching the gun's location through my binos, hoping to see a secondary explosion that would tell me we had blown the thing up. Nothing, though. But I do get a quick glimpse of men seeming to be wheeling something to the south.

"Man, Matt, I think we did some damage," I tell Dieffenbach. "Looks like they are moving the AA gun. I expect we have a few minutes to get birds in and didi before they get set up again.

"All right! Let's get to the pad." He grabs the radio and calls the lead bird. "Come down and get us now. We've got a tight-assed window before that damn AA starts in again."

"Roger," the pilot says, the beat of the bird's blades lopping his speech into chunks.

The trung sĩ nods as if he's understood this, moves as close as he can get to the last gun, works his way to the front of it, and tosses a final thermite grenade down its barrel. There is a whump! a belch of hot smoke, sparks, and then the last gun is spiked. We have done our job here. Now the task is to get off the hill before we get overrun. Through the rising hail of incoming small arms, we begin to make our way carefully up toward the pad watching the lead bird come up the hillside and make an abrupt flare to land. As we move, Recon's demolition sergeant joins us. He had gone to set a timed charge down at the rough magazines where the ARVN gunners had stored their huge load of artillery shells and powder.

"Ten minutes, LT," he tells Dieffenbach. "Then the whole shit and caboodle goes up."

"You heard him," Dieffenbach bellows, "we've got ten minutes before all that artillery ammo goes bang. Get on the bird. Get on now."

It is no good; the moment the slick lands, a dozen or so of the remaining ARVN marines come tearing out of whatever bunker they'd been hiding in and swarm the helicopter. They seem to be screeching, "Ra, ra, ra!" which sounds strangely like a cheer, though I know it is just a desperate cry for out, out, out! There is no room for us, no way to clear away the crazed ARVN. The trung sĩ has come up with us and is shouting to the marines to get away, but no use. They are desperate and demented and see the bird as the only way out of our trap. The pilot pulls pitch with what seems a ton of marines still hanging on. We are yanking the ARVN away from its skids. It lifts and slides away from the hill, dropping marines without a firm hold, some falling all the way to the riverbank. A second bird has been on its final approach and now touches down, taking away Recon's dead and wounded, a squad of Recon, and a couple of marines who have managed to push their way to it. It lifts, and a third bird drops in quickly behind it, loading more of Recon. Another follows, and it seems we are doing it. A fifth bird, the one LT Dieffenbach, his RTO, the demolition sergeant, I, and the trung sĩ are to board, makes its approach. But now, maybe eight of the ARVN marines, the last of them on the hill, come out of a bunker, screaming almost to a man, "Đưa tôi!" almost incoherently in their panic. Most manage to get on board before the worried pilot abruptly pulls up and away, circling back toward the river.

The lead pilot, with a bird full of terrified marines, is moving back toward the river. The pilot is on the radio telling Dieffenbach to "get those assholes under control before we come back."

Meanwhile, the demo sergeant who had set the charges in the ammo magazine is pointing at his watch and shouting anxiously to Dieffenbach, "Les than one minute now, LT!"

"Damn it! Damn it!" Dieffenbach screams. "Everybody to the trenches. Those artillery shells are going to blow." He grabs the radio handset from his RTO and, words tumbling in his haste, warns the flight of helicopters to get away from the peak. "It'll likely blow you out of the sky if you don't," he tells them.

So, virtually alone on the hill now except for a handful of ARVN, we get down. The whump of detonation as nearly two thousand artillery shells and powder bags go up is titanic and incomprehensibly violent, earth shaking, world shattering, time stopping. The concussion is so strong a wallop that it momentarily stops breath. The cloud of it is dark, its bloom ruddy, satanic, its noise a convulsion that leaves behind aching silence. Things, singing shell fragments, parts of howitzers blown up and out, shattered sandbags and timbers flying, an emulsion of the blood and bodies of ARVN marines who had not taken cover, their flesh in it, their bone—all shower on us amid a rain of clods and mud.

Eight more are dead, all of them ARVN marines who wouldn't heed and stayed at the pad. One marine has been crushed by the wheel of a howitzer blown off and fallen precisely into his piece of the trench. Four others are calling, "Bác sĩ!" Though the ARVN medics are all already gone.

Around the hillside's flanks, it is chaos as well. Four hundred thousand pounds of powder and high explosive have gone off in a detonation as large as that of a vest pocket nuclear weapon. The shock and overpressure stun and suspend the motion of even those at the base of the hill. For a few minutes, not a shot is fired from above or below. Down in the trench, fingers tight into my ears, mouth open to negate the effect of the blast, slammed by the shock of it, I can't locate the helicopters orbiting a klick away from the hilltop. Now I see that all the birds have survived, though smoke comes from the turbine of one slick. How much shock at a klick's distance? This was a monster detonation.

I can hear some, but my head aches. Pulverized muck and the detritus of the hill coat me; blood and human flesh are beaten together in it, inseparable from the soil of the hilltop.

Dieffenbach is on the radio again, calling for a bird to come in. This time, chastened, the few remaining ARVN marines behave, letting us board first. We lift and swoop forward and down, and now we are skimming above the river. No one is talking as we fly home.

CHAPTER 25

The marines are among the last of the ARVN troops to retreat from Laos. Some units come in an orderly withdrawal, fighting rear guard actions and emerging into Vietnam mostly intact. Other units have disintegrated into small desperate groups that escape and evade as best they can. Often, they have thrown away all their gear, lightening their load to didi faster through the jungle. We see them coming across the border in little groups, aimless, esprit shattered, running for home. The ARVN marines are the elite of the Army of Vietnam and mostly have shown courage and fortitude in combat. Still, they, too, run. Most of us on the American side had recognized that this incursion into Laos was a mistake from the beginning, the overall ARVN force neither disciplined enough nor well enough led to have any chance of success. We knew that the ARVN command structure was porous and unable to keep its battle plans confidential, ensuring that the NVA were forewarned. And, forewarned, the enemy had pressed a counterattack that overwhelmed the forces of the south. Despite small sorties like ours to LZ Bão, American forces did not enter Laos in any force. We knew we could have torn the NVA apart, torched their supply lines and depots, and set their war plans back by years. No dice. The Cooper-Church Amendment, passed just a month before Lam Son 719, made direct support from us inside Laos illegal and effectively emasculated ARVN operations there. It also told us that the war that had consumed some 58,000 American lives and left another 153,000 wounded had been a fatal waste.

Lam Son 719 is finished. A few rag tags of ARVN units are still exfiltrating from Laos; many wounded, most demoralized, all of them finished with this operation. LZ Linebarger's sole remaining mission is to slam shut the Highway 9 crossing from Laos into Vietnam, sealing it against NVA attempts to follow the ARVN back into Vietnam. Mostly it is quiet on the hill. The augmented Bravo Battery—with no observers left in Laos and thus no targets there—is firing few missions now except for close in defense or harassment and interdiction and occasionally destruction missions against abandoned ARVN combat vehicles. Far off near Tchepone B-52s are carpet bombing in the last of nearly 1,400 sorties. Their deep and resounding thunder has been a constant throughout the campaign's last days. All over Radio Hanoi, the North Vietnamese are strutting their victory, great but costly. American recorded deaths were 219; South Vietnamese 1,529. The North Vietnamese death toll was a dozen times as great, nearly 20,000 soldiers lost.

So who won? As victory in war is counted, this one goes to the North Vietnamese. MAJ Echols, CPT de la Croix, and I sit in the briefing bunker on LZ Linebarger, one of our last nights there, over a bottle of decent scotch, tearing apart Lam Son 719's concept, strategy, and execution. The drunker we get, the more derisive we are.

MAJ Echols calls it a "fucking rout."

Even less kindly, CPT de la Croix sees it as a monster disaster. "Worst goddamn defeat of the war. No way do the ARVN survive this. No way do they go on. Goddamn fall apart is what they are going to do. Kill ratios be damned."

"This war was lost a long time ago," I say. "There hasn't been any objective for a long time either except to inflict more damage on the dinks than they inflict on us. Intel says they lost enough troops to fill two full divisions here, and all that shows is that they will fight to the last man. The big brass above us think these past couple of months have kicked the NVA hard enough that they won't run any campaign here in I Corps this year. Maybe that's right, but I don't imagine American troops are sticking around much longer. ARVN showed they can't put up a real fight. I'll bet a month's combat pay that it won't be long after the U.S. didi maus from Vietnam until the North hits the south hard, knocks them to hell, and takes over. Makes you wonder what we've been doing here for all these years."

"Cheers to that," says Echols; we clink classes in an ironic toast.

Two days later, we get the word the battalion is pulling out of Quang Tri Province, headed back to the old Eleventh Brigade base at LZ Bronco. Scuttlebutt is that the brigade will be sent home in a month or two; other rumors say fall, leaving all of us wondering what we will be doing for the next few months.

I still hurt from the helicopter crash and, except for my hospital stay, have had no recuperation time.

"Hell," MAJ Echols says. "Have you had any R & R in the past year?"

I admit I haven't. "Not since Sydney last April."

"You can put in for it if you want. I'll support it if you do, but I don't know what will happen with the request this late in this damn war. Even so, take a week before you head to Bronco, find a hotel somewhere, sleep until you can't anymore. Eat something that isn't left over from WWII and doesn't come out of a can. Find a red-light district and screw your brains out. Then come back. We're going to be sitting on Bronco with not a damn thing to do and with four FOs who all want to prove they're as good as you. I expect your sergeant Morris can keep them in line for a week while you get some in-country R & R. Do you good, Captain."

CPT de la Croix seconds the motion, "Were I you," he says, stopping to take a taste of scotch, starting over again. "Were I you, David, I'd go to Huế. It got the shit bombed out of it during the Tet offensive, but it's still damn nice. I was there for a couple of days last fall. Good cheap hotels, good restaurants, and one hell of a variety of boom-boom."

I go.

Huế, the Forbidden Purple City, Vietnam's old Imperial capital. It lies along the banks of the Perfume River, a real city, the biggest I have seen in the country. I've never been to Saigon or seen the Mekong River. But the Perfume is wide and beautiful; a short stream only thirty klicks or so from its headwaters in the highlands to where it runs into the South China Sea eight klicks east of Huế. The name is from the fragrance of orchard flowers fallen into the water, though not so much of that during the war. Death, whose wartime stink permeates everything in Vietnam, is the stronger perfume now.

It is the end of the monsoons in the north of South Vietnam. Temperatures are in the sixties; rain is but a sprinkle in the evening. The hotel I find is the Saigon on the southeast side of the river, a venerable place with floors of dark wood, umbrellas like coolie hats under trees in a courtyard, air-conditioned rooms. The hotel overlooks the river and is a short walk to the Citadel, and the old Imperial City. Expensive, yes, some twenty-five dollars a night (but I've had nothing to spend my combat pay on in nearly a year). Feckless for the moment, carrying only a .45 as a weapon (my M16 and the rest of my field gear sent along with SGT Morris), I walk. Before Tet, the concierge at the hotel tells me the Citadel was magnificent. "Boocoo beautiful, Cap-tain. Not even VC ruin it." But like the rest of the city, it was bombed into a ruin when we took Huế back from the Viet Cong, leaving the Citadel a shadow of what it once had been. Even in tatters, the Citadel is a thing of phenomenal beauty, of intricately sculpted towers and pagodas, massive red doors, ornate Chinese-style lions, orange-tiled roofs, inlaid stone walkways, gardens with ponds full of water lilies. Oh, how it must have looked before the war's ruin!

Just three blocks from my hotel is the restaurant Les Jardins on Hoàng Hoa Thám Avenue ("A Slice of Paris," the sign in its window says). Many of the tables are outdoors, the food is French Indochinese (hell, after twenty months in Vietnam, I would eat most anything cooked fresh). Eating food much too rich for my C ration-accustomed digestion, I watch a stream of people walk by, Americans mostly in uniform, some in tropical civilian working attire. The Vietnamese are mostly in traditional dress, particularly the women who walk the avenue clothed in richly colored *áo dais*. I pretend there is no war, nor sound or sight of it. The military presence around me puts a lie to it, but I can imagine. There is almost no sound of combat (yes, from far off in the west, toward the rising Central highlands, there is the muted thrum and rumble of artillery fire so soft, it might only be imagined).

MAJ Echols was wrong about one thing: prostitution, long illegal in Vietnam, is not prominent in Huế. Yes, there is the Paradise Steam House, Huế's version of the Steam and Cream, the tame army brothel in Duc Pho near the Eleventh Brigade headquarters. It doesn't matter, a hand job is a kind of release beyond the sexual sort, though it is from a mama-san with a missing front tooth and a vacant smile (her mind elsewhere, only her strong right hand connected to me). Finally, on my fifth night there, a bellboy (in faded livery) comes up to me in the hotel lobby where I sit reading the *Army Times* and wistfully watching beautiful *áo dai*-clad young women walk past the hotel's front window.

"You lonely man? You want *làm tình*?" he says seriously.

"Làm tình?"

"Làm tình, yes, make love, good sex, good nooki. You want it?"

"I . . ."

"She nice, not *gái giang hồ* kind who walk street. She good, pretty. Make you feel like home. You want?"

I do. And so I spend that night and the next with Linh (no last name offered), a sweet and gentle soul. Maybe eighteen, her skin tawny, nose and cheeks freckled. She wears her hair in long braids. Her eyes are green (so perhaps some French in her ancestry). She is soft, slight, hardly shoulder high to me. Her English is fine with a tonal lilt to it.

Yes, we fuck and again and again. Yes, I pay her fifty dollars a night. It probably means nothing more than that to her. To me, holding Linh, whose name she says means "gentle spirit," holding her tucked against me, spoon-like in the soft hotel bed, the war seeps away, and all I sense is warm skin, a faint jasmine scent over the spice of our lovemaking. She sings as I hold her, "Tôi muốn được với bạn luôn luôn."

"It means?"

"It is an old love song. It means I want to be with you always." She snuggles to me, and we sleep.

In the morning of my seventh day in Huế, I am still half asleep as Linh puts a kiss on my forehead. I hear the rustle of my wallet, the door to my room close. And she is gone, though her scent remains on the sheets. Finally arising, I find exactly one hundred dollars in MPC gone from my wallet, precisely what I owe her, the rest of the cash untouched. In the lobby, the bellboy makes it a point to come up and tell me, "She think you nice. Is sorry no more for you too. Tells me to say good-bye for her. You come back, she say she love you again all over."

And so the war resumes.

On this last morning in Huế, I sit at down to a New Orleans sort of breakfast, coffee, beignets, two real fried eggs, thick cut bacon, slices of white, dark-speckled dragon fruit (expensive this time of year, but, as with Linh and the hotel, who cares?). The sun this morning in early spring is lovely, the air warm and only slightly humid with a bit of breeze in it, the sidewalk outside Les Jardins is filled with people, and yet I am having trouble sensing them as more than figments walking without meaning for me. The war is a damper on my feelings, and at once, I know I have enjoyed this beautiful ravaged city as much as I ever will. Three days before I got here, my waiter tells me in an accent I have to peel back to get to the meaning, some kid in black pajamas (a *tee-tee boy*, VC for sure) had lobbed a fragmentation grenade into a crowd on this street just a few doors down from the restaurant. "Down there, big bang, man, big. Many peoples get hurt, two blowed all *cockadau*. Boy ran away. Cockadau lots of people."

Hearing of the dead, there is nothing to say. "Very sad," I whisper. I get up and drop a pile of MPC on the table to pay for the meal. (It is illegal to use it in civilian commerce, but like the price of the dragon fruit, who cares?) I grab up my ruck—I've checked out of my hotel—and find a military bus stop for a ride to the airfield for a flight to Da Nang and then to Chu Lai and a bird to LZ Bronco. As I fly back into the war, it occurs to me that with this tour, I've had all the army I want, that I am not going to stay in after the war. It is a thought so sudden and startling that I yip aloud over the noise of the caribou flying me to Chu Lai, startling the corporal strapped into the netting seat across from me. Epiphanies come in strange packages. Yet I still have four months on this tour.

In Chu Lai, late in the afternoon, I'm told there is no transport to LZ Bronco until the next morning, and so I check into the visiting officers' quarters (just bunks in a dorm for company-grade officers like me—field grade officers get private cubicles, though the same bunks). I leave my ruck with a PFC at the desk and call in to Headquarters Battery of the 6/11 to let them know I will be delayed until tomorrow.

The familiar voice on the other end is the artillery battalion sergeant major. "CPT Weisman, where are you now?"

"I'm in Chu Lai, crashing at the VOQ tonight."

"It's good you called, sir. I'm supposed to tell you that COL Dolby wants to see you. He's at DivArty there in Chu Lai. You can see him in person."

"I don't suppose you know what this is about, Sergeant Major?" I've said that of all the senior officers I have worked under in Vietnam, COL Dolby is the one I respect most. Respect doesn't trump apprehension, though. Every meeting I've had with the colonel in recent months has brought an ugly assignment that I can't turn down.

"Not a clue, Captain. Good luck, though."

"Sure!"

A call to DivArty gets me a ride to its HQ between Chu Lai's main airstrip and the South China Sea. DivArty HQ is a one-story tropical-style building with a corrugated metal roof painted with the patch of the Americal Division: four white stars of the Southern Cross on a shield-shaped blue field. An ungainly antenna-studded observation tower higher than the building's roof rises next to its inland flank. The war near Huế may have been muted and faraway seeming. Not so here in the Americal's nerve center. Two distant bouts of crackling mark separate firefights in the high mountains to the west. Outgoing artillery bangs relentlessly, and the resultant far-off booms tell of the big guns' participation in these fights. Aircraft in their variety move on and off the airstrip, the searing engine noise of jets rising above the hum and blatt of rotary wing craft; a C130 Hercules drops from the south toward the strip's biggest runway in the wake of a Phantom jet. Nearly two years in Vietnam and I've been here only half a dozen times before. The driver leaves me on the unpaved and dusty parking area. I walk in under the pagoda-shaped frame holding the sign declaring this to be Headquarters

Americal Division Artillery. Both frame and sign are painted the bright red of the artillery's colors.

A staff sergeant shows me to COL Dolby's office at the end of a long corridor. It has a door made of real wood, not some canvas drape, his name neatly painted on it in red. Beneath the name is the designation G3 above the ornate black, red, and gold coat of arms of his last command, the 6/11th Artillery with its stylized lion, mythic birds, a centaur, and a six-pointed star. Dolby is division artillery's operations officer, a vital job coordinating artillery operations with the combat needs of all the Americal division's frontline units. On his desk as arty battalion commander back at LZ Bronco had been a plaque:

Artillery adds dignity to what would otherwise be a vulgar brawl.
—Frederick the Great of Prussia

Here in Chu Lai, it is the first thing I see on the colonel's desk as I knock and enter. On the wall behind him is a picture of a 155-howitzer firing with the caption "The King of Battle." Seeing such someone might think the old man had gone sentimental. Though not I.

"Colonel?" I come to attention in front of his desk.

"Yeah, yeah. For god's sake, sit down, David."

A knock at the door and a PFC comes in without waiting with a carafe of coffee, mugs, and fixings. I look at Dolby, who gets a half grin on his face. Coffee? A chair? This bodes nothing good.

The colonel sees as much and nods. "Yup, I've got something big and messy for you. As usual, I offer it as an opportunity, not an order. But your old, uh, friend, CPT Englander, has asked for you again. Seems you've got yourself some fans among the Snake-Eaters."

What the hell? "Sir, the last op I was on with them was supposed to be a diversion to drag some of the NVA units away from Lam Son 719 to take pressure off the ARVN." I see him nod. I add, "That fell apart before we really even got started. Lam Son is over. ARVN are screwed all on their own, and there's no benefit to sending a team back into Laos for that now."

"Right on all counts, David. But the war is winding down. The bulk of U.S. troops won't be in Vietnam for more than a few months more. Command down in Saigon has gotten a wild hair to deal with something now while we still have troops available: an operation inside Laos again, same general area you were in before. Because of that, CPT Englander's team has been tapped for it. You apparently did a good job of convincing Englander that artillery can be useful to him. He's asked for you back again. As I said, I'm not going to order you to go. If you like, I'll get someone else to go and you can stay with your current job with the 6/11 as LNO. I expect things will be quiet, mostly just winding down. By the end of the summer, fall at the latest, we likely will all be going home."

COL Dolby hasn't changed, an officer of fine intelligence and immense tactical skill in a rumpled, barely military wrapping. He pulls off his gold-rimmed spectacles and polishes them on a tattered handkerchief, puts them back on, and looks at me. He says no more, just looks at me, head thrusting slightly forward, eyebrows up in a question.

"Sir," I say, "I'll willingly take on any assignment you give me..."

"But?"

"But we both know Englander is ... unglued. We went into Laos last time ostensibly to rattle the NVA and distract them. But Englander's real mission was to find this nun he knows who used to work for Rev. Tom Dooley. He's monomaniacal on this. We didn't find her, and our real mission never got off the ground. He also has a bug about the Longshadows..."

"Yeah, U.S. deserters supposedly working with the enemy. He and I talked about them before."

I nod, not liking the direction of this conversation. Last time out with Englander, one of our unspoken missions had been to snoop and poop around to see if we could find intel on where the Longshadows might be. Apparently, the Longshadows are one of Englander's several obsessions, left over from the unsuccessful Operation Tailwind 2 he'd been part of. Didn't find anything, though. I remind Dolby about the old top sergeant for Bravo Company of the 7/31, 1SGT Schlagel, who was convinced the Longshadows were real, who thought that 1LT Schmidt, the leader of the 7/31's Recon Platoon who had been investigated for a war crime, had walked away from the battalion, and some thought he'd become a Longshadow. I told Dolby about seeing someone soon after who looked a lot like Schmidt walking with a Viet Cong convoy over on the Laotian border.

And I tell him about the helicopter crash. This was different, no rumor but real. "The third man following me as I tried to get the pilot out, I'd swear was a Caucasian and had a Ranger tattoo on his wrist. Damn, sir, maybe there are real Longshadows."

"Yeah, well, this isn't a hunt for Longshadows or any other chimerical hallucinations. The main point of this mission into Laos is to blow hell out of a regional VC supply depot about sixty klicks inside Laos in the mountains south of Attapu. The bigger part of the mission is that the depot is reportedly built right next to an NVA POW camp. Aerial photography is inconclusive on that. Weren't for the camp, we could just drop in an Arc Light strike and blow it all to hell. But if there are American prisoners there, we don't dare take the chance of killing them. If you find them, your unit is to capture the camp and provide security until we can get some birds in to rescue the prisoners.

"You'll have mostly the same full support you did on your first go-round in Laos, though this time, there will be just one ARVN artillery battery able to support you maybe halfway into there. You'll also have a whole squadron of birds, slicks, gunships, and even Phantom jets detailed to you, with more than enough ordnance to get you out of any conceivable trouble. Englander will be in charge. Your job will be fire support. This is to be an orderly reconnaissance mission. If it ever gets too hinky for you, call and we'll yank you out in a jiffy."

Jiffy is about as unmilitary a word as I can think of but completely in character for COL Dolby. Looks like I am doing this.

"Will you want the same RTO again?"

Cat? Would he want to go? "CPL Wilbur? I'll ask him. This is potentially a nasty mission, sir. If he volunteers, can we give him a bit of a reward, say promote him to sergeant?"

"Didn't I just make him a corporal a month ago?"

"Yes, sir, you did."

He sits and looks at me, finally saying with a slight grin, "Yeah, sure, sergeant. Fine, I'll have the orders cut."

"I guess I'm going, then, sir."

"Yeah, David, I guess you are."

COL Dolby is done, and I'd get up to leave, but the thing that SSG Olsson had said needs to be dealt with. I tell the colonel of SSG Olsson's and my conversation in Quang Tri, about the event on the finger of ridge in Laos where the enemy, whoever they were, had just stopped fighting, abruptly after a big bang and a series of pops.

"Englander had seemed agitated but relieved after that happened. I asked him what had happened, but all he would say was that it had been because of 'the worst of the worst.' He refused to say anything more."

Dolby rubs his hands together as if washing them and closes his eyes for a blink. "Son of a bitch," he says. "The worst of the worst is nothing but a rumor. Something the Hatchet Teams are supposedly empowered to use. I've heard it spoken of a few times at dark ops briefings. Just a note that it is available if things really go south."

"Something that stops a fight, like that," I say, snapping my fingers.

"Yeah."

"Is that why Englander had insisted everybody carry gas masks and atropine injectors on our last mission?"

COL Dolby holds up a hand. "No more of this. I'm going to do some asking. When I know, you'll know." He leans forward, his face softer, paternal. "Be very careful, David. Remember, as I said, if you have any reason to think things are unreasonably dangerous, call and you'll be out of there."

"Yes, sir."

I get up. Dolby nods at me, and as I leave his office, I see him sitting, eyes closed in what looks to be deep and troubled thought.

★ ★ ★

CHAPTER 26

The next morning, I fly into LZ Bronco and locate the 7/31's new battalion quarters in a cluster of big, somewhat raggedy tents, a row of freshly dug latrines on one side, a row of new, heavily revetted bunkers on another. A warm sun shines on the base, though puddles from recent rains pock it, showing the monsoon has at least a little punch left. Bravo Battery—big guns gone and miraculously back to its full complement of six 105s—is already set and laid in an old artillery position to the south of the base's airstrip. The battalion operations center has been set up in an unused barracks, lightly walled and roofed with sandbags. Inside, in a rear corner away from the infantry operations team, I find SGT Morris and Cat. Both are looking with surprise at a newly issued set of orders that promote Cat to sergeant (there are promotion orders for Malaby too, but he has boarded the freedom bird and is on his way home. He'll have to enjoy his promotion in civilian life). Also (surprise) there are orders promoting Morris to staff sergeant. In the packet are sets of camo-colored stripes. An included note, addressed to me from COL Dolby, tersely says, "Congratulate the both of them for me. They deserve the promotion, and this way, we'll preserve the rank separation between them."

"Congratulations from COL Dolby. He says you both deserve it," I tell them. "*Felicitaciones a los dos.* That's what my old RTO, Cisco, would have said."

"We're going out again, aren't we, sir?" Cat asks. He is looking at his new stripes somberly.

"Yeah, Sergeant, we're going on another operation with CPT Englander and his team. That is, I am going, and you are . . . I guess the word is *invited* . . . if you want to go." I look at him. "If you've had enough of carting a Prick 25 around in the field with me, arty battalion will assign me somebody else for the mission. Either way, you keep the new stripes."

"No, sir, I'll go. Who would want to miss out on all the fun?"

"That explains what *he's* doing here," Morris says, aiming his thumb at a young-looking PFC standing nearby. The kid (he really is one, younger appearing even than Cat, mousy brown hair, face still spotted with acne, sad sack sloppiness of fatigues hanging on a tall bony frame) stands uncertainly, leaning on the barracks wall. "Private Fostah here got in this morning. Battalion sent him over to us. Thirteen Foxtrot MOS and such, just out of advanced training at Sill. Fostah, come over and introduce ya-self to CPT Weisman. He's the boss of this shop."

The kid levers himself off the wall and comes stiffly over to us. On his new fatigue shirt is a nametag with "Foster" sewn on. I'd figured that was it, Morris's Gulf Coast roots showed in how he'd pronounced the name.

"Stand easy, Foster. We're not long on formality here," I tell him. "You have a first name to go with Foster?"

"Uh, yes, sir, it's Warren, sir. Warren Foster." He's slipped into the actual "at ease" posture, legs apart, hands clasped behind his back, upper body still at attention.

"Warren, huh? OK, I suppose you'll get a real nickname soon enough. Meanwhile, relax. I expect you to be military, do your job, give me the respect due an officer and that due SSG Morris and SGT Wilbur as NCOs. But this isn't the parade ground. Doing your job is the most important thing. Cat, uh, SGT Wilbur and I will be going out on an operation with the Special Forces for a while, maybe for a couple of weeks. SGT Morris will show you the ropes here and let you know when you're ready to do things on your own. Got it?"

"Yes, sir." He looks at me and, apparently realizing he is still standing stiffly at ease, relaxes a bit, letting himself loosen.

"Yeah, that's it, Fostah, you're gettin' it. Sit down where the sergeant was and let's get you started," Morris says, grinning.

I stick out my hand to Morris. "Congratulations again, Staff Sergeant. Cat and I will be out in the bush for a while. You've got your choice of any of the FOs in the battalion to sit in for me. Headquarters Battery already knows. Just make your pick."

SSG Morris smiles again. "Good luck, sir, Cat," he says. "Try and stay safe."

"Will do."

And with that, I go over to the infantry ops desk and greet MAJ Echols, who has already been briefed on my assignment. He winks broadly at me; the implication is "You poor son of a bitch." I wink back, and Cat and I head out for the supply shed for our field gear and souped-up radio. Then we go on to the nearby pad where we watch for the bird that will take us to the Téthian camp again.

Waiting for the bird, Cat and I sit on the bench outside the pad master's hooch. We have changed into tiger fatigues and reluctantly left our steel pots in the barracks, exchanging them for tiger boonie hats. This time, there is no pretense about the gear we carry: M16s, army-issue rucks, and web gear; Cat, the same enhanced radio we had used before; both of us with gas masks and a couple of sets of atropine and anticonvulsant injectors each (as CPT Englander has left word we are to carry that). Neither of us has cigarettes. Cat doesn't smoke, hasn't ever, he says, a rare thing for a soldier. I did, but I'd quit for good after smoking more than a whole pack while talking the terrified radio operator of a mortally wounded FO through a hellacious firefight a year ago in March. Done, I'd put down my radio handset and realized there were two dozen half-smoked Salems in the nasty hubcap-sized ashtray on our map table. I'd craved cigarettes through my R & R soon after in Sydney. Craved? Hungered for them as if they were sustenance but stuck to my resolve and haven't smoked since (not that I don't crave a smoke sometimes when stress or boredom lies heavily on me). Still, Vietnam can kill you dead enough.

"Captain, are we going out again to chase another fairy story about deserters from our side working for the VC?" Cat asks. His look is open as if he expects me to denounce it and hang this myth on Englander's gullibility. Before my encounter with the dead Ranger, maybe I would have done so unequivocally. Now? I'm not so certain.

"I don't think that's the mission, Cat. Looks like we're after an NVA supply dump and POW camp. But goose chase or not, we've got a job to give the team and the Yards the best artillery support we can provide."

Cat just shakes his head. "Wow, sir! A POW camp. Wow!"

The bird lifts us from Bronco and lofts above the coastal lowlands that are deeply green and fecund in the monsoon's aftermath, emerald rice shoots coloring the flooded paddies. We cross over the escarpment of the Central Highlands, flying maybe five klicks above the labyrinthine twists of the mountains and rivers there. Much of the jungle (save that which is dead from the application of Agent Orange by the Ranch Hand teams) is also a deep green, the withering heat of the dry season yet to come. We are too high to see birds or insects and too high as well to sense any signs of combat below. Though, with San Juan Hill closed down and no one replacing the battalion in these highlands, there is little in the way of battle here. It is, as they say, Indian country once again.

The Téthian camp seems unchanged from what we had left two months ago, speckled Yard chickens running free, dilapidated huts, thatching as bedraggled as before, smoke from chimneys the only sign they are occupied. The operations shack is also as before, leaden-colored smoke from its chimney whipped away in the wind from our bird's blades as we land. Puddles fill the camp's low spots; the water tinted the orange of the underlying clay. As with my first visit here, nobody emerges from any bunker or hooch to greet us. We debark, and the bird's crew chief hands down our rifles, radio, and rucks. The pilot pulls pitch, and the bird noses off to the north, climbs around the mountain to our east, and is gone.

Hugh Englander is his usual surly self, greeting me and Cat almost perfunctorily when we reach the ops shed door. Though noontime, he offers us only some bad barely lukewarm coffee. MSG Pat Flanagan and the Montagnard đại úy Y Giao are there eating, hardly looking up as we enter. (Seems like every time I come here, there's food on the hearth.) Finally, Englander's face brightening a little, he opens up.

"You know what you're here for, right?"

"Verbal orders say we are going after a POW camp and supply depot way inside Laos. But I've worked with you enough to know nothing is what it seems. I've an inkling this might mutate roughly into a hunt for Longshadows. Is that what we're really doing, Hugh, tracking down intelligence on the Longshadows? See if we can find the base camp where they are working and either bring them back or do them in?"

CPT Englander starts to laugh. "Shit, man, that what you think? That this is a real Longshadow hunt? Prove or disprove the myth for once and all, pull a Frank Buck and bring back some specimens dead or alive?"

"In a nutshell, yes, Hugh! That's what you were doing with Operation Tailwind 2 last year, wasn't it?"

"For all your technical smarts, man," Englander says, "it doesn't seem like you've got much of a sense of humor. No, this is exactly what it looks like: go after POWs and supplies dumped in Laos."

All I can do is shake my head. Stupid. But Englander is as irrational as ever. So maybe, though he says not, we *are* going looking for Longshadows.

"Get some food and let's go over the battle plan," Englander says. He pulls several maps from a stack on the table, shoos the first sergeant and the đại úy back, spreads out a couple of the maps, and sticks a finger down on the Laos-Vietnam border uncomfortably close to that spot where, with Bravo Company sixteen months ago, I had been in the battle of my life.

"No tramping through those swamps in Cambodia this time," he says. "Birds are going to drop us here on hill 1,000 on the ridge just north of the triple point where Laos, Vietnam, and Cambodia all meet. We'll walk about four klicks south along the line between Laos and Cambodia and then turn west into Laos here where the 110 Highway runs toward Attapu. Then we just follow the route of the 110 for about fifty klicks west. The NVA supply depot and the POW camp are supposed to be here on this mountain about ten klicks south of the highway."

Where Englander is pointing is a towering 1,400-meter-high mountain that slopes up steeply south of the open plain of Laos's Attapu lowlands. Its southern flank is especially sheer. A saddle connects it to another lower mountain about three klicks further west. Englander has the saddle marked as the probable location of the POW camp, along with a big penciled question mark on the higher peak with DEPOT written above it. The objective is about sixty klicks south of the town of Chavane where Tailwind 2 had gone in last fall. I note this to Englander, who grins. "Told yah. This is a whole different mission. More jungle and mountains for us, not so much civilization, roads, and such."

"I don't suppose we're just going to follow the open highway for fifty-some klicks to get there, are we, Hugh?"

"Nah, not as easy or exposed as that, man," he says. "Most of the way, there are rivers paralleling the highway with heavy tree cover around them. We'll stay off the road, moving through the trees by the water so that we're screened from the highway. This isn't a highway like back in the World. This is a gravel trail following the lay of the land, a lot like the crappy roads here in Nam."

"And here?" I ask, pointing to where the highway emerges onto the open lowlands skirting Attapu. "We going to move into the hills where the jungle is? Looks like tough going."

Englander laughs. "The A-Team will make it, and so will the Yards. You got any misgivings, let me know now."

I look at Cat, who seems unfazed by the prospect of pushing through fifty klicks of rough terrain. He nods back at me, mouths, "Piece of cake," and gives a slight smile.

"Nope, Hugh," I say. "Where you go, Cat and I go." I am hoping this isn't false bravado. It looks like a monster trek. "Last time, I gather, you had birds to take you most of the way and a convoy of jets and gunships for cover."

"Yeah, and we got our asses kicked. Birds gave away every move we made. Dinks knew where we were and where we were going all the time. They had to yank us out before we accomplished a damn thing. This time, we're going to be sneaky and furtive as hell. No birds to give us away unless we need their support. No resupply either—we're carrying everything we need with us: food, ammo, explosives to blow the supply dump. I'm not planning on calling any birds unless we're halfway dead already and extraction is the only way out."

I'd received a quick ops letter from COL Dolby describing the artillery support we'd have. He'd also sent along a sheaf of 1:50,000 scale maps of southeastern Attapu Province. Now, checking the easternmost of these maps, I find the location of the battery supporting us. It appears to be on exactly the same firebase just inside Laos as on our last go-round here. In keeping with the clandestine nature of the mission, Dolby reiterated that there would be no second battery positioned further into Laos. This single one, right on the border with Vietnam, will have four 155 mm howitzers and two 175 mm guns. Though not dealing in specifics in the ops letter, COL Dolby notes that the 175s will have the new experimental extended-range base bleed ammo available for us that will give the guns some forty klicks of range, at least ten klicks beyond their normal range, though the turbulence the base bleed creates makes their accuracy not great at its longest ranges. Still, that range is comforting coverage for two-thirds of our mission. But once we get to the Houay Hintho River, maybe seven klicks east of our objective, we will be entirely out of artillery range. At that point, Cat and I will be supernumeraries, effectively just two more guys with rifles.

I point this out to Englander, who grins cynically and says, "Yeah, I figured. Going in sneaky Pete means we likely have to watch out for ourselves. Just make sure you remind me when we get out of arty range."

★ ★ ★

CHAPTER 27

We come down.

Englander is screaming, "Hot LZ, Hot LZ; come out shooting!"

But we can't.

The snap of small arms tells us what but not where. So, hearts pounding, we get ready to jump off, wondering where the fight is. All of us on this bird are U.S. troops: me, Cat, Englander, SSG Olsson, and four other Snake-Eater sergeants who are new to me. We pile off, sensing bullets flying a distance away in the dark. The sound of battle is disorienting, and it takes me seconds to realize that the fight is to the north of the clearing where we have landed, up where the ridgetop road runs under a cover of trees. There is no incoming, no clear target.

"Who the hell is firing?" SSG Olsson asks. He gets no answer.

We scoot quickly away from the open stretch of highway where we are exposed in the bright and silvery light of a nearly full moon. Bad luck! For all the benefit we get from this well-lit night, we could have come down in daylight and been able to see where the hell we are going. Birds continue to come in behind us, bringing in the rest of the Yard company and the remaining American troops.

"Make a perimeter," Englander calls, and I hear the order passed to the troops by the đại úy, calling out, "Ngă po'dar," in Jarai. The order is repeated, and the troops move and begin to set in in an oval around the LZ as the last of the slicks drops its passengers.

The ammoniac stink of gun smoke drifts toward us on a slight wind. I pull Cat with me off to the west side of the highway under tree cover near where the ridge tips sharply down the long slope into Laos. Grabbing the radio handset from Cat, I call the battery to alert it, "No fire mission yet, but it's action three-two-hundred. Stand by."

"Roger, waiting," says the same American-sounding voice as before on the artillery push.

There is more fire crackling about fifty meters north of us, seeming to bounce back and forth across the highway, mostly small arms with some detonations that sound like grenades. In it I am down, prone, face planted, tasting dirt. From the direction of the firefight, I hear angry voices—Vietnamese or Jarai, I can't tell, maybe it's both—call back and forth. In it, I have no identifiable artillery target and can only lie pressed flat in the brush off the trail, Cat next to me with the radio. Englander has hit the ground near us. Still, the firefight continues, the strange snap and patter of bullets through the trees, but none of it incoming to our position. Clearly, given all the helicopter landings, they know we are here, though the battle goes on without us.

"What the hell, Hugh?" I say to Englander. "Sounds like this firefight was already happening when we put down here."

"Yeah, goddammit, I think it was." He calls to the Yard commander, "Đại úy? Move a squad that way and find out what the fuck is going on."

"OK, Cap, *bo'wuih*, will do," comes the đại úy's response in his Jarai-accented English. Then a couple of long sentences in Jarai, a response from another Yard, and now I can see maybe a dozen Yard troops, a couple of American soldiers accompanying them, break away and move up the highway toward the fight. There are more back-and-forth calls, one language I now recognize as Jarai, the other not Jarai's flat, almost German/English-sounding tongue, but something tonal. Not Vietnamese. Lao? I've never heard it, and I know only that the language spoken sounds far different from that the Yards speak.

As quick as that the firefight breaks off, the night grows silent, and in it, the squad of Yards comes back.

"Who were those sons of bitches?" Englander asks the đại úy.

"Don't know, Cap. They all didi away when my soldiers get there. No sign of who is who? Got two of mine, they *bị thương*, wounded, bleeding bad." The đại úy points to where two Yards are being carried back into our perimeter. SSG Olsson and a Yard medic quickly go over to them.

"These two guys need dustoffs, Cap," SSG Olsson calls. "Ain't dying, got the blood stopped, but they're shot up too bad to take with us."

Cursing, CPT Englander gets up and walks over to where Olsson and the Yard medic have the wounded soldiers stretched out under the trees. The Yard is holding an IV bag above one of them.

Englander, face picked out in the leaf cut of the moonlight, looks furious. "Goddammit, I'm not waiting here for a dustoff," he says and turns to the đại úy. "Tell trung sĩ Ksang to have a fire team and a medic stay here with the wounded men to wait for the dustoff. Tell him we're going south on this ridge on the side toward Laos. Have them follow us when they can."

"Ừ', I got it, Cap," says the đại úy. He moves off, calling, "Ksang, krăp dustoff, ră anai."

I call the battery and tell them to stand down but keep their guns pointed our way, "just in case."

"Roger," comes back the voice, relaxed as if he had not been much worried about us. "You are our only customer right now anyway. You need help, we're here."

We pull back from the perimeter into a spaced column formation and begin to move south along the patchy, graveled surface of the highway. Here, the road cuts through tall teaks rising out of heavy undergrowth on either side. Most of the trees are intact, though some, shattered and charred, bear the signs of an old battle. Who died here under these broken trees? Would I find their graves in the brush beneath the trees? In the moonlight, there is no color but silver and shades of gray and black, no tint of blood, though blood had certainly been spilled here.

We have moved a klick or so south when the muted sound of the incoming dustoff bips into the jungle. It seems down barely a moment before we can hear the turbine's blatt as it takes off again. I see Englander nod at that, his form barely a shadow where we walk in the dark under the trees.

Englander, Cat, and I are in the middle of the file, with Yard platoons and a split of the American troops fore and aft. Englander is a few steps in front of us, and I can't tell if the captain wants me walking near him or not. *The hell with it,* I think, and I step up until I am abreast with him. "Damn mess to start this mission wasn't it, Hugh?" I say. "We're not on the ground five minutes and already two are down and dusted off. Did the đại úy have any idea who all were in that fight? Some of the voices sounded like Yards."

Englander says nothing for a few paces. Finally, he turns to look at me. "Goddam Pathet Lao for one side, I think. Don't know who was on the other. Maybe VC. Assholes are supposed to be on the same side but don't like each other much. I don't think it was Yards."

Clearly, he's ignoring the fact that one set of voices was apparently speaking one of the uninflected Montagnard languages. No point in arguing about that now. Instead, I say, "So the idea of slipping undetected into Laos . . . ?"

"Blown, man. Looks like they didi mau'd when we got there. I don't think they know who all came in, though. I think all they saw were the Yard troops, but they don't know we are with them or where we are going. So maybe no harm."

I hear a snort from Cat, who is walking a meter or so behind us. My thoughts exactly: this is war; there is always harm.

Though raggedly surfaced with gravel over packed clay, the highway is passable and decently maintained. I see that its ruts have been filled in with heavy planks laid over spots where small streams cross the roadway; at places, rock outcroppings have even been blasted away to widen the road. Human footprints, hoof prints, the tracks of wagons and truck tires, many looking recently made, mark it. A well-used secret highway along the border.

About a klick and a half onward, we climb a steep slope, the road deeply cut between jutting banks to lessen the grade. Once again, I marvel: heavy grading equipment was surely used to level this road. That's more evidence of a war at the border far different from what I have fought these past twenty months. Carrying nothing but a rifle, a spare radio battery, water, and a lightly packed ruck, I'm not much bothered by the slope. I feel for those among the Yard troops who are loaded down with a dozen pounds or more of C-4 explosive in addition to their other gear. But they soldier on, seemingly unfazed by the weight or the climb. Frankly, Cat, loaded down with twenty-five pounds of PRC-77 radio, long antenna, and another extra battery, is hardly less burdened than the Yards, but he seems to be doing fine. A look from him suggests that I should worry about my own endurance here.

Finally, an hour or so later, we stop for a break on hill 1,000, exactly at the triple point where the borders of Laos, Cambodia, and Vietnam meet. There is an unwarlike silence here, strange in its calm. Few places in this war lack the noise of battle; this place does. Northwest, the jungle-covered ridge falls away from us precipitously into Laos, dropping more than one thousand meters of elevation into a deep valley in the space of just two klicks. The illumination of the full moon, now high in the eastern sky, chops that variegated slope into patches, some moonlit, others impenetrably dark. At the bottom, glinting here and there in the moonlight, is the course of a stream that runs northwest. The map shows the stream running after eight klicks into the Dak Xou River that flows northwest toward the plains around Attapu, the major town of this region.

All this is so odd to me. Most of my time in this war, I have been on ground made familiar by endless repetition of search-and-destroy traverses along the Sông Ba Tơ River, through the mountains and jungles of Quang Ngai Province and even across a small patch of the populous rice lands of the coastal plains. In Laos up north, while the land was new to me, the battlefield had the same familiar mental terrain of firebases and infantry patrols, big guns, and combat aircraft of all sorts. Yes, Cat and I had been out near here before with Englander and his Snake-Eaters and Yard troops, but only briefly and only for a few klicks across a tongue of Cambodia barely into Laos. This mission promises to be very different, a clandestine sortie deep into the Laotian south with scant support, our single connection to one lone artillery battery on the border as a lifeline, birds only as a final resort.

Rested, we push further along the Laotian-Cambodian broader ridge into a muffled night. The sounds that reach us are small ones in the otherwise silent dark: the faint tramp of booted feat, the now-and-again grunt or sigh at the uneven road, the once-in-a-while preternaturally loud snap of a twig, and the thrum of dragonfly predators chasing the keening of their mosquito prey. Around and over us, the tree cover is triple canopy, hiding the highway from aerial observation and blocking most of the light of the moon.

We move along the road's rise and fall at a steady pace for four klicks without cease. To track our progress in this dark, I am left to count my paces and observe the pointer of my compass's needle now southwest, briefly due west, now due south again, and finally a gradual turn back southwest. Englander no longer tests me on this, aware that I know—probably better than he does—exactly where we are at any given time.

An hour later, Englander calls another halt. Again, the only sounds are the subtle ones of men dropping to the trail and laying rucksacks down, along with the faint snick of cigarette lighters, most smokes hidden in cupped hands, though here and there the poorly concealed red glow of ember ends outshine the phosphorescent patches on the backs of jungle fatigues.

Englander comes up to me, map out, a slit of light from the red lens of his flashlight dimly illuminating it. "We're here, don't you think, redleg?" he says. The fact that he asks me is itself a token of his trust (though he damn sure wouldn't own up to it if asked). His finger indicates a spot on the border road maybe a quarter of a klick north of our position.

"Not bad map reading for a grunt," I say. I'd grin, but he wouldn't see it. "We're a couple of hundred meters south of that, right on this little prominence on the ridge at seven-two-four-two-two-three. We're about half a klick from where the 110 Highway takes off west into Laos."

"Uh!" is his response. He pulls the map up to stare at its contour lines, picked out in brown against the red that the light colors the map. He keeps looking at it, slaps at a mosquito on his neck, and says, "Fuck me, you're right."

"This is where we came up from Cambodia on this little finger out of all the bamboo last time we were here," I tell him, pointing to where the map shows that narrow stretch of rising ground. "We stay on this road another two klicks from here and we'll hit the hill we had our NDP on before we went down into the Khmer Rouge camp."

"Yeah, yeah, I see it," Englander says. "Everything looks different on a night move."

"So are we going to stay on this road or head west to follow the highway? How much farther are we going tonight, Hugh?"

"Yeah, yeah," he says again. "I want to head down into Laos near the highway. The map shows the land isn't too steep there. We can go near the highway but still stay off it in the trees. How long? Maybe four more hours. By then, it'll be close to sunup and we can find a place to bed down for the morning. I want to do most of our moving after dark."

He steps away, and I go over to where Cat is seated, back against the buttresses of a massive teak on the roadside. He has out a can of C ration peaches, spooning out the fruit, making little sucking sounds as he swallows.

"God, Cat," I say. "You're making me hungry with that. All I brought along are LRRPs."

"Yeah, me too mostly, Captain. But I have a few cans of the best part of Cs."

"You're carrying the radio and that too? It's going to get heavy before long."

"That's why I'm eating these now. Want some peaches? I've had all I want." He hands me the can with a few peach chunks and some syrup still in the bottom.

I shake the peaches and syrup out of the can and into my mouth, sweet tasting, kind of cool, maybe the slenderest flavor of real fruit there if you have a rich imagination. Still, I tell Cat, "Thanks. Good. Maybe I ought to have you carry more of these."

"Good luck on that, Captain." He laughs.

I kick a hole under some leaves, drop the empty can in, and push dirt and dead underbrush back over it. No sense leaving a trail.

We have moved another three hundred meters to just before where the 110 Highway diverges from the ridge when there is a yelp from the tail end of our file. The canopy here is not so thick, and moonlight filtering down makes the scene just barely visible.

"What the hell?" Englander says at the sudden low gabble from the rear of our line of march. "Quiet!"

But the đại úy, who has gone back along our file, now comes hurrying up the trail.

"Ala tueng čoh," he is saying urgently, "čoh ruă gŏ." The Yard medic near us jumps at the words.

"I can't understand that. What's he saying?" says Englander.

"Ah, čoh, bite, bite," says the đại úy, seeming to lose his English in his agitation. "How say, uh . . . say snake bite. Soldier is snake bite."

"Man!" Englander says. "Olsson, you hear that? One of the Yards has been bitten by a goddamn snake. Can you go back and see?"

"Yeah, Cap, on my way." He and the Yard medic trot back along our file.

The rest of the unit has now gone to ground waiting to hear what has happened to the bitten Yard.

"Captain," Cat whispers to me, "are they going to bring in a bird to dust him off if it's a dangerous bite?"

"I don't know," I say back. "A dustoff would give away that we're here."

"God, sir, oh god!"

It is at least fifteen minutes before SSG Olsson is back. "A green pit viper got him, Cap," he tells Englander. "The bastards live in the trees here. It got him on the hand when he was reaching for a branch to steady himself. His hand and forearm are already swollen big time. The Yard medic Y Jah was with me. Best I could make out from him is the bite won't kill him, just make him wish he'd die from the pain. I gave him some morphine. There's antivenin for that kind of bite, but I don't carry any. He'd have to go back to a hospital, Dak To at least, to get it administered. What do you want to do, Cap? Dust him off?"

"Is he going to die without treatment?" Englander asks.

"I don't think so. We got a lecture on poisonous jungle beasties back at Chu Lai a while ago. They talked a little bit about these vipers, said that they are dangerous. Their bite can cause defibrination, but they're not often deadly."

"What the fuck is defibrination?"

"It causes little blood clots, uses up platelets so that other bleeding can get worse. This was a little snake, not fully grown, so likely the dose of venom he got wasn't big. My choice, though, Cap, I'd dust him off to a hospital where he can get treatment."

"If we don't?"

"We'll, I expect he'll survive. It's going to be painful for him for a couple of days. There can be lasting damage from untreated bites. But the biggest immediate risk is that some of the little clots will clog the kidneys. That *can* be fatal. But whether clots would block both kidneys, I just don't know. Damage would take some days to manifest. Dialysis would be the treatment. They've got gear for it at Chu Lai."

All that Englander seems to have heard is that the snake-bitten Yard will likely survive. "No, have them bring the man along. Knock down the pain when you have to. I'm not giving away our position again by calling in a dustoff."

I can see SSG Olsson is far from happy about Englander's decision. I imagine much of his unhappiness stems from the fact that our mission is a loose one. Find a dink supply base in Laos and blow it up; see if there is a POW camp nearby. No specific objective. No reason for us not to be pulled out if men are in danger. But Olsson, a well-schooled soldier, knows how to follow orders after speaking his mind. So the snake-bitten Yard will be carried along with us. Getting him out for treatment will come later, if necessary.

"God, sir, if that happens to me and they won't get me out, shoot me, please," Cat says under his breath.

"Nah," I whisper back. "I'd shoot Englander first."

Cat gives me a strained chuckle.

Finally, we move again, turning west to follow the highway a klick down a long ridge into Laos. Here, the undergrowth beneath the jungle canopy is so thick that we must abandon our original plan of moving parallel to the road. Instead, Englander directs a small point squad (a fire team, actually) to walk maybe a hundred meters ahead of us along the highway carrying a radio. His orders are for them to hide and break squelch twice on the radio if they sense that any dinks or Pathet Lao are ahead of us. That will give the rest of us time to move off the roadway. A trailing fire team will walk drag offering a warning of three squelch breaks if they get wind of anyone coming up behind us. It isn't necessary, though; the highway remains empty, and we are undetected as we move another three klicks into Laos.

Exhausted to a man as the sun is just coming up into a hazy sky, we finally move off the road and find a low, well-wooded prominence about a hundred meters away from the highway where we settle in and at last get some sleep.

CHAPTER 28

Cat is shaking me. "Captain, wake up."

I've slept for hours. Noontime light is blazing. Cool day. Cloudless but misty blue sky. I'm still groggy and half asleep and would roll over again, but Cat has his radio with him. "Dinks," he is saying. "Dink tanks on the road."

"Jesus!" Almost awake, I'm pulling on my boots. From the highway maybe fifty meters away comes the clanking and roar of heavy tracks, moving east from the sound. Does Englander want to fight them? Purposely, we had buried ourselves in the heaviest jungle we could find to be hidden from the road. But the reverse is also true: we see nothing of the road from here. Above to our south, though, is a high rise of hill less wooded, maybe a hundred meters above the jungle canopy. From there, I can likely get a view of the highway.

Englander, antsy as I have yet seen him, is already over to us, prodding me to move. "Those are dink tracks. They sound like big-ass Russian tanks. They must be going up to the trail and then probably southeast into Cambodia and Nam. I'd like to take out those motherfuckers."

I can see a platoon of Yards already unpacking LAWs and looking as if they are ready to move. I have no doubt they can take out at least some of the tanks, but some will likely fight back, so it will be at a cost of some Yards wounded and dead.

Boots on, rifle and gear in hand, I say, "It looks like there's a good OP up there, Hugh." I point to the hill behind us where a military crest looks to provide a good spot to observe the highway. "I'd rather use artillery if you really want to take out these tanks. No point risking your troops. Give me a few Yards for security. I can get up there and get the battery cranking up to fire. Any tanks left should be easier picking for you." I stop. "Hugh, do you really want to hit these tanks? It'll give away our presence for sure. I thought we were doing this on the QT."

It is a mark of how far I have come with Englander that he nods immediately, saying, "No, man, it's the best target we've had in weeks. Can you really hit moving tanks with artillery?"

I want to say, "Hell, yes," but I just nod.

"So good, good. Go!" he says. He jumps away as if lightning has struck him, calling out softly for the trung sĩ to get some men to go up the hill with us. The Yard first sergeant bustles to gather a squad; whispers in Jarai pass back and forth as he assembles our escort.

So, thinking, *What the hell,* thinking that if our cover is blown now, we can just pull out of Laos. Map, binos, compass, and rifle with me, Cat and I and Englander and four Yard soldiers push our way south through the dense undergrowth. I'm wondering if we're going to be up the hill in time, but after fifty meters or so, the slope thankfully gives way to more open jungle. A faint trail, probably an animal track, heads up the shallow rise of the hill. We fight our way past some heavy-thorned wait-a-minute vines with me wanting to scream as a dozen or more needle-sharp thorns stick me in my arm, my thigh, and the side of my face on the way up. I yelp at their sting. The Yards, moving untouched through them, laugh. Cat is similarly unscathed, but Englander, bulling through them, is jabbed far worse than I am, his reaction to the pain only an angry grunt. Quickly, we get to a spot on the military crest I'd spotted where we can see a good stretch of the 110 Highway east and west, and on it, maybe half a klick away, are five boat-shaped, olive-painted PT-76 Russian amphibious tanks inching slowly single file to the east. Why they are going so slowly is unclear until later when we find that the road here had apparently been mined and they were following a squad probing for them. Hulking but light weight, they are Korean War relics that are almost antiques in a faster-paced war. These are hardly main battle tanks and are actually kind of tinny looking, with a bare three-fourth inch of armor and only a spindly 76.2 mm gun and a light machine gun for armament. But against dismounted infantry like us, they would surely be murderous.

"Man! Look at 'em," Englander says. He drops on the ground next to me on a grassy expanse among more wait-a-minute bushes. "Can you get 'em?" he asks.

"Yeah," I say, noting I have clear sight of the tanks on a stretch of road with a good distance before they turn out of sight. "I can get them, but you ought to send one of these Yards back down to tell our guys to saddle up and be ready. The moment I start shooting, the dinks are going to know an observer is nearby and come looking for us. Given that, maybe we should stick with stealth and let the tanks go by."

Englander seems to consider this for a moment. "Nah, take 'em out so we won't have to face 'em later."

The tanks are headed east, away from our line of march, so facing them again is unlikely, I think. But Englander wants them hit, so I grab the handset from Cat and duck behind a bush with my map to get the best target grid. I figure that target to be about two hundred meters ahead of the lead tank. At the rate it moves, it and the incoming artillery should meet exactly where I call it. I contact the battery and am happy to hear its RTO come immediately back to me asking for the target.

"Grid six-eight-seven-five, two-one-zero-zero. Tanks on a roadway, direction zero-niner-hundred, proximity six hundred meters. One round, HE in adjustment, battery two in effect."

"Roger, tanks, wow!" the battery RTO says and repeats my fire call. And I wait wondering if the ARVN gunners manning the battery can push out the rounds before the tanks turn the corner of the highway to the east and are out of my sight.

No worries, though. Hardly a minute later (stunningly fast for any heavy artillery unit), the RTO announces, "Shot!"

"Roger, shot," I respond.

Soon, the RTO comes back with "Splash."

The distance from the ARVN battery on the border to this road where the tanks are is only seven klicks, a minimal time of flight for the shells. From shot to splash is only fourteen seconds. The adjusting round comes screaming in, and now, through my binoculars, I can see it hit dead center on the highway about eighty meters right of the target.

"Left five-zero, fire for effect," I call, knowing that by the book, I should bracket them, but they are moving and are tanks, for God's sake. I'll take my chance that the adjusted rounds will hit precisely.

Hardly a minute later, the ARVN battery comes back with "Shot. Over!" and it is clear the dinks know what is coming, trying desperately to back the tanks up, to turn them on the narrow jungle-enclosed highway, crashing into the trees on either side as they try to maneuver.

Wham, wham, wham, wham, *wham, wham!* The big rounds, four from the 155 howitzers, two from 175 guns, land right in the middle of the line of dink tanks. One round scores a direct hit, blowing the tank apart into smoking scrap. Other shells land right among the tracks, the immense shock of the detonating rounds rocking the heavy vehicles. Dink tank crewmen come boiling out of all the damaged tracks. Smoke and dust obliterate my view as the second volley comes in, and two more of the tanks are hit. A fourth tank has lost a tread on one side and is able to move only in a circle. The last tank, undamaged at the rear of the column, has managed to turn and is moving at speed back to the west along the highway.

"Left three hundred. Repeat fire for effect," I call, and before the tank is able to get a quarter of a klick back down the highway, that volley of fire drops around it. None of the shells hits it directly, but they still do enough damage to stall it where it sits there on the road. As with the four others, the crew of this tank come rushing out and charge off into the jungle away from the highway and the dead tracks.

"Holy shit!" Englander says. "Holy fucking shit! Man, I've never seen shooting like that before." He is flushed red in the face with excitement, waving toward the smashed vehicles on the highway. "Did you see? Did you?" He punches me in the arm. I finally have a convert to the value of artillery!

Perhaps to rub Englander's nose in it, I call for the battery to fire an additional volley on each target, destroying the lone PT-76 tank on the west and blasting hell out of the four on the eastern side. "End of mission, man," I call to the battery RTO. "That was stunning. Five tanks destroyed. Great shooting!"

"Glad to oblige. Out," the RTO comes back blandly.

Englander just sits, glorying in the destruction wreaked on the dinks' armor. I shake his shoulder, and he comes out of it with a sloppy smile as if waking from a wet dream and looks almost bleary eyed at me.

"Hugh, we've gotta hump, now," I say. "The dinks are going to know an observer was here to call in that fire. We should didi before they come looking for us."

"Yeah," he says, "yeah!"

As we had down the hill, the ammunition in one of the burning tanks cooks off. We can hear the detonation and see its sides billow out as if a kid has blown up a balloon. Dark smoke pours out of a half-dozen orifices, especially from the open hatch in its turret. How many dink tankers are dead, I don't know; a bunch had taken off into the jungle, but some may still be on board. If so, they're toast. Englander sends a squad of Yards over to reconnoiter, and they come back with the word that there are seven dead enemy soldiers in and around the tanks. Maybe eleven have escaped, though wounded or not, I don't know.

We move west at a decent clip through the jungle along the tributary of the Dak Lay that parallels the highway, finally coming to a sheltered safe point a klick or so east of the small Laotian ville of Ban Phiadouang. Here, on the south bank of the stream, in a heavily overgrown slot between two fingers of ridge, Englander again calls a halt.

"We'll stay here until dark," he says. "I'll have the Yards snoop and poop a klick or so up the highway. But hidden like this, I doubt any of the dinks can find us here."

A good day. Englander calls in a report of the tank kill, grudgingly mentioning that it was artillery that did the trick. He gets a "Roger, nice work" in response and grins like a Cheshire cat at that.

Ban Phiadouang occupies a clearing on the north side of the 110 Highway about five klicks west of the Cambodian border. There are maybe thirty houses in it, mostly thatched and tiny, made of bamboo frames and slats, perched on stilts. A few larger structures—what must pass for houses of the affluent here—have corrugated tin roofs. One building set slightly apart from the rest is made of ornately carved teak beams and roofed with rounded shingles. It looks to be a small temple, maybe Buddhist, though I had thought that the Lao people here in the mountains, like the Yards, are animists. Whatever their beliefs, the building is the only structure in the ville bearing any color or art. A party of us hidden in deep undergrowth watch the ville from across the stream and highway: me, Cat, Englander, the weapons specialist SSG Ed Bohannan (one of the new American troops I have just met), and a fire team of Yards led by a young *hạ sĩ* (corporal) named Y Lan'do. Ban Phiadouang looks much like any rural village in neighboring Vietnam; several pigs in pens, chickens scratching at the ground under the houses, a couple of short-haired brown village dogs lying quietly (if they have sensed us, they make no noise about it), and a muddy area at the ville's west end where a pair of water buffalo wallow. The war, so immense yet local across the border, has touched only lightly here. The place would be peaceful and drab if not for the heavily armed squad of Pathet Lao that is standing around a pair of trucks in the ville's center. All veteran-looking soldiers, they are a mix of young and old in green fatigues and floppy hats, shod mostly in rubber tire-soled Ho Chi Minh sandals armed with AK-47s. One, by his garb of crisper uniform, red kerchief, and shined boots, looks to be an officer; three gold specks are on each shoulder, shapes hard to make out even with my binos.

Englander elbows me and whispers that the specks seem to be insignia of rank. "See, three five-pointed gold stars, that's a captain with them."

Why? I wonder. That's a lot of rank for the leader of a unit this small. Is there something special about these Pathet Lao troops?

The captain looks to be interrogating several of the ville's older men who stand shirtless and subservient, heads bowed and arms close to their sides, clearly nervous. The captain points off to the east where a smudge of black smoke from the still-smoldering tanks rises in the cloudless afternoon sky. He shoves one of the villagers and shouts something at him. Y-Lan'do, the Yard corporal with us, apparently speaks a bit of Laotian, but, hiding in heavy brush south of the stream some fifty meters away from the ville, we can hear only the sound of the questions addressed to the village elders in the lilting, tonal Lao language, but not their sense.

"They talking about the *hủy hoại*, the tanks, I thinking, Cap," Y Lan'do tells Englander. He is respectful but not servile. The Montagnards have little hierarchy in their civilian lives, and that flattened sense of leadership carries over to their troops. They dutifully take orders but have no compunctions about challenging even the highest-ranking officer when they question or disagree with those orders, nor does there seem to be any penalty for their doing so.

Englander is all for going in and taking out the entire squad of Pathet Lao. SSG Bohannan and I have counseled no, the Pathet Lao are not really our enemy but, at best, the allies of the enemy dinks. Though to me that makes them as much dinks as the Viet Cong are, there seems no point in stirring up more trouble here. Taking out the tanks seems enough. If we wanted to hit them, we'd have to do it from up close to have much effect, crossing the stream and the highway to do so, leaving us exposed and vulnerable. We could call for the rest of the company to saddle up and back us, but that would risk giving away the size of the unit we have here.

Better we wait and watch.

"We're supposed to be going in quiet, Cap," Bohannan says, "but, so far, we've been anything but—big fight up on the border ridge, now the tanks we took out. If we hit these Lao troops, we might as well paint a big 'here we are' arrow on all our heads."

"He's right, Hugh," I say. "Let's leave them be and move on west toward the objective."

"Fuck," Englander says. "Yeah, you're right, but in my book, they're as much dinks as the Viet Cong are."

The debate might continue, but at this moment, I see one of the Pathet Lao troopers fall, the crack of a gunshot following a second or so later. Spreading red on his chest and onto the ground shows how serious the wound is. A second shot a beat later takes down the captain, who looks wildly about for a flash before slumping to the dirt. The rest of the Pathet Lao platoon scatter, shouting their alarm. Most take cover behind one of the smaller houses. One of them, an older-looking man with a senior sergeant's gold chevron on his sleeve, is pointing to the low hills north of the ville. The shouted word "*tha-han*," a rising tone at the end, is all I can make out."

"He maybe say 'sniper,'" says Y Lan'do. "He pointing to where sniper is."

Once again, Englander makes to have us open fire on the ville. This time, SSG Bohannan puts up a hand to the captain. "Somebody's doing it for us, Cap. No need to give away our position. Let's just watch."

The first of the Pathet Lao hit by gunfire is clearly dead, blood dripping, head and one arm lolling as their sergeant gets two of his troops to load the man on one of the trucks. It appears the captain is only hit in his arm, and though wounded, he looks able to move. He, too, manages to climb aboard the truck with the dead man. More shots sound from the hill behind the ville as the rest of the Lao troops climb aboard the trucks. One truck starts with a roar; the other gives a clanging moan and stutter of a struggling engine that finally shudders to life. The two trucks, with all the Pathet Lao platoon aboard, take off west down the highway, and all at once, the ville is quiet. The dogs, which had darted yelping under one of the houses as the first shot was fired, have come out again and are both sniffing at the stain of blood in the dirt where the first soldier had fallen.

"What was that all about, Captain?" Cat asks me. I look at Englander for some help here, only to have him shrug as if it is a mystery to him too.

Covered by the Yard fire team, Y Lan'do, Englander, and I go over to the ville to see if we can find out the meaning of what just happened here.

A wizened gray-headed man emerges from one of the thatched houses and makes his way slowly over to where we stand by the bloody ground.

"Mee nyang geuht keun baw phee?" Y Lan'do asks him in halting Lao.

The old man's response is too fast to make out, though Y Lan'do apparently gets some of it, telling us, "He say, good soldiers on hill kill bad ones here. He say he saw good soldiers before down here on this morning."

"Who were the good soldiers?"

"Phai dee tha-han?"

"Kao sai see nam-tan keuang noong, tae ta-wayn awk," the old man responds.

Y Lan'do shakes his head as if he gets only a bit of what the old man says to him, finally telling us, "He say they wear brown uniform, come from east." The Yard corporal's eyes are big as if he knows what that means.

"I was afraid of that," says Englander. He stands for a few beats, looking at the old man and over toward the northern hills. "Let's get out of here."

Ever since we made first our combat assault onto the border ridge, I have had the feeling we were not alone. It was a gut feeling, no evidence to back it up. Things just seemed wrong: the border firefight, small noises along our line of march, and the PL tanks moving east looking for someone but not us. It was a menacing and vexing sensation just outside our perceptions.

"Brown uniforms, Hugh? What was the old guy talking about?" I ask as we move back across the stream and east to where the unit is set in waiting for dark.

"Damned if I know," he responds.

"Come on, Hugh. You seemed to know well enough back in the ville."

Englander walks on, mouth moving a bit as if chewing over what he wants to tell me. Finally, under cover of the jungle after we have waded a shallow spot in the little stream, Englander stops.

"The OLM," he says.

"The Montagnard rebels?" What's this? I'm thinking about what SSG Olsson had said about them. Are they defunct as Englander had suggested back in the cave, or are they functioning as SSG Olsson had proposed to me when we met at the Quang Tri hospital? If functional, what are they doing out here in Laos? I ask Englander that exact question.

"Damn OLM are alive and well," he says. "Some of our Yards were involved with them at one time, though not anymore. Their big base is in Mondulkiri Province in Cambodia, maybe a hundred klicks south of here. I don't know what the hell they are doing up here."

I don't know whether this is stunning news or not. It is certainly strange and would be an answer for the questions I had. "Did you get those papers we found in the cave translated, Hugh?" I ask.

He nods, looking reluctant to answer and finally admitting. "Some. Part of it was in a Yard language nobody around here knows. But a lot was in Jarai."

"And?"

"And it talks about an OLM plan to disrupt the Pathet Lao." He stumbles over his words a bit as if temporizing, finally adding, "They are allied with the Hmong here in Laos and are virulently anti-Communist. They and the Pathet Lao aren't the best of friends."

"Man, Hugh, so it looks like we are being shadowed by a bunch of OLM rebels here who seem to be the enemy of our enemies. But we don't have any connection or coordination with them. Or do we?"

"Hell, no," Englander says, and I wait for an expected "I'm as surprised as you are" from him, but he just shrugs. This does not make me happy—a rogue unit of Montagnard rebels traveling near us in Laos and shooting up the countryside without us having any contact with them. I am very tempted to tell Hugh we need to pull back to Vietnam and regroup, or if he is unwilling, then at least to call for a bird to take me and Cat out of this mess. Finally, I say as much to Hugh.

"No, please, David, this is an important mission, and I fully get it that your arty is important too. I'm going to send a squad out to try and contact the OLM troops to make sure their actions don't work against us."

Ahhhhh! is my main thought at that.

CHAPTER 29

We move for eight miserable klicks in a steady chill drizzle from Ban Phiadouang to the tiny ville of Ban Pakha at the confluence of the north and south forks of the Dak Lay River. Here, our chief enemy is not the NVA or the Pathet Lao. It is the wait-a-minute bushes that grow thick along the bank, their sharp thorns catching everybody.

The Yards don't complain, though the fight through the grasping branches must punish them as much as they do the rest of us. Y Pon, today's point man, slashes aside the worst of the thorn bushes; other Yard soldiers walking slack behind him widen the way. We are tempted to leave this grasping overgrown hell and make our way down the highway, but the risk of running into PL or NVA patrols is too great. At Ban Pakha, the 110 Highway joins the 96, the combined highways no better, a rutted, badly graveled track running along the slumbering Dak Lay. Southeast, the map shows the 96 Highway following the course of the river almost to Cambodia. Northwest, the river valley runs through open jungle canopy between low hills that offer little cover. Englander marches us along the stream's south bank where the wait-a-minute bushes thankfully grow fewer, but the jungle canopy thickens and the going is still miserable.

Two more men are down, one a Yard private named Y Talba, hardly more than a boy yet stoic after he badly sprained his ankle (or perhaps broke it, Doc Olsson doesn't know which) stepping into a hidden hole in steep, tortured terrain three klicks west of Ban Phiadouang. Y Talba is in pain and can hardly walk, two of the older Yards supporting him between them. The second is another of the new Hatchet Team members, a black commo sergeant whose name is Duane Ricks and who fell while trying to help Y Talba, fell and broke his right arm, his one utterance of pain at it a surprised "unh" before becoming as stoic as the Yard. Their injuries are not a danger to the injured men or the unit itself, but they slow us, as does that of the snake-bitten man. His arm has swollen to the size of his thigh, and every step he takes, he accompanies with a soft moan.

"Eighteen klicks are all we've gone. Not a shot besides artillery fired in Laos and already five men down," Englander says as we settle in to abide the daylight on a low hill south of the highway junction. The hill is triple canopy, spotted with thorn and bamboo thickets that screen us from Ban Pakha a couple hundred meters to our north. We are eighteen klicks west of the border now yet have traversed nearly thirty to get here, moving nearly a klick back and forth along the twists and turns of the river and hills for every klick we move west.

I am exhausted, too tired to more than wave at the mosquitos keening around me (keening but kept at bay by my repellent, one of the few items you can trust in the jungle) and too tired even to boil water for one of the LRRP rations I am carrying. I open one packet and pull out a tropical chocolate bar. The dense stuff won't melt in your mouth, so I gnaw it. (Guys with bad teeth shave off bits to suck on. It's said the WWII version was virtually inedible.)

"Do you want a can of fruit, Captain?" Cat asks me. It seems a kind gesture to this old man of twenty-five, and I would selflessly decline, but he tosses me one—pear halves in syrup—and I accept without a dissent. One day soon, I'll promote him to general, I say, for the compassion of this act.

"Nah, sir, I'm not cut out to be an officer. Give me these sergeant's stripes and an early out from Vietnam and I'll be happy." He grins. I attack the top of the can with my P-38, pull a pear half out with my Ka-Bar knife, take a couple of swallows of the juice, and pass the rest back to Cat. They are Cat's pears, and though thankful for his sharing them, I want to leave enough for him. The map, however, bears more scrutiny. By my measure, we are now well beyond the maximum range of the 155s on the border firebase. All that remains of our artillery support are the two 175 mm guns back there, presuming that they are firing the modified ammo that can reach nearly thirty klicks. That means we still have artillery cover for only another dozen klicks traveling west (barely seven more miles!). This realization is not encouraging. We've hit nothing heavy yet, but the signs of heavy enemy presence are strong, and my access to the big guns is my principal comfort. I thought about that several times as we hid in deep jungle watching Pathet Lao truck and armor convoys travel the highway. A few klicks back, we skirted a medium-sized base camp of Pathet Lao or maybe NVA (hard to tell which they were from a klick away on the other side of the river). Englander had been all for having me drop some arty on it.

"You could kick their asses and they'd never know who hit them," he said.

"I could, Hugh. But that's the problem—they wouldn't know who, but they'd know it was *somebody* unfriendly, and pretty soon, this whole river valley would be crawling with enemy patrols," I told him.

High on his own energy, Englander had waved airily, "Yeah, yeah, I guess you're right," and let it drop.

Ban Pakha is a tiny ville that makes Ban Phiadouang seem like a metropolis by comparison. It comprises perhaps ten thatched houses on stilts, their spaces cut out of triple canopy jungle. Pigs, chickens, water buffalo, and dogs are there too. It seems a sleepy place, placid, far from any signs of combat. The smell of soup and pungent aroma of grilling meat pervades it, making my stomach rumble. We are mortally tired, but out of an excess of caution, Cat and I and a squad of Yards reconnoiter it from a distance. We watch a trio of women, young by their energy but age indeterminate by their look, carry bundles of brightly colored clothing to the river and settle on rocks in the slight drizzle to wash the garments. Dunking, rubbing them with soap, scrubbing, and wringing the clothes, the women chatter to each other in a casual fashion that seems oblivious to war and danger. Y Lan'do is not with us on this foray. Our Yard squad is led by a young trung si who speaks some halting English but apparently no Lao.

When I ask him what the women are talking about, "No bic Lảo," he says to me and shrugs, a guileless smile on his face.

One of the women says something lilting, and the other two laugh. It is strange to hear a woman's laughter here so far into the bush. There is nothing else happening, and I tell Cat and the Yards we are going back to the company.

We get back to find yet another man down, this one an older Yard who, in clearing a place to sleep, managed to catch his machete on a branch, which deflected its course and slashed him on the calf, deeply. Doc Olsson has managed to staunch the worst of the bleeding but says the wound will likely reopen and the man bleed out if we try to move him very far. Olsson has cut away the leg of the man's fatigue pants, its tiger-patterned cloth blood soaked. The gash is maybe four inches long toward the inner part of the leg and very deep, white that may be bone visible in the bloody heart of the gash. The medic is working in it, his gloved hands red and dripping. The Yard, a rifleman named Y Ban, is stoic, gritting his teeth at the obvious pain, though bleary from a painkiller (morphine?) that Olsson has given him. Will the Yards attach shame to Y Ban's injury, which came not in battle but from his own hand, even if accidentally?

"Machete nicked his posterior tibial artery, Cap," SSG Olsson tells Englander. "I've got it stitched now. But if we try to move him far, those stitches can pull and maybe tear the whole thing open. I hate to say it, but we need a dustoff or this guy might not survive."

I know what Englander is thinking—that we aren't even halfway to the objective, and if we call in a dustoff now, it will blow any remaining chance of a stealthy move toward it. Still, even the gung-ho Englander isn't so hard-hearted as to let a man die just to protect our cover.

"Shit! Parnassus," he calls, "come over here!"

SSG Lyle Parnassus is Frank Rosenbaum's replacement. Chunky and short, he couldn't be more different looking from the hulking KIA'd commo sergeant.

"Yeah, Cap?" Parnassus says.

"Get us a dustoff. CPT Weisman will give you the grid. Tell them it's covert, just the dustoff bird, no gunships or other support. We'll make this as quick and quiet as possible."

"Got it, Cap." I read him a grid off the map, and he pulls up the handset of his radio to call our Hatchet Team Control, a small liaison unit set up on the same hill with the artillery battery that is supporting us.

Englander walks over to MSG Flanagan and asks him where he thinks the best spot is for an LZ for the dustoff bird.

"No place around here, Captain. All triple canopy around us on this side of the river. We'd have to blow down a bunch of these trees to open a spot for the dustoff. Might need to use a jungle penetrator even then. I think our best shot would be to carry the injured across the river and bring the dustoff bird down on the highway. We'd be in the open only a few minutes, and there wouldn't be any noise of our taking down trees. That's my thought, sir."

"Ah, Christ," says Englander. "Yeah, I think that's best." He looks at me and nods back when I nod at him. Is he asking my opinion or just making sure I know what's planned? Doesn't matter either way.

I tell them I think the best location for the pickup is grid 5952 1820, along the 96 Highway going south from our position. "There's cover there on our side of the highway and open space on the other, Hugh," I say. "That'll give us a clear field of fire if the enemy tries to hit the bird."

Englander looks over my shoulder at the map and says, "Yeah, good," and tells Parnassus to call in the corrected grid. The com sergeant relays the numbers to our control as I tell Cat to bring over the radio, so I can encrypt and call in the grids of a triad of targets on likely assault points around the LZ on the highway. These will give me quick spots—hopefully unnecessary—to adjust from if we get hit during the dustoff.

It is soft daylight beneath drippy cloud cover. The company is set in an ambush-like L formation; the long arm along the west side of the 96 Highway, the shorter one laid across it into a shadowed tongue of jungle on the southeast. We wait for the dustoff with Y Ban and the other three injured Yards. Cat and I and Englander are on the western leg of the position. The battery is primed. I've asked them to load both 175 mm guns with HE and ready them to hit the most likely target, a low single-canopy-covered hill maybe three hundred meters to our east. I'm banking on accuracy I'm unsure of. I'd prefer to shoot the target in advance, but that would give away our presence. So I sit.

"That's where I'd hit us from if I were the dinks," I tell Englander. He nods. "I think the same," he says.

About ten minutes after we set in there, we get a call from the incoming dustoff bird saying they are about a dozen klicks out from us, coming in from the northeast very high to avoid possible AA fire. This, I think, ought to be a classic in and out. The bird will come in high as it is now and a klick or so out will drop steeply to just above treetop level and slide down to a quick touch onto the highway. We'll load on the injured, and the pilot will pull pitch and didi mau back to Vietnam. Easy, except we are twenty klicks or more from any other American unit, with no gunships and only two 175 mm guns to support us if this hits the fan.

The pilot calls, "Berkeley Balder Eight-One, this is Dustoff Three-Seven, making our run now. Over."

"This is Balder Eight-One. Roger, we see you," SSG Parnassus tells him.

The hazy speck in the clouds to our north that is the dustoff bird grows larger as it drops from the overcast into clearer air. Englander whispers, "Ready," a whisper passed on down the line of the company. Medic SSG Olsson and a Yard medic *Binh nhất* (PFC) Y Tao'ma and a squad of other Yards wait just inside the jungle cover with the injured men, ready to load them on the dustoff as soon as it touches down. Right where the highways join to our north, the bird rounds the west side of a low hill and drops to treetop level just over the highway, the blatt of its blades growing louder.

"Coming, coming," says Englander.

Now the bird is just about to the LZ, and the pilot flares it for a landing, grit from the highway blasting up around it in a damp storm. And it is down, rocking, mostly in a restless hover barely touching earth.

Yard đại úy Y Giao, standing with the medics and the injured, hisses, "Hiu ră anai!" telling the troops to go now, and begins helping carry the injured men to the bird. I see the dustoff bird's crew chief beckoning urgently, his hand waving them in. SSG Ricks and the four injured Yards are on the dustoff now, and the crew chief is yelling something at SSG Olsson and the Yards, but his words are lost to us in the noise of the turbine and blades. They jump back, Olsson dodging away from the bird's slewing tail boom and viciously spinning tail rotor as the dustoff turns into the wind to take off. From three hundred meters up the hill in the east, machine gun fire hits the dustoff.

Englander screams, "No!" Damaged, the dustoff bird slips sideways, smoke puffing out near its rotor. It wobbles into the air, the machine gun fire tracking it.

"Fire, fire, you sons of bitches!" Englander screams at the company, and a huge volume of it from both legs of our L rattles into the hilltop where the enemy fire originates.

"God," Cat says, "is it going to go down?" A moan, as if a chorus to Cat, rises up from the Yards around us.

But I've already shouted "Fire!" to the battery, which responds almost instantly with "Shot!" and ten seconds later with "Splash." Though I have often derided the accuracy of the big guns, these are dead-on. A pair of detonations blossoms exactly where I had called for them on the crown of the hill. They impact with raging flame buried in deep gray smoke, a brighter secondary explosion following. "Repeat, battery two," I tell them, and I know that a minute or so later, four more of the 145 pound rounds will be detonating up there. Better, the dustoff bird stays airborne, limping up into the cloud cover and turning to the east. Will it make it back to Ben Het in Vietnam? I don't know. But now, away from us, the dustoff pilot can call for gunships to ride as wingmen on its return flight. Were any on the bird killed or injured? That, too, I don't know.

We hunker for maybe a minute there on the side of the highway, listening to the byplay of calls between the dustoff bird and Ben Het, listening to the pilot say that the crew chief had been hit and one of the Yards they are transporting (the man with the machete cut) had been killed. But he adds that the bird is still airworthy enough to make the thirty klicks back to Ben Het. (We learn later that the dustoff bird made it back across the Vietnamese border and set down on the 512 Highway six klicks short of Ben Het. Gunships rode guard on it until a unit from the Ben Het base could get there and pull them out. Remarkably, though some of the others were injured, all but the one Yard on the dustoff survived.)

With the dustoff complete, CPT Englander has given the order for the rest of our unit to didi mau northwest along the river "fast as we fucking can!"

"How the hell did they know a dustoff was coming in, Hugh?" I ask.

"Damned if I know, man," he says. But his face betrays uncertainty. The enemy would know only if someone breached the secret. Now it's my turn to say, "Fuck!"

We move, watching for ambushes and booby traps, watching for enemy who—clearly aware we are here—are surely trying to track us. We do our best to stay hidden, moving under deep jungle cover on the west side of the river, staying just in sight of the highway. On that highway as we move, we see a series of mechanized patrols. One patrol—probably Pathet Lao—is a mélange of worn vehicles, as if a parade of antiques engines of war: an ancient jeep, a Chinese BJ212 wagon that looks like the by-blow of a jeep and a Land Rover, and several battered troop-filled trucks that might date back to WWII.

Soon after comes another partially armored patrol with a pair of Russian light tanks and three battered armored personnel carriers. The other patrol of vehicles comes back a half hour later headed southeast, a tank and several tracks following soon after. None comes close to a stealthy move, their clanking alone enough to warn us, and we take cover in the deeper jungle until they pass.

Two klicks on, the front of our file gets into a brief firefight with half a dozen of the enemy apparently on a foot patrol. We hear the brief exchange of shots, an AK barking, M16s answering, and shouts. I am on the radio calling for the guns to get ready. There comes the bang of a grenade, soft sounding in the jungle, the harsh jangle of the blast muted. More shouts. A scream for "Doc!" and then silence.

In this fight, Englander rushes forward, and Cat and I follow. I'd been taught long ago by CPT Jack—the first company commander I'd worked with in Vietnam—that hitting the dirt in such a situation just sends the rest of the unit behind me to ground and deprives the commander the use of a maneuver unit in such a firefight. So Cat and I run up to find Englander standing among our point element. Three enemy soldiers wearing green NVA uniforms and pith helmets lie dead nearby, two of them blown apart almost beyond recognition by the grenade. The third is dead from a burst of M16 fire that has torn his chest open. The soldiers don't have a radio with them, but blood trails heading west mark the retreat route of the other three.

"Man, our cover is blown again," Englander says softly, shaking his head. "Hell, I guess there's no longer any secret about our moving here."

Wounded are SSG Larry Arguello, who had been walking second slack with the point element, and two Yards, though none are hurt seriously. Doc Olsson comes up along with a Yard medic named Y Mah, and they begin treating wounds. SSG Arguello has taken an AK round along the left side of his rib cage, tearing flesh and muscle and maybe cracking a rib, but not life threatening. One of the wounded Yards has been hit in the thigh, a wound also not life threatening, no arteries or bone hit, but it'll be painful for him to walk. The point man, a stringy-looking older Yard who is a true veteran, has taken fragments from the grenade, his face and left shoulder pocked with bloody wounds. He, too, will survive it with new scars over the old. I know that SSG Olsson would like to have them dusted off, but caught where we are, bringing a bird in would be much too risky. Englander and I have only to look at each other, and each realizes this truth.

I call the battery and tell them to stand down, look again at the map, and tell Englander that we are getting close to max range for the 175s.

"We are about six clicks away from losing artillery support, Hugh," I say.

His response of "No!" is eloquent and telling; a few months ago, I would have gotten only a shrug from him.

Englander is checking the condition of the three wounded men. "Can you move with us?" he asks SSG Arguello.

The weapons sergeant grunts and nods, saying, "Yeah, Cap, this ain't no biggie." But I note his wince as he turns toward the captain.

The Yard trung sĩ has come up and is talking to the two of his men who are wounded. He also turns to Englander and says, "They OK, numbah one, Cap-tain. No problem they move." Still, he sends them back into the file and moves two new men up to point. SSG Arguello refuses a similar offer from Englander.

"No, Cap," he says. "This is my spot." Englander doesn't argue.

So with another few of our men wounded, we move again.

It is not more than fifteen minutes onward that we find a hut hidden in deep jungle growth. The tell is a blood trail—surely from one of the NVA we had wounded—leading off from the riverbank and into the copse of heavy jungle. Approaching it, we find a round thatched structure with a bamboo slat door hanging open on leather hinges. Just outside is a body, a young NVA soldier lying near the doorway, an AK-47 still clutched in his hands. The front of his uniform, from chest to groin, is blood covered; his face has the placidity of one who has slipped quietly from life, pain leaching away, falling into death as into sleep.

"I thought the NVA took their dead with them, don't they, sir?" Cat asks me.

"Mostly," I say. "But I suspect they are too badly hurt themselves to manage to carry him. See . . ." I point to more blood trails heading off along the river. "We'll likely see the rest of them further on, unless they meet up with other NVA troops who can get them away."

The hut is a major find. Englander crows that it is "full to bursting" with weaponry and ammunition. Exploring further along the west bank of the river, we come upon six similar huts equally well stocked with weapons. We find one more of the NVA soldiers near the last of the huts, dead, lying in a small puddle of the last of his blood.

Altogether, we find nearly four hundred 122 mm rockets with half a dozen launchers, thousands of rounds of AK-47 ammo, and maybe five dozen RPGs. One hut is stacked with boxes of new AKs. Another is filled with HE and white phosphorous rounds for 82 mm mortars plus three .51-caliber machine guns with a large stock of ammo. Of the sixth and final NVA soldier, there is no sign. We have to assume he made it back to his unit, probably alerting them about us.

We open one last hut and recoil at the sight of several stacks of wooden cases, marked зарин with a baleful red skull and crossbones stamped next to the label on each. Something dark and oily has seeped from several of the cases, staining the wood. The top of one uppermost case is also stained, as if another case—now missing—had dripped down upon it.

"What the hell is that?" Englander asks. "Grenades, maybe. Some bad-looking shit for sure." He shows no interest in going inside the hut to look.

"Appears like they're labeled in Cyrillic, maybe Russian," I say. Like Englander, I stay well away from the hut's door, edging just close enough to look in at its evil contents. "I'd guess these are boxes of gas grenades, nasty stuff what with the skull and crossbones marked on them, I imagine these are full of poison gas. I'm not much interested in opening a box and verifying that, though," I tell Englander, who nods assent.

Cat, who has been peering over my shoulder, says, "Man, Captain, I don't smell anything. Isn't poison gas supposed to smell bad?"

"Depends," I say. We'd had a one-week chem weapons course at Fort Sill. The instructor had warned us, "Chlorine gas smells like bleach. Some World War I blister agents smelled like geraniums or new-mown hay. The worst stuff, stuff they have stocked for artillery shells or grenades today, sarin and other nerve agents, they're colorless and odorless. One nerve agent, soman, smells like Vicks VapoRub. The worst of 'em, nerve agent VX—a buffed-up cousin of sarin—isn't a gas. It's an aerosol, and clouds of it look faintly yellowish. No smell, though. Unless you're smellin' the daisies, you're going to be pushin' up." He'd cracked a mordant smile at that.

I look at the sinister death's head markings again and shiver; what rules of war there might have been in Vietnam are clearly inoperative here in the Laotian jungle. I am suddenly glad Cat and I are carrying gas masks and atropine injectors.

Most unnerving is the stain on the *top* of the uppermost case, suggesting there had been at least one more batch of grenades. I note that save for the stain, the upper surface of the top case is clean. Had someone taken away those grenades recently?

Control is ecstatic over this haul. Though I'm aghast at the idea of somebody running loose with gas grenades, to me, the stock of enemy matériel otherwise hardly seems worth gloating over. Our objective, the big supply depot that the NVA have west of here is reportedly orders of magnitude greater than this small haul. Still, Hatchet Control wants to retrieve this trove of weapons and ammo to display like a dead bug on a pin as support for why they had called for us to conduct this operation.

"Set in place and we'll send a Hook out to pick it up," Control comes to us over the radio.

"You're nuts," Englander comes back. "You want to cart this stuff back to Ben Het as a trophy? If you send a Hook out here for that, we'll have every dink and PL for miles around trying to take it down. I've got my commo sergeant taking pictures of the shit. If that doesn't do you, I'm sorry. Soon as he's done, our demo team is going to blow this stuff all to hell. Out." He pulls the plug on the radio's speaker. From a squawk on the handset, I can still tell there's a response on the radio from Hatchet Control, but Englander chooses to ignore it.

We move west a klick, leaving the demo team to set an explosive charge with a delay fuse in each of the huts. There, we hunker, waiting for the team to catch up. The distant detonations are huge, especially from those with the rockets and other heavy ordnance. We hear secondary explosions continue to pop off from the huts for more than an hour as we continue west.

Periodically, from across the river, we hear gunshots, which Englander says are signal shots to coordinate enemy movement. "Bastards are short on radios," he tells us, "so firing off rounds is the way they stay in touch." This appears to be only partly true, though. As we approach the point where the Dak Lay and two other tributaries join to form the headwaters of the much larger Nam Pouang River, we encounter a small ville of just a few huts across the river north of the highway, a settlement so small that the map does not show a name for it. Nearing there, we can hear the ringing of what sounds like a military field telephone. From the ville? No one can tell. Should we send a squad in to find out? No to that too. We know the enemy is aware we are near, but we'd prefer not to pinpoint our location in such a way. So we skirt that ville.

✯ ✯ ✯

CHAPTER 30

There come half a dozen shots from the front of our file.

"M16 fire? Our guys shooting?"

"Yeah?"

And SSG Lonell Pike, who has been walking second slack, comes trotting back to tell us that they've taken out a couple of NVA soldiers.

"You sure they're NVA?" Englander asks him.

"Yup, green unis, pith helmets and all. Not PL, definitely dinks. Place is crawlin' with 'em."

The Yards move quickly to conceal the enemy bodies in heavy brush to the side of our line of march. None of our troops is hurt in this exchange.

Another klick on, weary, having now moved steadily for nearly eighteen hours with only the brief stop near Ban Pakha, and with darkness coming on, we decide to settle into an NDP for the night, regroup, and figure out where we will head in the morning. The idea of moving only at night is as blown as many other of our plans. We continue to hear signal shots at intervals through the night, which seems to unnerve me more than it does Cat. Things are otherwise quiet, without a single enemy probe of our perimeter the entire night. As we rest in our NDP, light rain falls ceaselessly, its pattering through the canopy deadening the sound of any movement around us. Worried about being hit in the night, we've dug foxholes and put our poncho and mosquito net hooches up next to them. The nets are unnecessary; the rain has put down the mosquitos, their song absent from the darkness, but twice again in the night, we hear the brief distant ringing of that field telephone, as eerie as something from a ghost story. Exhaustion soon sends me to a fitful sleep where I dream of a file of Vietnamese girls wearing *áo dais* in a rainbow of colors walking endlessly past my foxhole without even a sideward glance at me.

CPT Englander and his commo sergeant have set their hooch up a few feet from the one Cat and I share.

Cat shakes me out of my dream. "CPT Englander wants to see you, sir," he says. I sit up on my air mattress and shake myself awake, the ripe dream of women melted away.

"Sir?" Cat says again, nudging my shoulder.

"Yeah, yeah, I'm awake," I say, and I stuff my feet back into my boots. I move over to Englander's hooch and duck inside out of the rain. The big Pole, SSG Dabrowski, pulls his feet in so I have room. The sound of the rain is a light drumming on the hooch's poncho roof. A red-lensed flashlight—lens stopped down to a slit of light—is on and hanging from the hooch's cross pole.

Englander, looking as if he has hardly slept, is working his teeth at a chunk of a chocolate bar and studying his map in the dim red beam. He holds the map close to his face and traces a finger along it, looking intently at the depicted terrain, tracing again. He looks up as I settle down. "I think I've figured our route for tomorrow," he says. "Follow me here." He turns the map so I can see it, stops, breaks off another chunk of chocolate, and holds it out to me, folksy as if I'm a guest offered a refreshment. I smile a little, take the chocolate, nod in thanks, and gnaw off a bit.

"Here," he says, "see where the highway makes a couple of turns and then heads northwest again. If we follow it, it'll take us out of these mountains and onto open plains headed toward Attapu. I'm thinking that, instead, about three klicks from here where a branch of the river splits off toward the west, we should leave the highway and follow the river. No road there, just a valley. By the map, the only marked habitation is maybe six klicks in. It shows just a few hooches, if the ville is even there anymore."

"Yeah," I say, studying the monochrome look of the map in Englander's red light. "Same as you, I'd rather get away from the highway, too much mechanized stuff and armor traveling on it. Just to note, Hugh, here, four klicks from where the ville is, though, is the farthest west the 175 guns supporting us can reach. Further west, we are out of their range. That will give us another twenty or so klicks to go from there without any artillery support."

"Yeah, you told me we were getting close to losing the guns. I'd hoped we would get farther on before that happened. We can call in air if we hit something bad, but it could be a long time before gunships or jets could get to us."

It is an irony that Englander finally seems sold on the value of artillery just as we are hitting the edge of where artillery will still be available. I suck on a bit of the chocolate, the taste at once sweet and bitter, and finally broach another irksome issue: the OLM unit that has been shadowing us.

"Do you know what they're up to, Hugh? They were noisy and visible the first bit of this trip but don't seem to have made any more noise for hours now."

"Word is they will be following the highway toward the north and will maybe draw off any PL or dinks following us."

"Word is? Don't they communicate with you?"

"Sometimes." His voice gets smaller as if chagrined that he doesn't have closer contact with this chimerical unit of rebel Yards.

"So we won't have them as a shadow anymore?"

"Hell, Weisman, I don't know. They keep in touch most of the time, but damned if I can get them to coordinate any of their movements with ours." He jerks as if suddenly shivering. "I just don't know."

I watch him for a beat, only his face and hands illuminated in the bubble of red light from his flashlight. "A diversion is good, Hugh," I say, "especially if the tanks and other vehicles follow the Yard unit while we head west."

"Yeah," he says. "Man, I need some sleep. We'll explore this more before we leave in the morning."

Dawn. Though there is a lowering and threatening sky, the rain seems done for now. It has left everything dripping, though, and sent the river up half a foot or so from yesterday. In the wet, leeches are out, and Cat finds one on his pant leg. Usually a tough, combat-tested kid, Cat freaks out at the leech, slaps it off, and quickly drops his fatigue pants to check for more.

"Any on me, Captain?" he asks. He turns his back to me so I can inspect his legs.

"Nary a one." I grin. I tell him the story of my trek across the swamp up north with all the sated leeches I'd found in my pant legs.

"Cripes! I hate those things," Cat says, his face reddening under the freckles.

Pushing on through the bush, we are now about two and a half klicks west of where we'd had our NDP last night. We're at the point where the highway makes a sharp turn to the north. We hear the squeak and clank of tracked vehicles on the highway. We've just recrossed the river, actually a tributary of it running from the south into the Nam Pouang, and are at a small open spot clear enough we can look across this river branch to the highway. There are six tanks there, substantially heavier than the amphibious tracks we'd taken out back near the border.

"Russian T54s," says SSG Pike, now walking with me, Cat, and Englander. "Those suckers are armored for sure. Four inches of it on the front of the hull, eight on the front of the turret, nearly three on the back. Nasty armament too. Got a hundred-millimeter gun and a .30 cal machine gun on it. A LAW will take one out if you can hit it right, but that's a tough target."

"Man!" says Cat.

"Yeah, you don't want to mess with one of them," Pike says. "I'm happy as hell the dinks don't have those on our side of the border."

"Can you pull that trick again, drop some arty on 'em and take 'em out?" Englander asks.

"We could do a job on them if we can get the shells close enough. But with those monsters, near isn't like horseshoes. What the sergeant says about their armor, I'd have to hit them directly while they are moving to do any damage," I tell Englander. "And trying to do so will let them know we have an observer close enough to adjust fire on the target. Do you want to do that or go stealthy?"

The answer comes from what must be the OLM company. Several streaks of fire—RPGs by their look—lance out toward the tanks from the jungle on the other side of the river. One hits the turret of a tank with a sharp bang of the shaped charge, doing little apparent damage. The turrets of all the tanks turn in the direction the RPGs came from and let go an intense volume of fire from their 100 mm guns and coaxial machine guns. Their firepower is stunning, shredding the jungle in a storm of leaves and broken branches on that side of the highway. Whether they got any of the rebel Yards over there is unknown. Apparently unharmed—though one of the tracks has darker smoke coming from its exhaust but seems able to keep up with the others—the tanks continue on the highway to the east.

"Does that answer your question?" Englander asks me. "I don't know what those Yards' plans are, but it looks like they are still doing a diversion as cover for us." He turns to the Yard first sergeant. "Saddle up, let's go."

"Ữ, we move!" The Yard trung sĩ nods and calls out, "Mo'go'i ră anai!" to his troops.

We are two klicks past the point where the highway makes its stair-step turn north when we run into a reinforced Pathet Lao platoon moving in a file along the highway in our direction. Our point element emerges from a tree line onto an open, soggy expanse of grass and walks almost into them. Still under tree cover, I hear the contact before I see it: AKs fire several stuttering bursts; an M60 opens up, M16 fire backing it. A trio of grenades detonate sharply, and there are shouts in English, Jarai, and Lao.

A pang of dismay bursts in my chest, sending me lurching forward. "Come on, Cat, let's get up there," I tell him, and we take off running toward the tree line. First thing I see as we move into the open is a line of our guys down in the clearing firing at the PL who have gone to ground on the highway and in a ditch running along the highway's far side. Four of the PL on the highway are obviously dead, lying in a broken repose amid running blood. The remaining PL, perhaps thirty of them, are exchanging intense fire with the Hatchet Team in the clearing.

Cat and I drop there, and Englander comes up next to us, calling for the rest of our company to come up and take positions along the tree line to our left.

"Flanking fire," he calls. "Keep 'em pinned so we can maneuver."

I have already grabbed the radio handset from Cat and begun calling a fire mission, giving the target grid, direction, and proximity. Proximity is a serious problem, though. We are only about fifty meters from where the PL are set in along the highway and the ditch. We are also exactly on the gun target line, the PL straight ahead, the guns directly behind. That's nowhere you want to be with guns like the 175s, especially near the end of their range where they can have accuracy problems if the gunners are not precise in their settings. So, for safety's sake, I've given the battery a starting grid about two hundred meters beyond where the PL are set in (still danger close) and plan to adjust subsequent rounds closer by short distances.

As I am getting this fire mission off to the battery, I can hear an American voice from our guys in the clearing calling, "Doc," and several Yards calling, "Poj'rao" ("doctor" in Jarai). One of the wounded Yards is a few meters from us. Cat, shucking the radio and his ruck, crawls over to him and pulls him back out of the line of fire so a Yard medic can get to him.

"Wow!" I say to Cat, who shrugs, "He was hurt, Captain." A bullet had smacked in a meter or so from Cat as he was pulling the wounded man back, eliciting a yelp. But Cat's not hit.

Set in where we are, we're not able to move easily. The tree line to our left tapers off into swampy ground where the going would be hard. We could back away, but somewhere to our east are the enemy tanks, and I have no doubt the PL trapped on the highway have called them to come in.

At this point, I hear, "Shot!" over the radio, say back, "Roger, shot," and tell Englander I've got artillery coming in.

"They're right on top of us. Can you get it in close enough to do any good?"

"I think so," I tell him, though I admit that's optimistic. At this distance from the guns, range probable error is large, and where exactly the big rounds hit is anybody's guess. Finally, I hear, "Splash," from the battery RTO and the rumbling thunder of the 175 mm rounds coming in. As they detonate, the PL hit us with a quartet of RPGs that sizzle in from across the highway and crash into our position in fire and smoke. Again, there is a call for "Poj'rao," signifying another Yard hurt. The artillery has dropped in maybe 180 meters beyond the PL, and so I call, "Drop 100, repeat," to the battery.

Englander, meanwhile, frustrated at my careful adjustment, demands, "Can't you get that shit closer to 'em?"

"Doing it, Hugh," I say.

"Hurry, then."

The second volley drops maybe sixty meters behind them (remember the probable error), shell fragments sing through the enemy position and on over our heads, screams of pain from the PL follow. At that, the enemy soldiers pack it in and did mau east along the ditch past us and away.

I call, "End of mission, nice shooting," to the battery, and the American-sounding voice of the RTO comes back with a cheery "De nada!"

With the tanks almost certainly coming back, we take little time for damage assessments. Seven PL bodies lie on the highway, and four more with shrapnel wounds are in the ditch. At last, half a dozen blood trails follow the path the PL had taken in their getaway, speaking of more PL wounded either by our fire or the artillery. The water in the ditch bottom is red at intervals with blooms of their blood.

SSG Olsson comes up to Englander to tell him that we have eight wounded. "Four pretty seriously, Cap. I'd like to dust them off."

"I'd like to too, Mike, but this is no place to bring in a bird," he says. "Maybe five hundred meters on, we'll turn west along a side stream away from the highway, looks like another klick in, and we'll have a spot where we can set up an LZ."

It's obvious the medical sergeant doesn't like it, but Englander only shakes his head. "Best we can safely do, Mike. How many of the wounded can walk?"

"All but two. One of the Yards has lost most of his lower leg. SGT Parnassus has a shattered tibia from an AK round. I've splinted it, but he can't walk on his own. A couple of more have serious upper body wounds, but Y To'ma and I have them bandaged, and the bleeding mostly stopped. They'll need dusting off soon, but they can walk for a klick or so if necessary."

"The rest?"

"Sundry flesh wounds, Cap. Worst is a Yard machine gunner with a smashed ankle. I really want to dust him off too. In fact, I'd like to get all our wounded out. Better for them, better for us in the long run."

"I hear you," says Englander. "We'll see what it looks like up ahead."

CHAPTER 31

Off the highway to our left, the going looks hellacious: a series of steep hills covered with a low dense scrub that would be impossible to cut through in any good time. The base of the hills is right at the highway, and we have no choice but to use this road for half a klick. Thus, we have to move out in the open, visible to anyone who might be observing from the hills to the north. To the highway's right lie rice paddies stretching to these hills, a perfect field of fire if there are enemy machine gunners in the tree line some two hundred meters away.

We move with care. Englander has sent two fire teams ahead to reconnoiter the roadway and put another out as a screen to our right flank along a paddy dike that parallels our line of march. A fourth team trails maybe two hundred meters behind us as a following screen watching for dinks or PL who might be moving up on us from that direction. And so—on as much alert as we can be—we walk up that half klick of highway and turn off it unimpeded into a long valley stretching west along a shallow tributary of the Nam Pouang. The going here is no better.

This end of the valley is low, covered with much the same heavy scrub as the hills.

"Wide open and soggy," Cat remarks. "No easy way to move here."

The only ingress is a tight path—as much an animal trail as a footpath—that runs alongside the stream. As before, the scrub is thick with wait-a-minute bushes, and everyone in our file is scratched and stuck.

It is quiet, no sign of any enemy following us.

"I don't trust it," Englander says to me. "That firefight wasn't likely to send them running. I imagine they're just regrouping to hit us again."

This time, I'm the one to say nothing, grunt agreement, and point to a grassy space ahead, mostly scrubby with just a couple of ratty-looking teaks and several fallen trees. "Open enough up there. We can bring in a dustoff pretty comfortably, Hugh," I tell him.

Englander remains hyper vigilant when he calls a halt there.

"Christ, we're exposed here," he says and turns to 1SG Flanagan. "Set up a loose perimeter around the area, Top. Put out listening posts front and rear and a squad up on the open face of the hill to our north. That'll give a good warning if they try to hit us here."

Englander, Cat, I, the commo sergeant, and Flanagan are sheltered in a boulder-strewn outcropping that will offer us some cover if we are hit. Though we have likely been followed, it is not the enemy that is our first concern but the weather, which has been iffy all morning and now, with thickening cloud cover piling over us and the resumption of a moderate rain, may make it dangerous for the dustoff bird to try and get in.

SSG Dabrowski has put a long antenna on his radio and called our Hatchet Control on the border. "Dustoff's coming, Cap," he tells Englander after a short conversation on the radio. "ETA is twenty, maybe thirty minutes."

"Goddammit," says Englander. "That's too long to sit here. Rain's going to be a problem if it gets heavier, and likely the PL a problem too if we set in here that long."

Dabrowski has another brief exchange over the radio and tells Englander, "No dice for anything quicker, Cap. The birds are coming from Ben Het. That's sixty klicks, and they say the ceiling is down to nothing in places in between, slowing them down a lot."

"Crap, what the hell happened to the plan for them to have birds in the air on the border at all times for us, so if we call them, they won't have so far to travel?" Englander looks as if he's searching for something on which to punch away his frustration. It's all rocks around us, though. With clenched fists, he just spews more and nastier curses under his breath.

Fortunately for me, we do still have artillery support available. The 155s can't shoot this far, but we are maybe a klick within max range for the 175s with no intervening hills close enough to interfere. I know that by the time we hit the western end of this valley that support will be lost to us. As we wait, the clouds drop further, and the rain gets heavier. Right now, those big guns are the ace in my pocket. Meanwhile, no fan of being soaked, I've pulled my poncho out of my ruck and sit huddled under it next to Cat, who's done the same.

Ten minutes on, the rain growing heavier, our east listening post begins a transmission, saying, "Movement! South . . ." Then a sharp cry from the Yards along the stream, "Số thâu vào!" (Incoming!) just as an RPG lances in from across the stream. It strikes open ground maybe a dozen meters short of where our small command unit is hunkered among the rocks. The blast, coming right at us, is fierce, a gut punch that kicks a storm of dirt and rock our way. The debris smacks viciously off the rocks around us. AK fire follows, coming at us from the same direction. Almost immediately, our troops respond, their fire aimed at the RPG's apparent point of origin on the tongue of a hill maybe a hundred meters south of us across the stream.

I grab for the radio. "Grid four-niner-zero-zero, two-four-two-five," I tell the battery. "Direction three-eight-zero-zero, proximity one-five-zero, one gun HE in adjustment, battery two in effect."

The battery RTO repeats that back to me, and I wait for his announcement of shot, trying as always to bring my racing heart under control as the volume of small arms fire from the hillside grows heavier. The Yard đại úy is the first hit, a bullet piercing his thigh, and he goes down with a bellow of pain. One of the Yard medics, disregarding the danger, darts out to drag his captain to cover and begin treating him. MSG Flanagan is hit seconds later by a ricochet off a rock hardly a foot from me, the bullet singing off it right past my face and catching the first sergeant high on the right side of his chest. Flannagan's response is a dull "Uh" at the pain, and he drops behind a boulder, clutching his chest. SSG Olsson comes skittering over from where he has been sheltering behind a huge fallen teak trunk to treat him.

The medical sergeant drops his aid bag and pulls Flanagan's fatigue jacket and T-shirt open to expose an ugly wound oozing blood along the first sergeant's rib cage. "Ain't in the lung, Top," he tells Flanagan. "Not even into the ribs. You're lucky as hell. Looks like it glanced off the rib cage, maybe broke one, and came out under your shoulder. Not bleeding enough for it to have hit any arteries." He is pulling out battle dressings and a morphine syrette as he talks.

"No morphine," says Flanagan. "I've gotta be able to know what's going on." He says this through clenched teeth, words shuddering out.

"Nah," says Olsson, "I see you're hurting like hell. With pain like that, you can't do anything anyway." He sticks the syrette into the first sergeant's shoulder, squeezes the morphine in, and pins the empty tube to Flanagan's collar. Seeing the narcotic begin taking effect, he starts readying the wounds for a dressing.

Flanagan's face softens as the pain recedes. "Yeah, better," he says, his eyes wandering now. Olsson tapes down the dressings, a star of blood seeps through the one over the entrance wound, and shakes his head, saying, "Not too serious, Top. You're going to be OK."

The battle has picked up further. Now mortar rounds drop among us, their fragments snarling in the grass. On the perimeter of our position, all are frantically digging in. Cat has tried to dig a hole for us, but a hard rock shelf lies just beneath the dirt where we are, and he can get no more than a few inches down. Surrounded by big rocks as we are, though, I'm hoping we aren't likely to catch any incoming. *Tell that to MSG Flanagan*, I think. His wound may have been a fluke. Still, despite their cover, the rocks deflected a bullet right into him. Some protection! A lot of AK fire snaps around our rocky lair, the PL clearly seeing that we here are the command element and trying to take us out.

As the mortars pick up their pace, I get the word of "Splash!" from the battery and soon hear the burst of the round and watch through the rain as a gout of smoke and flame go up on the hill just right of where the enemy seem to be set in.

"Left five-zero, fire for effect," I call and get a "Roger" back from the battery. Soon, two of the big 175 mm rounds come thundering in and impact right on the spot where much of the enemy fire has been coming from. Almost immediately, the incoming mortars, small arms, and RPGs slack off. We are not out of danger, though. As the incoming from the south slows, the Yard squad up on the hillside to our north begins taking fire of its own. The squad leader there, a trung sĩ the Yards have nicknamed Kra (the Ape) for his tough cunning, calls in to tell us, "Dinks coming, five, six maybe coming." (Hard to tell if he is saying five or six or fifty-six. I hope the former.) Englander tells them to come back into our perimeter as soon as they can manage.

"OK, Cap'n. *Ta truh.*"

Stunningly, they make it in virtually unscathed except for one Yard creased on his forearm. Soon as they're in, I have the battery drop a volley on that position on the hillside. Englander wants gunships, maybe even Phantoms or a Spooky, but the weather nixes the idea.

"If it lifts, we'll get some to you," Hatchet Command says to Englander's disgust.

So we sit, dug in now, fighting a mostly unseen enemy in the underbrush around us, sitting for maybe an hour through spates of incoming AK and mortar fire. With no sign of the dustoff, SSG Dabrowski finally reports in frustration that "they're not coming, Cap. They say weather's got too bad. Gotta be awful back there for a dustoff to turn back." It must be awful; the dustoff pilots I know would fly through the fires of hell to pack up a wounded man if they had to. Now, with the incoming fire diminished to an occasional AK round, Englander issues the order to saddle up. "We'll get out of here while we can," he says.

And then over Dabrowski's radio, we can hear, "Berkeley Balder Eight, this is Dustoff One-Four. We are five klicks to your east, coming in. Can't see a damn thing here. Can you give me a strobe to guide me?"

"Fuck me, they are coming in after all," Englander says. He pulls a palm-sized red plastic-cased strobe light from a nylon pouch in his ruck, snaps it on, and tosses it out into the clear area where he wants the dustoff to land. Its snapping light judders across the LZ.

"Ask him how many he can take."

Dabrowski relays the question.

"I can lift six," comes the response from the pilot. "Make them the worst hit. I don't think I can get back here again."

Dabrowski rogers that, and Olsson tells Englander who the worst are. "Have him take Top here. No arguments, Top. You ain't moving with that wound. Take the Yard with the bad leg wound, the one with the broken ankle, and the one with the smashed arm. Parnassus too. He can't walk with that bullet in his leg. And the Yard đại úy with that bad thigh wound."

The đại úy argues and then begs to stay. "My men, Cap-tain. I stay, they mine." His eyes look wet, whether with rain or tears of frustration, I don't know.

"No, no," says SSG Olsson. "You try to move on that leg, you'll bleed out and die. You go back, get it fixed, and *then* come back."

"Biến đi, biến đi, biến đi . . ." ("Fuck off" in Vietnamese), the đại úy says softly to himself. I have heard no profanity in Jarai.

Olsson throws up his hands.

Englander steps in, saying sharply, "You go, Y Giao. You hear me? No argument. It's no good for you to be stubborn. If you die out here, you're no good to anybody. You go on the dustoff or you bleed to death, hear?"

"I hear," says the đại úy. "I go, biến đi!" He shakes in his misery.

"That's it, Cap. We've got two others who oughta go back, Larry Arguello and the Yard corporal with the fragged up face, but they can move OK, so they can wait. Others I can deal with here."

As the dustoff comes in, I have the battery drop rounds on the hillsides north and south to suppress incoming. The dustoff bird's blade noise seems to suddenly well up from the clouds, and the bird bursts from them, flares in a seething shower of blade-stirred rain, and settles, bouncing next to the flashing strobe. Olsson and two of the Yard medics rush to get the wounded onto the bird. The đại úy is last, still complaining hotly about his fate in Vietnamese. A few AK rounds crack in as the bird finishes loading; one hits the tail boom with a metallic "tunk" but appears to do no real damage. With our wounded loaded, the pilot quickly pulls pitch. The dustoff bird lifts and turns, its blades bite air with a harsh blatt, and then it is up and off, heading east again. I hold my breath, but no AA fire tracks it, and it is soon gone. With its exit, we are now down a dozen men including two American troops, with three more wounded men still here with us. We are still a good twenty klicks from our objective. If there was a point to saying it, I would tell Englander we should turn back, tell him that we are losing men with no reason, a dozen wounded, one of them later killed as the first dustoff took its load out. *Nothing gained,* I think, *nothing gained,* a phrase that seems more than ever a version of the war in miniature.

"Man!" says Englander. "I'm glad to get that done. Let's get the hell out of here." He retrieves and extinguishes the strobe, darting out to it quickly so as not to draw fire.

We move.

The heaviness of the rain masks our exit from this dangerous end of the valley. Our trek west is a slog between jungle-covered ridgelines north and south, through marshy ground and clouds of mosquitos that the rain, now slowed to a drizzle, doesn't put down. My repellent laid on all my exposed skin is only moderately effective in this mosquito haze, and I am bitten a dozen times. (Wondering absently as I slap them if the antimalarials I've been taking will do their job.)

Nor are we alone. Twice, snipers fire at us from the hills to our north. A young Yard named Y Poe—nice kid, younger even than Cat—is hit, grazed really, across his forehead. He is really not badly hurt, but he bleeds there as profusely as all scalp wounds until one of the Yard medics can get a dressing on it. The kid is stoic under treatment in the way all the Yards seem to react to pain.

I have had the battery shoot a recon by fire along our route into the valley, one of the big rounds every hundred meters, placed alternately on the trail in front of us and on the hills to either side. I want to make the most of the big guns' support before we lose it. Finally, four klicks into the valley, with the sun going down and heavy rain returning, Englander calls a halt for the night. His initial plan was to move stealthily at night and lie low during the day, but it's a truism of war that what you plan for the most carefully never happens.

The map marks the river course here as intermittent, but even with the rainy season tapering off, the stream's flow is strong. The water here is often at least knee deep, and crossing it, as we've had to do three times now on this part of our march, is tough but not dangerous. Finally, we dig in for the night on a low wooded hill just south of the stream. Soaked, exhausted, ready for a real rest, we lay out the perimeter of an

NDP woven into tangled undergrowth and heavy jungle canopy. To our west maybe three hundred meters is a ville too small for the map to name. It occupies the narrow bottom of the valley on both sides of the stream. Tomorrow we will have to go through it to continue our march to the west.

Lesson learned from being caught in the open this past afternoon, we all dig in. The men punch deep foxholes into the red Laotian dirt of the hill and take the time and care to add grenade sumps and pack the excavated earth into berms along the holes' front edges. Cat begins to dig ours as I call in a set of defensive targets for our position. I do so relieved that we still have artillery to call, the uncertain effect of the base bleed ammo giving it more range than I had expected. But I know that we have reached the maximum range of the 175s supporting us and that these are the last delta tangos I will be able to call in until we get back east of this location. Although the ground is wet, the digging is hard going through rocky soil. So, done calling in my targets, I spell Cat on the digging.

With the đại úy dusted off, a Yard lieutenant, *Đại úy hải quân* Y Lam, is now in command of the Yard company, and he sits with me and Englander, looking surprised and nervous at suddenly assuming authority. Y Lam is young, and with his black hair cut short and spiky, and with his tiger camo uniform shabby and ill fitting, he's nowhere as military looking as Đại úy Y Giao. Y Giao's English had been middling, though decent enough to get his point across and understand Englander's orders (couched as suggestions so as not to offend a man supposedly of equal rank, but they were orders in reality). Y Lam seems lost in our conversation, and Englander finally calls for our translator, Y Aguăt, to come up from the line and help him and the đại úy hải quân communicate.

In the dark, the PL have thrown a few Chicom grenades at us. Only two of the poorly made things go off. The rest just rattle among the trees and fall harmlessly. The pitch dark of this storm-whipped night is already our friend, and to go with it, Englander wants absolute noise discipline.

"No talk, understand? No rifle fire," Englander orders Y Lam. "No giving away our position that way. Throw grenades back at them. You bic?"

Y Aguăt repeats Englander's orders in Jarai.

"Ữ' kâo hluh! I bic, Cap-tain." The Yard lieutenant nods, his face a study in eager seriousness.

Englander also orders full light discipline: no fires or cigarettes or use of flashlights outside hooches. That means pouring water into cold LRRP rations, which make a soggy unappetizing mess that tastes like muck. Cat offers me another can of peaches, but I decline, knowing it is his last.

Past midnight, with many of the unit asleep, the PL launch their first probe of our position. Again, it is with Chicom grenades, nasty things that sometimes go off with a smelly, throaty bang and sometimes with just a harmless pffffft!

And so—with rifle and machine gun fire *verboten*—now ensues the strangest battle I've yet been part of in Vietnam, a battle fought mostly without a word uttered in pitch darkness and pouring rain. Our position sits above the stream's south bank on the top of the small hill, our perimeter tight, our holes well-spaced and deep. Often as not, the grenades the PL are throwing at us whack against tree trunks and go off there, harming no one. Our guys respond with grenades of their own, some bursting in the trees but most falling to ground where the PL seem to be.

RPGs snarl in, most smashing into trees and blazing in their detonation. More than a few of our guys are lightly wounded by flying teak splinters. Only a few of the RPGs miss the trees to impact near our position; their impacts throw off spurts of dirt and debris. Mortar rounds fall also, but lacking a precise target, few hit close enough to cause danger. I call in artillery fire on the targets I had already planned. You can hear the sequence: "Shot," "Splash," an orange flash, and resounding boomer-boom far up on the hills. Seeing nothing of where they are landing, I adjust the big shells by sound alone, painstakingly bringing them in as close as I dare, moving them toward us until the power of their detonation sends tree and rock fragments into our position.

Englander wants gunships or a Spooky with its phalanx of miniguns, but the deteriorating weather makes it impossible for them to fly.

"Christ!" he says. "It's just us now and the arty. Nothing else for support."

As the fight proceeds, I have been hearing sharp klicks and whistles out in the jungle below us. At times, it is a single klick and with it, far off, the muted sound of groups of the enemy moving in the trees. At other times, it is a pair of klicks or whistles, and almost immediately after, there is a rain of grenades from the same side from which we had heard the movement.

It is quickly clear these sounds are signals the PL are using to direct their troops. With two lengths of bamboo, Y Aguăt shows us how they do it. "Hit together, make noise, use to give orders." He shows us, tapping them so softly, there is only an almost inaudible click.

"How many PL are there, do you think, Hugh?" I ask.

"A shitload of 'em," he whispers back.

And I have to laugh at that. "A shitload, huh? That a military term?"

"Best one there is. Actually, I think from how many grenades they throw at once, there are a couple of companies of PL out there at least. We're OK here, though. PL don't have a firm fix on how we're set in. Not knowing, they aren't likely to try to overrun us."

Overrun, the word chills me. I've been there before. The sense of not knowing who—foe or friendly—is coming toward you or how close they are can be petrifying. Years after the war, the memory of being overrun will animate the worst of my dreams, the kicking, moaning, sweat-soaked nightmares that will sometimes drive my wife from our bed. But this night, I believe Englander is right. The PL aren't going to try a mass attack. It will be these grenade and mortar and RPG strikes coming at us all night. Nobody is getting any sleep in such a formless rumble.

This inconclusive action continues for at least two hours. I'm told this by SSG Arguello: we have lots of small wounds among us, grenade fragments, tree shards, a wrenched shoulder from one ducking fast into his foxhole. The only man hurt seriously during this time is SSG Richard Arno, a Special Forces engineering sergeant loaned to the Hatchet Team taking the place of the late Gary Greenwood. Arno is a small guy, maybe five feet six inches and 125, soaking wet, already balding at age twenty-two, but with the guts of a giant. He is dug in with an M60 on the west flank of our perimeter along with a squad of Yards (to preserve our concealment, Englander orders he use the machine gun only as a last resort). Englander's hooch and the one with me and Cat are just up the slope from it. Arno's position overlooks the Laotian ville a couple of hundred meters further west. The trees are thinner there, the canopy more open. Arno has set out trip flares defining his field of final protective fire on a narrow bit of trail that runs from our hilltop downhill to the ville. The flares, fifty meters out from our perimeter, are too far down the hill to give away anything about our location. At about 0230 hours, one of these trip flares ignites, the bloom of yellow light it casts illuminating a handful of PL troopers making their way up this trail. Running from the light, one of the PL turns and smacks headlong into a tree, hard enough to fall and lie still.

"Son of a bitch knocked himself out cold," I hear Arno say. He tells the Yards with him to cover him. He's going to go out and grab this PL as a prisoner before the guy can come to. He gets most of the way down the trail to the guy, ready to grab him when two other PL pop up. One shoots Rick in the hip. He starts yelling, runs in agony halfway back up the trail, turns around, and lobs a grenade at the three enemy. By then, the flare has burned out and there is no telling if the grenade did any damage, though a yip of pain suggests it did. Rick is goddamned lucky. The bullet he caught misses arteries and the hip joint and buries itself in the meat of his butt. Doc Olsson's got him patched up, but his moving with us in the morning is going to be a bitch.

Hours after Englander had called for one, an AC-47 Spooky comes on station above us at about 0400 hours. Englander has a radio transponder to use to mark our position for the big gunship, but the Spooky can't seem to read it.

"Roger," the bird's pilot tells us, "understand you've got the transponder deployed. Negative on reading a signal from it, though. You sure it's on?"

"Fucking A, it's on," Englander comes back. "Its yellow telltale light is on. It's got a new battery and all that shit."

"Man, my gear here is old, that's probably why I can't read you," the pilot responds. "But in this stuff, I don't think I can help you. Clouds are too heavy to see many ground flashes."

We can hear the Spooky circling above us, its murderous bank of miniguns tantalizingly close. It orbits us for twenty minutes while the tech on the bird tries to read our transponder. Finally, he gives up.

"Can't find a target in this soup. I'm going to leave station and head back before the dinks aim a redeye at me."

"Christ! The bastards have no such thing. I need your help, man. Can't you stay on station a while longer?"

We begin pointing out the flashes of enemy RPG fire, and the Spooky pilot takes several runs above and far out from where the fire comes from, blazing back into it with multiple miniguns. Finally, the pilot apologizes. "Sorry, I'm leaving. That's all the help I can be. Visibility's getting worse. Good luck." And with that, the Spooky and its immense yet unused firepower depart our sky.

As sort of a consolation prize as it leaves, the Spooky blasts hell out of the side of the towering mountain across the stream to our north. The map shows that the mountain's southern face verging on the river is very steep; no PL are likely to be there. But the sound of a half-dozen miniguns ripping into it is comforting if unprofitable. I hear later that the pilot reported he'd killed as many as sixty-seven of the enemy in that sortie. I don't know how he came to that number since nobody could see a thing outside our perimeter.

At intervals during the night, we respond to enemy grenade volleys with grenade volleys of our own.

After one such exchange, I hear yelps of pain and misery coming from the jungle north of us. "Hear, Hugh? We got a bunch of 'em this time. Hear, they're dragging their dead and wounded away."

"Sure sounds like it," Englander says. "I'd much rather they all went away." That's what happens just before dawn with the hill downslope all around going silent. In the growing light, we send out several squads to recon, and reports come back of just two grenade-blasted bodies but many blood trails.

"Kicked their asses, I think." Englander grins.

CHAPTER 32

The next Laotian ville is the meanest and saddest yet, a clutch of rude thatched huts around a bare muddy patch set along the banks of the stream.

"Looks like folks live here. But ain't any of them to be seen," SSG Dabrowski says. "Must have run off from our little set-to last night."

A squad of Yards snoops and poops around the huts a bit but finds nothing.

"All gone, go didi mau, no more peoples living here, he say," Y Aguăt says, translating the report of the squad leader (very roughly, I imagine).

"Pesthole of a place anyway," Englander comments.

A blood trail, dark splats of it fly covered and half coagulated, crosses the center of the ville. Further on, where the trail enters the jungle again, a footprint has been impressed into one blood splash, telling us the wounded man had been carried away. Not far, though. A dozen paces past the ville, the body lies dumped at the side of the trail, limbs akimbo and heaped dishonorably in death. Already it stinks of decay, flies covering wounds in the shoulder and back. Some creature, probably a village dog, has torn at the meat of one leg.

"These ain't like the NVA. Don't carry off their dead, just leave them like so much garbage," Dabrowski says. "Ain't right, ain't right." He shakes his head in disgust.

We pay no more attention to the ville and resume movement west. After we are a klick or so on, I call the battery and have them drop a couple of volleys on the hilltop we had occupied during the night. The big rounds coming in behind us are a sort of so-long-until-later from the guns. We are now out of their range.

I tell Englander, who just grunts as if told he is out of rations (annoying but hardly an emergency). I suspect he is more bothered than he shows.

It is clear that SSG Arno cannot keep up. The wound in his buttocks is obviously excruciating, his whole leg stiff from it. He has cut a tree branch, wielding it with painful effort, desperate to show he can use it as a cane, but his progress is agonizingly slow.

"We gotta dust him off, Cap," SSG Olsson says. "He ain't going to make it much farther like that, and he's got us all slowed down."

Englander agrees, but the narrowness of the valley and the heavy jungle canopy combine to make this locale impossible as an LZ for a dustoff bird. He sends a squad ahead to recon a space a klick and a half on that the map shows as open and see if it is really a likely spot to bring in a bird. Meanwhile, Olsson has had a stretcher rigged from a poncho and a couple of saplings so that Arno can be carried. The engineering sergeant doesn't like the idea but accepts that it's better than trying to limp along on his cane and wounded butt.

"Man, Captain," he says to me at one point, "wasn't the way I wanted to go home, shot in the ass like this." He grins at me through the pain, but it's one of disappointment as much as mirth.

The Yard squad we've sent ahead comes back and reports that the area upstream is open enough to accommodate a dustoff, and Englander tells the company to saddle up and head that way. He sends the first platoon forward to secure the LZ with the rest of the unit to follow.

"One squad in a blocking position here," Englander points to a spot on the map where the trail and stream converge. He tells Y Aguăt to tell Đại úy hải quân Y Lam to have them set into the tree line. "In an ambush formation, bic?"

"I bic am-bush," says Y Lam, nodding. "They know how. You see."

"Are there any Yard LTs who speak decent English?" Englander asks.

Y Aguăt doesn't translate this, and Y Lam only smiles.

"Another squad same, same ambush here," Englander says, pointing out a spot on the river a couple of hundred meters further west of the LZ. "Same, same, you bic?" he says to Y Lam.

The Yard lieutenant studies the map as if this is all new to him, finally grins, and says, "Yes, yes, I bic." He trots off to organize his troops.

Englander shakes his head and mutters, "Fuck me."

The spot for the dustoff LZ is a barely usable clearing with two small stands of brush and one massive teak in the middle. SSG Arno, cursing his stiffened buttocks and thigh, levers himself off the makeshift stretcher and rummages through his rucksack for det cord and C-4 to blow down the tree.

SSG Olsson grins cynically at me and says, "If there's any of the damned PL don't know we're here, blowing down this tree will educate them."

A few minutes later, Arno bellows, "Fire in the hole!" waits a few seconds for all of us to find shelter, and then sets off the blast. The base of the big tree shatters, shards of wood flying out violently in all directions, and the huge meter-thick trunk falls thunderously. Three of the Yard soldiers squawk at its fall and burst out from where they've taken cover right next to where the trunk comes down.

We laugh the laugh of the exhausted at this, our tension relieved by their antics. Đại úy hải quân Y Lam laughs until tears run down his cheeks. Such is the tension we've been under. One of the Yards who had jumped free of the falling tree—an older corporal named Y Pol—is furious at first at our laughter and stands red faced until the realization comes of how they must have looked leaping out of the path of the falling teak. Then he begins to guffaw as well.

This is where I almost lose Cat. We get a whispered call from the unit moving into an ambush position to our west. "Movement! One hundr'd meters. Maybe squad size."

"Set in and take 'em when they hit your kill zone," Englander responds.

Some thirty beats later, M16 and M60 fire erupts from their direction followed by the sharp detonation of grenades. Into this comes a vast volume of fire that sounds like AK-47s, with their lower, more growling note.

"It's a mob of 'em," Englander yips. He grabs a squad of Yards and heads west at a fast clip, Cat and me following. The Yards we had sent to set up the ambush have been ambushed themselves. They are down in the open along the stream bank, having gone to ground while still in the kill zone of the PL's ambush. Maybe a platoon of the PL is set up across the stream, firing into the flank of the Yards. Another enemy squad or so is arrayed across the trail ahead of the Yards in a blocking position. A third PL group has moved in behind the Yard squad to cut off retreat. Sure, SOP says that when ambushed, you turn into the long flank of the ambushers and charge them, moving out of the kill zone and trying to break through. People get killed that way, but staying put means the enemy can continue to rain fire on you. Here, though, the stream is deep enough that it is a barrier blocking such a charge.

"God!" Englander says. "They're stuck. The PL'll butcher them." We've got to take down that bunch on the east, so our guys can pull back. He grabs the arm of the Yard squad leader with us, points to the nearest group of PL, and says, "Go there. *Nao adih!* Fast, fast, *ho'măr.* You bic?"

"Ye-es." The squad leader grins and shouts directions to his squad, who quickly begin to move.

SSG Albert Mays, our lone weapons sergeant now that Larry Arguello has been dusted off, has come up with the Yard squad, and he and his Yard assistant gunner move forward with them carrying an M60. Fifty meters from us and maybe twenty meters from the PL, they engage, hitting the Pathet Lao troops from behind and putting them in a crossfire.

Cat and I are down next to Englander, lying behind a small swerve of the bank that gives us some cover. I am itching to grab the radio and call in some artillery on the PL, itching but that's all. We are beyond the artillery support area and must rely on small arms alone. Caught in the crossfire, the PL unit nearest us begins to panic and to retreat into the tree line on the north. Our troops start to pull back out of the ambush's kill zone, dragging two dead and three wounded Yards with them. The Yard rescue squad comes back with them.

As they pull back, SSG Mays is hit and falls, clutching his gut. The retreating Yards, including Mays's AG, either don't notice or don't care. They come back toward us, leaving Mays alone behind them.

Englander is beside himself, fury animating him as he screams, "Get him! Get him! Bring him back. *Djă gŏ'!*" But the Yards pay no attention and continue their pullback, leaving Mays out there alone.

"Goddammit," Cat says. "Can't leave him." And he jumps up, shucks his ruck and radio, and moves out in a crouch toward the downed sergeant.

There is no point in telling him to come back. He's doing what he thinks he must, and all I can do is to tell him to get down and low crawl toward Mays. By now, the Yards are back from the kill zone, and Englander, now beyond fury, is pushing and kicking them to go back and get the weapons sergeant. "*Ră anai*, you bic?"

Cat is all the way to Mays, and I am up now, rucksack shucked, ready to move forward if the Yards won't. Cat raises up to get a grip on Mays. There is a shot from across the river; Cat's head snaps back, his boonie hat flies, blood spattering from beneath it. Cat cries out with a sort of bark of pain, tumbles backward, and is down unmoving. And now, up myself, rifle up, I am already moving toward where Cat and the weapons sergeant lie, Cat fallen atop Mays's legs. I see maybe a dozen of the PL come out of the tree line and head toward Cat and the sergeant. There are too many; I can't move toward them now, my courage subsumed. I can't get there, and if I do, there will be three of us fallen there because the PL have reached Cat. One, wearing the gold inverted chevron of a senior sergeant, stands over Cat and reaches down to pull his head up. Beneath it, blood has spilled down over Cat's scalp, his red hair redder still with the blood soaking it. The sergeant shakes his head, grunts something in Lao I can barely hear, lets Cat's bloody head fall back, and begins to move his troops back toward the tree line. I am up, unhinged by Cat's injury. I bellow, "You son of a bitch!" at the PL sergeant and blast a burst of ineffective fire at him from my M16. Englander grabs my arm and yanks me back down. "Get behind some cover, you stupid jerk," he says.

Now, the Yards who had retreated from the ambush begin to move back toward Cat and Mays, pushed by their squad leader, who is shouting a torrent of angry Jarai. Slowly, watching for more PL troops—though the PL seem to have gone—the Yards get back to Cat and Mays and pick them up. Although their demeanor is rough, they bring the two American soldiers back gently, carefully.

And I see that Mays, gut shot, is alive, breathing. Cat, they lay at my feet, the squad leader shaking his head, saying, "Sah-ree, dại úy," and putting his hand on my shoulder.

SSG Olsson has brought a platoon of Yards up to reinforce us. He drops his aid bag and takes a first look at Mays. He puts a pressure bandage over Mays's wound (there is no exit wound; the bullet is still inside the engineering sergeant) and sets up an IV for him. Now I see that Cat is alive. My god, Cat is alive! He is breathing. His eyes are half open though wandering in a sort of daze. The wound in his scalp seeps blood, but the worst of the bleeding has stopped.

"Grazed, that's all," says Olsson. "He's one lucky sucker, but best if he gets back to the rear for stitches sometime soon. Good that his skull ain't fractured. Almost surely a concussion from this. Going to have a monster of a headache when he's good 'n' come to. Aspirin'll knock that down some. Still going to hurt like a bitch."

He begins cleaning the blood from Cat's face, pulling out a dressing he soaks with water from his canteen, and wiping away the already clotting blood. Looking at Olsson treat Cat, I can't get the idea out of my head that I'd been stupid to have us trade our steel pots in for boonie hats. A steel pot would have deflected the bullet and prevented Cat's wound.

"No," says Cat at the suggestion that he should be dusted off. It's more a moan than speech. "No, Captain. I want to stay out here for this. No hospital until we're done."

I look at Olsson, who shrugs. "Ain't life threatening, sir. I can put some bacitracin ointment and a field dressing on it. Tape won't stick where the wound is, so I'll tie it under the corporal's chin. Going to look like some no-tit gal with an Easter bonnet. Sorry, I wish I could do better." Seeing that Cat is awake and functional, Olsson gives him some aspirin and some penicillin tablets to ward off infection. He puts a few more of the tablets and pills into a vial and hands it to Cat. "Aspirin when you need it, take the 'cillin twice a day."

"You look one hell of a mess, Sergeant," I tell him. I'd retrieved my camera when we were last at LZ Bronco, and I take a picture of Cat. "Something to show your kids. What you did was both the stupidest and the pluckiest thing I ever saw." I grin at him, joking. "Cat, if they'd killed you, I would have had to carry the damned radio by myself."

He half grins back, the injury obviously paining him. Seeing Cat lying there like that—as with my old RTO Cisco who had been badly wounded in the hip—I had felt tears of misery start to well up. But Cat is alive, and I stifle it. A tearful captain is not a heartwarming sight. (I will write Cat up for a Medal of Honor, knowing he will get no such thing for this action. But he does receive a Silver Star with a V for valor on it. Not an insignificant honor itself. The scar will part his hair nearly dead center from just above the hairline on the front to where it curves down just before the parietal arch on the back. An inch lower and the bullet would have blown his skull apart!) I tell Cat I will carry the radio for a while. He doesn't need the jouncing of its twenty-three pounds. He argues but gives in after a moment.

The dustoff comes in to our now quiet LZ and carries out SSGs Mays and Arno and the dead and wounded Yards. So—counting today's action—five of our American troops are in hospitals back in the rear along with fifteen Yards wounded and three dead.

Whatever the reason, this battle seems to have taken the fight out of the Pathet Lao, who have melted back into the jungle, leaving the little river valley to us. Here, the stream turns southwest, and we follow it for eight uneventful klicks, much of it through a bamboo forest just as thick as that around the Khmer Rouge base camp we had taken weeks ago back in Cambodia. Just at nightfall, we arrive at a place where the stream joins another and becomes a modest-sized river that turns northwest. Here, we dig in for the night once again. By the map, we have maybe half a dozen klicks today toward our first objective, the NVA's regional ammo and supply depot. The POW camp, if it exists, is a few klicks farther on.

Cat and I set up our hooch, and, seeing he is in pain and exhausted, I let him crawl in to sleep while I dig us a foxhole. The night is chilly but dry for a change and the sky clear. Better: it is quiet with no sign of the Pathet Lao or the North Vietnamese. I boil some water and add it to a LRRP ration bag of beef stew. I sit alone eating and looking up through the branches of broken jungle canopy at stars in a pitch-black sky. Finished, now working my teeth into a bar of tropical chocolate, I wonder what will be coming next.

★ ★ ★

CHAPTER 33

The new day is brighter than recent ones. Watery light from the late-morning sun penetrates a hazy sky. It is cool, but not so chill as recent past days. We are concealed on a south running fork of the Houay Loumphou River. North the river runs into the great Xe Xou and thence to the grasslands of the Attapu plain. South, this nameless arm of the river has cut deeply into the mountain's shoulder, leaving a long limestone bluff that looms above the river, almost sheer, perhaps six hundred meters high. It runs to the north for at least two klicks and to the south as far as we can see. Maybe a klick north of us part of the cliff has slumped, tumbling into the river valley. It's a fairly new wound upon the mountain, steep and full of broken rock covered with low sparse undergrowth. I stand with Englander, studying my map and comparing it to the terrain. The map, its data dating back to just after WWII, does not show the broken place in the cliff. It is apparent that a heavy bomber strike—mostly an Arc Light strike from B-52s—had recently been directed at the mountain. I count sixteen craters, including one where a bomb had caused this slump in the cliff.

"This is not where you had showed me the depot is," I say. "You'd marked the peak of Phou Kanghông as our destination. This mountain is Phou Kanthoung."

Englander sneers, "Yeah, well you gotta admit they sound alike."

"Dammit, Hugh, they're miles apart!"

The accusation in my voice is justified. By my map location, our objective is on the similar mountaintop of Phou Kanghông, ten klicks further west. He's done this obfuscation dance again, enjoying it, enjoying keeping me in the dark about our real objective as if I might let it out of the bag. But to whom and for what reason, I can't fathom. Secretiveness seems just part of Englander's nature.

"No," he says, "this is the place."

I'm not going to argue the point. I have no doubt the captain knows where we are going. "That's a damn big mountain, Hugh," I say. "Where does intel say the depot is?"

"The dink supply depot is supposed to be up there. See way south on the peak where it looks like there's the mouth of a cave? I think that's the entrance," Englander says. "The intel is fuzzy... Christ, it's goddamned hairy. Just somewhere up there. They told me the most likely place is that secondary peak with the cave. The depot is supposed to mostly be in caves, so it can't be hit from the air. That's why they sent us. We blow that thing, intel says the boom'll knock the whole top off the mountain."

Our column is visibly diminished. We'd started with eighty Yards and a dozen Americans. We are down to sixty-five Yards and eight American troops, plus me and Cat. That's little more than half the company. Of the U.S. troops, only I am uninjured, not counting the ache in my still-healing side and wrist. A large proportion of the Yards have wounds of varying severity, though all are still reasonably fit for combat. Every one of the Americans is also wounded, though none seriously enough to be outside the fight. In our last battle, Englander was grazed in the same shoulder he'd been wounded in months before. The wound is not deep, but the shoulder has stiffened up again, making it hard for him to use his left arm. Early on after his wound, Cat complained of a bad headache, but Doc Olsson gave him some blockbuster of a pain pill, and he's settled down. Oddly, our unit's morale is sky high. We've penetrated more than forty klicks into Laos, taken out a bunch of enemy tanks, fought off numerous attacks by PL and NVA forces, destroyed some big enemy weapons stores, and made it within sight of our objective. We've done that with the unit largely intact, despite only sporadic air support and the last dozen klicks without artillery support. All, though, will be without benefit if we don't reach at least our primary objective of the supply depot. We'll measure real success if we also find and liberate the POW camp.

We study the broken place in the bluff. "I'm going to send a squad of the Yards up that way to recon it, see if it is suitable for the rest of us to go up that way."

I've been checking out that route with my binos and frankly don't like it at all. To me, it's an open invitation to a massacre. "Hell, Hugh, I'd think about that again," I tell him. "We'd be going up in the open for at least five hundred meters without cover. Its straight slope is a clear field of grazing fire for the dinks if they are set up there. And why wouldn't they be, given that that's the most obvious route up?"

Englander most always bridles at being challenged, and he's not liking it now, I see.

"Here," I continue pointing to the map, "if we go around to the other side of the mountain, the going would be a lot easier. We could . . ." Englander is suddenly red in the face, as unaccountably angry as he'd been when he'd been pulling the fingernails out of the Khmer Rouge soldier he'd been questioning back in the Cambodian bamboo forest. His outburst now is as sharp and impulsive as a rifle butt smash.

"Listen, you goddamned redleg snot." He waves a hand in my face and then swings it to point to the collapse in the bluff. "That's the way up. That's where we're going. It would be eight klicks through some hairy jungle to get around to the other side. We wouldn't make it until tonight and have to NDP there before going up in the morning."

There's no profit in getting in a pissing contest with a madman, I think. So I just stick to my opinion. "Fish in a barrel going up this side, Hugh. If they can catch us in the open there, the mission would be done for. And you know it."

Englander, face redder than ever, has picked up his M16, and for an instant, I am afraid he's going to try and shoot me. Softly to my side, Cat has brought his own weapon up a bit. Englander glares at me for half a dozen beats; his eyes flick to Cat and then back at me, his fingers almost white on his rifle's pistol grip. He looks again at Cat, whose freckled face is impassive and a bit scary with the bits of dried blood still clinging to the hair around his forehead and in his beard stubble where he hadn't been able to wash thoroughly. I see that Doc Olsson has come up near us as well, now watching intently.

Englander heaves a sigh and lets the muzzle of his weapon drop. "OK, Christ," he says. He stands, breathing hard for a few beats, finally saying, "Sorry, I'm just edgy here. We're just so damn close. How about we split the difference on the plan? I'll take a platoon of the Yards on this route up the bluff. You can take the rest of the company and go around the back side. We'll wait here to go until you tell us you're in place. That'll be after dark, and if there are dinks guarding this access point, maybe they won't see us coming." He leans in at me. The redness has faded from his face, and he seems less angry, though unnervingly intent. "Better?"

Now it is my turn to let go the breath I realize I've been holding. "Yeah, Hugh, much better," I tell him, though I remain certain that his way up the bluff on this side is likely suicide.

So Englander, along with twenty Yard troops and two of the Americans—Olsson and Dabrowski—set in behind the tree line to wait for us to go around to the west side of the mountain. Ours turns out to be a horrible, joyless slog through swampy jungle at the base of the bluff. To our left, the mountain rises steeply, a ragged near vertical climb up treacherously rotten limestone. To the right, the Houay Loumphou River rushes northward through a deep narrow channel, the moving water too fast for any crossing back to the east. The morning is still cool, but we sweat in the humidity that the rain of the previous days and the watery sun's slight heat have brought up. There is no trail, so we take turns cutting our way through heavy growth around the mountain's base. Tough as the going is, I am almost ready to admit Hugh's more exposed route up would be the way to go. Finally, at its northernmost point, the bluff makes a sharp turn back to the southwest where we can cross a narrow ridge to find the northwest-flowing Houay Hintho, which is yet another tributary of the Xe Xou River. Once across this ridge, shallow, tempting valleys run back southeast toward the bluff. Should we try and shorten our trek by taking one? No! The map clearly depicts how doing so would bring us right back to the eastern bluff at a point halfway up. There would be no way to go on from there except back to the same broken-down stretch Englander will be climbing. The continued, arduous, sweaty, mosquito-ridden path around the mountain I'd first charted out seems to be the only real way up.

Not long after that, we encounter a gravel road that does seem to head up a ridge in the direction of the supply depot. If so, it would be an easy shortcut. The road is wide enough for a heavy truck to negotiate it, and fifty meters or so to the east there looks to be a turnout where trucks can move over to let those from the other direction pass. A regular superhighway in the Laotian wilderness!

We send road guards up the road east and west to watch for any traffic and then make a quick careful crossing. There is a huge temptation to take the road straight up to the dink depot. But with the danger of meeting a well-armed NVA convoy on this road with none but ourselves for support, I opt to go the long way around. Though there are tire tracks on the road, they appear old, partly washed out by the recent rains. We encounter no vehicles, trucks or otherwise, during this crossing.

"One thing, Captain," Cat says to me, "this is supposed to be an active depot, but look at the road—a lot of stuff growing on it. Some in the tire tracks look like it's been growing there awhile."

From the mouths of babes! Of course, he's right. We'd been looking so hard for enemy that we missed the fact that there don't seem to be any. I call Englander to report our progress and the fact that the road to the depot seems not used recently.

"Bastards are there for damn sure," he says. "Keep on truckin' and give me a sitrep when you get there."

"Roger," I say. "I'll let you know. Out."

It gets to midafternoon; we're taking a break on a bit of high ground where the mosquitoes are less, about halfway along toward our objective. For the first time in hours, we're able to enjoy having our feet out of the mucky water. Most are savoring a quick rest and smoke.

SSG Dennis Sullivan, the other American medic, comes up to me. He's new to the team and one I have not gotten to know yet: a burly guy not quite my height, brown curly hair salted with some premature gray (though I suspect he can't be more than a couple of years older than I am), eyes dark as sinkholes. His drawl is pure Gulf Coast West Florida, so thick that my liaison sergeant Malcom Morris sounds like a northerner by comparison. (Though the more Sullivan talks, the more I think the depth of the accent is put on on purpose.)

He tells me he's from Pensacola. "Close 'nuff, you could spit from there into Alabama." He smiles. "We're the hurricane capital of America. But we've got beaches so fine, like they only wish they had out in Mexifornia."

"Do you speak English there too!" I grin.

"Ya, when we havta, fo' da toorists," he says in an exaggerated accent, grinning back. He smokes, watching the cigarette's ash as if wondering how long it will grow before falling. "You and CPT Hugh getting along OK? He's a hard one, sure."

"Mostly," I say. "He's smart, a real tough Snake-Eater officer."

"But . . . ?"

"But, well, best just to say he doesn't seem to like anyone else's opinion."

"Yeah, he's that fo' sure." The ash has grown to more than an inch. He begins to take another drag, the ash falls, sparks extinguished in the sweat on his fatigue shirt.

"I hear they call you Whitey. That right?"

"Yeah, that's me. You'd think it sounds racist, but it ain't. I was just the only white kid in my neighborhood. Nickname stuck. You all can call me that, I won't mind."

"OK, Whitey, a question, what do you know about this OLM unit of Yards supposedly shadowing us?"

"Them? Fuck!"

"By that you mean?"

"I mean, I been hearing they out there, but I don't know why. They supposed to be a diversion. But we still getting the shit shot outta us. Haven't heard nothing from them for a while." He shakes his head, drops the cigarette, and crushes it into the mud. "I guess we better get moving."

"Yeah," I say, "let's saddle up."

Night. The mosquitos swarm. We have traversed four more klicks, and to our left, a long stretch of hill begins a climb east toward the peak of Phou Kanthoung. Under the jungle cover, it is very dark. The moon, approaching its third quarter tonight, will still cast some light but will not rise until 2230 hours—long after we've reached the peak. Our endurance nearly tapped out, we rest for a half hour at the foot of the ridge, making a hot meal, drinking some crappy LRRP ration coffee, and, finally, at 1900 hours, I try to call Englander. Nothing. Is the mountain blocking commo? Does he hear us but can't respond? Cat doesn't think so. I call over those of the American team who are with us plus Đại úy hải quân Y Lam and his senior sergeants and Y Aguăt to translate.

"I can't get a hold of CPT Englander," I tell them. In this dark, I seem to be speaking to undefined, ghostly shapes. "Maybe this damn mountain is cutting off commo, or maybe he's in a situation where he can't call. Suggestions?"

"I say we go on up," SSG Martin says. "We got to get there anyhow, and there's enough of us to fight if we have to, even without the captain and the Yards he's got with him." There are short sounds of agreement from the other American sergeants.

"Y Lam, are your men ready for this?" I ask. Y Aguăt repeats the question in Jarai.

"Yes, *kâo arăng pre*, my men ready!" Y Lam comes back ardently.

"OK, send a squad with a radio ahead to recon, you bic?"

"Yes, yes, I bic."

"Gibbs?" I say to the weapons sergeant who had replaced SSG Pike.

"Sir?"

"How about you walk slack with that squad and snoop some up there to see if we have a clear trail?"

"Will do, sir."

We move. The Yard recon squad goes first and then, after a ten-minute wait, the rest of us. I've had Cat repeatedly try to call Englander but with no success, not even the break of squelch to tell me he's heard.

"It's not the radio, Captain," Cat tells me. "I've been able to raise the battery clear back on the border with a commo check just now. CPT Englander's just not answering."

From far off, as faint as if it is the voice of a revenant, over the slight noise of our movement, I am sure I can hear rifle fire. In these tangled mountains, it is impossible to tell for sure the direction of that sound, but it seems to be from the northeast, the direction where Englander should be. I call a halt, and the soft sound of our unit's footsteps cease.

"There it is," I say to Cat. "Can you hear it?"

"A firefight? I think I might, Captain."

There is brief silence and then a dull boom and a couple of beats and then two more. They are much like the distant, muted slam of grenades bursting and the steady ticking of far-off machine gun fire. It goes on for perhaps two minutes and briefly stops.

"Son of a bitch!" I say. "Let's move, move!" And we resume our march up the steep lower end of the ridge through the jungle's pitch darkness. Twice more, I think I can hear the rattle that most surely must be a machine gun and another small arms exchange; a trio of faint booms finishes it. Then it all stops. Cat, continuing to call for Englander, still gets nothing. *I had warned him*, I think. I had told him going up that stretch of broken-down bluff was foolhardy. What has he run into? Is he even still alive?

Once past the first difficult stretch, our climb isn't hard. It is long, though, nearly two and a half klicks up a steady, heavily overgrown slope. It takes us more than two hours, the rising last quarter moon just nosing above the mountaintop as we approach our objective. When we are about two klicks up (by my count of paces), I get a call from SSG Gibbs, a whisper over the radio. "We're up here on the summit. Whole hill drops down sharp as hell to the south and east. Northside, from what I can see, there's a road. Looks like the entrance to the supply dump is a big opening in the mountain like a cave or mine under where we are. Big sucker, you could drive a truck right in."

"Guards? Do you see any?" I ask.

"Don't, but there are guard posts at the road and another looking back down the ridge the way we came up. If there are guards, they must have missed us 'cause we turned off and climbed to the very top of the hill. We'll recon it and call you."

"Roger."

Finally, the company makes it to the top of Phou Kanthoung. We are exhausted, mosquito-bitten, and sore, but safe. Comes the question: what to do now? We have found the depot. It is in a sheltered cavern, deep in the limestone mountain, likely impervious to bombing and, given even a few defenders, likely also impervious to our assault.

CHAPTER 34

And now it all starts to go to hell.

We come down around the east side of the peak, and the point man pokes into the first guard post. He finds a single guard, and rather than trying stealth, a Ka-Bar knife or such, the Yard point man shouts, "Buh ha!" and lets go a rip of full automatic fire from his M16. Damn! No chance for stealth now.

A second guard comes running out of the cavern's gaping front, AK-47 up, right into the fire from the M60 held by SSG Gibbs, who has reconnected with the point team. This guard, too, falls, as do three more enemy soldiers who come along behind him from the dark depths of the cavern. Then? Nothing. No boiling anthill of enemy, no colossal firefight, no battle royal with the guardians of a massive supply depot. Just nothing.

I direct SSG Gibbs plus Đại úy hải quân Y Lam and two squads of Yards to set up security just inside the cavern's mouth. It's tomb quiet in there, but I want no surprises. Sullivan, in turn, takes one of the squads and moves deeper into the cavern, which corkscrews down into the body of the mountain. They are gone maybe five minutes, and then there comes a rackety-rack, the sound of small arms echoing from down in the tunnel. Then, as with CPT Englander, silence.

Man! I grab SSG Sullivan (thinking there could be need for a medic) and a squad of Yards, and together we move into the cavern. It's immediately clear that the cavern entrance had been widened artificially, most likely with explosives, leaving a talus slope of broken rock. One turn into it and the moonlight is gone. It is dark as night. Red flashlights flick on from the men around me, and we walk further around the cavern's first turn.

"SGT Sullivan?" I call, and though my voice is soft, it echoes, and soon, from close up ahead, comes, "Yeah, Cap. We're here."

We round another turn and find the sergeant near three dead enemy—NVA from their look as I play my light over them. One of his squad is wounded in his right arm. "We're going to need a dustoff soon for this one," SSG Sullivan says. "But he can likely walk for now. Bullet's gone thru 'n' thru, though." He bends to his work, patching the Yard rifleman, who is stoic throughout. Sullivan sticks him with morphine anyway.

"What happened?" I ask SSG Gibbs.

"They walked right up on us, three of 'em, flashlights shining and all. We saw each other at the same time, and that's when the shooting started. We popped all three, but they got this Yard, Y Mot." He points his flashlight beam up at the cavern's ceiling. "You see that? A string of lights. Must be a generator in here somewhere."

"Could be," I say, "but they were using flashlights, so if there's a generator, it may be broken or out of fuel."

"Yeah, Cap, or they might just be preserving it. I'll send a team to look for one."

Maybe ten minutes later, there is the sputtering of an engine up near the cavern's entrance, and the bulbs strung down the cavern come to life. They are not overbright, leaving the passageway a hodgepodge of light and shadow. But once it's lit, the truth is apparent enough.

"Ain't nothing here," SSG Gibbs says. "Looks like shelves for stuff in that tunnel. Lots of broken-down ammo boxes. But in this whole place, there is nothing. No weapons, no ammo, no rockets or mortar shells. This place hasn't been used for months, maybe longer. I'm going to have some of the Yards snoop and poop further in. But I don't think we'll find anything worthwhile."

So we sit. There are passages that go deeper into the mountain. One side passage has an array of rifle racks. There is one AK-47 still in it, but useless, its stock pocked and cracked and a slight bend to the barrel, the look of a weapon that had been hit by a grenade. The rifle's trigger mechanism is missing, likely cannibalized to repair another weapon. Our biggest find is a box of a dozen egg-shaped M26 fragmentation grenades. At the cavern's deepest accessible point (beyond which it degenerates into twisted, impassable passageways) is a dormitory with a couple of dozen makeshift bunks. Only eight have blankets and sleeping mats.

"Eight of them," Cat says. "We killed two outside, the three back near the entrance, and the other three in the cavern. That's all, I think, Captain. We really came all that way for this?" He shakes his head, disgusted.

Now the generator is running out of fuel, the lights flickering and turning a dim yellow. We pull out of the cavern and settle down to try and figure out our next step. Our biggest challenge is that we have no idea what happened to Englander, the two other Americans, and the two squads of Yards. Were we all together, I'd push for calling birds for extraction. Yeah, there is the unconfirmed report of an NVA POW camp near here to consider. But Englander's first location fix for this disused supply depot was ten klicks from its true location. There may really be a POW camp. But who knows if it is anywhere near the ville of Ban Gnangteu that Englander had claimed? Further west, the mountains only get higher and more rugged, and if the POW camp is not at its purported location, the hunt for it in these mountains would be an impossible task.

It is nearly 0300 hours. We have spent some four hours searching the abandoned supply depot, continuing with flashlights in the dark even after the generator went down for want of fuel. To a man, the unit is exhausted, and I have no intention of moving until we have had some sleep and, more importantly, until we can confirm what has happened to Englander and those with him. I'm not pleased with how exposed we are in the mouth of this cave, and so I direct the unit to climb back up to the mountain peak and set up an NDP for the remainder of the night.

Meanwhile, hoping for word on Englander, I send Y Lam and a squad of Yards to recon the road and see if they can find them. The Yards are gone for an hour and come back reporting they have found nothing. SSG Gibbs says he believes the squad didn't look, just walked out of our sight and hid there before coming back.

"Fucking likely," I say, though Y Lam denies it. But the company's energy is spent, there's not a sound indicating any further action, and so, pissed though I am, I decide to wait until dawn to look further.

Just at sunup, there is the sound of movement on the road below, low talk, careless of noise discipline. Though the words are unintelligible, the voices sound American. Around me on the hilltop, I hear soldiers, alert to the sounds below, getting ready. This may be a ruse by the enemy, but the voices do sound like those of friendlies.

I move to a sheltered overlook where I can view the cavern entrance and the road. "Englander?" I call. A sudden hush below. "Englander?"

"Yeah! Is that you, Weisman?"

"We're set in up here."

"God! I'm glad to find you. Can you send down help? I don't think we can make up to you without help."

In the gray beginnings of dawn, I can pick out a small group of men on the road, maybe eight I count. There'd been twenty-three when we'd left them. Where are the others?

SSG Gibbs takes a squad of Yards and goes down to Englander and the others. Soon, some limping, a couple badly shot up and barely able to move, all that's left of those who'd stayed with the captain come back up the hill. The three Americans, Englander, Olsson, and Dabrowski look like hell. Olsson has a shattered wrist where grenade fragments had hit him. Dabrowski has a gunshot wound in his hip and can barely hobble up the hill. Englander has added a jaw wound to accompany that of his already damaged shoulder. The left side of his face bloody and badly swollen, he has a hard time speaking clearly. One handed, Olsson has dressed all their wounds, medicated them as best he can. The five Yards with them have assorted wounds, none life threatening. (Three who had such bad wounds had been left back there on the bluff's edge along with the dead, Englander admits, shaking his head.)

I want to know what sort of enemy meat grinder they had run into (I have to contain a huge urge to tell the arrogant captain Englander that I had warned him). First things first, though, SSG Sullivan spends time with Englander and the two sergeants, cleaning and redressing their wounds, after which he joins a Yard medic in treating the surviving Yards. Their injuries range from frag and bullet wounds to one whose lower right arm has been blown off and the stump of it tightly bound with a tourniquet. Their desperate but quiet talk with the other Yards serves as background for Englander's story of how some unit (NVA, PL, or other) had ripped them apart.

Englander clutches a canteen cup of warm coffee and sips at it now and again, holding the cup to the unwounded right side of his mouth. "Don't know, don't know who they were," he says. "We'd got about halfway up the place where the bluff had been knocked down. I'd sent a fire team of Yards up ahead. Then it was like the mouth of hell yawned open and vomited all this monstrous volume of fire. The Yard squad got knocked down right away. The rest of us went to ground. There was no cover there at all. They hit us with frags and RPGs and rifle fire. We fought back, but they had the high ground and chewed us up. I thought we were done, dead but just not buried yet, when somebody above shouted a command to cease-fire in Vietnamese." It all stopped then, but too late—most of the Yards were dead and the rest of us shot to shit."

"We never saw who they were," SSG Dabrowski interjects. "We didn't. It was like an ambush. Halfway up that slope, they just started pouring fire into us. There were a lot of 'em. Fifty, sixty, maybe more."

"Weapons? Do you know what they were shooting, Hugh?"

"It was dark, Weisman! We couldn't see. How do I know what they were firing?"

"It was AK-47s," Dabrowski says. "No mistaking that. AK-47s. NVA for sure." He looks at me for a moment, drinking coffee that dribbles into the stubble on his chin. Finally, he asks what we found. "Is this the dink supply depot?"

I nod and see a glimmer of interest brighten in Englander's eyes. "And?"

"And nothing, Hugh. There's nothing up here, no base camp, no supply depot, just an abandoned cavern guarded by a squad of left-behind NVA where the dinks once stored guns and ammo," I say. "So what the hell caused the NVA to set up there on the bluff as if they knew you were coming?"

Tears are still on Englander's face, but his eyes have gone cold again, looking hard at me. "You don't get it do you, Weisman. Do you?"

But I do get it, all at once. This whole fool's mission suddenly falls into place. "The OLM company did this, didn't they, Hugh? They leaked word to the NVA that you were headed up that broken bluff." I stop and stare at Englander. "Dammit, man, they're not our diversion, are they, Hugh? It's the other way around. We are their diversion. We're just here to make noise and draw the NVA and the PL away from the POW camp so they can go in and take it? They don't give a damn about us."

Englander tries a rueful smile. His wounded face won't let him. "Playing dead there in that graveyard half the night, I had time to think about it. I came to the same conclusion. We're along here to draw the dinks' fire while OLM goes in and burns down everything in that camp, takes out all the damn Longshadows, and gasses the lot of them."

That last stops me. I hadn't even thought about gas, but it makes sense. Without artillery or air support, that is the only likely way for a small unit of renegade Montagnards to pack enough offensive punch to take out the camp full of NVA.

"Gasses them with VX, that's the worst of the worst, isn't it, Hugh? Nerve gas? Like what killed the Khmer Rouge in that battle at the border. We couldn't use it because you almost got caught at it last time you came in here. We'd be crucified by higher command if we used it. So the OLM troops use it, and nobody gets blamed?"

"Christ, no! Nobody is nuts enough to use something that evil."

"You saw, they used it back there where we were trapped by the Pathet Lao. They'd surely use it here where it really matters. Wouldn't they, Hugh?"

He just sits there, looking into the steaming swirl of his coffee, saying nothing.

Man! My frustration comes out in a gush. "Maybe these renegades hate the NVA. They'd have good reason. But there are plenty of enemy dinks for them to go after in Vietnam. Why come fifty klicks into Laos to hunt them? I'd say this *is* really a Longshadow hunt, isn't it? We track down info on the Longshadows. Higher command doesn't trust us to do the necessary and kill them if we find them, does it, Hugh?"

He's lost his obstinate grin, just looks at me as I continue. "We're supposed to see if we can find this base camp and see if they are working here and either bring them back or do them in. Prove or disprove the myth for once and all, bring back some specimens dead or alive? The OLM bunch are the insurance. They are supposed to kill all the Longshadows if they can't be brought back, right?" Christ! All I can do is shake my head, laugh as sardonically as Englander had, and add, "It *is* all a fool's errand, Hugh, as worthwhile as looking for Prester John or Jack the Ripper or the Loch Ness Monster."

Englander sighs; with his wound, it is kind of a bubbling sound that is chilling. "In a nutshell, yes, Weisman! We're fifty klicks inside Laos and we haven't found a damn thing worthwhile. You saw that there's no supply depot here, just an empty cave that might have been a base camp one time. I should have figured. We came in to look for the Longshadows before, last year. Found shit. Just an empty camp just like this with hooches and tunnels and hardly a soul there."

"So can we pack it in, then, Hugh? Neither Olsson nor Dabrowski can travel. We have to call in a dustoff for them anyway. Your wound needs attention, along with a bunch of the Yards. Let's call for extraction. Let the damn OLM hunt for the POW camp if there is one."

"Bridget," Englander says.

"Christ, Hugh, do you really think she's out here? How long has it been since you've seen her? Months? This company is already hurting, a bunch of the Yards dead, hardly a man not wounded. Let's pack it in, Hugh. This hunt of yours isn't worth getting the rest of the company killed, is it?"

"I'll call for the dustoff, but we're going on to the POW camp."

"Alleged POW camp, Englander."

"Whatever." He waves me away.

"We going to stay with them?" Cat asks me.

"Maybe,' I say. "Right now, I don't fucking know."

CHAPTER 35

The dead litter the slope where our Yards had fought the NVA. Waiting for the dustoff bird, I walk among their bodies. I should feel fury at the waste of their lives, of men who died as a diversion. But I feel only sadness for these victims of a useless campaign. I watch the big CH-53 Sea Stallion helicopter come in and take them away, take away the bodies and the few wounded like Dabrowski and Olsson and like the two wounded Yards we'd found still alive on this small battleground. There will be another funeral dance at Téthian. Missing will be the souls of the men whose blood has seeped down into the slope and saturated it so that to bring them all entirely home, we would have to dig up and transport the whole mountainside back to the camp on the Sông Re. There are also eight bodies of Vietnamese soldiers in NVA uniforms scattered at the top of the slope, fatalities of our fire in response to that ambush. We let those bodies lie. Maybe the NVA will come back and bury them. Surprisingly, our Yard soldiers mourn them as well as our own dead, mourn them as fallen brothers, even if enemies. A chant rises from them for all the dead here because they are of the same human tribe as the Yards with us. It humbles me to think that the Yards grieve even the enemy dead.

I try to make Cat get on the bird with the wounded. With us out of artillery range, I don't need his radio or him anymore.

"Get on," I say. "Go back to Duc Pho."

"Due respect, Captain, I'm staying."

"I could order you."

"And I could disobey. What are you going to do, send me to Vietnam?"

"This is a useless mess, Cat. I'm staying because the company needs someone with rank to fend off the worst of Englander's decisions. But I don't want to risk you any longer for no damn reason. You've been wounded, leave it at that and go."

He gingerly feels the scabbed-over gash on the crown of his head, smiles a bit too brightly, and says, "Nah, I'm staying, Captain. Somebody's got to ride herd on you."

We watch the big helicopter drop onto the road above the slope, watch the Yards load up the dead and the wounded, watch the machine climb up again, hear its huge blades grab air with an ear-shattering blatt. And gone.

There are now just forty-five of us, about half the original company, all but me at least lightly wounded. None is much interested in cutting our way off the mountain through the jungle, safer, though, it might be. So we stay on the road following fresh tracks. Dispirited, we go through the motions because this is the mission we've been handed.

"OK, Hugh, where the hell are we going now?" I ask.

"Ban Gnangteu, where else? That's the best location we have for the POW camp. Do you agree?"

This last surprises me. Englander is asking my opinion, either as a ruse to keep me thinking I'm involved in the decision or as a sign the captain is feeling the pain and misery of his (and everyone's?) wounds.

"Yeah, Hugh, Ban Gnangteu. And if not there, then let's go home."

He grunts as if he means it.

West of Phou Kanthoung Mountain, the terrain is a jumble of low hills and winding streams, all covered by grasslands pocked with bamboo thickets and a few lonely trees. Further west, toward the mountain of Phou Kanghông, the map shows the jungle encroaching again. At least here on these grassy hills for a few klicks, the openness of the landscape diminishes the chance of another ambush. As we move, the day warms to perhaps sixty degrees under a deep blue sky marked with just a scattering of clouds. Beneath that sky, the land steams, the vapors rising into a low stratum of fog over the grass, the land it covers bright but fuzzy in its haze.

The bird that had taken away our dead and wounded had brought us some resupply of ammunition and food, LRRP and C rations, and so we had feasted before we hit the road, most including me and Cat, eating the heavier (and better-tasting) Cs so as not to have to carry their weight later. So, stomach full, dry, and sun-warmed, I walk with only the care that I have no idea what new hell we are heading into now, following a continuing trail of creped NVA boot prints overlaying earlier sandal prints that most likely belong to the OLM renegades.

"I want to meet those motherfuckers again," Englander tells me. "Meet them in a fair fight with our whole unit, air support, and even arty if you can arrange it, and not just a platoon caught in an ambush."

"Do you know how many of the NVA there are?" I ask him.

"Sixty, maybe. They travel in small companies, so they can spook around in the jungle without being seen."

"You killed a lot of them there on the bluff. Maybe there aren't so many as that now," I say.

Englander grunts. "Yeah, maybe, maybe."

The going is relatively easy compared to that of the past few days. The road is open and decently maintained. Twice, our point element discovers and tags with white tape some mines recently placed in the road, more likely left by the OLM than the NVA and more to warn us off than to injure anyone.

"OLM wants us to go away," Englander grins. His smile is big but lopsided, favoring the wounded left side of his face. SSG Sullivan has left the wound treated but undressed, allowing it to dry and start to heal in the sun. Still, it leaves Englander bearing a bit of the rictus of Baron Sardonicus from the old movie. If he survives, he's going to have a hell of a scar on that cheek.

Three klicks on, the point man calls a halt, and the word comes back from him that there are a lot of antipersonnel mines in the road. Some are newly buried. Others are older, still functional but set in weathered spots among the gravel patches.

There is some push from the Yards for us to leave the road and chance moving through the grass parallel to it. Đại úy hải quân Y Lam is among them, saying, "We not go road, OK? Boocoo mines on it," repeating it in Vietnamese, "Oài đường và đi bộ ở đó?"

Englander doesn't like the idea, and neither do I. Mines are relatively easy to spot on the road's sparsely graveled surface, while mines in the grass will be almost impossible to see. The Yards are persistent, though, and Englander gives in, saying, "OK, I bic you want to stay off the road. OK, but you watch, you bic?"

They move off into the grass, taking care at first to push it aside looking for the mines. Three hundred meters on the inevitable happens. The Yard walking point, a kid named Y Bannat, steps on a mine. There is a click and a hiss. Y Bannat has an instant to utter half a yelp. He has half spun, and I can see his eyes go wide, his hand starts to come up in futile defense. The mine bounces up waist high and detonates. He comes apart, the steel of the mine, the ball bearings inside dismembering him. The detonation catches the Yard soldier walking slack half a dozen meters behind, a small, tough kid I don't really know, named Y Litt, knocking him down and chopping him apart, dead. Third in the file, SSG Gibbs, catches one ball across his cheek and another in the flesh of his thigh, through and through, adding to his collection of miseries. A fourth man goes down shrieking, blood on his shirt, but it is only a fragment of the mine's shell that has torn a gouge in his shoulder. No harm beyond that. Gibbs's is the voice calling, "Medic!" the loudest. Y Bannat and Y Litt are dead. A dustoff will do the young Yard soldiers no good, and both Gibbs and the man walking behind him are not badly injured. So we leave the two young Yards there in grass to retrieve later—bodies in pieces, blood everywhere there where the mine detonated—covering them with a mound of the long elephant grass blades.

I am choked up, shuddering at the sudden deaths. Englander is dispassionate. His face twists, but whether in agony over the two dead Yards or in the pain of his own wound, I can't tell.

"Use the road," Englander says blandly to Y Lam. "Maybe more mines on it, but at least we can see them."

Chastened, even stoic, the Yard lieutenant says, "OK, OK, I bic."

Over the next klick, we find and mark more than two dozen mines. Almost certainly, there are more unseen in the grass.

A Shepherd to Fools

Englander is both furious and perplexed. "Why the hell mine this stretch? We're in Laos, for Christ's sake, not much war here. Why waste the mines?"

To me, it is obvious—they've mined the approaches to the POW camp. "It's a hint that we're on the right track, Hugh." I say. "The mines aren't just to keep us out. They're there to keep the POWs in, to let them know escape won't be easy."

As if to punctuate the point, half a klick later, we encounter a Caucasian man lying near where a mine has blown one of his legs off at the knee. The heat of its detonation looks to have seared arteries of the stump shut, so he is not bleeding much. He lies on the side of the road, moans escaping him, the mine's blast having thrown him partly into the tall grass. A sandaled foot and the remains of the dismembered leg lie in the center of the road almost as an arrow pointing to the spot the blast had scorched into the roadway's gravel. The mine has left only a small hole in the road, likely because it had been tilted so that most of the blast energy went into the one leg, leaving the man otherwise intact. Surprisingly, he seems to have been armed, an AK-47 lying just beyond where he has fallen.

SSG Sullivan treats him, covering the wound's shredded surface with antibiotic ointment and bandaging the stump with a battle dressing. The man is incoherent even before Sullivan sticks him with a morphine syrette, and we get nothing but babbles out of him.

"Guy's strange," Englander says, looking at the fallen man. "Looks well fed, clean, no signs he's been mistreated the way the NVA generally do to prisoners. Wearing black pajamas and Ho Chi Minh sandals like the VC wear. Do you know what to make of him? Do you think he's American?" he asks me.

I do, but I'm not going to encourage Englander's aggressions by saying it. I think to myself that the man is a deserter who has been working with the NVA, a Longshadow. His disjointed speech seems to be in an American accent. Like the soldier I had seen on the ridge trail while evading the NVA up north, the man also has a tattoo, this one on his right forearm. It is of a Jayhawk, the mascot of the University of Kansas (I'd almost attended KU before deciding on UC Berkeley and know the Jayhawk symbol well). Almost certainly, that says he is an American, though this tat is not evidence as clear as the Ranger tattoo on the man I'd killed up north. But if this is an American deserter working with the NVA, then the myths about them have been vindicated, if only in a small way. The injured man is tall and as blond as CPT Englander. Instantly, I am reminded of the rumor of the Salt and Pepper Longshadows supposedly harrying our old area of operations in Quang Ngai Province. Could this be Salt, the tall blond one of the pair? Whatever, this man is in no shape to communicate, now hardly conscious in his morphine haze. It is not apparent, though, which direction the man had been traveling. If east, then he was likely running from the POW camp. Escaping? Running from whom, NVA captors or the OLM renegades? If west, then he was headed *toward* the camp. To help defend it? The enigma begs answers of equal possibility.

"What are you going to do with him, Hugh?" I ask. "We can't carry him with us in the shape he's in. That'd kill him sure. If we could, we should dust him off. If we leave him here, he's likely to die in a few hours, and, humanitarian gestures aside, we would lose the chance to get intel from him. That intel's important. Frankly, I'd call in a dustoff now."

Englander shakes his head. "I'm not waiting for a dustoff. We'll put him there," he says, pointing to three sparsely leaved trees that stand together on a bit of a rise just off the road. We are now moving into the ragged outliers of a new forested area, and trees are more common here. "Put him under the trees. Shade will help him keep alive for a while. We'll dust him off on our way out."

"Man, Hugh, it's a bird in the hand. The biggest reason for our coming here, other than to rescue POWs, if there are any, is to gather intel. Maybe there are Longshadows up ahead, maybe they're gone or dead. Maybe it's a myth. But this guy being here tells me there may be something to it. I say dust him off now. Otherwise, he'll likely be dead *if* we even come back this way."

"OK, Weisman, OK. You want him dusted off, you wait here for one. I'll leave a squad with you for security." He looks at me.

"I'd rather . . ." I start.

"Best offer, Captain."

"OK, put him under the trees and call a dustoff. Cat and I will stay here with the squad. We'll catch up with you again once the bird takes him out."

"You ought to get on the bird and go with him."

"Nah, we've come this far. You'll need somebody who can read a map to get you where you're going."

"Screw you!" Englander says, the right side of his mouth twitching into a small grin. "See you in hell, then."

That would be it except that while Englander and I argue, SSG Gibbs has been searching the wounded man and has come up with a sheaf of papers in Vietnamese and a packet of paper items in a plastic bag that is cloudy with age. That cloudiness almost causes us to miss the fact that what is in the bag are photographs, black and white, moisture having stuck most of the photos together, ruining parts of the images.

"Man, Cap, look at these," he says to Englander, who takes the photos and begins to look through them as I watch over his shoulder. The first photo is of a couple of thatched huts on a mountainside in a jungle clearing. Off in the far distance is a set of twin mountain peaks that looks just like Phou Kanthoung.

"Hugh, I think this was taken from a mountain looking east toward the peak we have just left."

"Yeah, looks that way to me too."

Englander carefully peels the second photo off the back of the first, obliterating part of it in the process. What we can see of it is of a group of grinning soldiers in NVA uniforms pointing AKs at several others, prisoners by their look, huddled in a bunch. All that remains visible of them is legs and feet.

"Goddammit, it's all torn up in the center, I can't make out who the hell are being guarded in this picture."

"No more, Hugh," I say. "The intel guys can get them apart without ruining the photos."

"Yeah," he agrees. But he pulls a few more apart just a bit. Several others show more of the jungle huts. A couple show several westerners dressed as the wounded man in front of us is dressed, in black pajamas, all obviously free and carrying rifles and other combat gear. Longshadows?

"God, David, this is a trove. Unbelievable intelligence. What was this guy doing with all of it?"

I watch several of the Yards pick the wounded man up, lay him behind the trees, and settle into a rough security circle around him.

With the photos in hand, I'm now sure the man wasn't running toward the battle; he was escaping it, carrying evidence. Maybe he'd had enough of fighting for the NVA. Maybe he figured that by bringing these pictures back, he could trade the info for better treatment when he surrendered to our forces.

I would tell all this to Englander, but he is suddenly still, holding another photo up, fresh looking and ragged only at one side. He peers at its slightly unfocused image as if through a microscope trying to find fine details.

"God! That's Bridget. Look, see her!"

He pushes the picture toward me. There's no way to make out detail, but it does look like a woman. She's standing next to two others who look to be prisoners, barefoot and dressed shabbily, clearly not with the Longshadows.

"That's her, David, that's Bridget. She's up there on the mountain in the POW camp."

All I see is a photo of what looks to be an old woman, details too fuzzy to make out. But Englander is sure, antsy suddenly to be off and away to that mountain.

"I'll stay with the Yards here, Hugh. You go. We'll catch up as soon as we can. With these photos, it is more important than ever to get this man back to where he can be treated and interrogated."

"Yeah," says Englander, "yeah," and he hands me the packet of photos and leaves me and Cat and the squad of Yards under the trees, while he takes the rest of the company west almost on a run.

Wondering at it all, wondering if the blurry photo is really Bridget O'Meara as Englander thinks, I look at the man who may well be one of the storied Longshadows. Who the hell are you?

I shake myself out of this thought, pull out my map, and give Cat our grid coordinates. He gets on the horn and calls for the dustoff.

"Roger, sending a bird," comes the response, the voice faint and full of static.

"Where are you calling from?" Cat asks.

"Ben Het."

"What the hell?" I say. I grab the handset from Cat. "There are supposed to be birds on station at the border for quick response."

"Negative today. They've been pulled back here for security's sake."

"Dammit, then how long for a dustoff bird?"

"Got one cranking now. But it's seventy klicks to your location. So expect ETA to be in an hour, maybe forty-five minutes if you're lucky."

"Roger, chop-chop, quick as you can. We've got a badly wounded prisoner and some important intel to send back with him," I say, full of disgust and frustration at the slowness. On a whim, I click the radio back over to the artillery push and call the battery on the border.

"Commo check. Over," I say.

Their signal is strong, and the battery's American-sounding RTO answers with alacrity, "Roger, I've got you five by. What's your sitrep? Over."

I bring him up to speed on our situation.

"Anything we can do?" he asks.

"If we weren't twenty klicks past your max range, I'd call in some defensive targets. Best would be for you to pick the battery up and move it thirty klicks west into Laos so we could get some support from you."

To my surprise, he doesn't laugh but instead says, "I'll relay your request. Over."

"Roger. Out," I say, wondering if he's serious.

We settle in. The slight rise we are next to is an elongated grassy mound some five meters from the roadside. Lying in the elephant grass behind it, we are concealed from the view of anyone traveling along that road. That is a good thing, because half an hour later, with the dustoff still at least forty klicks away, an NVA patrol comes toward us along the road from the east. Y Gat, the young *hạ sĩ* (corporal) who is the Yard squad leader, orders the squad to take cover, and they do so, burying themselves in the tall grass, weapons ready. We watch the NVA soldiers approach. There are about a dozen in the patrol. They are walking carefully among the mines.

"Nhiều mỏ hơn có" (Many more mines over there), one says, pointing.

"Đi cẩn thận lính, bạn cần chân của bạn" (Walk carefully, soldier, you need your legs), says an older man, probably the patrol leader.

"Có, trung sĩ, tôi muốn giữ chúng" (Yes, Sergeant, I want to keep them), the younger soldier laughs.

They come toward us. I have tried to tell Y Gat not to engage them. But neither he nor any of the Yards with us speak much English. One raises his rifle, and I reach out and push it down, looking at the hạ sĩ and shaking my head. He ignores me.

As the patrol comes abreast of us, Y Gat barks, "Bắn chúng!" an order to shoot them, using the Vietnamese words for it, and a volley of fire pours out from the squad. They are good shots, and within moments, all the NVA soldiers are down on the road, most dead, a couple wounded. Two of the Yard soldiers jump up and move to the road, calmly dispatching the wounded. Without ceremony, they pick up the enemy bodies and throw them off into the high grass on the other side of the road.

Y Gat looks at me, smiles, and says, "Nó là tốt hơn theo cách này," also in Vietnamese, as if he thinks I speak that better than Jarai, telling me, I guess, that it is better this way. What's done is done, though, and all I can do is smile ruefully and shake my head.

"God, Captain," Cat says, "shooting like that is going to bring somebody out to investigate."

"I know, Cat. We'll move as soon as the dustoff arrives."

Providentially, things remain quiet for the next half hour. Either the dinks have not heard our brief shoot-out or they give it no priority given the likely attack on the POW camp. The sun is high, moving toward 1200 hours, when the dustoff bird, accompanied by two Cobra gunships, appears in the east and makes its way above the grassland to us. I pop cherry smoke, and the bird flares and lands on the road. The gunships orbit like circling wasps a hundred meters or so above. Their blatt and the whap of the dustoff bird's blades make conversation difficult, but I introduce myself as CPT Weisman, telling the dustoff's crew chief that this is a special prisoner.

"Probably a deserter working with the dinks," I say. I hand him the packet of photos. "Treat him carefully. Make sure the word about him gets back to COL Dolby with DivArty at Duc Pho. This man is likely a rich source of enemy intel. Tell them the photos are especially important intel. Some of the pictures show what looks like Americans working with the NVA."

The crew chief is startled. "Is he one of the Longshadows, Captain?"

"Looks like it. Treat him like he's fragile as glass."

"Will do." He slips the bags of photos and documents into a pocket on the leg of his flight suit, carefully zipping it closed.

The dustoff bird lifts and climbs back toward the east, the gunships accompanying it.

"Let's go, hạ sĩ," I say to the Yard corporal. He just grins and looks at me uncomprehending.

"*Đi, đi đi!* You bic?" I say, exasperated, and point down the road toward Ban Gnangteu.

"*Vâng, vâng,* OK, I bic," he says, nodding agreeably. And we move away from the trees and bloody grass, where clouds of flies are already thickening over the dead.

We move along the road toward the west carefully, watchful for the mines likely buried there. Far off, perhaps half a dozen klicks away, the higher ramparts of the mountain of Phou Kanghông, covered in heavy jungle, grow visible above the upward slope of the grasslands around us. From it, fitfully, as if from a small series of brief firefights, we can hear quick exchanges of gunfire, their sounds faint and delicate in the distance.

"Some fighting up ahead, Captain," Cat says to me. The sun at zenith has burned off the morning's fog and now gives just enough warmth to make us sweat. Cat blots it from his forehead with his fatigue shirt sleeve. At our current pace, the location of those fights is about an hour away.

I nod. "Looks like Englander and the company may have found the POW camp," I say. "I'd like to get up close enough to get a view of what's happening."

"Me too," Cat says.

I gesture to Y Gat to pick up the pace to a fast walk; he moves at a slightly faster slog, which I estimate may cut a whole ten minutes off our time to the mountain.

CHAPTER 36

The mountain of Phou Kanghông rises above low hills west of us like a giant's castle, crenelated and deeply covered in triple canopy jungle all the way to the peak. Like Phou Kanthoung, the mountain we left this morning, it tops a wide rocky massif. On a secondary crest southwest below the mountain's peak, the map shows the ville of Ban Gnangteu, where the POW camp is supposedly located. For much of the time it has taken us to move the last bit of distance toward the mountain, we have heard the far-off, sporadic sounds of firefights, just quick exchanges as if there is a running battle with brief moments of contact. I have repeatedly tried to call Englander, who answered only once with a terse "Later! Out."

We have come to a spot where the road winds down toward a rapid-filled river the map labels the Houay Bouy. A hundred or so meters on, the road crosses a timber bridge at a narrow spot and continues up the mountain on the far side in a series of switchbacks almost buried in jungle.

"What in the world are those?" Cat says, pointing across the river to dark shapes visible in a treeless space at one turning point on the upslope. "Are they bodies?"

Binos out, I study the broken forms. "Yeah, three of them. Not our guys, though. They're in khaki uniforms like NVA." The NVA take their dead away from most contacts, so the fact that they haven't yet confirms the fast-moving nature of this battle.

"*Chúng ta đi đâu?* Go, go?" Y Gat asks me.

"Yes, didi, fast, fast," I say.

"Nao ho'mǎr," Y Gat orders the others in Jarai, and we move again, following the road's broken surface down to the river and across to where it climbs the mountain.

The Yard soldiers with us are on extreme alert, weapons at the ready, moving quickly, though with care to be quiet. Once again, I'm impressed with the Yard soldiers' discipline: none utters a word, responding instead to Y Gat's quick hand signals. We pause at the first switchback only briefly to look at the trio of bodies. All three have been riddled with small arms fire and sprawl so inertly, they seem almost boneless.

Through the filter of the trees, the sound of the firefight is louder, if more spasmodic than before: a scattering of gunshots, a pause, a shot or two, more silence, and then a quick hail of fire and the detonation of grenades before more silence. It sounds to me as if the battle has broken up into small exchanges between fragments of the forces at the ville. We move again, watchful now, weapons ready, getting off the road and under the heavy tree cover as soon as the lay of the land allows.

We reach a high point on the climb. From here, the road descends gradually for perhaps half a klick into a wide, heavily overgrown space of several acres spotted with tiny clearings occupied by huts and other structures: the camp. It has grown briefly quiet below, so it comes as a terrible surprise when, all at once, from the cover of heavy jungle fifty meters or so on our left, there is a volley of small arms fire that rakes the front of our group.

An American voice from that direction rasps, "Die assholes and go to hell!" as the fire envelopes us.

I sense more than hear the bullets flying past me, their hum a flicker of sound. Just in front of me, a bullet catches Y Gat in the head, tossing it back in a spray of blood, and he spins and falls without a word, instantly dead on the gravel. Instinct throws me back into the brush on the opposite side of the road as bullets pepper the trees around me. The same instinct makes me reach futilely toward Cat for the radio handset. Two more of our Yard squad are down on the road, one thrashing and screaming from a gut wound. The other, shattered by automatic weapons fire, is as dead as Y Gat. The rest of our Yards take cover while pouring fire into the bushes on the other side of the road. Not an infantryman, though realizing a call to the artillery battery would be useless, I have no quick impulse to bring up my own rifle, the sense that I need to fire back taking an instant to register. Cat is already firing at the enemy. They seem to be a small group in the bush across from us, and they either die or didi almost at once when we return fire. Y Gat's death is so sudden and unexpected, I hardly comprehend it for a beat or two. Finally, I join one of the Yards in poking into the bush where the enemy fire had come from. There are no enemy dead there, only a pair of blood trails, thick splashes of it. The voice had been American and perhaps a western face, glimpsed, and then lost to my view as he ducked away.

Damn, damn, damn, I think, shaking my head to clear it. I see one of our Yards kneeling over Y Gat's body, looking from it to the other dead Yard near it. We have no medic with us, but Cat has a field dressing that he is pressing to the remaining man's lower leg where a wound gapes. Blood soaks the man's pant leg and pools on the ground beneath him.

"Captain, he's going to die if we can't get a medic up here," he tells me. He leaves off pressing the battle dressing and cuts away a strip of the man's shirt with his Ka-Bar to make a tourniquet that he tightens around the upper thigh. The pain must be excruciating, and, teeth clenched, the man jibbers at it, unable to contain his moans.

Getting a medic up here is unlikely to happen right away, I think. Looking at the remains of the running battle below, it is difficult because of the distance to differentiate friend from foe. Men dart among the structures in and out of the trees to the sound of gunfire and a few sharp detonations that are likely grenades. Several, ours by their tiger fatigues, move into a small open space in the middle of the ville, clearly firing at others behind a hut. There looks to be return fire. One in tiger fatigues falls. The others move forward, and one throws an object (grenade?), and there is a detonation behind the hut. Searching with my binos for a way to get a medic up here, I see mouths open as if in screams, but distance and the sound of gunfire cover those voices.

We can't sit here watching while Englander and the rest of the Yard company are in this fight.

"Đi?" one of the older Yards from the squad asks me.

I nod, and he nods back, an up-and-down headshake in the Yard way, his grin nervous, and tells the others left in the squad in Jarai to "Hiu!" and we move.

Y Gat and the other dead Yard lie in the road. A fourth Yard from the squad sits with the wounded man as Cat and I and the remainder of the Yards with us make our way cautiously down the slope toward the ville. Now I see that Cat is limping, favoring his left foot. There's no sign of blood there, but something is wrong.

"Man, Cat, you're limping. Were you hit?"

"No, Captain, I turned it getting down there on the road. Maybe sprained. I can walk on it OK, though."

Seeing the pain in Cat's eyes as he walks, I don't know what to say. Cat and I seem to share the same charm of invulnerability. Not a perfect one, my ribs still give me twinges, and I have scars from battles months ago. But like Cat, the core of my being is intact. My wounds like his, mostly internal, few on my body, most of my scars marked on my spirit. Cat's doggedness in the face of this new injury shows that no matter how much of a kid he was when we first went into the bush together six months ago, he is a seasoned soldier now. Is that a good thing? I don't know.

We move, stepping quickly but with care, watching for enemy soldiers as we head toward the scene of the battle. By the time we get there, the firing has stopped. There is a stone-rimmed well in the ville's center where we had seen the last bit of firefight. Near it gathered are CPT Englander, SSG Gibbs, and some twenty of our Yard soldiers, all looking wounded to some extent. SSG Sullivan and a Yard medic move among them dressing their wounds. One of our Yards goes up to the medic, points up the hill to where the wounded man is, and the two of them head away up to help him. As Cat comes up to him, Sullivan makes him sit as he binds the sprained ankle, smiling a little at the futility of telling Cat to stay off it as much as possible. SSG Gibbs whacks down a sapling, trims off the branches with his Ka-Bar, and gives it to Cat as a walking stick.

With the soldiers gathered here are four others, three men and an old Caucasian woman, the image of the woman in the photograph. Two of the men are also Caucasian; one is black. All three look worse for wear, starved looking in ratty clothing, the men bruised and filthy. Englander has been shot again, though his rucksack took the brunt of whatever hit him. The woman sits with Englander, holding his hand as Sullivan comes up to him and begins to patch a bloody place on the captain's side.

Englander sees me, smiles wolfishly despite the obvious pain of his wound, and says, "CPT David Weisman, meet Sister Bridget O'Meara."

So she exists and is alive! I don't know what to say except, "Hello, Sister O'Meara. It's good to finally find you."

She nods without responding, all her attention on Englander, helping Sullivan to clean away Englander's blood and put a dressing in place. It is affectionate care, but their vast age difference suggests they could never have been lovers, even were she not a nun. Rather, the care is such as a mother gives a child.

The battle seems over for now, but I feel nervous just waiting in the clearing. So I tell Englander I'm going to take Cat and a fire team of Yards and begin to snoop through the ville.

"Yeah, good," he says, waving me toward the buildings indifferently.

Everywhere are bodies, most of them in NVA khaki uniforms. A few others are of Montagnards, clad in green jungle fatigues. They are surely OLM troops like those we killed on the hill up above. The renegade Yards and NVA alike were armed with AK-47s, weapons easier for guerillas like the OLM troops to maintain in the jungle. Also among the dead are Montagnard soldiers in the tiger fatigues our troops wear, at least fifteen of their bodies by my count. We've lost two-thirds of the company!

We push across the ville past the bodies and gunfire-riddled buildings that show just how vicious the fight had been here. In a rise toward the far side of the ville, we find a series of dugout holes looking to lead to tunnels going down into the mountainside. Scattered among them, we find more than a dozen other dead men who, from their posture, had obviously died in agony. Most have the look of Americans, one a Yard. All look well-fed like the Longshadow we had found back on the road in the same sort of VC black pajamas. None is marked by gunfire.

"What the hell, Captain," Cat asks. "What killed these guys?"

I flatly don't know. There is no blood on them, no visible wounds. None of the men looks starved or beaten. They seem sleek and neatly clothed but horribly dead. Whatever killed them has left the pupils of their eyes tightened to pinpoints. Snot has flowed freely from their noses. Several have vomited, peed themselves, and defecated before dying. One, pupils also pinpointed, lips and chin covered in mucus, lies in an impossible, horrifying contortion, his knotted muscles looking as if they had nearly torn him apart.

Cat makes to go toward one of the tunnel entrances, and I grab him, something telling me a deep evil of war waits there.

"Poison gas, I'd say," I tell Cat. "It was nerve gas from the look of their eyes. The pupils are shrunk down to nothing. Man, yes, this was nerve gas. Heavier than air, it must still be down in those holes."

"Nerve gas? Goddammit. Who the hell would use that?" Cat looks dumfounded at the idea.

"Think of the case of VX grenades we found in the hut by the river. The stuff with the Russian markings," I say. "I don't know who used it, but let's get the hell away from here, Cat. If it is VX, it is death waiting to happen."

"But we've got the masks and injectors, sir."

"Yeah, God only knows if that will protect us." I pull my instamatic from my ruck. I've been taking pictures right along on this march, but there are still a few shots left on the camera, and I carefully photograph the gassed Longshadows. Evidence, self-protection? I don't know, but I feel safer having such photos.

Back in the center of the ville, I tell Englander about the gassed men. "That's monstrous, Hugh."

"War's monstrous. What difference does it make how they died?"

"Christ, Hugh, they suffered. Did you see them?"

"You suffer just as much from a bullet. Any way you go is bad. I doubt this hurt any worse than getting gut shot and dying by inches. Pain is pain."

"The worst of the worst, Hugh."

He looks startled and stares at me for a few beats. "Who gives a damn?"

"You knew, though, man. That's why we are carrying these gas masks and injectors, isn't it?"

He doesn't evade, admitting freely, "Yeah, it is. These damn outlaw Yards use VX sometimes. They have a stock of it they stole from the NVA, who get it from the Chinese, who get it from the Russians. Hell, I think we have it too."

"Maybe," I admit. "But we don't use it. That'd be a damned war crime."

"You sure we don't?"

"I'm sure, Hugh."

He just snorts.

I decide to drop it for now. I can raise the question back at brigade, though I think Hugh is probably right about nobody giving a damn since it wasn't U.S. troops who used the VX. "Look," I finally say, "we've found the POW camp. We've rescued three prisoners. It looks like we've even found more men who look like Longshadows. They're dead, but, hell, I've got pictures. And you've found your friend Bridget. Are there are more prisoners here for us to find?"

"If there are, they are down in the tunnels with the nerve gas. I'm not going down to find out," Englander says. "You're welcome to check if you want."

I shake my head. "I say we call it mission accomplished and go home."

"Yeah," he says, "home," saying it as if it's a benediction. He's rescued Bridget, and to him, the rest is just egg in our beer.

Getting out, though, won't be as easy as that. The jungle around the POW camp is deep and thick, likely full of NVA and probably Pathet Lao troops, with no place large enough to land a bird to extract us. The OLM troops are out there too, maybe trustworthy, maybe just out for themselves. It is no better on the path down the mountainside. In fact, the map shows the closest decent LZ is two klicks back down the road to the river and then another klick south to a wide area of only gradual slope at the foot of a low ridge. We are also down to the bare bones of a company, not even twenty-five counting me and Cat. Two-thirds of those who started with us are dead or dusted off. All the remaining troops except for me are hurt. The three POWs had been repeatedly beaten and look hardly able to travel. Even Bridget, though showing fewer marks of maltreatment, had apparently been starved to the point that she looks too weak to move quickly.

I study the map image of the likely LZ. "It shows a fair amount of bamboo there," I say to Englander. "Don't know if it's a decent place to put birds down, but we'd have to cross the river and go another three klicks to get to anything that looks better. Given our condition, I don't know if we'd make that."

"Yeah, yeah, I know," Englander says slowly. He looks around as if realizing for the first time what went on here. "Yeah. Let's do it."

CHAPTER 37

Bridget limps badly but refuses help except over some of the worst spots in the road. "They beat me on the soles of my feet. Hurts like a beast," she tells me with a shudder. "I don't know what they hoped to gain."

As we walk back along the road out of Ban Gnangteu, I look at this woman, rail thin, the top of her head barely up to my chin. Her face is deeply tanned, lined and liver spotted, her hair like a close-cropped gray helmet. Her expression is stern but hardly commanding, yet the Yards show her great deference, the sort they would show a respected leader or elder. Two offer to carry her, but she declines.

"You walk, I walk," she tells them. Her accent is American, faintly Bostonian.

"How long have you known Hugh?" I ask, though Englander had already said he had met her maybe a year and a half ago. I ask because I don't know if I can trust anything he says.

"I've known him the better part of two years. I met him when I first settled in down on the Cambodian border. He had command of a Special Forces A-Team there. At least that's what he called it. To me, it was spooky stuff, things better not known." She turns to look at me as we walk. "Yes, I know he's irascible and hot-tempered. Some people have called him a real bastard . . . bastard." She seems to test the word, pausing at it as if a nun should not be possessed of such language. "The Montagnards tell me he is a good commander, though, smart, wily, very effective in counterinsurgency actions."

That last stops me; it is not the sort of specific military term I would expect from a noncombatant. Tom Dooley had been CIA. I wonder if Bridget is also, or at least a collaborator.

She smirks when my eyes widen at the term and shrugs, saying, "You don't hang around in a war zone for as many years as I have without picking up the lingo."

We walk silently for a moment, and then I ask what's really the central question of this whole adventure, "Why did the NVA kidnap you?"

"I work with the Montagnards. I suppose they wanted to know how familiar I am with the NVA's operations."

"About the Longshadows?"

A pause. "I suppose. But they're hardly a secret."

"Maybe not here, Bridget, but back in our war, they're a myth like the gremlins in World War II who supposedly fucked our planes up for the hell of it." (She's tough; my rough language doesn't faze her.) "As a myth, the Longshadows are unnerving. If they're real, then our higher-ups would have to admit that American soldiers are disillusioned and deserting."

She nods, whether in agreement or just response I can't tell.

I add, "The brass would do anything, including another illegal operation like ours here in Laos, to keep *that* word from getting out. The enemy sure in hell doesn't want that. They have an interest in keeping the Longshadows a legend, hairy and menacing. They kidnapped you so you wouldn't tell the truth about the Longshadows. Didn't they?"

Turning her head away, she says nothing, and that silence alone tells me I'm right. It says that we'd use every means to erase the evidence, even—God forbid—to go as far as allowing OLM to use nerve gas to make sure all the Longshadows are dead. It also means that our higher command surely doesn't want Bridget to come back and tell her story to the press. That, I suddenly see, is the real reason the OLM renegades are here.

"The OLM isn't here as a diversion, not as our partners in freeing the POWs, but as a hit team to ensure you never get back to tell that story."

Bridget's face has become an obdurate mask. The thoughts behind it I cannot read.

"It's a wild theory," I tell Englander. But he listens without a twitch, not surprised when I tell him that's why I think the NVA kidnapped her, not surprised when I tell him I think that it is our own side that wants her silenced. "Isn't she as dangerous to the NVA as she is to our side, Hugh? So why did they capture her instead of assassinating her?"

"Because she's a damned hero to the mountain people out here," he says. "The NVA don't want the kind of trouble they'd get if they killed her."

"OLM doesn't seem to see her as a hero."

"OLM is a cat's paw of the CIA—the company pays them, and OLM does what they direct."

"Fuck!" I say. That had never occurred to me.

"Fuck, it is, for sure."

We have no idea if the LZ we hope to use is safe, and so Englander dispatches SSG Gibbs and six Yard troops to recon the area first. The rest of us move down the mountain road to a sheltered switchback near the bottom and set up security to await their report.

Maybe a half hour later, Gibbs calls in to Englander, his voice barely above a whisper over the radio. "Three places where you could set a bird down here, Cap. Best is an open rocky stretch at the south end. Jungle isn't heavy there, so good visibility, but the drawback is there's not much separation from the trees. Means the enemy can get close without coming out into the open. Only other problem is a knob on the other side of the river where the dinks could set up an AA gun if they have one. Other two possible LZs are smaller and even more exposed to enemy fire."

"OK, we'll chance it," Englander responds, if not happily. "You should set up in a secure spot there and wait for us. With the wounded, we're moving slower than you. Expect us in an hour or so. Out." The plan is to have Gibbs split his group between the two lesser LZs to make some noise and draw any enemy troops away from the real one we want to use. When the Hook comes in there to pick the rest of us up, it will hopefully draw the enemy back to our LZ, and that will open one of the smaller ones for a feigned extraction of Gibbs's team by Huey. With a bit of luck, the enemy will be left in confusion, not knowing which LZ is the real one.

Our call to Ben Het for extraction again elicits a scratchy, barely intelligible response. "Roger, we'll send a Hook. ETA is about ninety minutes."

We'd prefer it faster. Ninety minutes means a wait of a half hour or so at the LZ. But the big passenger bird is coming from somewhere east of Dak To. So much for the theory of a quick reaction to our needs.

The biggest change in our situation—and it is a huge positive for us—is that we have artillery back, at least partially. Somehow, some way, the ARVN artillery battery that had been supporting us from the border took my request seriously and was able to relocate west thirty klicks to a mountain peak in Laos. Their 175s were too heavy for even a CH-54 Skycrane to lift. So the only guns they have with them are their four 155s, leaving us still a couple of klicks beyond their max range. But if the extraction fails, we will have their support if we have to make a run for it.

"It's good to hear your voice, man," I tell the battery's RTO.

"Good to hear yours," he comes back.

"Are you safe there?" I ask.

"Safe enough. We're on an isolated peak. Got a company of ARVN for security. We don't want to be here long, though. You've gotta chop-chop getting out of there."

"Roger that," I say, and I ask what I have wondered for weeks now, "Who are you, man? You sure don't sound like an ARVN."

There's a pause for a few beats, and then he comes back. "Nah, not ARVN. I mean, the battery is, but I'm not, and the FDC isn't. Let's just say you and I are on the same team and leave it at that."

"Roger," I say. "Thanks. That explains a lot. Glad to have you there even if I hope we won't need you."

"Same here. Out."

Who knew there were black ops artillerymen in Vietnam? It is a thin reed to grasp at if we need it, but better than no support at all.

"We'll have artillery support if we move two klicks east," I tell Englander.

He stops and stares at me for a moment. "How?"

"Battery moved west. Guns were doing us no good where they were."

"Wow!" He grins lopsidedly.

"Yeah," I say.

Still, we keep with our present plan for the time being. We could leave the bodies of our dead if it came to that. (God! It can't. There's hardly a sin worse than leaving our dead behind, especially here where we likely could never return for them.) But we've also got wounded who would have trouble moving much farther. We are nearly at our planned extraction point. The nearest LZ in range of the guns where we could get artillery support is across the river, three klicks north and east through a narrow, steep saddle. Moving to where we'd get arty would be tempting if it were clear all our folks could move with us. We walk, taking our time for more than an hour as we get repeated sitreps from the incoming Hook and its gunship escort. With luck, we'll be up on that bird and out of here, headed back to Ben Het.

If anyone is watching us move the rest of the way down the mountain from Ban Guangteu (my bet is there are watchers), we must look to them like refugees from Ragnarök's bloodiest doom: lame, halt, badly shot up, carrying a big load of our dead. The sun, now behind us, is almost as low as the peak, casting the mountainside around us in sharp relief. This early in the spring, we will not have much more sunlight. East of us, the Houay Hintho River is in full-throated flood, its brown waters rushing north toward the torrent of the Dak Xou and on to the great muddy Xé Kong River in the heart of the Attapu plain.

We walk south along the bluff above the river, seemingly alone, no sign of North Vietnamese, Pathet Lao, or even the OLM (the latter, though ostensibly our allies, we trust hardly more than the others). We move carefully, staying toward the wooded inner edge of the trail, trying to be silent. We succeed only partially as we learn when an AK-47 barks from across the river and a bullet smacks the damp dirt of the trail a few feet ahead of CPT Englander. No one is hurt, and whoever the rifleman on the other side is, he is invisible against the dark-green wall of jungle over there.

"Đại úy hải quân, Y Lam," Englander says, beckoning to the young lieutenant now in command of the Yard company's remnant. "Tell your point man to stay off the trail. Move through the trees. You bic?"

He does bic, if not the words, at least the forceful gestures Englander makes in giving the order.

"Ő, I bic, sure, sure," Đại úy hải quân Y Lam, says. The sleeve of his tiger-patterned fatigue shirt is bloody, most of it torn away from the wound below, covered in a field dressing, red seeping in. Still, he grins wolfishly and gives a quick order in Jarai to the Yard soldier walking point. With that, we move off again, now hidden in the thicker growth to the right of the trail. This going is slower, but we are at least screened from the eyes of the enemy this way.

As we move, we get another call from SSG Gibbs. "Dinks think they have us figured out, Cap. They've got all three possible LZs staked out, ready to give us some trouble if we try to bring birds in any of 'em."

"Hang tight," Englander calls back. "We'll use the big one. I'll give you the word when to start the diversion at the other two spots."

"Roger, we're ready."

We've come down to the base of the mountain, the bank of the Houng Bouy just a few meters below us, the river too deep and savage to cross here. It's a fact that has a double edge: we'll have trouble if we need to get to the other side, but any enemy on that side would have hard going to cross and get to us. The clearing we hope to use as an LZ is about a hundred meters south along the river. Englander, Y Lam, and a fire team of Yards move out ahead of us to scout it.

"Looks like the only dinks there are on the southwest end of the space. None at the north end," Englander tells me. "You keep coming. Extraction bird is about one five minutes out from us. I'll set up security here. You move in at the north end and do the same."

We arrive at the LZ. Mostly relegated to hand signals, nods, and grins, I manage to tell the Yards to put out security along the tree line bordering the open space.

Cat is looking a bit gray from pain, his bound-up ankle clearly troubling him more than a little. He sags to the ground behind a big teak tree a couple of meters shy of the opening. "Are we in range of the guns yet, Captain?" Cat asks me.

I know we're not, but I pull out my map again to check. "No." I show him what I'd figured earlier—that to get into its range, we'd have to cross the river and traverse some rough terrain.

"Man," he says, "I hope it doesn't come to that."

"Me too," I say.

The Hook contacts us again, saying it is now about ten klicks out, headed our way. There is no noise from it or its gunship escorts yet, but far off to the east, just south of the sunlit peak of Phou Kanthoung, I think I see dark specks drawing closer.

"That's our birds," I tell Cat. "Coming now."

Apparently, Englander sees it as well. The Yards near me have a radio tuned to their company push, and over it, I hear Englander call to SSG Gibbs. "Birds inbound, start your diversion then didi over here fast."

"Roger," Gibbs says.

Almost at once, there is a deep triple beat of explosions as Gibbs's fire team throws grenades at the place where the enemy soldiers are hidden. A volume of small arms fire erupts there; a machine gun fires in a quick trio of three round shot groups. At the south end of our LZ, there comes the sound of Vietnamese voices, and then the brush there shakes as a unit of NVA hidden there takes the bait and moves toward where Gibbs is located.

It seems as if it has worked. The NVA have left us alone here and have gone to take on Gibbs's team. The bulky Hook comes stuttering in, its heavy twin rotors bashing the air, dropping toward our LZ. The Cobra gunships come down alongside it. Warned that Gibbs's team is on the east side of the LZ, the gunships focus their suppressive fire along the west side, some twenty meters out, giving us a clear corridor to get on the bird. Doc Sullivan and the Yards with me make it to the bird's open rear door. Cat and I follow. Moments later, Englander, Y Lam, and the Yard fire team pile on. A sweaty few minutes later—as the Hook sits on the ground, rotors turning, vibrating as if fretful to be in the air again—SSG Gibbs and his team of Yards join us. The Hook's flight engineer from his station at the rear gives the word to the pilot to lift. The big blades smash air, and we rise sweetly upward. The fierce ripsaw sound of the Cobras' miniguns tear at the ground us as we climb out of the mountain's shadow, out into the gold of late afternoon light, up into the darkening eastern sky, up into a spray of AA fire that comes up at us from the long low ridge on the east bank of the Houng Bouy.

The sound of the heavy AA rounds hitting the side of the Hook is a rattle of thuds and shrieks of tearing metal. Holes full of dusk's light pop into the roof of the Hook. The big bird shudders and tilts. Its engines falter and then catch again, and we climb again out of the jungle. On the bulkhead across from me, oil freed from its reservoir in one of its turbines gushes down, puddling on the floor of the bird. The AA fire has ceased. Out a window, I see the Cobras raking the ridge where the AA came from. Smoke rises from it, though too late.

"Going to make it out in one piece!" the flight engineer shouts to us above the shriek of the failing turbines. "This sucker will fly on one engine."

But the bird has more damage than that, something perhaps in the transmission also failing, and we lose lift, the heavy bird shaking as if in a monster's grip. We tip and begin to drop. A spasm catches my throat and chest as if I've been flung back into the helicopter crash I'd endured in Laos. Outside, I see the trees come up at us. We fall into them. The bird cants slightly onto its right side, and all I can envision are those huge rotor blades carving like a giant's butcher knife into the guts of the bird, into us.

But we are down, mostly intact. The turbines scream into silence. In the front of the bird, through the open doorway into the control cabin, I see the pilots scrambling to get out of the cockpit, one first reaching for a radio to call in a fast Mayday before we leave. Wondrously, no one in the Hook is further injured in the crash. The flight engineer pulls a release, and the rear door drops open.

"Get out, get out!" he bellows. "Don't know if this thing will catch fire or not. So get the fuck out!"

We move. Outside, I see we have come down on a bamboo-cluttered open space along the far side of the ridge and on the bank of yet another small river. We are perhaps two klicks east of where the Hook had picked us up. Above, the two Cobra gunships orbit like two nervous birds of prey, watching the thick jungle around us. Already the call has gone out for another bird to come and lift us away from this place. Like the others, it, too, is coming from Ben Het, an hour and a half away. There is nothing to do but to move a safe distance from the downed Hook, set up security, and wait. Biggest worry, how much flying time do the Cobras have left? Roundtrip from Ben Het is nearly half their range. They have maybe half an hour remaining before they will have to break station and head back for fuel. The one positive of where we are being that, by my calculation, we are now within range of the relocated 155 battery. Meanwhile, all we can do is set up security, hunker down, and wait for rescue.

We dig in. Englander has put a listening post out on the nose of the ridge to our northwest, two hundred meters from our position. About forty-five minutes after the crash, the LP reports movement in the jungle between them and the Houng Bouy River.

SSG Gibbs is with them and reports, "A good-sized unit headed our way. Only getting glimpses of them through the trees, so I can't get a firm count. But I estimate fifty. They're moving carefully. Going to be too dark to see them soon."

"Roger, stay put. You can hit them from the rear if they come at us," Englander responds. "No place for us to move to. We've been digging in here. Damned Hook is still nearly an hour away."

"Roger."

We have no gunship support. The Cobras, low on fuel, have been forced to break station and head back to Ben Het. Others are headed our way but are too far out to be of immediate help. Artillery is our best fallback. I take the handset from Englander. "I've got artillery support again," I tell Gibbs. "Can you give me a good grid for the enemy's location?"

"Yeah, yeah, I think so, wait . . . OK, good grid is two-nine-seven-five, one-eight-one-zero. That's toward the front of their file."

"Got it," I say, looking at where a path is depicted crossing a narrow stream. I scribble the numbers from SSG Gibbs onto the plastic over my map with a grease pencil and call in the fire mission. "Fast, fast," I tell them. "A bunch of enemy is coming our way."

"Roger, no worries, man. We'll be shootin' right away."

Between me and the target is nothing but jungle, no way to tell where anything hits, no way to see how to adjust it. "I'm going up to the LP," I tell Englander. "I can get a better view there." I grab the radio from Cat, who, with his bad ankle, wouldn't be able to move fast enough to stay with me on the run up the ridge. He doesn't like it but agrees he'd be more hindrance than help.

"Hang here, Cat. They can use you. Banged up as we are, every rifle is going to count."

I run, mostly in shadow now. The sun is now fully behind the ridge where the LP is located, its light a halo around the high ground there, gone from my side of the slope but deepening into sunset gold on the low rise east of the fallen Hook. I need daylight to do the best job of adjusting fire, but not much is left now.

I'm about halfway up the ridge when the battery announces, "Shot!" and I find a clear spot below the LP to watch for where the 155 mm rounds impact.

"Splash!"

"Roger, splash."

No first marking round here. I want to hit the enemy fast and hard, so I'd called for the full battery to fire in adjustment, wanting to get as much fire on them as quickly as I can. Thankfully, Gibbs's target grid had been accurate, and the sheaf of impacting artillery lands right on top of where the enemy file apparently is. The fire of the shells' bursting is a ruddy wink against the dark jungle behind them. In the fading light of dusk, I can still see the bit of exposed trail the enemy is using, the part of it at least that is coming down from the high ground. Closer to us, I can see nothing of the enemy soldiers, but I would bet that some at least have already come past where the artillery impacted. So I tell the battery, "Drop one hundred. Repeat fire for effect."

I have the guns drop further in another adjustment, the big rounds now edging into danger close territory hardly a couple of hundred meters from where I am. The LP, I know, must be getting nervous, the incoming artillery surely landing hardly a hundred meters below them at the northern low point of the ridge. I don't really care. Our guys are in no condition for a big fight, and I've come to trust the skill and accuracy of this black ops artillery battery.

I have no hope that the artillery will be able to take out all or even most of the enemy. But it will force them to move north into the open to get away from it. Doing that, they effectively flank us to the northeast, but I think that in the open, we'll be able to see them from our high ground position where the Hook went down. Seeing them, hopefully we'll give them enough of a fight that they'll turn tail rather than take us on.

CHAPTER 38

"No way out, you!" an enemy soldier hardly fifty meters northeast of us calls from the trees, his voice heavy with a Vietnamese accent. "You *chieu hoi* now!"

"Up yours," and a burst of M16 fire is the response.

In the last flush of daylight, we can see that the hillside behind us opens onto a bare stony slope, good to land the Hook supposedly inbound soon. Good for that, but bad, very bad for a retreat from the oncoming enemy who can rake that open space with grazing fire if we try to cross it unprotected. The artillery I've called has cut off the larger mass of the enemy to our front, the blasts of the 155 mm shells muffled but titanic in the defile west of us. More enemy troops, coming from somewhere east, are behind us, cutting off that escape route. Across the open space, we can hear the voices of the enemy, low and careful as they move to block us.

I'm back down from the low ridge, back along with SSG Gibbs and the rest from the LP. We're too few to be effective if we remain split up, and so we've linked back up with Englander's group.

Englander looks at me, eyes wide, face flushed with anger and frustration. We are so damn close to escape. If the extraction bird could just come in here and set down on the shelf of the hill no more than fifty meters ahead of us, if it could come down despite the withering fire of the nameless enemy AA gun on the knob to our right, come down in the protection of a blaze of supporting fire from the new pair of gunships. But the gunships are gone, shot down in the jungle by another of the enemy AA guns, seemingly abundant in these Laotian mountains. The gunships are burning hulks, pilots dead, the ships' fires sending up pillars of smoke, dark near the ground, golden where they emerge into the sunset. Only the big Hook orbits above us, circling high above the AA gun's two-klick maximum ceiling, its pilot wanting to bring it down to extract us but wary of the power of that gun.

"So close," says Englander, looking up toward where it circles in the sky. His voice is raspy, unhappy. Bridget, sheltering in a small dugout nearby, looks on with almost motherly concern.

"Right four hundred, add two hundred," I tell the battery. It feels good to have artillery support again, to be able to call them and call down their murderous fire on the enemy. Strong. It's the only real defense we have now, as the big 155 shells thunder in from the east, thunder in and crash down around the high ground where the enemy fire comes from. Again, the AA gun sends its fire skyward toward the orbiting Hook. The fire I'm calling in hasn't hit the AA gun yet, and I call the battery again trying to fix on the gun's position in the fading light. "Right one hundred, drop five-zero, repeat."

Englander, Gibbs, Sullivan, Cat, and the ragtag of the remaining Yards with us hunker intently in quickly dug holes among the trees, firing back at the enemy, whether PL or NVA it is not clear. Incoming AK fire rattles among the trees. I can still see the sweat on our men's faces, have the sense the heat from them, the heat of fear and fury. The enemy are so close, we can smell their sweat, its rankness different from the sweat stink of our own guys.

One mockingly calls, "Đầu hàng" (Surrender), and then in heavily accented English, "We are more than you!"

"Fuck you, dink," Englander calls back, and the Yard troops take up the call, "Fugyou! Fugyou! Fugyou!"

An RPG sizzles in at us in response and bursts in the trees, sending wood fragments sharp as shrapnel singing into the woods behind us. One of the enemy troops back there shouts urgently, "Yud than no mai suan rai thi kai sid koen pai!" (Stop. You are shooting too close to us!) The words in Lao telling us we appear to have NVA to our front and Pathet Lao to our rear.

Some of the enemy have gotten through onto the low stretch of open space north of us. It is almost fully dark now, the waning moon and its helpful light hours away from rising. We can hear the enemy below moving up, and I call the artillery fire to our front in even closer, hardly seventy-five meters away. Two of the battery's guns are shooting there. Two more I've called in behind us to block the other element of the enemy. They don't dare move at us through the artillery fire. But we are caught.

There is nowhere for us to run. Left, the slope rises too steeply to climb. Right is the open space and then the river where we might take a chance, its rush and roar a seeming good alternative only compared to the threat of the enemy's guns. North and south, the enemy blocks us. Our only real chance of escape is the Hook orbiting overhead.

A handful of the NVA have broken past the falling artillery and into the clear space in front of us, coming up the slope, firing, yelling, "No way out, you! *Chết bây giờ! Chết, chết, chết!*" (Die now! Die, die, die!)

AK fire snaps among us. Our M16s and the one M60 we still have with us reply. Meanwhile, in the dark, finally seeing its telltale flashes of fire, I've figured out where the AA gun is.

"There," I tell Englander. "On that open point of the ridge. That's where the dinks have their gun."

"No," he says, "can't get there. All the damn enemy between."

But on my map, I can see the grid of the gun now, 3138-1679. "New fire mission," I tell the battery.

"Send it," the RTO says.

"Grid three-one-three-eight. Over."

"Roger, grid three-one-three-eight. Out."

"One-six-seven-niner. Over."

"Roger, grid one-six-seven-niner. Out."

"Direction three-zero-zero-zero, proximity two hundred, enemy AA gun in the open. Two guns, VT in adjustment. Battery two, VT in effect. No marking round. We're close enough that it won't make a damn bit of difference."

"Roger that. Out."

Soon, the point where the enemy gun is emplaced erupts with bright airburst flashes of artillery. The thunder of its detonation resounds off the surrounding slopes. The AA gun's fire ceases. I call in another barrage to be sure.

"Call the Hook down now!" Englander tells SSG Gibbs. "If it comes in fast, we can get away."

The Hook, high up as it is, is still catching the last dregs of the setting sun as if caught in a spotlight's gelled bastard amber beam. It breaks away from its orbit and begins a long sweep south in a spiral that will soon bring it down onto the LZ.

"When it's down, we run!" Englander bellows.

Now, the enemy, with a last push to get us before we can lift out, come up from the jungle and down from the high ground behind us. They come, yelling, shooting, hardly thirty meters away, their AK fire slapping around our foxholes. They come flinging Chicom grenades. They move between our position and where the Hook is aiming to come down, blocking our escape. Too many of them to fight through. The bird lowering.

There comes a pop and then another and then maybe a dozen more, a fizzy sound as if from soda cans bursting. The air around us is suddenly full of a mist, some of it rolling down right onto us from the high ground behind us where many of the PL were. More of the grenade bursts blossom among the NVA in front of us. Within seconds, all enemy fire stops.

I know! VX, the worst of the worst!

"Gas!" I shout. I grab for the M17 gas mask I've carried since this mission began. Yes, I know. This was what had killed the Longshadows up on the mountain. This was the nasty stuff in the Russian grenades we had found. There is no time to think. Just do. Already, I'm starting to choke in the mist. *Fit and clear the mask,* I think. *Grab for the antidote autoinjectors.* A PL soldier staggers out of the trees and down the slope toward me. His eyes are streaming with tears, mouth foaming. He bends over to vomit and collapses, twitching, flopping side to side. My mask is on now, but a faint sort of cooling mist has touched the bare skin of my arms. A shiver runs through me, a sudden tightness of breath and a wave of nausea. I already have an autoinjector in hand, pulled from a pouch in the mask carrier. A moan escapes me that becomes a wheeze, my lungs tightening. I press the atropine injector against my thigh, feel the needle stab, a shock of sudden injection, holding it while I try to count to ten. I fall. Breathe, breathe. Nausea overwhelms me. I hold it. The mask must stay on, the air through its charcoal filter has a faint campfire odor of burned wood. I can't let myself vomit in it. There is a smell of vomit around me, of feces as men around me shit themselves in their convulsions. My muscles relax as the atropine clears my nerves. I press the other injector, it with pralidoxime, to my thigh now, push until I feel that needle penetrate and the stuff flow in, neutralizing the VX. The moans around me are like the mewling of infants. Men convulsing, pissing themselves, breath hissing into clogged lungs. No one is standing now.

Breathe, breathe! I think. I am on my knees, vision starting to clear. Cat is right in front of me, sprawled on his back, arms wide and flailing. The darkness, which had seemed suddenly complete in my failing vision, full black, recedes, and I can see again.

"Cat!" I'm screaming. His head flops, and he looks at me dimly through pinpointed pupils. Thick streams of snot glisten on his lip. I find his gas mask in its pouch, pull it out and tug it over his head, and push it into place. I grab the autoinjector from his mask carrier and stab the atropine into his leg. He had been crouched in his foxhole, and I drag him out and away from the heavy mist of nerve gas settling into it around him. He stirs but is not conscious, and I grab the second injector from his bag, stab that into his leg too, and stab us both with the CANA diazepam anticonvulsant injectors. I'd been trained and tried dummy injectors at Fort Sill. My actions are automatic; none of this comes back to me consciously. It is strange how the mind works automatically at such times.

My muscles are still spastic, though settling down as I pull Cat up onto a slight rise of ground above where the mist is flowing. It is VX, I am sure. No nerve agent deadlier. No odor or taste. Faintly yellow in color. Persistent. Does not evaporate. It will lie in low places here for days now. The worst of the worst.

Around me, not a shot has been fired since the grenades full of VX were thrown. All purposeful motion, of us, of the enemy, all has come to a convulsive halt. Some others of us have also managed to get their masks and VX antidotes out in time.

Near me, Englander is on all fours, vomiting. His mask is on the ground beside him, left where he had pulled it before the gas overcame him. I move to him, grab the mask, and start to pull it on him.

He croaks, "No! Not me. Not me." He waves a hand toward Bridget, who is in her dugout convulsing, her breath coming as a deep wheeze, arms flopping purposelessly. "Her," he manages to say. "Her!"

Bridget is looking at me with a barely conscious appeal. "No!" she seems to be pleading. "Not me." But there is only one mask, one pack of autoinjectors in Englander's pouch. I see what Englander wants. His is not selflessness, not bravery, not the noblesse oblige expected of an officer (that he who claims to be noble must conduct himself nobly). It might be repayment of a debt he owes Bridget, though were it that, it would diminish Englander's sacrifice to the status of a transaction. Not even love (at least not romantic love). It simply is an act both gallant and right.

The Hook on short final flares toward landing. The huge twin rotors blow away much of the settling VX mist. No matter. It is persistent death and will kill wherever and whatever it settles on. The Hook rocks and sets down among stands of bamboo, the back door grinding open, the flight engineer shouting for us to come aboard.

Of us, there are only nine moving. Me, Cat, Bridget, Gibbs, and Sullivan (both of the latter had their masks and autoinjectors and had managed to get their masks on and the antidote to the VX injected). Also alive are four of the Yards who had kept their masks and antidote kits through the long trail here from Vietnam.

Englander lies rigid and shaking, eyes pinpointed, breath barely moving in and out in a horrible wheeze. We carry him aboard and do the same for the pilots and flight engineer of the other Hook. The Yards carry some of their own fellows on. I have scrounged a mask and some injectors off of one of our dead. I pull it onto Englander and stab both injectors into his thigh. In time? I don't know. Bridget sits on the floor of the bird holding the Hatchet Team captain's hand. The trip back to Ben Het is long, the VX's action quick and strong. Some of those we brought aboard—those like Cat and Gibbs (and me?) whom the nerve gas touched only lightly—may survive. Englander? I will write Englander up for the highest honor for valor I can. Our actions here in Laos are lost, buried in the annals of things officially not. Englander's medal, a Distinguished Service Cross, will be formally awarded for bravery in a battle never fought on soil he never stepped on. Only those who cannot say will truly know.

At Ben Het, they will strip away my tiger fatigues, my boots and hat and gear, all going into a fire to evulse the poison of this mission. Nothing of it but memories and dreams will stay.

We lift into a dark and star-filled sky.

GLOSSARY

Agent Orange: one of the toxic chemical defoliants used by the American military in Vietnam to deprive the enemy of food and hiding places in the jungles by killing all vegetation. Nicknamed "Agent Orange" because of the identifying orange stripe on its steel drum containers.

AK-47: A Soviet-manufactured Kalashnikov semiautomatic and fully automatic combat assault rifle, it fires a 7.62 mm bullet at six hundred rounds per minute; the basic weapon of the NVA. A simple but very reliable weapon. It had a distinctive deep popping sound when firing.

AO: area of operations, the formal limits of the territory in which a unit operated.

Arc Light: code name for B-52 bomber strikes.

Article 15: the least severe form of nonjudicial military punishment. Generally administered at the company level, often resulting in loss of rank and pay. From Article 15 of the Uniform Code of Military Justice.

APC: armored personnel carriers. The Pathet Lao had a few Russian-made BTR-40s first manufactured clear back in 1947. They were lightly armored, protected from small arms but worthless against anti-vehicle mines or artillery.

ARVN: Army of the Republic of Vietnam; the South Vietnamese Regular Army.

Back to the World or back in the World: back in the United States (sometimes wryly called the land of the Big PX—post exchange, a big military-type variety store).

base bleed: A Swedish invention, this is a type of extended-range ammunition that adds a small smoldering charge to the base of the shell. This "base bleed" system adds pressure to counter the vacuum created by the flight of the shell and adds as much as 30 percent to the range, though the turbulence of airflow this creates reduces accuracy a bit. Practical base bleed rounds were tested in the late 1960s, though not in common use in Vietnam.

battery: the basic unit of artillery, equivalent to a company. It generally has five or six 105 mm or 155 mm howitzers or two to four eight-inch howitzers or 175 mm self-propelled guns.

battalion: In the Vietnam War, it generally comprised a unit of about seven companies with some 1,300 soldiers typically commanded by a lieutenant colonel. Several battalions were grouped to form a brigade.

beehive round: an explosive artillery shell, like an oversized shotgun shell, that fires thousands of small arrow-like fléchette projectiles. Used for close-up final defense if an artillery battery was attacked.

berm: perimeter line of a fortification, especially a foxhole; usually raised above the surrounding area.

bic: Vietnamese slang for "understand."

bird: general slang term for a helicopter, usually a UH-1H "Huey," though any rotary wing craft was termed a bird.

black magic: Black magic is a real, if rarely used, last-chance procedure for when all other methods of artillery fire direction have been lost. *U.S.*

Army Artillery Field Manual FM 6-40, chapter 14, "Emergency FDC Procedures," details this rump process for getting steel on the target in the most extreme of combat conditions.

Black soldiers: About 13 percent of those who fought, and of those U.S. troops who died in Vietnam, were black, about the same as the proportion of blacks in the U.S. population. But only about 4 percent of the officer corps were black.

blood trail: a trail of blood left by a fleeing man who has been wounded.

blue line: any water feature on a map, so called because of the color used to designate water on topographic maps.

body bag: plastic bag used to transport dead bodies from the field.

body count: the number of enemy killed, wounded, or captured during an operation. Washington and Saigon used the term as a means of measuring the progress of the war.

boocoo: bastardized French from *beaucoup,* meaning "much" or "many."

boonies: the jungle from "boondocks," first used by U.S. soldiers in the Philippines following the Spanish-American War. Also called "the bush."

Bravo: military phonetic for the letter *B*. LT Weisman was the FO for Bravo Company (see *phonetic alphabet*).

break squelch: a quick pulse of radio noise that comes when you depress the transmit bar on your radio handset. Often done as a quiet radio signal when speaking aloud was too dangerous.

brigade: a tactical and administrative military unit composed of a headquarters and one or more battalions of infantry or armor, with other supporting units.

brother: a black soldier.

buck sergeant: a three-stripe sergeant, lowest in rank of the sergeant classification.

bush: infantry term for the field (also see *boonies*).

C-123: cargo airplane; larger version of the Caribou.

C-4: plastic putty-textured high explosive carried by infantry soldiers, stable without a detonator. It burns with a hot flame when lit and was often burned to heat C rations in the field.

CA: combat assault, a tactical airlift of troops into the field, usually via Huey helicopters. Generally preceded by heavy artillery fire as a preparation around the landing zone.

cache: hidden supplies, usually rice, weapons, or ammunition.

carbine: a short-barreled, lightweight automatic or semiautomatic rifle.

Charlie: slang for Viet Cong or Mr. Charles or Chuck. It was short for the phonetic representation Victor Charlie for VC.

chieu hoi: the open arms program, promising clemency and financial aid to Viet Cong and NVA soldiers and cadre who stopped fighting and returned to South Vietnamese government authority. To chieu hoi was to surrender to the U.S. forces.

claymore: an antipersonnel mine, which, when detonated, blasts eighth-inch steel balls in a sixty-degree fan-shaped pattern to a maximum distance of one hundred meters. Used as perimeter defense. The claymore mine was nasty and lethal. A trick of Viet Cong sappers was to sneak in and turn the claymores around so that the lethal side faced toward the U.S. troops.

clusterfuck: a disastrously chaotic situation where everything seems to go wrong because of incompetence, communication failure, or a complex environment.

Cobra: the AH-1 Cobra attack helicopter, an angular, vicious-looking bird designed exclusively as a gunship. It carries a pilot and gunner and is armed with turret-mounted miniguns or grenade launchers, plus rocket pods and 20 mm cannons.

company: a unit generally consisting of three rifle platoons and one weapons platoon (usually a mortar platoon) and a headquarters unit in its Vietnam War iteration, all together numbering about one hundred men commanded by a captain.

concertina wire: coiled barbed wire with razor edges (also called razor wire).

conex container: corrugated metal packing crate, approximately eight feet in length width and height.

coño: Cuban slang for "fuck."

Crane: CH-54 Skycrane heavy-lift helicopter. An insectoid-looking craft that could lift twenty thousand pounds of cargo.

C rations: the common term for what were Meal, Combat, Individual rations. (The actual C rations were used in WWII and phased out in favor of the Individual rations.) The C ration was replaced in 1958 with the Meal, Combat, Individual (MCI). Although officially a new ration, the MCI was derived from and very similar to the original C ration and in fact continued to be called C rations by American troops throughout its production life as a combat ration (1958–1980). They consisted of an M-unit can (meat-based entree item), a B-unit (bread item) composed of the crackers and candy can and the flat spread can, and a D-unit can (dessert item). Each C ration weighed nearly three pounds, which made them heavy to carry in the field. Troops often discarded the packaging and stuffed the cans in socks for easier carrying. Lightweight freeze-dried LRRP (see *LRRP*) rations were a prized alternative.

đại úy: a captain in the Vietnamese army.

danger close: the warning "danger close" is given by the artillery observer to caution that friendly troops are within injury distances to the target. A recommended technique is to initiate fires at the minimum safe distance and to then "creep" those fires onto the target. Danger close distance for a 105 mm shell is six hundred meters; minimum safe distance is four hundred meters.

dap: handshake and greeting that may last up to ten minutes and is characterized by the use of both hands and often composed of slaps and snaps of the fingers. Used by black soldiers, highly ritualized and unit specific.

Delta Tangos: defensive targets. The FO for each unit in the field designated a set of preselected artillery targets for the company's night defensive position (see *NDP*) to be called in if they had enemy contact during the night. The FO would "fire in" those targets in the early evening by having the artillery battery fire on the target location and then calling in adjustments until the preselected target was precisely located.

DEROS: Date of expected return from overseas. The day you went home from Vietnam.

det cord: detonating cord used with explosives, often used to string several charges together. It has a very high-velocity rate of explosion.

deuce and a half: two-and-a-half-ton truck.

diddy-bopping: walking carelessly.

didi mau*:* Vietnamese slang for "go quickly."

didi: slang from the Vietnamese word *di,* meaning "to leave" or "to go."

dinks: What we called the Vietnamese, primarily applied to the Viet Cong and North Vietnamese Army, though it could mean any of the Vietnamese people, a pejorative to dehumanize our enemy. In the region of I Corps where I served, the term "gook" was not commonly used to describe the enemy.

dinky dau: to be crazy, from "dien cai dau."

DMZ: the demilitarized zone, the nominal boundary between North and South Vietnam. As the name implies, it was supposed to be free of military activity but was in fact a hotbed of troop movement on both sides.

doc: a medic.

Duc Pho : coastal village in Quang Ngai Province, adjacent to the Eleventh Brigade headquarters on a firebase known as LZ Bronco.

dustoff: medical evacuation by helicopter. Originally, Dust Off was the radio call sign of the Fifty-Seventh MDHA, or Medical Detachment (Helicopter Ambulance).

E & E: escape and evasion, a getaway maneuver troops train for.

elephant grass: razor-edged tropical grass plant taller than a man, indigenous to many parts of Vietnam.

FAC: forward air controller; a person who coordinates air strikes. The FACs generally fly in an OV-10 Bronco, a small, fast twin-engine, twin-tail aircraft.

FDC: artillery fire direction control center. It calculates the firing data for the big guns, elevation, deflection, time fuse settings, and such. Each artillery battery has its own FDC, which cross-checks firing data with the FDC at their artillery battalion HQ.

firebase: a fixed, fortified headquarters position for a unit generally of battalion size or larger. Most firebases include an operations center, a battery of direct support artillery (usually 105 mm howitzers), a platoon of 4.2 (four-deuce) mortars, a rudimentary medical aid station, and a helicopter landing pad. Often also called an LZ.

flare: illumination projectile; hand-fired or shot from artillery, mortars, or air-dropped.

FNG: fucking new guy; somebody newly arrived with no prior experience in the war.

foo gas: also called fougasse; a mixture of explosives and napalm-like gasoline and oil jellied with detergent, usually set in fifty-gallon drums placed around the perimeter of a firebase.

forward observer: "Fox Oscar" was the common slang (from the phonetic alphabet for the initials FO, Foxtrot Oscar) for an artillery officer, generally a lieutenant, attached to a field infantry unit to coordinate the placement and adjustment of direct or indirect fire from ground, air, and naval forces. LT Weisman was the FO attached to Bravo Company.

four by four: a command for artillery to fire in a grid pattern of four bursts across, four down.

free-fire zone: an area, generally in the countryside away from large populated villages, where everyone was deemed hostile and thus a legitimate target by U.S. forces that could be fired upon without the need for permission. The entire area of operations that LT Weisman worked in around San Juan Hill was a free-fire zone.

friendly fire: accidental attacks on U.S. or allied soldiers by other U.S. or allied soldiers.

garratrooper: a noncombat soldier (generally one who has a rear area assignment) who has no combat skills but excels at essential military skills such as highly shined boots and starched uniform. Also see *REMF*.

G-3: division level tactical advisor; a general staff officer.

grids: topographical map broken into numbered thousand-meter squares.

grunt: an infantryman.

gun: a high-velocity, low-trajectory, long-range artillery piece with a flatter trajectory than a howitzer (see *howitzer*). The M107 175 mm gun was used in Vietnam. It has a range of thirty-four kilometers (twenty-one miles). Because of its flat trajectory, the 175 was not considered as accurate as lower-velocity, higher-trajectory howitzers. The M107 was retired from the U.S. Army in the late 1970s, but it continues to see use in many armies around the world.

gun target line: also called the Golf Tango; the direct line between an artillery piece and its target. Since the most likely errors in setting data on an artillery piece were those that would cause the round to fall long or short on the gun target line, this line close to the target was not the best place to be when artillery was firing.

gung ho: rabidly enthusiastic (sometimes to the point of craziness).

gunship: attack helicopter armed with heavy weapons, generally miniguns and rockets (see *Cobra*).

H & I: harassment and interdiction fire. These were random artillery fires used to make terrain more dangerous in enemy areas. A battery would get a regular list of areas where it could fire H & I to scare and disrupt enemy in the area.

HE: high explosive.

heat tabs: flammable tablet used to heat C rations. Took a long time to heat the food and gave off harsh fumes.

hide: slang for a place of concealment like a cave or thick copse of trees.

hip shoot: an emergency artillery technique where a battery being moved is pulled into a quick temporary firing position, laid, and fired as swiftly as possible.

Ho Chi Minh sandals: Vietnamese sandals similar to flip-flops made from used automobile tires.

Hook: a Chinook CH-47 helicopter. This was the Vietnam War's main large cargo and troop transport helicopter. Sometimes irreverently called a "shit-hook."

hooch: a hut or simple dwelling, either military or civilian. Also tentlike structures made from ponchos, sticks, scrounged plastic, and sometimes mosquito netting put up by troops as shelter in the field.

Hooch maid: Vietnamese woman employed mostly on major military bases as maids or laundress.

horn: radio handset.

hot LZ: a landing zone under enemy fire.

howitzer: a short-barreled cannon used to fire shells at medium velocity and with relatively high trajectories. The 105 mm howitzer was the artillery piece of choice for direct support of units in the field. The 105 had a range of 11,500 meters. The 155 mm and eight-inch howitzers and the 175 mm guns were on call if greater range or firepower was needed.

HQ: headquarters.

Huey: a UH-1H helicopter, the direct support workhorse for frontline troops. A "slick" was the standard model, "slick" of heavier armament or modifications. It was armed with two door-mounted M60 machine guns and used for transporting troops and light cargo and for medical evacuations from the field (generally called "dustoffs.") A Huey modified to contain a sophisticated radio console was used as a command-and-control (or C & C or Charlie-Charlie) helicopter, generally by commanders at the battalion level and above. The Huey could also be modified with miniguns and rockets for use as a gunship. The gunship version flying in the Americal area of operations was called a "shark" and was painted with an open, tooth-filled shark's mouth on its nose.

hump: grunt term to march or walk carrying a rucksack in the field.

I Corps: For military purposes, South Vietnam was divided into four Corps. I Corps was the northernmost military region, stretching from the DMZ (demilitarized zone) in the north—the boundary between North and South Vietnam—southward to the southern border of Quang Ngai Province. The action in this novel takes place in the southernmost and southwestern-most regions of I Corps.

in-country: to be within Vietnam.

Indian country: also often called the bush, the boonies, the field. It refers to areas away from U.S. firebases or larger installations. Often areas where U.S. control is light and NVA and Viet Cong operate freely.

indigs: slang term for any of Vietnam's indigenous peoples, usually applied to minorities like the Montagnards.

insert: to deploy troops into a tactical area, generally by helicopter.

Jody: the person who wins your lover away while you are in the Nam. From the marching song or cadence count, "Ain't no use in goin' home / Jody's got your girl and gone / sound off . . . one-two . . . sound off . . . three-four . . . etc."

John Wayne: the macho action of someone who exposes himself to danger—after the tough actor of the same name.

jungle boots: canvas boots designed like traditional leather combat boots. Canvas dries easier, while leather boots rot in the jungle. Black leather lower part, black leather and green breathable canvas uppers. Jungle boots also had a steel shank in the sole of the boot to protect the wearer from booby traps and "punji" stakes.

jungle fatigues: lightweight tropical fatigues.

Ka-Bar: (sometimes called a K bar) a Marine Corps survival knife, though with its seven-inch blade, it was designed less for survival than for killing "when you run out of bullets," as Marine DIs would say. Though it was issued to the marines, army grunts also prized the knife for its better heft and sharper point than the bayonet for the M16 rifle.

KIA: killed in action.

killing zone: the area within an ambush or close to the burst of a grenade or artillery shell where everyone is either killed or seriously wounded.

Kit Carson scout: former Viet Cong who defected to the South Vietnam side who acted as guides for U.S. military units.

klick: military slang for a kilometer.

laager: a defensive position generally with a circular perimeter, mostly used for a night encampment, most often referring to a defensive position for armored vehicles. From the Afrikaans term for a position in which war wagons are drawn up into a circle. See also *night defensive position*, or *NDP*.

LAW: A light antitank (or antipersonnel) weapon, M72, which supplanted the much heavier Bazooka that had been used in WWII and the Korean War. The LAW was a lightweight one-shot launcher with a 66 mm armor-piercing rocket sporting a shaped-charge warhead, also sometimes used as an antipersonnel weapon against dug-in troops.

LBJ: Long Binh Jail, a military prison stockade in Long Binh.

Lima Charlie: phonetic alphabet for "loud and clear." Those are the words you hope to hear when you call the artillery battery and ask for a commo (communications) check.

Loach: OH-6 Cayuse light observation helicopter, a four-seater often used for reconnaissance and close support missions.

Lam Son 719: a major ARVN incursion into northern Laos in February–March 1971, designed to showcase the power of South Vietnam's military and its readiness to carry on the fight without U.S. involvement. The United States provided logistical, aerial, and artillery support to the operation, but its ground forces were prohibited by law from entering Laotian territory. It is seen by most military observers as a failure that ultimately led to ARVN defeat and North Vietnamese victory in 1975. See *Into Laos* by Keith William Nolan, a fine and thorough retelling of Lam Son 719 that informed my understanding of this last great American action in the war. Chapter 18 details the U.S., ARVN and NVA battle losses.

LP or OP: listening post or observation post with several men. OPs were often permanent establishments; LPs were mostly set up temporarily at night outside the perimeter away from the main body of troops; both were designed as an early warning system against attack.

LRRP: long-range reconnaissance patrol. An elite team usually composed of five to seven men who went deep into the jungle to observe enemy activity without initiating contact.

LRRP rations: a lightweight freeze-dried meal developed in 1964 during the Vietnam War for use by Special Operations troops on long patrols deep in enemy territory, where the bulky canned MCI ration (formerly known as the C ration) proved too heavy for extended missions while afoot. As it was a freeze-dried (dehydrated) ration, it required 1.5 pints (700 ml) of water to cook and reconstitute it.

LT: a first or second lieutenant.

LZ San Juan: (also called San Juan Hill) westernmost Eleventh Light Infantry Brigade firebase; in this story, it is home and headquarters for the Seventh Battalion Thirty-First Infantry. In reality, San Juan Hill was the firebase that was headquarters to the Fourth Battalion Third Infantry. It occupied the hilltop of Núi Suôi Loa, a 1,200-foot-high peak overlooking the Sông Ba Tơ Valley in central Ba Tơ Province. Originally established by marines, hence the name.

LZ: landing zone; usually a small clearing secured temporarily for the landing of troops in a combat assault or for resupply helicopters. Some become more permanent and eventually become base camps.

M16: the standard U.S. military rifle used in Vietnam from 1966 on. It fires a 5.56 mm round at high velocity of 3,110 ft/sec, with an effective range of 550 meters for a point target.

M60: the standard lightweight machine gun used by U.S. forces in Vietnam. It is an American general purpose 7.62 mm machine gun, reliable and accurate with a max range of nearly a quarter of a mile.

M79: a U.S. military handheld grenade launcher with a maximum range of four hundred meters, firing a high-explosive round powerful enough to produce over three hundred fragments that travel at 1,524 meters per second within a lethal radius of five meters.

mad minute: When the grunts were in a free-fire area, it was a brief crazy minute where everybody in the company had permission to fire his weapon, generally on full automatic. It sounded like a full-fledged firefight and was a way to let off steam and frustration.

mama-san: pidgin used by American servicemen for any older Vietnamese woman.

marking round: the first round—generally white phosphorous or smoke—fired by mortars or artillery. Used to adjust the following rounds onto the target.

MARS: Military Affiliate Radio System. Used by soldiers to call home via Signal Corps and ham radio equipment.

maximum ordinate: the highest point of an artillery shell or rocket's trajectory, commonly called the "max ord."

mechanical ambush: euphemism for an American-set booby trap.

Mermite can: large insulated food container used to carry hot meals to troops in the field. Its capacity was a cubic foot, about seven gallons.

minigun: rapid-fire Gatling-style machine gun with multibarrels that is electronically controlled, capable of firing up to six thousand 7.62 mm rounds a minute, primarily used on choppers and other aircraft.

Montagnard: a French term for several tribes of mountain people inhabiting the hills and mountains of central and northern Vietnam.

mortar: consisting of three parts a steel tube, base plate, and tripod. A round is dropped in the tube, striking a firing pin, causing the projectile to leave the tube at a high angle. Infantry companies generally carried one or two 81 mm mortars. Larger 4.2-inch (four-deuce) mortars were situated on firebases.

MPC: military payment currency. The scrip U.S. soldiers were paid in. It was supposed to be good only for sanctioned transactions at the PX and the like. But MPC became the de facto currency—used even more than the official Vietnamese currency, the piastre—for paying Vietnamese workers and making purchases on the Vietnamese economy.

napalm: a sticky jellied petroleum substance that burns fiercely.

nav rounds: a location technique often used in terrain where there are no clearly identifiable landmarks. Nav (navigation) rounds are smoke or white phosphorous marking rounds fired over known points (such as grid intersections). An observer would call for two of them to be fired and measure the azimuth to each. The observer's location is at the point where the two lines intersect.

NCO: noncommissioned officer, any rank from corporal through sergeant major.

NDP: Night Defensive Position, where a unit digs in to spend the night.

NVA: North Vietnamese Army.

obturating ring: a ring of relatively soft material (often copper) used to provide a seal between the hard casing of an artillery shell and the rifling of the artillery piece's tube.

OCS: Officer Candidate School. A military training school for officers. LT Weisman (and I) received this training and commission at the Artillery OCS at Fort Sill, Oklahoma.

ogive: the curved nose of an artillery round or rocket.

P-38: a tiny collapsible can opener supplied with C rations.

perimeter: outer limits of a military position.

Phantom jet: F-4 fighter-bombers. Range: 1,000 miles. Speed: 1,400 mph. Payload: 16,000 lbs. This workhorse of the tactical air support fleet carried all sorts of armament including high-explosive bombs and napalm.

phonetic alphabet: We used it to clarify the letters of the alphabet, generally for radio communications, but also for other uses such as unit designations (e.g., Bravo Company, Alpha Battery) and slang identifiers such as Charlie Oscar for "commanding officer." The alphabet is **A**lpha,

Bravo, Charlie, Delta, Echo, Foxtrot, Golf, Hotel, India, Juliet, Kilo, Lima, Mike, November, Oscar, Papa, Quebec, Romeo, Sierra, Tango, Uniform, Victor, Whisky, X-ray, Yankee, Zulu.

piss tube: a vertical tube—often the casing for a 105 mm artillery round—buried two-thirds in gravel for urinating into.

platoon: a subdivision of a company-sized military unit, normally consisting of two or more squads or sections, generally twenty-five to thirty men. Commanded by a lieutenant.

point: the forward man or element on a combat patrol.

point man: generally a very experienced rifleman who walked in the dangerous front position in a file of troops.

poncho liner: a quilted nylon insert to the military rain poncho, used as a blanket.

pop smoke: to ignite a smoke grenade to signal an aircraft and provide an indication of wind direction for landing.

PRC-25: (often nicknamed the Prick 25) Portable Radio Communications, model 25. A backpacked FM receiver transmitter used for short-distance communications. The range of the radio was five to ten kilometers, depending on the weather, unless attached to a special nonportable antenna that could extend the range to twenty to thirty kilometers. Cat and Cisco carried this radio for LT (and then CPT) Weisman. See also *secure radio PRC-88*.

PSP: perforated steel plate often used to create landing pads for helicopters. The perforations made it lighter and allowed water to drain.

Puff the Magic Dragon: AC-47—a fixed-wing, propeller-driven aircraft equipped with three miniguns, each capable of firing six thousand rounds per minute per gun for a total of eighteen thousand rounds per minute. The miniguns were mounted on one side of the plane. The plane would bank to one side to fire.

pull pitch: using a helicopter's collective pitch control to increase lift, a term used by helicopter pilots that means they are going to take off.

punji stakes: sharpened bamboo sticks used in a primitive but effective pit trap. Often smeared with excrement to cause infection.

Purple Heart: U.S. military decoration awarded to any member of the armed forces wounded by enemy action. Any soldier who was awarded three Purple Hearts was allowed to leave Vietnam.

Quad .50: a four-barreled assembly of .50-caliber machine guns, generally truck mounted, which saw its first use in WWII as an antiaircraft weapon. The .50-caliber round is high velocity and very heavy and capable of knocking down a full-grown tree at a kilometer's distance.

R & R: rest and recreation. There were two types: a three-day in-country and a seven-day out-of-county vacation. Bangkok, Thailand, and Sydney, Australia, were popular destinations. Married soldiers could obtain R & R in Hawaii.

recon by fire: artillery or small arms fire directed into an area before a company moved there. Designed to scare and rout out enemy that might be there.

Redeye FIM-43: a man-portable surface-to-air missile developed in the 1960s. It used infrared homing to track its target. The NVA used heavier SAMs in defense of Hanoi and were rumored to have some Redeyes as well.

Redlegs: slang for artillerymen. Red is the artillery color. After he left the field and moved into the command bunker on San Juan Hill, LT Weisman (and I) slept in the red room, the quarters reserved for the battalion's artillery liaison officer. The term originated in the Civil War where Union artillerymen had red stripes on their pants.

red ball: slang for a paved road; from the map symbol of a solid red line marking hard pavement of a highway, a dashed red line marked a gravel road.

refugee: used as a verb, it described the act of forcibly moving a population of Vietnamese from their home village.

REMF: rear-echelon motherfucker, a derogatory term used by grunts in the field to describe troops who rarely got out into combat. They had comfortable housing, hot meals, and access to entertainment. Also see *garratrooper*.

Rome plow: mammoth bulldozer on a tank chassis used to flatten dense jungle or clear wide paths through it.

ROTC: Reserve Officers' Training Corps. Program offered in many high schools and colleges geared to prepare students to become military officers. West Point trained officers looked down upon OCS officers, who in turn looked down on ROTC (rot-see) officers.

round: any piece of ammunition, from those for small arms to those for large artillery pieces.

RPG: a rocket-propelled grenade. A handheld Russian-made antitank rocket, originally designed by Germans for use in WWII and called a *panzerfaust*. A nasty high-velocity explosive rocket that will penetrate armor.

RTO: radio telephone operator. Each company had two RTOs in its headquarters section (one to communicate with the platoons, one to communicate to higher command levels—battalion and above). Each platoon had an RTO as well. The FO also had his own RTO.

S-1: Personnel **S-2:** Intelligence **S-3:** Operations **S-4:** Supply **S-5:** Civil Affairs. These are staff officers for battalion and brigade level commanders. Higher levels, divisions, corps, and above had G-level officers, generally corresponding in duties to the S-level officers. MAJ Connelly was the S-3—and later battalion commander—for the 7/31 Infantry Battalion.

saddle up: put on one's rucksack and get ready to move out.

salvo: firing an artillery battery in unison.

sapper: a Viet Cong or NVA solder who gets inside the perimeter, armed with explosives.

search and destroy: an operation in which Americans searched an area and destroyed anything useful to the enemy. Most infantry operations in Vietnam were of the search-and-destroy sort as opposed to clear-and-hold operations designed to take and stabilize an area.

Secure radio PRC-77: a heavier version of the standard PRC-25 radio carried by units in the field. The secure radio had an encryption device built in. When the radio's secure system was set and activated, it would transmit an encrypted signal, enabling open communication between units without having to manually encrypt the message. The radio weighed about twenty-five pounds, five pounds more than the PRC-25.

Shark: A Huey modified with miniguns and rockets for use as a gunship. The version flying in the Americal area of operations was called a "Shark" and was painted with an open, tooth-filled shark's mouth on its nose.

shit burning: sanitizing latrines by burning the excrement in kerosene; it was a nasty, smelly job.

short round: an artillery round that falls short of its target. Generally caused by a gunnery miscalculation by the Fire Direction Center or a firing error from using the wrong powder charge or the wrong elevation setting on the artillery piece. (See also *gun target line*.)

short-timer: soldier nearing the end of his tour in Vietnam.

short-timer's stick: When a soldier had approximately two months remaining on his tour in Vietnam, he might take a long stick and notch it for each of his remaining days in-country. As each day passed, he would cut the stick off another notch until, on his rotation day, he was left with only a small stub.

shotgun: walking shotgun meant walking second in line behind the point man.

shrapnel: pieces of metal sent flying by an explosion (originally a nineteenth-century artillery shell containing metal balls, designed to explode in the air above enemy troops).

sitrep: situation report.

six: any unit commander, from the company commander on up. ("Let me talk to your six," meaning, "Let me talk to your commander.")

slick: nickname for Huey helicopters, slick of arms except for M60 machine guns. These are the workhorse helicopters that lift troops and other supplies for close support of units on the ground.

smoke grenade: a soda can-sized grenade that released white or brightly colored smoke. Often used for signaling helicopters.

snake and nape: 250 lb. Mk 81 Snakeye bombs and 500 lb. M47 napalm canisters.

Snake-Eaters: slang, how the Special Forces troops refer to themselves.

SOP: standard operating procedure. The written by-the-book or unwritten-but-expected way to do something.

spike: to disable an artillery piece. Sometimes done when retreating troops had to leave the weapon behind. A term from earlier times where metal spikes were driven into the touch holes of cannon to render them useless.

steel pot: the standard U.S. Army steel helmet.

STRAC: acronym for Strategic, Tough, Ready Around the Clock, a squared-away, ready-to-fight soldier (one of a number of similar meanings for STRAC).

strobe: handheld strobe light for marking landing zones or friendly troop positions at night.

syrette: a hypodermic needle connected to a collapsible tube, like a toothpaste tube, which generally was used for giving a dose of morphine.

tee-tee: pidgin for very small, from the French "petite."

Tango Sierra: phonetic alphabet shorthand for "top sergeant," the company's first sergeant.

Tet: Buddhist lunar New Year. Buddha's birthday.

thermite: a mixture of powdered aluminum and metal oxide that produces great heat for use in welding and incendiary bombs. Often used to disable equipment such as artillery pieces that could not be moved.

thousand-yard stare: the stone-faced stare of many grunts who had been in the field too long.

thump guns: nickname for the M79 grenade launcher, a single-shot, shoulder-fired, break-open grenade launcher that looked like a sawed-off shotgun on steroids. It fired a wide variety of 40 mm rounds, including explosive, antipersonnel, smoke, buckshot, and illumination. Those who carried them were called grenadiers or "thump gunners" (see *M79*).

TOC: tactical operations center, the nerve center of a battalion, with communications, tactical information, and intelligence-gathering and liaison functions.

top: a top sergeant, the company first sergeant.

tracer: a round of ammunition chemically treated to glow so that its flight can be followed.

trip flare: a ground flare triggered by a trip wire used to warn of the approach of an enemy at night.

trung si: a sergeant in the Vietnamese army.

VT: a variable time fuse, first used in WWII. It contains a small radar transceiver that detonates the round in the air when within a certain distance of the target on the ground. It is far more accurate than time fuses when the exact distance to the target is unclear.

ville **or hamlet:** a small rural village.

web gear: canvas belt and shoulder straps for packing equipment and ammunition on infantry operations.

WIA: wounded in action.

wood line: also tree line, a row of trees at the edge of a field.

XXIV Corps: the headquarters that had overall command of all forces in I Corps, the northernmost military sector of South Vietnam.

Lightning Source UK Ltd.
Milton Keynes UK
UKHW010413190821
389088UK00008B/368/J